UKRAINE: *PERESTROIKA* TO INDEPENDENCE

Ukraine: *Perestroika* to Independence

Taras Kuzio
Honorary Fellow
Ukraine Centre
University of North London

Second Edition

St. Martin's Press
New York

UKRAINE

Copyright © 1994 by Taras Kuzio and Andrew Wilson
Copyright © 2000 by Taras Kuzio
First edition 1994
Second edition 2000

St. Martin's Press, Scholarly and Reference Division,
175 Fifth Avenue, New York, N.Y. 10010

Published in the United States of America

This book is printed on paper suitable for recycling and
made from fully managed and sustained forest sources.

Printed in Great Britain

ISBN 0–312–21674–2 clothbound
ISBN 0–312–21675–0 paperback

Library of Congress Cataloging-in-Publication Data
Kuzio, Taras
Ukraine : perestroika to independence / Taras Kuzio. — 2nd ed.
   p.   cm.
Includes bibliographical references and index.
ISBN 0–312–21674–2. — ISBN 0–312–21675–0 (pbk.)
1. Ukraine—History—Autonomy and independence movements.
2. Nationalism—Ukraine.   3 Perestroika—Ukraine.   I. Title.
DK508.84.K89   1999
947—DC21
                                                    98–7135
                                                      CIP

I would like to dedicate this book to my parents for their
help and understanding.

Contents

Acknowledgement

The author acknowledges the assistance of Andrew Wilson, the co-author of the first edition, in removing some of the inaccuracies of that edition, but understands that he has no wish to be associated with this edition. Any remaining faults are the author's own.

List of Maps and Tables

Maps

Tables

List of Plates

1. Ukrainian Cossack, Summer 1990
2. Demonstration outside KGB headquarters in L'viv, Summer 1990
3. Young men and women take an oath of allegiance to an independent Ukraine, Summer 1990, Kryvyi Rih
4. Pre-election rally in Kyiv, February 1990
5. Ukrainians wearing the uniforms of the 1917–20 'Sich Sharpshooters' in Kyiv, January 1990
6. Mass demonstration by 100 000 people in Kyiv on 30 September 1990 against the signing of Gorbachev's Union Treaty
7. Members of the 'People's Council' lead demonstration in Kyiv, Autumn 1990
8. Celebration of the 500th anniversary of the 'Days of Cossack Glory' in Dnipropetrovs'k (Sicheslav), Autumn 1990
9. Levko Lukianenko addresses a rally in the forest of Bykivnia near Kyiv, where, according to 'Memorial', up to 240 000 Ukrainian victims of the NKVD lay buried, May 1989
10. Ivan Drach addresses rally in support of Lithuania's declaration of independence, Kyiv, March 1990
11a. Searching for a lost relative, 7 May 1989
11b. Human bones uncovered at the Bykivnia site, April 1989
12. Radical MP, Stepan Khmara, speaking at the Supreme Council of Ukraine before his arrest in November 1990
13. Viacheslav Chornovil. Ex-dissident, (former) chairman of L'viv *oblast* council and leading challenger to Leonid Kravchuk in the December 1991 presidential elections
14. Levko Lukianenko, leader of the Ukrainian Helsinki Union–Ukrainian Republican Party, 1988
15. Leading ex-political prisoners, now all deputies, on the day of the Ukrainian Declaration of Sovereignty, 16 July 1990
16. The catacomb Ukrainian Catholic Church holds a service in the woods, Ivano-Frankivs'k, Christmas 1989
17. Patriarch Mstyslav, (formerly) leader of the Ukrainian Autocephalous Orthodox Church
18. The Second *Rukh* Congress, October 1990, Kyiv

List of Acronyms and Abbreviations

CPSU	Communist Party of the Soviet Union
CPU	Communist Party of Ukraine
DPU	Democratic Party of Ukraine
GWA	Green World Association
IPA	Inter-Party Assembly
IWU	Independent Workers Union
OUN	Organisation of Ukrainian Nationalists
PDRU	Party of Democratic Revival of Ukraine
PPU	Peasants' Party of Ukraine
PUSP	Popular Union in Support of *Perestroika*
ROC	Russian Orthodox Church
Rukh	Ukrainian Popular Movement
SDPU	Social Democratic Party of Ukraine
SPU	Socialist Party of Ukraine
STUU	Solidarity Trade Union of Ukraine
UANTI	Ukrainian Association Independent Creative Intelligentsia
UAOC	Ukrainian Autocephalous Orthodox Church
UCC	Ukrainian Catholic Church
UCDF	Ukrainian Christian Democratic Front
UDU	Ukrainian Democratic Union
UHU	Ukrainian Helsinki Union
UNA	Ukrainian National Assembly
UNS	Ukrainian Nationalist Union
UPA	Ukrainian Insurgent Army
UPDL	Ukrainian Peoples Democratic League
URP	Ukrainian Republican Party
USCPS	Ukrainian State Committee for the Protection of Society
USDPU	United Social Democratic Party of Ukraine
VOST	All-Ukrainian Union of Workers' Solidarity
WUU	Writers Union of Ukraine

Introduction

The vote by the Ukrainian parliament to declare independence in the aftermath of the failed August 1991 Soviet coup, and the subsequent ratification of that decision by popular referendum on 1 December 1991, was a crucial factor that helped bring an end to the old USSR, and thrust a hitherto under-researched nation of 52 million people into the limelight. This book aims to redress that past neglect and analyse the events that led up to Ukrainian independence.

Chapter 1 examines theoretical work on the development of nationalism, particularly on the role of the intelligentsia and state elites in generating national revival movements. In the context of the disintegrating USSR and its previously all-powerful state, it is argued that although the cultural intelligentsia played a crucial early role of initiating national and democratic protest as political conditions began to open up in many republics in 1987–90, it tended to be state 'national communist' elites that led this movement to success in 1991.

Chapter 2 discusses the specific weaknesses of the Ukrainian national movement, which made it even more unlikely that the Ukrainian intelligentsia could take power alone.

Chapter 3 examines state and dissident politics in the postwar period, and stresses how the 'era of stagnation' proved exceptionally durable in Ukraine, lasting until at least 1989.

Chapter 4–6 trace the slow and uncertain rise of opposition politics during the early Gorbachev era.

Chapter 7 discusses the crucial turning-point of the 1990 republican elections in Ukraine, which gave the opposition a quarter of the seats and a foothold on power for the first time.

Chapter 8 describes the uneasy transition period of 1990–1 when elements in the communist hierarchy began to build bridges with the new opposition. More conservative elements resisted this process, however, resulting in stalemate, with neither side able to overwhelm the other.

Chapter 9 describes how the failure of the August 1991 coup broke this deadlock, and by shifting virtually all political forces into the 'national communist' camp, helped to ensure 90.3 per cent support in the referendum for Ukrainian independence on 1 December 1991 (and victory for ex-communist President Leonid Kravchuk), that helped bring an end to the old USSR.

Spellings are transliterated throughout by the Library of Congress system. Ukrainian names are used in preference to Russian (for example, Donbas rather than Donbass), except for Russian politicians. Soft signs are translated with an apostrophe for place names, but the convention of excluding them from proper names is followed. The terms 'Moldova' and Belarus are preferred. The area on the Left Bank of the river Dnister is referred to as the 'Dnister Republic' or, from the Russian, 'Prydnistrov'ia'. Kiev is transliterated as Kyiv. 'Gorbachev' and 'Boris Yeltsin' are kept as well-known Anglicisms.

Of the too numerous people that the authors would like to thank, the following should be mentioned: the University of London for generous financial support, Eugene Pathia at RFE/RL for kind permission to use quoted materials, Valentin Yakushik, Dmitrii Vydrin and all the staff of the International School of Ukrainian Studies in Kyiv, especially Natalka and Iurii Petrus, Dominique Arel in Canada, Dominic Lieven, and especially Helen Skillicorn in London for her invaluable support.

We are also grateful to the Prolog Research Corporation, the Ukrainian Press Agency and many, many people in Ukraine who helped in the collection of valuable primary materials that made the book possible.

TARAS KUZIO

1 Theories of Nationalism and the Soviet Ukrainian Context

INTRODUCTION

On 24 August 1991 the Ukrainian parliament, or Supreme Council, declared national independence, their action subsequently being confirmed by 90.3 per cent of the population in a referendum on 1 December 1990. The central task of any contemporary political history of Ukraine must be to try to explain how this occurred. This opening chapter seeks to place Ukrainian nationalism in a theoretical context, without, however, arguing that Ukraine's entire recent history can or should be retrospectively analysed as a necessary development towards the nationalism of today.

As Ukraine, in common with the other constituent parts of the former Soviet Union, has recently experienced a self-styled national 'revival', the main theoretical question is whether it has anything in common with the great European or colonial revivals of the last two centuries.

The literature on such revivals is enormous.[1] There are very many potential theoretical explanations as to why national movements develop, although not all have been specifically applied to the contemporary Soviet context, and still fewer to Ukraine itself. As recent works by Alexander Motyl, Lubomyr Hajda and Mark Beissinger have noted, Sovietology's coverage of nationality problems in the USSR has often been lacking in theoretical perspective, or has failed to make its perspective sufficiently clear.[2] Even when political science approaches to Soviet studies became more common after the decline of the 'totalitarianism' paradigm in the 1960s, they rarely paid commensurate attention to the national question.[3]

This chapter will, however, consider the work of those authors who have looked at the recent development of nationalism in the Soviet Union and Ukraine in a theoretical context. Their approaches reflect changes in the theoretical approach to nationalism over the past three decades. Teresa Rakowska-Harmstone and Bohdan Krawchenko's work is based on the traditions of the 1960s and 1970s, which stressed the primacy of socio-economic factors in political science analysis. Hence they draw heavily on Karl Deutsch and Michael Hechter. In contrast, Alexander Motyl's work reflects the increasing emphasis on the role of the state that became popular from the mid-1970s onwards, and Kenneth Farmer's emphasis on nationalism as a cultural phenomenon has much in common with the work of Anthony Smith.[4]

DEFINITIONS

Anthony Smith has defined nationalism as 'an ideological movement for the attainment and maintenance of autonomy, cohesion and individuality for a social group deemed by some of its members to constitute an actual or potential nation'.[5] This definition will be followed throughout this book. 'Autonomy' in the Soviet context could, however, have a variety of meanings, ranging from seeking to defend and maximise Ukrainian interests within an all-Union context to outright separatism; hence the term 'nationalism' is reserved here for the latter phenomenon; namely, the pursuit of an independent nation-state.

The 'social group' deemed to be a 'nation' is defined by Smith as: 'a named human population sharing a myth of common descent, historical memories and a mass culture, and possessing a demarcated territory, common economy and common legal rights and duties.'[6]

The first half of this definition identifies the primarily *cultural* markers of ethnicity, which can be transformed into nationhood by the addition of the civic attributes mentioned in the second half of the extract. That is, ethnic communities, or *ethnie*, have been in existence almost as long as recorded history; modern nations simply extend, deepen and streamline the ways in which members of *ethnie* associated and communicated, by adding higher levels of territorial and political organisation to the community.[7]

If ethnicity is cultural and the state is a civic system, the attempt by nationalists to combine the two is often problematic. Nationalism is taken to be a series of propositions designed to argue that the only legitimate basis for establishing a modern community is the nation, which is argued to be a more effective alternative to purely legalistic methods of social bonding. The attempt to create such bonds can either come from below via the intelligentsia, or from above via the state.

Not all national groups are possessed of states, however. Nor is the reverse true. The nation and the state are not codeterminous. In fact, in the Soviet Ukrainian context, the conflict between the nation or *ethnie* and the supranational state was of paramount importance.

The relationship of cultural nationhood to the state or to socio-economic factors is a complex one. Three possibilities will be considered below.

For both socio-economic determinism and the state-centred approach, culture is an intermediate variable, operated on from below by socio-economic change in Krawchenko's perspective, or manipulated from above by the state in Motyl's. The third possibility, that culture itself is always the dependent variable, is rejected because of the difficulty in granting causal power to such an abstract variable.

In the light of this analysis, the basic argument of this book is that Ukrainian independence was the joint work of two elite groups. As with many previous national revivals, the initial stages involved a groundswell from below led by the local cultural intelligentsia.[8] However, given the nature of Soviet-type societies and the specific weaknesses in Ukrainian society discussed in Chapter 2, the cultural intelligentsia was not strong enough to achieve power and universalise the national message alone. It was therefore the 'national communists' – those members of the *apparat* who embraced Ukrainian nationalism at a relatively late stage – who finally made the decisive contribution by providing all-important state resources.

In other words, of the three theoretical possibilities, the one that makes most sense in the Ukrainian context is the manipulation of nationalism from above by elements in the state. Despite the intelligentsia starting the push towards independence, national communism in the end was decisive.

What theoretical arguments, then, have been put forward concerning the development of nationalism in the Soviet Ukrainian context?

MODERNISATION THEORY

Teresa Rakowska-Harmstone[9] and Bohdan Krawchehko[10] have emphasised the importance of modernisation processes and socio-economic change in generating nationalist discontent. They argue that the silent social revolution that transformed the Soviet Union after 1917 was the primary causal factor in a rising tide of nationalist discontent, clearly visible even before Mikhail Gorbachev came to power in 1985.

Although the regime may have been able to contain most of its manifestations, it was nevertheless faced with a growing problem of systemic instability engendered by the nationalities issue. Whether or not such discontent would have had the capability to overhaul the system, its existence was more a cause of Gorbachev's reforms than a consequence of them.

Both writers base their analysis on the writings of Karl Deutsch, which ironically had much in common with official Soviet ideology on the nationalities question in this period.[11]

Both Western and Soviet approaches rested on the amorphous concept of 'modernisation' – meaning processes of industrialisation, urbanisation and a rising division of labour and consequent mass production of education, plus a progressive tendency towards growth first in manufacturing and then in services. Modernisation supposedly replaced traditional social relations, with their emphasis on ethnic or loculist identities, with, on the Western perspective, universal economic rationality, and, on the Marxist perspective *rastsvet* (flourishing) of ethnic groups, but then their *sblizhenie* (drawing together) and eventual *sliianie* (union) as the 'Soviet People'.[12]

The argument that national identities and nationalism are the product of traditional societies, and are therefore doomed to transcendence by the march of modernisation, is still popular.[13]

Deutsch's work did not necessarily imply the decline of nationalism, however. Deutsch suggests a formula whereby in multi-ethnic societies the relative strengths of competing tendencies towards differentiation and assimilation depend on the relative powers of the dominant and minority social groups in social communication.

Whether ethnic groups diverge or unify, according to Deutsch, depends on whether there is choice or compulsion involved, perceptions of material costs and benefits, frequency and nature of inter-group contact, symbols and barriers between the groups, and so on. Most important, however, is the relative strength and similarity of social communication networks. If modernisation provides an ethnic group with sufficient resources (school systems, linguistic networks, densities of economic intercourse, and so on) to increase their levels of internal social communication, and hence their sense of identity, such groups are more likely to differentiate than assimilate.

This is related to Samuel Huntingdon's general theory of political stability. Whether a social and political order is stable or unstable in the face of such growing national mobilisation depends on its ability to 'institutionalise', i.e. provide a sufficient supply of channels of political participation to match the growing demand for it. Political, and social, disorder 'is in large part the product of rapid social change and the rapid mobilisation of new groups into politics, coupled with the slow development of political institutions'.[14]

John A. Armstrong and Teresa Rakowska-Harmstone both applied this perspective to Soviet, and specifically Ukrainian, nationality problems in the 1960s and 1970s.

According to Armstrong the Ukrainians were 'younger brothers' to the Russians. The Ukrainians were relatively low on the scale of social mobilisation and culturally close to the Russians, hence the former's assimilation was likely, given current policies and demographic trends.[15]

Rakowska-Harmstone argued, from the same perspective, that for many key republics in the Soviet Union since the 1950s, particularly Ukraine, 'the rate of development of ethnic nationalism has outstripped the rate of national Soviet integration'.[16] The tendency of socio-economic development to foster increasing levels of ethnic awareness, (*rastsvet*, in other words), had simply swamped the state's ability to assimilate people to a Soviet, or even Russian, identity. In any case, the Soviet system's denial of truly equal participation opportunities for all nationalities made assimilation less likely, she argued.

In terms of national integration, the system was caught in a dilemma. Its ideological and institutional matrix lent legitimacy, even if only a secondary one, to ethnic claims. At the same time, the exercise of ethnic rights and autonomy was effectively denied in conditions of political centralisation and one nation's hegemony.[17]

The result was ethnic discontent, although the regime's coercive capabilities ensured that 'the ethnic nationalism phenomenon remains clearly within the constraints imposed by the system'.[18]

The argument rests on the tension caused when newly, or already, mobilised ethnic groups are able to achieve some *partial* degree of 'participation', but not to the degree warranted by their level of mobilisation. Otherwise, there would be an obvious contradiction between arguing that ethnic discontent is caused by inadequate participation, and simultaneously arguing that it results when ethnic groups come to control some parts of the state and make demands on the centre.

As argued by Krawchenko, participation, in the sense of representation in the leading bodies of society (state, cultural and economic institutions), has been disproportionately reserved for the dominant Russian nationality, and in the sense of access to political decision-making, reserved for the communist elite.

SOCIO-ECONOMIC THEORIES

The arguments of Bohdan Krawchenko and Wsevolod Isajiw are similar.[19] Although also based on the Deutschian theory outlined above, the authors also use Michael Hechter's concept of a 'cultural division of labour'.[20]

Krawchenko stresses that nations are always made by elites.[21] The growth of any particular group's national consciousness depends on first, the creation of specifically national elites by modernisation processes, and, second, the manner in which the same processes furnish national elites with the necessary tools (schools, modern means of communication), and the necessary audience (concentrated urban populations), for the propagation of the national message, though this also depends on 'the central state's toleration of the national message they communicate'.[22]

Krawchenko, therefore, argues that the attempt to create a Ukrainian state in 1917–20 was fatally handicapped by the relatively under-developed Ukrainian social structure. In Otto Bauer's sense of the term, Ukraine was a 'non-historical nation', not because it lacked an historical past, but because it lacked a social structure of indigenous elites to lead and disseminate the development of national consciousness.[23]

Ukrainian society in 1917 was overwhelmingly rural (80 per cent of Ukrainians lived in villages, and 97 per cent of them were peasants) and 87 per cent illiterate.[24] Ukrainians accounted for only 30 per cent of the urban population, were under-represented in the working class (40 per cent of 'workers' were Ukrainian, but the figures were considerably less in the large industrial centres, which were a bulwark of Bolshevism), and were a minority amongst educated elites on Ukrainian territory, which tended to be Russian, Jewish or Polish (for example, Ukrainians accounted for only 13 per cent of those engaged in trade or commerce and only 30 per cent of the liberal professions).[25]

Not only did the Ukrainian national movement lack much of a base in urban centres, the intelligentsia or the working class in 1917, but the latter acted as the carriers of a specifically *anti*-Ukrainian ideology. The predominant 'cultural infrastructures' on Ukrainian soil before the revolution equated empire with civilisation and Ukraine with barbarism, and the working class was either apolitical or inclined to socialism.[26]

Alternative channels of nationalist social communication had been slowly revived since the early nineteenth century, but the above-mentioned weaknesses in the Ukrainian social structure, combined with severe state repression, made it difficult to make significant inroads into the dominant imperial consciousness (conditions in Habsburg Galacia were more favourable). Consequently, even many mobilised Ukrainians suffered from a 'Little Russian' or 'younger brother' complex, which made them relatively willing subjects of the empire.[27] Therefore, Krawchenko argues, 'the policies of the Central *Rada* [the short-lived Ukrainian parliament of 1917–20] existed, to a large extent, in thin air'.[28]

Since the failure of Ukraine's bid for independence in 1917–20, however, the social structure of Ukrainian society has been transformed (as has the nature of other national social groupings on Ukrainian soil, the Russians included). This ironic by-product of Soviet modernisation has, according to Krawchenko, helped overcome some of the strategic structural weaknesses of Ukrainian society, as large numbers of Ukrainians were drawn from the countryside to the cities, creating by the 1960s and 1970s indigenous majorities in most of the leading sectors of society.

This can partly be explained by Deutschian formula, since, whereas in the nineteenth century relatively small numbers of Ukrainians were more easily co-opted into the dominant imperial culture, after 1917 the influx of Ukrainian humanity into the cities swamped the system's assimilational ability, thus increasing indigenous capacities for social communication and culture formation. Therefore,

> the [newly mobilised] Ukrainian ethnos is a good deal more stable [i.e. non-assimilated] than some theorists of the merging of nations would hope.[29]

More fundamentally, however, mobilisation did not take place in a vacuum, but within the confining and distorting context of a hierarchical cultural division of labour' (i.e. a division of social labour which also corresponds, albeit imperfectly, with cultural [here ethnic] divisions, so that Ukrainians tend to be over-represented in low status positions, and Russians predominant in higher-status areas).[30]

Newly mobilised Ukrainians, confident of their right to equal status in a manner impossible in 1917, found themselves in competition for education and employment with growing numbers of Russian immigrants (there were 11.4 million Russians in Ukraine by 1989), as the Ukrainians tried to move up the social ladder.[31] The over-concentration of Russians in leading positions of society created a social blockage and a displacement of resulting tensions onto ethnic relations.[32]

If such an over-concentration of Russians was not the result of overt discrimination, it was supposedly the inevitable consequence of the structure of Russian society being more urban, educated and mobile than Ukrainian society, and of state support for the Russian language.[33] This was also the theme of one of the most famous Ukrainian dissident works of the 1960s, Ivan Dziuba's *Internationalism or Russification?*[34] Motyl has, however, pointed out that Ukrainians who accepted the imperial priorities of the state enjoyed considerable upward social mobility as 'younger brothers' in the Soviet period.[35]

Therefore, the idea is again that a previously powerless ethnic group has increased its degree of mobilisation sufficiently to allow it to resent the fact that its further progress is artificially inhibited.

This was not, of course, a smooth or continuous process. Krawchenko argues that the purges of Ukrainian elites in the 1930s were designed to forestall the first early effects of such 'Ukrainianisation' (although the purges also destroyed much of the Russian intelligentsia in Ukraine).[36]

After 1953, renewed Ukrainianisation again brought Ukrainians close to a hegemonic position in 'the strategic centres of social, economic and political life'.[37] Hence, for Krawchenko, postwar nationalism was being incubated throughout society, but most importantly in the local apparatus of the state, the result of a long march through the institutions by new Ukrainian elites. It would only be natural to expect them to seek to gain control over their own society as soon as they were given the opportunity to do so.

There is much merit in Krawchenko's approach. It helps to explain why, *ceteris paribus*, any Ukrainian national movement would be stronger in 1989–91 than in 1917–20, particularly in terms of elite leadership.

The problem with such an analysis is that opportunity is all-important. It will be argued in this book that the immense power of the Soviet state must be recognised by assigning primary causal power to the state rather than to socio-economic processes. No groundswell of popular protest from below was conceivable until the state was reformed from above. Even when Gorbachev's reforms allowed pressure from below to develop, the primary political actors were still state elites. They could, as in previous eras, have put the nationalist genie back in the bottle. The fact that they did not do so, and that the logic of their situation impelled them to politicise national culture from above, was ultimately decisive.

RATIONAL CHOICE THEORY AND THE STATE

Our analysis will largely follow that of Alexander Motyl, who has stressed the primacy of the state in permitting or promoting the development of nationalism,[38] first, because truly nationalist politics were only really possible in the drastically changed political circumstances of the late 1980s; and, second, because nationalism was more of an unintended product of *perestroika* than a problem it sought to address and contain. '*Perestroika* has not so much *released* pent-up forces waiting to assert themselves as it has *created* them.'[39] Hence nationalism was not much of a threat to the Soviet regime until the late 1980s, although the repression that kept it hidden would also account for the violence of the subsequent nationalist upsurge.

As Tilly has argued, vague notions of 'modernisation', 'discontent' and 'disequilibrium' are simply too broad to serve as useful analytical tools. Any analysis that over-relies on them will fall into the trap of determinism. Concrete political actions create history not abstract forces, and therefore any explanation of events must always concentrate on describing the available channels of political activity and genuinely active agents: individuals, groups and the state, with the latter being particularly important in the Soviet Ukrainian context.[40] To this end, Motyl proposes a much clearer distinction between what he calls the 'private sphere', 'the public sphere' and the state, because the political factors determining the possibilities for national self-assertion in each sphere vary enormously.

The first, the 'private space' of home and family, has largely been free of state interference since the death of Stalin, and purely private channels of social communication have been left to operate freely.[41] Second, there is the 'public sphere' which is 'located between the individuals comprising society, or the private sphere, and the state, the public sphere is the site of organised public activity and discourse'.[42]

Motyl uses rational choice theory to argue that the necessary conditions for nationalist collective action against the state in the public sphere would be anti-state interests and attitudes, followed by their 'de-privatisation', organisation and mobilisation by elites; and finally opportunity, or the ability to use public space for collective action.[43] However, the state, defined by Motyl as an instrument of potential control and regulation over private and public society, still retained enough of its totalitarian character in the post-states era to prevent any challenge to its monopoly control of public space (that is, only the first of the four conditions was met).[44]

The most important factor in the appearance of nationalist discontent in the public sphere is simply the last factor of opportunity. Before the late 1980s, although ethnic grievances and even specifically nationalist sentiments may well have been present, the Soviet state's willingness to use severe repression against any trespass of rivals onto its jealously guarded monopoly of public space, kept such attitudes 'privatised'. The balance of costs and benefits likely to accrue from nationalist opposition to the state mean that only the most committed of dissidents would risk challenging its monopoly of the 'public sphere' (see Chapter 3). In Ukraine, this period lasted until 1989, when the retirement of the first secretary of the Communist Party of Ukraine, Volodymyr Shcherbytskyi, who had held his post since 1972, brought the Brezhnev era to a close in Ukraine.

The 'public sphere', therefore, was insulated from whatever effects modernisation processes and the emergence of new national elites may have produced. Motyl's *Will the Non-Russians Rebel?* implied that this situation could have continued almost indefinitely, whereas the logic of Rakowska-Harmstone's and Krawchenko's arguments would be to suggest that the state and the public sphere were more permeable or to predict a pressure cooker model of social change welling up from below, and leading to eventual crisis.

As political factors, and especially the state, are always of primary importance, and the state effectively prevented any challenge to its monopoly control of the public sphere, the only possibility for the expression of national demands was within the state itself. Having originally argued that the totalitarian Soviet state could survive indefinitely, immune from the influence of nationalism, Motyl later abandoned the view of the totalitarian state as a monolithic and impenetrable entity, and argued that the federal system itself had an inherent tendency towards the production of certain types of nationalism, or 'national communism', of which the state had continually to purge itself, even before 1985.[45]

The origins of the term 'national communism' lie in the Austro-Marxism of Otto Bauer and in the politics of 1920s Ukraine.[46] Ukrainian leaders such as Mykola Skrypnyk and intellectuals such as Mykola Khvylovyi sought a national route to communism, but shared its utopian ideals. They argued that a national route was a necessary means to the construction of communism, as it was the only way to ensure popular participation, but they also considered that national and cultural particularities were quite compatible with a socialist system.

The phrase 'national communism' however, by the 1980s no longer implied a commitment to the building of utopian goals in a national context. It simply referred to those members of the CPSU who chose to pursue their goals in a specifically national context, and whose politics were based primarily in the defence of national interests, despite whatever ideological baggage they still carried with them.

Motyl's argument differs from that of Krawchenko, in that national communism is a consequence of the implosion of the central state, whereas from Krawchenko's bottom-up perspective national communism is the result of previous processes of socio-economic change which mobilised an ethnic Ukrainian majority into the leading positions in the state.[47]

Although the Soviet federal system was not decentralised in terms of offering local elites a genuine share in day-to-day decision-making, the system had a chronic tendency towards creating advocates of national interests from within its own ranks.[48] Soviet officials in the republics, appointed to administer power downwards over a particular national group, tended to develop a natural tendency to promote the demands of that group upwards, and utilise the group's resources to strengthen their own hand in relations with the central state.[49]

That is, although the central Soviet state had totalitarian ambitions, its overreach would periodically lead to a declining ability to control the periphery (such as in the 1920s, the Krushchev era and the 1980s). Nationalism within the regional state apparatus itself, in the sense of the local elite starting to pursue its own interests, could then no longer so easily be kept in check. In other words, the federal system was the one fault-line along which the otherwise seemlessly totalitarian state would begin to split, once it began to decentralise. However, the pre-*perestroika* state always retained sufficient centralised coercive capacity to complete the cycle by recentralising, and beating local demands down again.

Although *perestroika* has been interpreted, at least in part, as an attempt by the metropolitan centre to eliminate this cyclical tendency towards 'penetration crises' caused by the expansion of local ethnic power networks with the power to resist or block central initiatives and create a more efficiently centralised state, its practical effect was the opposite.[50]

Through *glasnost* and his own struggles to assert himself as a figure, Gorbachev undermined the power and prestige of the key central institutions, particularly the Communist Party, while his failure to reform the economy decreased the periphery's traditional material dependence on the centre. 'Attempting to pursue reform and power simultaneously, and thereby repudiating the traditional pattern of Soviet succession dynamics, guaranteed failure on both counts', and ensured that the inevitable attempt by the centre to repeat the cycle of the past and recentralise was a failure.[51] As the centre could no longer offer resources or legitimacy, republican leaders had to seek both among their local populations.

Second, developments in state politics were paralleled by a growing tendency to oppositional collective action which went far beyond previous phases of the cycle, once coercion and control were relaxed or became ineffective, and by an eventual alliance between such movements and national communist republican leaderships.

Motyl returns here to rational choice theory to explain why oppositional nationalist challenges to the state in the Gorbachev era became not only possible, but also logical.

The traditional rational choice paradigm, as stated by Olson, is that many types of collective action (such as trade union action or a nationalist campaign to increase the language rights of the indigenous ethnic group) face potentially debilitating organisational problems.[52] If individuals are rationally self-interested, then any cost-benefit analysis will lead to under-participation in collective action. The costs to be borne by individuals who join in collective actions are immediate and obvious (personal expenditure of time, energy and resources, the possibility of suffering sanctions in the Soviet context), whereas the benefits tend to come in the form of 'public goods'. That is to say, for example, a law favouring the use of the language of the indigenous nationality would benefit all members of that nationality, regardless of whether they contributed to the actions which helped secure the benefit, or not. Hence, rational individuals will 'free-ride' on the original action, seeking to enjoy the benefit from which they cannot be excluded, but avoiding the personal costs of taking part. As this will be a near-universal calculation, many forms of collective action will be chronically short of participants.[53]

Motyl argues that Olson's stress on the provision of additional material 'selective benefits' to encourage participation in collective action (such as a trade union offering insurance schemes to its members) is only one way of overcoming the problem of how to organise such action. However, as Zald and McCarthy have observed, 'a number of factors, including interest in individual goods, interest in collective goods, and solidarity with others interested in collective goods, may all move actors to mobilise for collective action.'[54] That is to say, collective action can also be based on group solidarity, a commitment to moral purpose, and on the existential impulses of group identity, as much as by a desire for material personal reward.[55]

Motyl states that once the state reduces coercion and constraint sufficiently to create a 'public space' large enough to permit collective action, such action will take place if prior problems of organisation, leadership and resources have been overcome. Without the material resources to provide selective benefits, and overcome the 'free-rider' problem, 'the major task in mobilisation ... is to generate solidarity and moral commitments to the broad collectivities in whose name movements act.'[56]

National identities, as Motyl points out, may be particularly, if not uniquely, well suited to such a task, namely generating strong feelings of the community as a collective subject, which can then serve as the basis of its collective action.

As Rachel Walker has said,

a society cannot operate coherently or efficiently without a recognisable, reasonably inclusive and, most important, persuasive sense of the 'we' ... a persuasive social construct of this sort must exist if a society is to be recognisably social rather than simply a nominal amalgam of fractured and alienated parts. And it is one of the central functions of political discourse to construct this hegemonic 'we' ... it is the identity of the group which makes political (and for that matter economic) action possible.[57]

Cultural feelings of national identity and solidarity are then the perfect cohesive for collective action, especially when all other possible focal points for group organisation, such as class, had been disorganised and atomised as a consequence of the long period of domination of public space by the Soviet state. 'The communist revolution ... has weakened or destroyed competing political currents, with the exception of nationalism, and thereby upgraded the last.'[58]

Soviet rule effectively destroyed civil society in the sense of self-organising social spheres independent of the state, which in any case had lacked much of a history in pre-communist Ukraine (apart from Galicia). Channels of organisation that would seem natural in Western Europe (interest groups, social classes) have yet to be created, as the (re)building of civil societies in the old Soviet Union is a painful process still very much in its infancy.[59] Hence the growth of ethnic, and eventually nationalist, demands in the public sphere was, by default, a logical development, which was given extra intensity by all sorts of other demands (environmental, social and economic) being sublimated into nationalist movements, because of the lack of any alternative outlet.

The same arguments, when combined with the problems connected with the sheer size and diversity of Ukrainian society discussed in Chapter 2, helps to explain why bottom-up nationalist collective action was relatively difficult to organise, relatively late in appearance, and never encompassed a majority of the population in the manner of the Baltic states.

In Ukraine it was unlikely that a nationalist movement could create a situation of 'dual power', from whence it would proceed to outright victory over an enfeebled state.[60] There is no specific logic that makes the relation between the power of the state and of the national movement that seeks to challenge it a necessarily zero-sum game (that is, one always expands as the other contracts). Indeed, in Ukraine the mobilisational ability of both was in simultaneous decline, after the nationalist challenge peaked in October 1990.[61] Instead, Ukraine had to wait for an alliance between the opposition and dissident forces within the state, as in the Baltic States and Armenia as early as 1988–9, although this was delayed until as late as the spring of 1991.

From then onwards the situation was transformed. The elections of 1990, and the referendum of March 1991, showed that support for the national opposition was confined to 25–33 per cent of the electorate. Once the state began to politicise the population from above, near-unanimous (90 per cent) support was achieved for independence by December 1991.

Certain elements within the state were more vulnerable to nationalist sentiment than others, and therefore more likely to make common cause with oppositional nationalist agitators in the *perestroika* period. These would include members of the cultural intelligentsia's own bureaucratic *apparat*, and those officials who wish to maximise their independence from the centre for the sake of maximal personal freedom of action, or rational-technical opposition to an irrational, overcentralised bureaucracy.[62] Against this, however, must always be set the fact that empires always function through the placement of representatives in the periphery whose primary loyalty is to the centre, to function as the 'bridgehead which the centre in the Centre nation establishes in the centre of the Periphery nation'.[63]

In Ukraine, the latter were comparatively numerous. This meant that state elites did cross over *en masse* to national communism, even in 1990–1, but rather the Communist Party was effectively split, with a substantial body of conservatives in resistance to bridge-building with the opposition.

THE STATE, CULTURE, IDENTITY AND NATIONALISM

Kenneth Farmer has examined the cultural basis of Ukrainian nationalism, and its origins in concepts of personal and collective identity.[64] If the idea of culture as the main independent variable is rejected, then national identity is either provided from below, by the intelligentsia, or from above, by the state.[65]

Although at times Krawchenko implies that the groundswell of socio-economic tension from below is sufficient in itself to generate a politicised national identity and consequent nationalist discontent, his argument more normally emphasises the intermediary role of elites. The social change that produced upward Ukrainian mobility is instrumentally important in so far as it affects the composition of the elites who control the process of culture formation or replication, and whether this will have a specifically national content.

For Motyl, culture only becomes important when the state allows it to. Either the state loses control and national cultures become the perfect cohesive for collective action against the state, or national communists politicise and manipulate culture from above in order to create a power base for themselves. The power of the pre-Gorbachev state meant that its 'Soviet' culture was indeed stable. It should not be argued retrospectively from the collapse of any sense of Soviet identity that it did not command significant support in the pre-*perestroika* period (or during the latter's early stages). Farmer's analysis, written in 1980, shows that, in the competition between the rival myth-symbol complexes of 'proletarian internationalism' and 'national moral patrimony' (i.e. traditional Ukrainian national identity), the pre-*perestroika* Soviet state was possessed of a considerable comparative advantage.

If the strength of any given nationalism in the cultural sphere is a joint function of its own cultural resources, its relationship to the state system and of any possible interaction between the two, then the purpose of Chapter 2 is to show that the cultural resources available to Ukrainian nationalism have traditionally been relatively weak, despite the strong Ukrainian national revivals that took place in the 1920s and 1960s. Hence, although the Soviet regimes in the Baltic republics were relatively easy prey for resurgent nationalisms in the *perestroika* era, the Ukrainian movement that began to challenge the state in 1988–91 was not strong enough to finish the job.

The key factors tipping the balance in the struggle for Ukrainian independence were the appearance of the national communists and the total collapse of the centre. In an extraordinarily short space of time, the Soviet empire failed the periphery in all key respects. The Soviet connection had offered at various times a Utopia, access to a wider world, the prestige of empire, the hope of technical and mater-ial progress, of raising individual and community standards of living. Messianic belief in Utopia had disappeared by the 1960s, however, and the flow of material benefits and related social mobility to all intents and purposes ground to a halt sometime in the mid-1970s.

More importantly, the official Soviet ideology and identity system's key failure was its inability to create and sustain the moral and cultural constructs by which a community can order its existence once *glasnost* was unleashed on people's historical myths and memories. (Ironically, it could be argued that the High Stalinist period, with its evidence in blood, was more stable and effective in this sense – at least it gave people some sense of where they were going.)

Therefore, the crisis of the state in the *perestroika* period was also one of identity and legitimacy. Gorbachev's failure to recognise this and his consequent blindness to the need to develop some kind of reintegrative strategy allowed the crisis to worsen. As argued above, only nationalism could provide an alternative set of unifying myths, symbols, values and principles, a sense of identity (a 'we') and once unleashed proved a powerful successor to the Soviet identity (which of course never fully suppressed national identities in any case).

As Smith points out, 'nationalism provides the most compelling identity myth in the modern world' through its power of 'transcending oblivion through posterity the restoration of collective dignity through an appeal to a golden age, the realisation of fraternity through symbols, rites and ceremonies'. To this might be added the powerful way in which nationalist notions of 'homeland' help to situate the indi-vidual, and the manner in which the notion of national uniqueness give a sense of worth to the identity in question.[66]

Nationalism was therefore grasped by the national communists both as the best means of legitimating their challenge to the centre, and as a reintegrative strategy for the territories they hoped to control.

This time the failure of the centre to recentralise meant that a certain critical point of no return was passed (in Ukraine in early

1991) whereafter the material, cultural and authority resources in the republics outweighed anything the centre had to offer, and the USSR was effectively doomed. The loyalites that are generated in the cultural sphere are distinguished from material or political interests precisely by their capacity to meet deep-rooted individual and collective psychological and identity needs, and therefore tend to be 'either-or': (in this case Soviet or Ukrainian) that is, not divisible or easily transferable. It may be possible for some individuals to feel 'multiple' or 'situational' loyalties, in more stable social epochs, but a Gresham's law tends to operate in more conflictual periods, as the strongest loyalty squeezes out the rest.[67]

In Chapter 2 we turn to an analysis of the specific weaknesses in the Ukrainian situation referred to above. Although the logic of the argument is that attention needs to be devoted to events at the centre, it will be assumed that the story of the USSR's last days is well enough known, and the analysis of Chapter 3 onwards will therefore concentrate mainly on Ukraine.

2 Strengths and Weaknesses of the National Movement

INTRODUCTION

In nearly all respects modern Ukrainian society is characterised by diversity. The lack of a single consolidating centre such as the Roman Catholic Church in Lithuania or Poland has made the organisation of a national movement relatively difficult. Ukraine's vast, sprawling territory, the size of France, has always contained many different regions and traditions. Moreover, throughout the modern period, Ukrainians have not possessed a Ukrainian nation-state, and it is normally the state that is the most powerful instrument in overcoming such diversity.

Ukraine's last true periods of independence were in the seventeenth century (the last vestiges of which, Cossack autonomy within imperial Russia, were abolished by 1781) and under the always fragile governments which sought to revive the national idea in the unfavourable circumstances of 1917–20.

Consequently, in the modern era Ukrainian ethno-linguistic territory has rarely been governed as a unit, but has been continually subdivided in shifting patterns among several states (although its core, the lands on either side of the Dnipro, was ruled by Tsarist Russia and then the USSR for two centuries) until most, but not all, Ukrainian lands were incorporated into the Ukrainian Soviet Socialist Republic (Ukrainian SSR) in 1945. However, these lands have always been administered as regions in a broader system of empire. This is not to make a value judgement, but is simply a recognition that Ukraine has not possessed its own autonomous political institutions.

The analysis here follows Eisenstadt's definition of an empire as a supranational or supra-ethnic political system, which exists by virtue of its possession of sufficient 'free-floating resources' to give it political autonomy. An empire is then defined by its very ability to act freely, and therefore does not necessarily involve any specific set of social or economic relations, exploitative or otherwise. (This is not the same thing as saying that an empire is immune from all outside influences.)[1]

The struggle to escape from empire and invest the institutions of the Ukrainian SSR with real political content will be the theme of later chapters. The present chapter seeks to analyse the effect that such a lack of autonomy has had on Ukrainian politics and society, and the consequent key strengths and weaknesses of Ukrainian nationalism today, in terms of territory and demography, regionalism, culture, society and economy, and then relate this to the arguments presented in Chapter 1.

TERRITORY AND DEMOGRAPHY

Map 2.1 shows the post-1945 boundaries of the Ukrainian SSR within the Soviet Union (the Crimea was added to the Ukrainian SSR in 1954, and declared itself an Autonomous Soviet Socialist Republic in January 1991). The 25 administrative sub-units of the Ukrainian SSR, known as *oblasts*, are also shown, together with the city administrations of Kyiv and Sevastopol. It should also be noted because of shifting historical patterns of political rule and migration, significant groups of ethnic Ukrainians live in adjoining territories. On the other hand, many border regions within the Ukrainian SSR also contain potentially worrisome minorities.

Ukrainians living outside of the Ukrainian SSR can be divided into four main groups. The first two live within the Soviet Union, in adjoining areas of Moldova, Belarus and the Russian Federation (RSFSR), part of the Ukrainian ethno-linguistic territory in the past; the second two further afield. Map 2.2 shows Ukrainians in neighbouring territories. The 1989 Soviet census recorded a total of 44.2 million Ukrainians, of whom 37.4 million lived inside the Ukrainian SSR and 6.8 million in other republics.[2] The largest numbers of the latter lived in the RSFSR (3.7 million), Kazakhstan (0.898 million); Moldova (0.561 million) and Belarus (0.231 million). Smaller concentrations of ethnic Ukrainians, such as those in the Baltic states, tend to be among the most highly denationalised.

Ukrainians in Moldova are concentrated on the left bank of the Dnister centred around the town of Tyraspol', where a large proportion of Moldova's heavy industry is concentrated. The area, also known as 'Prydnistrov'ia', was part of the Ukrainian SSR until 1940,

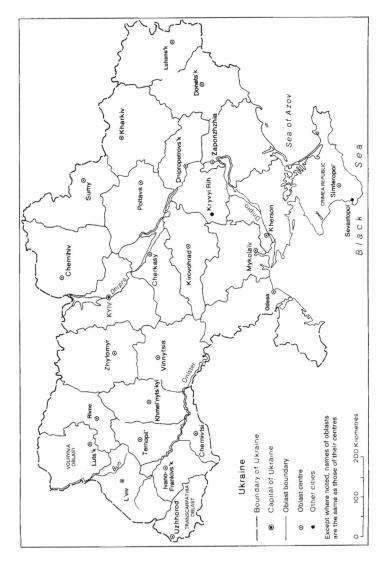

Map 2.1 **Post-1945 boundaries of the Ukrainian SSR within the Soviet Union**

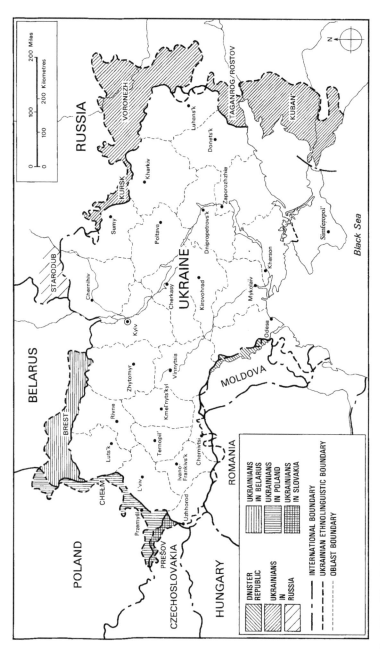

Map 2.2 **Ukrainians in neighbouring territories**

when it was added to other lands gained by the USSR from Romania to form the Moldavian SSR.[3] The mainly Russian and Ukrainian (60 per cent) population of the region showed markedly separatist tendencies when the Moldovan Popular Front came to power in 1990.

Ukrainians in Belarus live predominantly in the south-western region of north-eastern Polissia, south of the River Prypiat' and around the town of Brest (this area is now the Brest and Homel *oblasts*).

In the RSFSR, ethnic Ukrainians are mainly concentrated in southern Kursk and Voronezh *oblasts*, in the Taganrog and Shakhty regions at the mouth of the River Don which were part of the Ukrainian SSR until 1924, and in the Kuban' and Caucasus.[4] (The Kuban' was settled by Zaporozhian Cossacks in the eighteenth century after Catherine II destroyed their military stronghold, the 'Sich'.)

Tsarist and Soviet internal borders have been frequently redrawn, always with the interests of the centre in mind, and hence have tended to lack more than symbolic legitimacy. Those Ukrainians who have found themselves on the wrong side of such borders now tend to be heavily denationalised. The future Ukrainian state, therefore, is likely to become increasingly vocal about their interests,[5] and for those of the second group of Ukrainians, dispersed more widely throughout the USSR, either in large cities (in 1989, 247 000 Ukrainians lived in Moscow, for example; 94 000 in Kishinev; 51 000 in Minsk; 44 000 in Riga), or as migrant labour further afield.[6] Under Soviet rule, Ukrainians outside the Ukrainian SSR have never enjoyed the same levels of educational and cultural facilities as Russians outside the RSFSR.[7]

A third group are the Ukrainians living beyond Ukraine's western borders: approximately 300 000 in Poland, 50 000–150 000 in the former Czechoslovakia, 50 000–70 000 in Romania, and isolated communities of around 30 000 in the Vojvodina autonomous region of Serbia, and in Bosnia-Herzogovina.[8]

The Ukrainian border with Poland and the status of the minorities on either side have posed a particularly thorny problem in the region. The border established after the Polish-Ukrainian war of 1919 left millions of mainly Galician Ukrainians under Polish rule, and neither of the more westwardly borders established in 1939 and 1945 coincided with the ethnic boundary. The Ukrainians from the Chelm region and the 'Lemko' Ukrainians from the areas around the town of Przemy´sl in the south-east of Poland (see Map 2.2) were largely dispersed from their traditional homelands during Operations 'Vistula' in 1947.[9] Only 30 000 remained, but Polish Ukrainians have been trickling back to the area since the end of communist rule in Warsaw in 1989.

Ukrainians, or Lemko-Ukrainians, in Slovakia are concentrated in the Prešov region of northeastern Slovakia. The former Czechoslovakia also governed what is now Ukrainian Transcarpathia from 1919 to 1938.

The Ukrainians left in Romania after the mainly Ukrainian region of North Bukovyna was transferred to the Ukrainian SSR in 1940 live in the most northerly areas of the counties of Maramureş, around the town of Baia Mare, Dobrudja, around the town of Constanţa, and Suceava, and suffered from severe pressure to Romanianise under the Ceauçescu regime from 1964 to 1989.

Finally, the fourth group (not shown in Map 2.2) are the Ukrainians of the wider diaspora. It is difficult to give a precise figure for this group, as emigrants, particularly to the New World, are not usually required to be precise about their origins, and many left Ukraine around the turn of the century, at a time when Ukrainian national consciousness was at a low ebb. However, the diaspora may number some 2–3 million, with the largest groups in the USA (1.5 million), Canada (750 000),[10] Argentina (100 000), Brazil (50 000–100 000), the UK (30 000) and Australia (20 000).[11] (Additionally, a disproportionate number of the 400 000 Soviet Jews settled in Israel by end-1991 have come from Ukraine, as the former heartland of Soviet Jewish settlement.)

There have been two great waves of westward Ukrainian emigration. The first, in the late nineteenth and early twentieth centuries, was because of economic hardship and the relative openness of Austro-Hungarian Ukrainian lands to the west. The second was due to the dislocations of the Second World War. Hence, Ukrainian émigrés in the West have tended to be from Western Ukraine, and therefore to be more nationally conscious and politically radical (on Western Ukraine, see below), whereas Ukrainians under Russian or Soviet rule have tended to migrate eastwards within Russia/the Soviet Union itself.

Western émigré groups have considerable political influence, particularly the Canadian Ukrainians, who make up 3 per cent of the total population of Canada.[12] Well-financed and politically prestigious, they have had a strong impact on domestic Ukrainian politics since 1988.

On the other hand, as Map 2.3 shows, Ukraine has substantial minorities of its own and therefore faces the possibility of territorial claims or political interference from its neighbours.

As stated above, there were 37.4 million Ukrainians in the Ukrainian SSR in 1989. The rest of the population of 51.5 million was officially made up of 11.4 million Russians, 490 000 Jews, 444 000

24

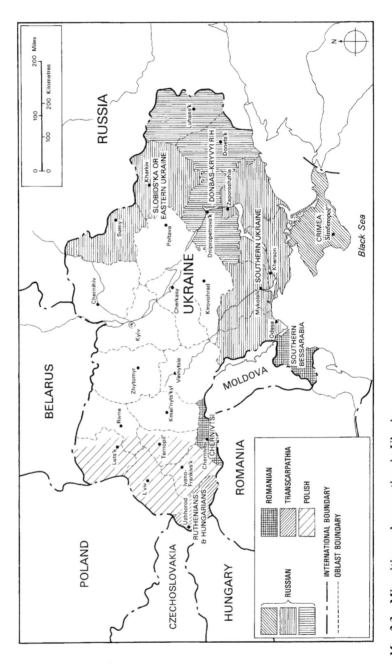

Map 2.3 **Minorities and separatism in Ukraine**

Belarusians, 325 000 Moldovans, 234 000 Bulgarians, 219 000 Poles, 160 000 Hungarians, 135 000 Romanians and 596 000 others; in all 14 million, or 27 per cent of the total population.[13]

The Russians are, of course, the largest and most significant minority. Russian peasants have lived on Ukrainian territory for centuries, especially in what are now the Kharkiv, Sumy and Luhans'k *oblasts*, and as settlers of the southern coastal region, conquered by Catherine II in 1768–83. Greater numbers arrived in successive waves of industrialisation starting in the 1870s, and continuing under Soviet rule in the 1930s and 1950s to 1970s. There were 2.5 million Russians in Ukraine in 1897, 7.1 million in 1959 and 11.4 million by 1989.[14] The Russian population therefore is still heavily concentrated in the industrial regions of eastern Ukraine, and the port regions of the south.

In addition, under Tsarist rule, the imperial elite (military garrisons; administrative, business and cultural elites) tended to be Russians, or Russified Ukrainians. The Soviet empire has not been staffed so exclusively by ethnic Russians, and consequently the institutions of the centre's rule in the periphery have become more Ukrainian. Since the 1950s, the composition of the Communist Party in Ukraine, and therefore of the ruling elites in Ukraine, has become broadly proportional to the relative size of the Ukrainian and Russian populations in Ukraine.[15] However, the potential for conflict between Ukrainian and Russian elites remains.

The figure of 11.4 million Russians, however, is derived from Soviet census questions which rely on self-identification of nationality. One school of thought holds that this is a considerable underestimate, because many nominal Ukrainians are in fact acculturated to a Russian identity and/or are Russian-speaking. Thus, Ukrainian-speaking Ukrainians accounted for only 64.7 per cent of the Ukrainian SSR population in 1989, and were in a minority in southern (40 per cent) and eastern Ukraine (44 per cent).[16] Together with Russian-speakers from other minorities (see below), and because of the cultural and religious closeness of Russians and Ukrainians, on this argument the 'Russian' minority in Ukraine is close to 40 per cent of the population.[17]

The counter-argument would hold that assimilation processes are of course reversible (although this is more difficult in the case of language), especially as many self-declared 'Russians' may in fact be Russified Ukrainians, and that local Russians can be mobilised to the Ukrainian national cause by a mixture of territorial and economic nationalism.[18]

The social composition of the Russian population, and the consequent patterns of Ukrainian–Russian interaction, is substantially different from that in the Baltic states and Central Asia, however.[19] In the Baltic states, Latvia and Estonia especially, the Russian presence is mainly a result of the postwar factory construction and relatively high standard of living that drew large numbers of Russian immigrants into the domestic working class. Few have learned the local language. Hence in the late 1980s they were susceptible to the politics of economic populism and opposition to indigenous attempts at cultural revival.

In Central Asia, by contrast, Russian immigrants tended to occupy privileged positions, both economically and politically, owing to the lower education levels and limited labour mobility of the indigenous group. Additionally, many Central Asian republics fit quite closely the 'internal colony' paradigm of Michael Hechter.[20] That is, the locals are largely confined to the bottom of a relatively undeveloped and undifferentiated social structure, employed in agriculture or a commodity monoculture, or as an unskilled working class with Russian supervisors. Hence the Russians have often behaved like the settlers of European overseas empires.

Ukraine's Russians, on the other hand, have a much longer tradition of living on Ukrainian soil, are more evenly spread throughout the social structure, and as fellow east Slavs, feel less threatened by the Ukrainian language and culture. (Although they can also be dismissive of it – only 4.9 per cent know Ukrainian.) They are more likely to make common cause with their Ukrainian cousins than would Russian colonists with the indigenous nationality in Central Asia, but, on the other hand, Russians feel a cultural affinity with the Russian Federation, or with the former USSR. They are not likely to be attracted by the myths and symbols of either the Ukrainian People's Republic of 1917–20 (which had no practical jurisdiction over eastern and southern Ukraine), or by the wartime struggles of the Organisation of Ukrainian Nationalists and Ukrainian Insurgent Army (which were again largely confined to Galicia and Volhynia, and often fought against eastern Ukrainians).[21]

Other minorities in Ukraine can be divided into three camps: (1) those subject to Russification, such as Jews, Germans, Belarusians and Greeks; (2) a smaller group that has gravitated towards the Ukrainian language and culture, mainly Poles and to a more controversial extent Rusyns; and (3) those who have retained a distinct identity, such as Hungarians, Moldovans-Romanians, Bulgarians and Crimean Tatars.[22] Overall, postwar Ukraine, although still a multi-ethnic state, has become slightly more homogeneous, as minorities have declined and assimilated, most, but not all, Ukrainian ethnic territories are now in the same state, and modernisation has Ukrainianised the cities.

Poles, Jews and Germans are three minorities whose importance has declined sharply in twentieth-century Ukraine. Until the partitions of Poland in 1772–95, a large swathe of Ukrainian territory west of the River Dnipro (the 'Right Bank' – see below), was under Polish rule, and a landowning Polish ruling class predominated in the area until 1917. In Habsburg Galicia (see below) Poles and Ukrainians vied for supremacy, a rivalry that continued under Polish rule of Galicia from 1919 to 1939. War, revolution and population transfer have, however, reduced their numbers from 2.194 million in 1926, to 219 000 in 1989, according to the official census.[23] The largest remaining Polish communities are in L'viv and Zhytomyr *oblasts*. (Polish exile sources, however, have claimed that 500 000 Poles remain on Ukrainian territory, their numbers underestimated because of high levels of Polish linguistic assimilation.)[24]

Jews have lived on Ukrainian territory since the Middle Ages. The Tsarist 'Pale of Settlement' until 1917 confined Jewish settlement to the area of the old Polish–Lithuanian Commonwealth (which included most Ukrainian lands from 1385 to 1648), and out of Russia proper. Therefore, there were over 2 million Jews in Ukraine in 1897.[25] Their social position as middlemen between Ukrainian peasants and their Russian or Polish overlords caused much resentment. War, pogroms, the Holocaust and emigration (including to Israel from 1971 onwards) have reduced the Ukrainian Jewish community to a shadow of its former self (840 000 in 1959, and around 300 000 in 1991).

Unfortunately, as postwar Poland has shown, the near-disappearance of Jews does not necessarily mean the disappearance of tensions between Jewish and indigenous communities. In Ukraine, memories of the murder of Jews in 1648 during the Cossack-Polish War and in 1768 during the Kolïvshchyna uprising, the pogroms of the 1880s and early 1900s, and the massacres of 1919–20 by troops of the Ukrainian People's Republic and Volunteer (White) armies and during the Second World War, will make reconciliation difficult.[26]

In 1926, 394 000 ethnic Germans lived in Soviet Ukraine, and 610 000 overall within what became the postwar boundaries of the Ukrainian SSR.[27] In 1928–9 they even enjoyed the status of six specifically German *raions*. War, deportation by Stalin and resettlement, however, virtually eliminated the German community, with only 39 000 remaining in 1989.[28]

In Transcarpathia there is much dispute as to whether the majority population (some 75 per cent of the *oblast*'s 1.1 million) is Ukrainian or an ethnically distinct group known as Rusyns or Ruthenians.[29] The area also has a substantial Hungarian minority and a small number of ethnic Romanians in the Tiachiv region.

The Hungarians are highly compact territorially and predominant in the Berehove and Vynohradiv *raions* (which border Hungary), though their cultural centres are in Mukachiv and Uzhhorod. They remain overwhelmingly attached to their mother tongue (97 per cent continuing to use it as their first language in 1979), and are basically a rural community (75 per cent in 1989).[30] Problems in the past between Ukrainians and Hungarians are the result of a legacy of forced 'Magyarisation' during the period of Hungarian rule of Transcarpathia from 1867 to 1918, the Hungarian destruction of the short-lived Carpatho-Ukrainian Republic of September 1938–March 1939 (formed as the result of the break-up of the Czechoslovakian state, of which Transcarpathia had been a part since 1919), and the Hungarians making common cause with the Ruthenians against the Ukrainians.

As regards the majority, Paul Robert Magocsi has argued that, as late as 1945, the inhabitants of Transcarpathia did not have 'a clear-cut understanding of their own national identity. The Russian, Ukrainian and Rusyn orientations each had enough adherents to prevent any one of them from becoming dominant ... this balance was broken after 1945 by the Soviet regime, which gave exclusive support to one orientation, the Ukrainian.'[31] Since 1989, the Rusyn identity, fuelled by linguistic peculiarities, a sense of a separate past and of relative closeness to central Europe, has revived, although even Magocsi had thought it to be in terminal decline.

Ivan Rudnytsky, on the other hand, states that the

> Russophile and Rusynophile orientations were moribund by the 1930s and the victory of the Ukrainian national movement resulted from the dynamics of the internal development of Transcarpathian society, and not from the intervention of outside *deus ex machina*. The Soviet regime did not impose, after 1945, a Ukrainian identity on the people of the Transcarpathian *oblast*; it only ratified the outcome of a preceding spontaneous local development.[32]

The struggle between the two conceptions in Transcarpathia itself after 1989 is described in Chapter 9.

Ukraine's Romanians and Moldovans (some differences between the two groups do exist, but they were exaggerated in order to justify the division of the Moldavian SSR from Romania in 1940) live mainly in the Hlyboka region of Chernivtsi *oblast* and in southern Bessarabia (the territory west of the River Dnister that since 1954 has been part of the Odesa *oblast*). These areas, long disputed between Tsarist Russia and Romania, were seized as a result of the Nazi–Soviet pact in 1939, and its general unravelling prompted both Moldovan and Romanian revanchist claims by June 1991.[33] Romania has also supported Gagauz and Bulgarian separatism in southern Bessarabia, but has opposed similar attempts by Ukrainians, Russians and Gagauz to dismember Moldova.

The Crimean Tatars were the original inhabitants of the Crimean peninsula, their Khanate having been absorbed into the Tsarist state in 1783 after the Russo–Turkish wars of the eighteenth century. Migration had reduced the Tatars' share of the population from 78.7 per cent to 19.4 per cent by the time of the mass deportation of the remaining 200 000 or so in 1944, for alleged collaboration with the Germans.[34] A long campaign for rehabilitation resulted in the partial restoration of civil rights in 1967, but the Tatars have only been able to return after a USSR Supreme Soviet investigation in 1989. Some 130 000 had already returned by mid-1991 rising to 260 000 by 1993.[35] However, fear of their return among the (mainly Russian) settlers who have taken their place has helped fuel separatist sentiment in the Crimea.[36]

Other minorities include the Belarusians. According to the 1989 census, 33.5 per cent of Ukraine's 440 000 Belarusians gave Russian as their first language, and only 18.6 per cent gave Ukrainian.[37] Hence, they and other highly Russified minorities are often regarded as effectively an addition to the Russian minority in Ukraine.

As a result of late eighteen-century immigration, 240 000 Bulgarians remain in Ukraine, 170 000 of whom live in southern Bessarabia as a compact and largely rural community around the town of Bolhrad. The 1989 census reported 62 per cent as maintaining Bulgarian as their mother tongue.[38] On the Azov coast, 37 000 live in Zaporizhzhia *oblast*, having been resettled there after the Russo-Moldovan conflict in 1861–2.

Ukraine's 99 000 Greeks, on the other hand, despite a history of settlement on Ukraine's Black Sea coast since *c.*1000 BC are now heavily Russified; only 8 per cent gave Greek as their mother tongue in 1979.[39]

Table 2.1 gives an ethnic breakdown of the Ukrainian SSR in 1989, by *oblast*.

Table 2.1   National composition of the Ukrainian population in 1989 (per cent)*

Oblast	Ukrainian	Russian	Other
Galicia			
L'viv	90.4	7.9	2.7
Ternopil'	96.8	2.3	0.9
Ivano-Frankivs'k	95.0	4.0	1.0
Volhynia			
Rivne	93.3	4.6	2.1
Volyn'	94.6	4.7	0.7
Other West			
Transcarpathia	78.4*	4.0	17.6†
Chernivtsi	70.8	6.7	22.5‡
Left Bank			
Kyiv (city)	72.5	20.9	6.6§
Kyiv (*oblast*)	89.4	8.7	1.9
Kharkiv	62.8	33.2	4.0
Poltava	87.9	10.2	1.9
Sumy	85.5	13.3	1.2
Chernihiv	91.5	6.8	1.7
Right Bank			
Kirovohrad	85.3	11.7	3.0
Cherkasy	90.5	8.0	1.5
Vinnytsia	91.5	5.9	3.6
Zhytomyr	84.9	7.9	7.2
Khmel'nyts'kyi	90.4	5.8	3.8
East			
Donets'k	50.7	43.6	5.7
Luhans'k	51.9	44.8	3.3
Zaporizhzhia	63.1	32.0	4.9
Dnipropetrovs'k	71.6	24.2	4.2
South			
Mykolaïv	75.6	19.4	5.0
Kherson	75.7	20.2	4.1
Odesa	54.6	27.4	18.4¶
Crimea	25.8	67.0	7.2**
Total	73	21	6

Source: *Natsional'nyi sostav naseleniia SSSR, po dannykh vsesoiuznoi perepisi naseleniia* (Moscow: Finansy i statistika, 1991).
*   Ukrainians and/or Ruthenians.
†   Including 12.5 per cent Hungarians.
‡   Including 10.7 per cent Romanians and 8.9 per cent Moldovans.
§   Including 3.9 per cent Jews.
¶   Including 6.3 per cent Bulgarians and 5.5 per cent Moldovans.
**   Before the large-scale return of the Crimean Tatars.

REGIONALISM

Because of their different populations and divergent historical experiences, Ukraine can be divided into the following six regions, and their specific features examined as follows.

Galicia

The three western *oblasts* of L'viv, Ternopil' and Ivano-Frankivs'k first came under Soviet rule in 1939. Their previous experience of Austrian (1772–1918) and Polish rule (1387–1772, despite the Ukrainian revolt in 1648 and 1919–39) had been relatively mild, and a strong revival of national life had taken place in the late nineteenth century. Galicia had been a part of the kingdom of Kievan Rus', and had enjoyed its own period of independence as the Principality of Galicia–Volhynia' until the fourteenth century. Its latterday revival was, however, based on the local Uniate, or Ukrainian Catholic Church, established in 1596, and the Habsburg desire to bolster Ukrainian nationalism as a counterweight to the Poles. Already strong by 1917, Ukrainian national consciousness in Galicia was further strengthened by the armed struggles of the Western Ukrainian People's Republic of 1918–19, the Organisation of Ukrainian Nationalists (OUN) from 1929, and the Ukrainian Insurgent Army (UPA) from 1942 against Polish, German and Soviet rule. (The latter fought on against Soviet rule in Galicia until 1954.) The Galician population has remained over 90 per cent Ukrainian despite Soviet rule, and since 1945 has become even more ethnically homogeneous after the death or resettlement of most of the pre-war population of Poles and Jews.[40]

Galicia has seen itself as the 'Piedmont' of Ukrainian nationalism since the late nineteenth century, but the tension between Galicia's sense of mission and those regions of Ukraine which are Russian-populated, Russified or simply more ambivalent about links with Russia (the south, east and Left Bank), has also been a key *leitmotiv* throughout modern Ukrainian history.

Volhynia

The two modern *oblasts* of Volyn' and Rivne have a level of national consciousness that rivals that of Galicia. Most of the area was not under Soviet rule in the inter-war period, but was under Tsarist rule after the Polish Partitions of 1793 and 1795 and hence has had strong

Polish Catholic and Russian Orthodox influences which justify the region's separate treatment.

Transcarpathia and Bukovyna (Chernivtsi *oblast*)

These two *oblasts* are geographically in the West, but have been much more loosely and ambiguously linked to Ukraine as a whole. Transcarpathia has been discussed above. The treaties of Saint-Germain (1919) and Trianon (1920) gave the region to Czechoslovakia, although far-reaching promises of local autonomy were never implemented. Hitler's dismemberment of Czechoslovakia led to the short-lived Carpatho-Ukrainian 'autonomous republic' of 1938–9 under the Uniate priest Avhustyn Voloshyn, destroyed by Hungarian invasion. Since the war, the Soviet state has pursued a policy of Ukrainisation. The dominant religion in Transcarpathia is also Uniate, but there is some resentment at Galician domination of the Church.

Although Czechoslovak rule in Transcarpathia may be remembered with some nostalgia, Romanian rule of Bukovyna in the inter-war period abolished the autonomy the area had enjoyed under the Habsburgs, and meant forced Romanianisaion after 1924, despite (or perhaps because of) the declaration by a North Bukovynan assembly of November 1918 to seek union with Ukraine. The legacy of this period, a strong Orthodox tradition and the fact that the local population is now 70.8 per cent Ukrainian, have probably tied the region more closely to Ukraine than is the case with Transcarpathia.

The phrase 'Greater Ukraine' is used to refer to the rest of the Ukrainian SSR, i.e. those Ukrainian lands under Soviet rule in the inter-war period (not counting ethnically Ukrainian territory in other Soviet republics, but including the Crimea added in 1954). It has three sub-regions.

Central Ukraine

The heart of historical Ukraine. Its ten *oblasts* can be divided into the Left Bank and Right Bank-Podolia regions (east and west of the River Dnipro respectively). The former – Kyiv, Kharkiv, Poltava, Sumy, Chernihiv – have been under Russian rule since 1654. The latter – Kirovohrad, Cherkasy, Vinnytsia, Zhytomyr and Khmel′nyts′kyi – were under Polish rule until 1793, and are mainly agricultural, especially in the west. (The division between 'Left' and 'Right' Bank is here fairly arbitrary because of shifting administrative boundaries, but is important in terms of the longer history of the Russian connection on the Left Bank.)

Eastern Ukraine

The four *oblasts* of Luhans'k (formerly Voroshylovh-rad) and Donets'k (the Donbas), and Dnipropetrvs'k and Zaporizhzhia are highly industrialised and Russified.[41] Although important Ukrainian historical and cultural centres, their character was changed utterly by successive waves of industrialisation from the late nineteenth century, which developed the area's water, coal and iron ore resources. The Donbas working class was a bastion of Bolshevik (or, on occasion, Makhnovite) support in 1917, and are equally radical today. Immigration has produced a Russian population of 43.6 per cent in Donets'k, and 44.8 per cent in Luhans'k, and a lesser 32 per cent in Zaporizhzhia, and 24.2 per cent in Dnipropetrovs'k.[42] The high numbers of Russian-speaking Ukrainians in these *oblasts* (34.3 per cent of Ukrainians in Donets'k and Luhans'k gave Russian as their first language in the 1979 census) also need to be added to such figures, however.[43] Much of the area's traditional industry is now highly uneconomic, environmentally hazardous, and therefore facing closure.[44]

Southern Ukraine

The three coastal *oblasts* of Odesa, Kherson and Mykolaïv and the Crimean peninsula have the weakest historical links to Ukraine. The south was not part of Kievan Rus or the Hetmanate and was added to Tsarist Russia by Catherine II's wars with the Turks in the late eighteenth century. Its ethnically mixed population of Ukrainians, Russians, Greeks, Jews, Bulgarians, Moldovans and Gagauz is the result of subsequent in-migration. Under the Tsars, the area was known as 'Novorossiia' (New Russia). Ukrainians are in a minority in many areas, and national consciousness is low, particularly in the Crimea, where the Ukrainians account for only 25.8 per cent of the population. Crimea was only added to the Ukrainian SSR in 1954 as a gift from Khrushchev to mark the 300th anniversary of the Treaty of Pereiaslav (which led to the 'reunion' of the Left Bank with Russia). The original inhabitants of Crimea, the Crimean Tatars, were deported in 1944.

Eastern and southern Ukraine (Crimea included) were never in any practical sense under the jurisdiction of the various Ukrainian governments of 1917–20, nor did the Ukrainian independentist forces have much impact on these areas in the 1940s.

It is, of course, also important to consider the relative population in each area. The three *oblasts* of radical Galicia, for example, contain just 10.4 per cent of Ukraine's population.[45] Volhynia contains 4.3 per cent; Transcarpathia and Bukovyna together 4.1 per cent; central Ukraine 39.8 per cent (divided between 23.8 per cent on the Left Bank, and 16.0 per cent on the Right); the highly industrialised eastern Ukraine has 27.2 per cent (with 16 per cent in the Donbas alone); and finally southern Ukraine, including Crimea, has 14.3 per cent. Therefore, the national movement's areas of greatest strength, Galicia and Kyiv, do not represent a large section of the republic's population.

Hence, Ukraine is characterised by an unusually high level of regional diversity. Its borders historically have not been those of a nation-state. Some of Ukraine's marginal lands', which have always been a problem for the process of state-building, now lie outside its borders, such as the Kuban' or the Brest region; others, such as Transcarpathia and Bukovyna, lie inside, but the fullness of their incorporation is an open question.

CULTURE AND RELIGION

In this sphere, modern Ukraine faces three main problems. First, a degree of cultural pluralism (partly related to regional divisions), which has made the organisation of a united national movement highly problematical. Second, while western Ukraine is closer linguistically and culturally to Poland and Belarus, and historically has closer ties to Central Europe, the existence of large minorities in Ukraine and the pressures of Russification have resulted in perhaps 40 per cent of the population, especially on the Left Bank and in the eastern and southern regions, feeling closer to Russia. Thirdly, although general Ukrainian culture has maintained a surprising level of vigour, the lack of recent statehood means that Ukrainian political culture is chronically underdeveloped. With the major exception of Galicia, which developed some of the elements of civil society under Habsburg and Polish rule, Ukraine lacks strong political traditions to draw on as it tries to build a post-communist society.

In Galicia, the myths and symbols of national moral patrimony were well established by the early part of this century.[46] In retrospect, the postwar Soviet regime seems only to have enforced the privatisation of such sentiments and modes of social communication, while proving incapable of transcending or eradicating them. If anything, the addition of a new myth of the wartime struggles of the OUN and UPA helped to further underpin nationalist sentiment.[47]

In addition, the Soviet federal system has helped to bolster Kyiv, since it regained capital city status in 1934, as a 'centre of national culture and consciousness'.[48] The Ukrainian population of Kyiv increased from 60.1 per cent in 1959 to 72.4 per cent in 1989.[49] This recreation of a L'viv–Kyiv axis, for the first time since the Middle Ages, has been vital in cementing a sense of nationhood in the leading urban areas where the national movement was so weak in 1917, and in the modern period, the original strongholds of the anti-Soviet and national opposition were Galicia in 1987–8 and Kyiv by the late 1980s (see Chapters 6–8).

The cultural symbolism of Galician-Kyivan nationalism, however, cannot but have a highly differentiated appeal in the other regions of the Ukraine. The OUN-UPA myth, for example, is not easy to disseminate, because its military struggles were confined to western Ukraine, and because the population of Greater Ukraine have been long accustomed to an interpretation of the Second World War which glorified traditional Soviet myths and symbols.

Additionally, the non-Galician population of Ukraine remains more deeply attached to the welfare and egalitarian values of the Soviet era. In those territories with a much stronger tradition of links with Russia, the Ukrainian national movement has stressed the importance of linguistic distinctiveness, precisely because Greater Ukrainians and Russians are similar in some other respects, particularly the shared Orthodox tradition. Again, however, the attempt to reassert Ukrainian linguistic rights will risk alienating the Russian and Russified sectors of the population, outside western and Right Bank Ukraine. Hence, the Ukrainian national movement in the past has often divided between a messianic element, which seeks to raise the level of national consciousness in all areas to that of Galicia or Kyiv (by force if necessary), and those who have been prepared to play down the cultural card and make a pragmatic and basically economic appeal to the east and south in order to attempt to transcend regional and cultural differences.[50]

Certainly, the OUN and UPA quickly found that they had to adapt their programme towards greater consideration of bread-and-butter issues when they tried to expand their appeal beyond Galicia during 1941–4, and the ideology of authoritarian 'integral nationalism' was dropped after the third extraordinary Congress of the OUN in summer 1943.[51] (The organisation had already split into 'moderate' [Melnyk] and 'integral' [Banderite] factions in 1940.)

Although a dire economic situation may help to unite all Ukrainians in a kind of short-term territorial patriotism, the long-term unity of an independent Ukraine is more likely to depend on the development of the kind of symbolic cultural unity, which Chapter 1 sought to argue was a more effective form of social cement than purely civic bonds, or ties of material interest. Such a 'single psychological focus' would have to transcend the particularistic cultural loyalties of different groups and regions. The attempt to rely exclusively on the Kyiv–L'viv tradition, narrowly conceived, for the cultural resources of the new state would simply create centrifugal forces.

Religious diversity is another longstanding problem in Ukraine. Ukraine has been Orthodox since the adoption of Byzantine Christianity by Volodymyr, Prince of Kyivan Rus' in 988 AD, but since the thirteenth century the faithful have divided their loyalties between Moscow and Kyiv. In keeping with Orthodox traditions of religious support for secular power, the separate Ukrainian Church was first dissolved and subordinated to the Moscow hierarchy in 1686, and then reborn after the formation of the Ukrainian People's Republic in 1917–20 as the Ukrainian Autocephalous (Independent) Orthodox Church in 1921. The Autocephalous movement's attempt to create a National Church independent of Moscow made considerable headway in the 1920s, until it was suppressed in 1930.[52] Despite the constitution of a new hierarchy in German-occupied territory during World War II, the Church was again repressed in 1945, although it continued to exist abroad.

In Galicia, the Uniate (or Ukrainian Greek Catholic) Church was established during the period of Polish rule at the Union of Brest in 1596 in the attempt to proselytise Catholicism in the East. Although under the authority of the Pope, the Church has an Eastern rite. The vigorous strength of the Church in Galicia, and to a lesser extent, Transcarpathia (it was effectively suppressed by the Tsars in the rest of Ukrainian territory in the early nineteenth century), has helped to maintain a Westward orientation among its flock, and its married clergy historically have been a leading elite in the Galician national movement. Its hold on the population was clearly not destroyed by its forced incorporation into the Russian Orthodox Church in 1946.[53]

The strength of religious traditions in Ukraine, and the way in which the Uniate and Autocephalous Churches have reinforced national sentiment (whereas the Russian Orthodox Church has been an unabashed vehicle of Russification), have been major strengths of the national movement, but the division between the three has also been a major source of weakness. (In Lithuania or Armenia, by contrast, the National Church and national movement have tended to be strongly mutually reinforcing.)

SOCIETY[54]

Changes in the social structure of Ukraine in the twentieth century have already been momentous. A backward, socially undifferentiated and largely illiterate peasant society has become urbanised and educated. Ukraine is now a more 'modernised' society, but one that still bears the birthmarks of its passage into modernity. By 1966, a majority of the Ukrainian SSR's citizens were urbanised, and a majority of its Ukrainians by 1979.[55] Ukraine's population of 51.9 million in 1991 was 68 per cent urban (35.1 million).[56]

The total workforce in 1990 was 23.301 million, including 3.481 million collective farmers (15 per cent of the total), 13.674 million workers (59 per cent) and 6.146 million 'sluzhbovtsi' or 'employees' (26 per cent).[57] An alternative to the notion of 'employees', as a measure of the Ukrainian white-collar population, are specialists with secondary or higher education, who numbered 6.969 million in 1990 (30 per cent of the workforce).[38]

However, although the decline of the countryside and corresponding urbanisation and the creation of a Ukrainian working class and intelligentsia have been the most profound social changes of the Soviet period, most social groups in Soviet-type societies tend to be amorphous. Deprived of the capacity for self-organisation, groups such as the peasantry or working class exist more as labels than as concrete social entities.

The growth of a specifically Ukrainian intelligentsia ought to be an important strength of the national movement, one that first manifested itself after the Ukrainisation of the 1920s. Although this trend was cut short by the purges of the 1930s, it resurfaced again in the 1960s. (A united intelligentsia of nearly 7 million would clearly provide the Ukrainian national movement with the leadership it lacked in 1917–20.)

Even the intelligentsia is far from homogeneous, however, and its different segments will clearly be differentially receptive to nationalism. L. M. Drobizheva's paradigm of the development of the Estonian national movement under *perestroika* can usefully be compared with Ukraine.

Nationalist discourse was initiated by the academic intelligentsia, and then given a wider hearing through the artists and writers of the creative intelligentsia. A wider audience was reached through the mass media intelligentsia (editors and journalists), before a mass movement was finally created through the agency of teachers and other intelligentsia 'working in the sphere of production'. They in turn connected 'the elite groups of the intelligentsia with the wider masses of the population'.[59]

In Ukraine, the occupational and emotional interests of the artistic and cultural intelligentsia as a whole can be expected to make them strongly supportive of a national movement which stresses the importance and unique value of the national language and culture. Other sections of the intelligentsia, however, are predominantly Russian-speaking, because Russian was the language of their work-place and their means of access to their peer groups in the world at large. Scientific and technical institutes, for example, and the employment opportunities for those they produce, have long been heavily concentrated on the Left Bank and in highly Russified eastern Ukraine.

The working class, on the other hand, is much larger than in Western economies at a similar level of economic development, a structural legacy of the excess demand for manual labour in all Soviet-type economies.[60]

As in all of the Soviet Union's western republics, extremely rapid industrialisation and urbanisation, founded on labour-intensive economic growth, plus highly concentrated urban housing developments, has created mass *laagers* of relatively undifferentiated working-class culture, which are difficult for intelligentsias to penetrate. This impenetrability is likely to have been further compounded by the crisis in upward social mobility following the economic stagnation of the 1970s onwards. Again, this working-class sub-culture is heavily concentrated in industrialised Left Bank and eastern Ukraine, often in the more Russified areas.

The working class, deprived of independent organisation and lacking even the limited channels of political expression available to the intelligentsia, has primarily been oriented towards basic economic and welfare issues, an attitude often crudely characterised as the so-called 'kovbasa' (sausage) mentality. This insensitivity to the national question was demonstrated during the Second World War, when *pokhidni hrupy* (nationalist agitators from Western Ukraine) found little enthusiasm for their idealistic message.[61] Nor were the *shestydesiatnyky* (the new generation of cultural activists in the 1960s) able to establish Solidarity-style links with the working class.

Ukraine has collective farmers rather than a peasantry. Although under the Tsars Ukraine had a strong tradition of individual rather than collective farming (as the land was more fertile than in Russia proper), a peasantry in the sense of an independent class of smallholders has long since ceased to exist. Collectivisation and the Great Famine in 1932–3 destroyed the Ukrainian peasantry as a political force.[62] The present-day rural population is disproportionately elderly and female, as younger elements have been drawn into the cities, and economically dependent on the collective farm. However, much of the urban population is first-generation, and links with the countryside are maintained by family ties and by the absence of a sharp dividing-line between urban and rural spheres of employment, particularly in small towns. Hence, there is a steady, two-way cultural diffusion between town and country, so that the latter is not as isolated as it would at first seem.

ECONOMY

The economy is important in so far as it has shaped the pattern of interests in Ukrainian society. Much recent economic dispute, not least in Ukraine itself, has centred on the question of whether the Ukrainian SSR can be characterised as an 'internal colony' of the USSR.[63] An 'internal colony' lacks the political or economic institutions with which to shape its own destiny, and therefore is subject to the imposition of economic priorities decided elsewhere. That is to say, its economy is instrumental to that of the core area. The effects of this instrumentality will vary, but may include imbalanced development (regionally and sectorally), national income transfers and resource exploitation. This could logically happen to any region, or even within a region; therefore the significance of 'internal colonial-ism', according to Michael Hechter, who coined the term, comes when this economic pattern overlays an ethnic boundary, thereby creating a highly politicised 'cultural [i.e. ethnic] division of labour' (see Chapter 1).[64] It also places Ukrainian economic elites in a paradoxical situation – economically dependent on the centre, but simultaneously resentful of this fact.

Apart from the partial decentralisation of the *sovnarkhozy* period of 1957–65 and the NEP period of 1921–9, over 90 per cent of economic activity in Ukraine has always been controlled by the central all-Union ministries, thus satisfying the first condition above. Ukraine's economy also shows abundant evidence of the predicted consequences. It suffers from uneven regional development, despite the Soviet system's initial emphasis on equalisation between regions through industrialisation.[65] The economy is also sectorally imbalanced, because Soviet planners have concentrated on maintaining Ukraine's role as a supplier of food-stuffs, coal and iron, and metallurgical and chemical products (rather than light or consumer industries). Like all Soviet republics, it also has its share of localised all-Union monopolies (its share of USSR mili-tary-industrial production, such as the Iuzhnyi rocket-producing complex in Dnipropetrovs'k, is possibly as high as 40 per cent),[66] but its self-sufficiency in many key areas, energy especially, is doubtful.[67]

Most observers, from Mykhailo Volobuiev, the Ukrainian national communist economist of the 1920s, onwards have calculated that Ukraine has suffered from a net outflow of its national income and wealth, both under the Soviet Union and under the Tsars.[68] The centre has rarely invested in Ukraine in proportion to the taxation revenue extracted from the republic. In addition, Ukraine has suffered from more indirect forms of income transfer, owing to relatively low fixed Soviet prices for its agricultural and raw material exports, and relatively high prices for the finished goods it has to import.[69]

The ecological situation in Ukraine is nothing short of disastrous, and this can be attributed primarily to the unaccountable operations of Moscow ministries.[70] The effects of the Chornobyl' disaster are well known, but Ukraine also has endemic problems with industrial and water pollution, and public health in general. These are common to the whole of Ukraine, although they are particularly acute among the rust-belt industries of the Donbas.[71]

However, even if it is possible to argue that Ukraine has been an 'internal colony', it is not so easy to identify the corresponding exploit-ing metropolis. It is not another national group (i.e. the Russians), because there is no evidence that the RSFSR has received net benefits in exact counterpart to Ukraine's net costs, and the Soviet political system cannot be simply characterised as an ethnic hegemony.[72] Rather, all the Union republics have been subordinated to the Great Power interests of the leading elements in the Union system itself, their economies subordinated to 'the geopolitical demands of the state as perceived and acted upon by the state leadership'.[73] Ukraine has, of course, derived some benefits from the all-Union command economy, such as some economies of scale and guaranteed access to cheap energy supply, but never as a result of its own republican decision-making processes.

The pattern of economic relations described above has several political effects. Ukrainian elites have usually been deprived of the economic resources that would otherwise have empowered any political challenge to the centre. On the contrary, those who have controlled Ukraine's economy have tended to act as representatives of the centre. The bureaucrats of the command economy function as the 'representatives of the centre in the periphery' that Galtung has argued are a key aspect of any system of imperial rule.[74] However, there has also undoubtedly been a structural tendency for republican level sub-elites (the term 'sub-elites' is used to stress that indigenous economic elites are still normally subordinate to all-Union bureaucrats, even on their own territory) to seek to expand their power, whenever the system of vertical integration above them has broken down, as in the 1920s, 1960s and, most importantly, in the economic chaos of the early 1990s. An alliance between 'national communists' in republican political institutions, and republican economic sub-elites can be a potent nationalist force, as seen in the rise of the 'sovereign' or 'national' communist group under Leonid Kravchuk in 1990–1.

CONCLUSIONS

Overall, although the same forces leading to an upsurge in nationalism in the late 1980s may have operated throughout the USSR, as argued in Chapter 1, Ukraine's ability to support a national movement lay somewhere in between that of the Baltic states and Russia. Ukraine's diversity, sheer size and lack of any recent tradition of statehood made collective action harder to organise than in the Baltics, but, on the other hand, Ukraine did not have the identity problems produced in Russia by the confusion between Russia and the Empire.

In Ukraine, the process of forming a unified nation would have to take place as much *after* the nationalist takeover of the state as beforehand.

3 Ukraine on the Eve of the Gorbachev Era

INTRODUCTION

The Brezhnev era ended late in Ukraine: its chief representative, Volodymyr Shcherbytskyi, who had kept Ukraine in a tight grip for four Soviet leaders since his appointment as first secretary of the Communist Party of Ukraine (CPU) in May 1972, managed to survive until September 1989 – four and a half years into the *perestroika* era.

Even his successors, Volodymyr Ivashko (September 1989–July 1990) and Stanislav Hurenko, who led the CPU until its banning on 30 August 1991 by the Supreme Council of Ukraine, failed to embrace fully the logic of national communism outlined in Chapter 1. Therefore in the early years of *perestroika* nationalist yearnings were not as marked in Ukraine as in other Soviet republics, although Ukraine caught up rapidly after 1990.

Shcherbytskyi's rule was characterised by repression, economic and spiritual stagnation, and a determined campaign for the Russification of Ukrainian language and culture. The media, cultural and educational circles were purged of nationally conscious elites, and national communist elements were removed from the CPU. In the words of one author:

> Thanks to Shcherbytskyi and his associates, Moscow succeeded in cultivating a following of loyal 'Little Russians' in Ukraine, who were willing to subordinate the republic's interests to those of the centre. As the leader of this group, Shcherbytskyi may well go down in history as the *maloros par excellence*.[1]

SHELEST AND SHCHERBYTSKYI

Analysis of the pre-Gorbachev era in Ukraine usually contrasts Shcherbytskyi's ultra-loyalist and pro-Moscow Brezhnevite orthodoxy as first secretary of the CPU from May 1972 until September 1989[2] with the supposed national communism of his predecessor, Petro Shelest, who held office from June 1963 to May 1972.[3] As will be argued below, this is enlightening, but a simplification.[4]

Some of the key changes within the CPU that supposedly encouraged the growth of national communism can be traced back to the Eighteenth Congress of the CPU in 1954, and the rule of Shelest's two predecessors, Oleksii Kyrychenko (June 1953–December 1957) and Mykola Pidhornyi (December 1957–June 1963). This period, inaugurated by the death of Stalin in March 1953, saw the renewed Ukrainianisation of the upper echelons of the CPU. Henceforth, the first secretary of the CPU would always be an ethnic Ukrainian (Kyrychenko was the first), as would a majority of leading figures in the party and the state apparatus. (The second secretary of the CPU, responsible for cadre appointments, was also an ethnic Ukrainian until 1976, though in many other republics this sensitive post was always reserved for Russians.) The percentage of Ukrainians in the CPU, only 23 per cent in 1922, rose and stabilised at levels first reached after the first wave of Ukrainianisation in the 1920s (although still less than the Ukrainian share of the population of the republic).

The Ukrainian party grew more rapidly than the CPSU as a whole, reflecting the same desire to increase its Ukrainian membership.

According to Krawchenko, therefore, 'The [1954] congress marked a turning point in the history of Ukraine. It saw the emergence of a new Ukrainian political elite.'[8] Shelest did not appear from nowhere.

Table 3.1   Percentage of Ukrainians in the CPU[5]

1920	1922	1927	1933	1937	1940	1950	1960	1971	1980	1988	1990
23%	23%	52%	60%	57%	63%	59%	62%	65%	66%	67%	67%

Table 3.2   Growth of the CPU[6]

1918	1922	1933	1936	1940	1945	1954	1959
4 301	73 804	555 433	241 330	505 706	164 743	795 559	1 159 207
1966	1971	1976	1981	1986	1989	1990	1991
1 961 408	2 378 789	2 625 808	2 933 564	3 188 854	3 302 221	3 294 038	2 500 007[7]

Rather, his regime's relatively tough defence of Ukrainian interests was the product of a long incubation period under his predecessors, during which the post-1917 modernisation of the Ukrainian social structure had resulted in the local state structures being captured for national communism from within.

On Motyl's alternative interpretation, however, the Shelest period was the product of the 1960s leadership transition in Moscow, and the consequent relative tolerance of troublesome republics. Brezhnev did not allow control of the periphery to atrophy in the same manner as Gorbachev, and was therefore able to recentralise in the early 1970s.

The analysis of the politics of Shelest and his circle, as they were actually conceived and implemented at the time, is however complicated by 20 years of mythologising since his dismissal on charges of aiding and abetting nationalism in 1972.[9] The official explanation of his ouster was late, partial and based on a caricatured identification of Shelest with the 'national-separatist' straw men of communist propaganda.[10] Similarly, Shelest has also been retrospectively claimed by nationalists as one of their own, without too much supporting evidence, other than the mere fact of his dismissal. Shelest himself, after his belated reappearance in 1988, sought to defend his period in power as a forerunner of the politics of *perestroika* and *glasnost'* rather than remembering them in the true context of the time.[11]

In fact, Shelest was neither a separatist nor a precursor of the modern era. According to Pelenski, 'Shelest can best be compared to the Ukrainian Hetmen of the first third of the eighteenth century ... political leaders who attempted to maintain correct relations with the imperial centre, on the one hand, and who tried to defend the autonomy of the Ukrainian Hetmanate, its institutions and its special interests, on the other.'[12] However, another author believes that 'Shelest did aggressively assert a claim of national equality and reciprocity within a communist "internationalist" framework, and this claim did increasingly diverge from the integrative-russifying trend in official policy.'[13]

Shelest was never a separatist but he did lobby for Ukrainian cultural and economic rights, reflecting the preponderance of such elites in Ukrainian leadership circles at the time.[14] In the manner of the dissident Ivan Dziuba (see below), he called for a return to supposed Leninist orthodoxy in nationalities policy, demanding equality of treatment for all Soviet nations, and respect for Ukrainian freedom of action within spheres of traditional republican autonomy. Additionally,

Shelest could be seen as a product of the periodic tendency described in Chapter I for Soviet federalism to generate advocates of local interests, whose authority-building strategies, patron-client networks or technocratic desire for full competence over their own sphere of expertise tended to create centrifugal forces when the centre relaxed its control of the periphery.

His agenda cannot be retrospectively identified with the *shestydesiatnyky* dissident movement however. They and the Shelest group represented two different issue and interest networks, which overlapped, but did not coincide.[15]

In the economic sphere, Shelest would often present himself as a spokesman for republican interests (in the 1970s he was condemned for *misnytstvo*, or localism). He opposed attempts to shift investment priorities eastwards to Siberia and Central Asia, and called instead for investment in Ukraine's already dilapidated capital base and infrastructure, especially in Ukraine's traditional bedrock industries of mining and metallurgy.[16] His argument that Ukraine's share of 'inward' investment should match its contribution to all-Union output paralleled those of 'national communist' economists such as Volubuiev, who had developed the notion of Ukraine as an 'internal colony' in the 1920s (see Chapter 2).

Shelest's speeches, for example, to the Twenty-Fourth Congress of the CPU in 1971, and in Donets'k in July 1971, contained barely veiled attacks on all-Union authorities, and Gosplan in particular, for neglecting Ukrainian needs.[17]

In the cultural sphere, Shelest's rule coincided with increasing outspokenness amongst the Ukrainian intelligentsia, who had been largely silent since the last national revival was abruptly terminated in the early 1930s. Having tentatively found its feet under Khrushchev's partial liberalisation of the late 1950s and early 1960s, the intelligentsia began to take its campaign for cultural and linguistic renaissance into the Party-state apparatus. Although political constraints prevented Shelest making an open alliance with the cultural intelligentsia, nevertheless his remarks to the Ukrainian Writers' Congress in 1966, were unambiguous: 'We must treat our beautiful Ukrainian language with great care and respect. It is our treasure, our great heritage, which all of us, but in the first place you, our writers, must preserve and develop ... Your efforts in this direction always have been and always will be supported by the Communist Party.'[18]

Similar comments at the Twenty-Fourth CPU Congress in 1971 echoed demands first made by the Ukrainian intelligentsia at a conference on the state of the Ukrainian language in February 1963.[19] In response, Shelest's Minister of Education, Iurii Dadenkov, circulated a plan for the Ukrainianisation of higher education institutions in August 1965, although not surprisingly this was blocked by Moscow.

Despite the arrest wave of 1965–6, Shelest was at least more tolerant of the 1960s generation of dissidents and their cultural agenda than others in Moscow or the CPU desired. The most telling evidence for this is that the 1972–3 purge of the cultural intelligentsia coincided largely with his removal in May 1972, and that portion of the purge which preceded his downfall from January 1972 onwards can, in retrospect, be seen as a sign of the growing dominance of those who would eventually replace him.

None of this, however, meant that Shelest was a 'rebel', or that he did not operate within the rules of a system to which he was fundamentally loyal. His post-1988 interviews revealed a loyalty to Leninist principles that was by then somewhat outdated. Shelest's contradictions were also evident in his calls for more effort in atheistic propaganda, his criticisms of nationalist émigrés and his demand for an 'intensification of the ideological struggle', especially between 1970 and 1972.[20] Indeed, his 1970 book *Ukraine – Our Soviet Land*, was nationalist only in the sense of being not in tune with 'the pro-Russian atmosphere of forced assimilation of the late 1960s and early 1970s', although it sought to rehabilitate certain specifically Ukrainian historical symbols.[21]

Shelest's desire to return to Leninism reflected the then prevalent mood within *samizdat* and independent literature (which coincided with the early Gorbachev view) that the faults of the Soviet system could be laid at the door of 'Stalinism' (and also 'Brezhnevism') – but not at that of the Communist Party or Lenin. This view was most famously expressed in Ivan Dziuba's study *Internationalism or Russification? A Study in the Soviet Nationalities Problem*, presented to the CPU and government in December 1965 and then circulated among regional leaders for comment.

Brezhnev (a Russian from the Dnipropetrovs'k region, which was also Shcherbytskyi's home base), the ideological secretary Suslov, and their supporters in the CPU, perhaps had a better understanding than Shelest of the centrifugal tendencies encouraged by his policies, and of how the logic of national communism rhetoric always tended to stimulate demands by local elites for progressively greater autonomy. Hence, centralist circles in Moscow, led by Suslov, but also those CPU elements dependent upon all-Union structures, began manoeuvring against Shelest as early as 1968, as the conservatives began to consolidate their position in Moscow.[22]

An early sign was the campaign by the Dnipropetrovs'k-Donets'k CPU against the book *Sobor* (The Cathedral), published in 1968 and written by the chairman of the Writers' Union of Ukraine, Oles Honchar. As there was a simultaneous campaign against 'Ukrainian bourgeois nationalists' in the area,[23] the campaign was interpreted as Shcherbytskyi attacking Shelest by proxy.[24] After initially favourable reviews, the book was withdrawn from sale.[25]

In July 1970, Shelest's client, V. F. Nikitchenko, was replaced as Ukrainian KGB chief by Vitalii Fedorchuk, widely perceived as a representative of the centre.[26] All of the regional heads of the KGB were also replaced in Ukraine at the same time. Fedorchuk moved immediately against the dissidents that Shelest had tolerated, and finally against Shelest himself in May 1972.[27]

A press campaign was followed by mass arrests and purges, resubordination of academic institutions to strict Communist Party control and a campaign against Ukrainian national distinctiveness. 'The KGB completely slipped out from under the control of the CPU leadership', the *samizdat Ukrainian Herald* stated, after Shcherbytskyi successfully convinced Moscow 'that Shelest was a nationalistic deviationist'.[28]

The Shcherbytskyi regime, by contrast, therefore, is normally seen as representing the triumph of the centre in the locality. The purge of the early 1970s indeed went far beyond the removal of Shelest himself, as it was designed to expunge completely the temptations of national communism. Between the Twenty-Fourth and Twenty-Fifth CPU congresses in March 1971 and February 1976, six new replacements were appointed to the (11-man) Ukrainian Politburo, while 41 per cent of the Central Committee, 63 per cent of *Obkom* secretaries, and 8 or 9 of the 25 *oblast* and city first secretaries were changed.[29] (The figures include changes made at the Twenty-Fifth Congress, but still understate the total upheaval, as the purge arguably started in 1970–1.) Official figures, which are also almost certainly an underestimate, cite 37 000 expelled from the CPU in 1973–4, or 1.5 per cent of the total membership.[30] The purge fell particularly heavily on those involved in propaganda and culture work, on the universities of L'viv and Kyiv, on the editors and journalists of organs suspected of heresy, and, of course, on dissident circles as well (see below). It did not, however, appear to encompass economic elites.[31] The new regime had a clear understanding, therefore, of the nature of Shelest's power base.

Accordingly, Shcherbytskyi's surprisingly slow consolidation of his power was based in a shift in the balance of governing forces towards those more directly concerned with purely 'political' work or administration, and more politically reliable agricultural specialists, whereas the representation of the cultural intelligentsia, i.e. the group most prone to national communism, diminished.[32] The higher elite also tended to be disproportionately recruited from the more Russified and again, therefore, politically 'safe' areas.[33] The Donets'k and Dnipropretrovs'k party machines, both traditionally highly integrated into all-Union economic and political structures, were particularly important in this respect, whereas Galicia and Kyiv provided few members of the new governing elite.

Politically, the Shcherbytskyi coterie therefore represented those portions of the CPU who were more prepared to do Moscow's bidding. Thus, under Shcherbytskyi, the CPU no longer raised object-ions to the centre's investment and resource allocation policies, and the rearguard action fought under Shelest to protect the Ukrainian language gave way to collaboration in the policies of intensified Russification adopted after the Twenty-Fourth CPSU Congress in March 1971. As a result, the number of Ukrainian schoolchildren edu-cated in Ukrainian-language schools fell below 50 per cent in the second half of the 1970s (it did recover until the mid-1990s).[34] Fewer books were published in the Ukrainian language under Brezhnev than under Stalin.[35]

Whereas Shelest had been willing to provide symbolic sustenance to Ukrainian national consciousness in the areas of language, culture and historiography, as with the book *Ukraine – Our Soviet Land*, largely ghost-written for him by Oles Honchar in 1970, the cultural and polit-ical discourse of the Shcherbytskyi regime placed it firmly within an all-Union context. Shcherbytskyi would even speak Russian on most public occasions. According to Pelenski, 'throughout Shelest's speeches and writings there are, of course, positive references to the Russian people. But, they do not include even an iota of that enthusi-astic servility that is so familiar to readers of documents of both the Stalinist period and the period since 1972.'[36]

The Shcherbytskyi regime maintained a rigid monopoly over public political activity until well into the Gorbachev era, despite premature predictions of his demise, or that he would be forced to trim his policies.[37]

In 1979, for example, the downfall of the chief scourge of dissi-dents and 'national communists' since November 1972, the Propaganda Secretary Valentyn Malanchuk,[38] together with the dis-missal of Education Minister Marynych and the appointment of a new editor, Perebyinis, for *Literaturna Ukraina* (the main organ of the Ukrainian cultural elite) in March 1980, was interpreted as in-augurating a policy of partial reaccommodation with the cultural intelligentsia.[39]

Similarly, on various occasions in the 1980s, the departure of key colleagues (such as Fedorchuk in January 1986, Prime Minister Oleksandr Liashko in 1987, and Second Secretary Aleksei Titarenko in December 1988), policy disagreements (over Chornobyl' for example, or Shcherbytskyi's reported criticism of Gorbachev's Geneva summit with Ronald Reagan in November 1985) and setpiece CPU/CPSU Congresses or plenums were all minutely examined for evidence of a Gorbachev-inspired move against Shcherbytskyi.[40]

However, there was no real evidence of a centrally coordinated campaign against him.[41] Nor did policy changes under Shcherbytskyi ever amount to more than his bending with the climate of the times to the degree necessary to ensure his survival.[42]

The latter stages of Shcherbytskyi's rule, therefore, cannot be inter-preted simply as an unwanted conservative hangover into the Gorbachev period, which the centre was anxious to remove. Rather, the CPU, although challenged by the gradual rise of opposition groups, loyally fulfilled the key instrumental role of control of the periphery for the centre until at least autumn 1990.

The Shcherbytskyi regime was founded on a 'younger brother' logic, the CPU elite receiving local predominance, and the possibility of all-Union promotion in return for resisting the national communist temp-tation[43] (a role comparable to that of the Scots in the establishment and policing of the British empire). The CPU, therefore, remained largely passive during the initial phases of *perestroika* because they only occupied intermediate and instrumental power positions.

As Gorbachev tried to recentralise in response to the 'penetration crisis' suffered by the centre (i.e. its increasing inability to direct and control republican bureaucracies), he gradually undermined the basis of the informal 'younger brother' contract, and the republican elec-tions of March 1990 introduced a state- (and authority-) building logic that began to conflict with all-Union interests. However, predictions of anything more than cosmetic change under Shcherbytskyi before these structural changes took place were premature.[44]

The consequences of Shcherbytskyi's longevity in office and the fact that, unlike in some other republics, Ukraine's momentum had been away from, rather than towards, national communism since 1972, were, in terms of the analysis presented in Chapter 1, threefold. First, it was comparatively difficult for the Ukrainian opposition to establish itself as a legitimate public force until its take-off in autumn 1989 and breakthrough in mid-1990. Second, the possibility of securing political change through a split in the ruling elite and consequent alliance with opposition forces, as in the Baltic republics or Armenia, was ruled out until the rise of 'sovereign (i.e. national) communists', led by Leonid Kravchuk, between winter 1990 and spring 1991. Third, even when this possibility eventually emerged, it was on terms more favourable to the maintenance of communist power than in many other republics. Indeed, the Declaration of Independence on 24 August 1991 was arguably an attempt by the CPU to hold on to power in an independent state.[45]

However, several complicating factors deserve to be mentioned. First, the 'Communist Party of Ukraine' (from 1918 to 1952 it was called the 'Communist Party [Bolshevik] of Ukraine') was never an autonomous organisation. It simply referred to those members of the CPSU who were resident in the Ukrainian SSR. The CPU did not even have its own programme until its Twenty-Eighth Congress in June 1990. Its leadership never had full 'horizontal' competence over Ukrainian affairs and it was often bypassed by alternative channels of power.[46] Therefore, the idea that the history of the CPU can be divided into clear eras defined by the political priorities of its first secretary (for example, the so-called 'Shcherbychchyna') is partly fictional.

As Hodnett argues, 'Neither Shelest nor Shcherbytskyi have come close to being the centre of an all-dominating patron–client network at the top leadership level in the Ukraine.'[47] Some elements within the CPU undoubtedly did owe their loyalty to the first secretary (for Shelest, the Kharkiv group, for Shcherbytskyi the Dnipropetrovsk organisation), but others owed it to past leaders, or saw their careers within an all-Union context. The CPU, therefore, was always a factionalised body, with arguably no true existence as a systematic whole. This, in turn, undermines the notion of a strict dichotomy between the Shelest and Shcherbytskyi eras, and helps to explain the otherwise unexpectedly sudden re-emergence of a sleeping national communist tendency in winter 1990-Spring 1991.

The long-term logic (socio-economic for Krawchenko, institutional for Motyl) towards the regular recurrence of national communism meant that the renewed rise of 'sovereign communists' in 1990-1 in Ukraine was to be expected, because the conditions that gave rise to it in the 1920s and 1960s remained 'part of the historical agenda'.[48]

NATIONALITY POLICY UNDER BREZHNEV

Article 71 of the 1977 Soviet constitution guaranteed each republic 'the right to freely secede from the USSR'. But there would never be any need to exercise this 'right', as 'each nation is aware that its freedom and progress are reliably assured precisely within the Union'.[49] In reality the republics of the USSR had less autonomy than the states of the USA or the cantons of Switzerland.[50] For advocating the 'right' to secession many Ukrainian and other non-Russian dissidents were imprisoned in the Gulag prior to 1987.

As mentioned in Chapter 1, Soviet nationality policy was based on the concepts of *rastsvet* (flourishing), *sblizhenie* (drawing together) and the eventual *sliianie* (merging) of nations. During his speech on the fiftieth anniversary of the formation of the USSR in 1972 (the year Shelest was removed from office), Brezhnev refined official doctrine with the introduction of the new concepts of *vsestoronnee sblizhenie* (all-round rapproachement), and *splochenie* (cohesion) leading to *edinstvo* (unity), which was already reflected in the 'new historical community of people', the 'Soviet people' whose formation Brezhnev had announced at the Twenty-Fourth CPSU congress in 1971.

The drawing in of the Ukrainian 'younger brothers' into a ruling partnership with the Russians was perceived by Moscow in the 1970s as the crucial component of this process, as rising Muslim birthrates threatened to reduce the Russians' share of the Soviet population below the psychologically important 50 per cent mark.[51] Ukrainians were also the best targets for the plans to accelerate the adoption of Russian that were given extra emphasis in the 1970s.[52]

Hence the common past of Ukrainians and Russians was repeatedly stressed. The 375th anniversary of the 'reunification' of Ukraine and Russia in 1979, the '1500th' anniversary of the city of Kyiv in 1982 and the millennium of the Christianisation of Kievan Rus' in 1988 were celebrated as the joint heritage of all three East Slavic nations.[53]

The portrayal of the USSR as the logical successor to Kyivan Rus' was meant to deprive Ukrainians 'of a separate and distinct identity either in the past, present or future.'[54]

During the Brezhnev period, the numerical and proportionate role of Russians in the republic dramatically increased. The Ukrainian share of the republic's population dropped steadily from 76.8 per cent in 1959 to 72.7 per cent in 1989, as the Russian share grew from 16.9 to 22.1 per cent. The rate of increase of the Russian population between 1970 and 1979 was 15 per cent, or 1.3 million, exceeding the numerical increase of Ukrainians.[55]

As Krawchenko argues, 'These were not the immigrants that one found in most other countries in the world – newcomers moving into subordinate positions in the host society. Rather this immigration resembled the movement of population which occurs from an imperial core to a colonised periphery.'[56] It is difficult, however, to determine retrospectively how much this was an issue at the time, although similar complaints can be found in *samizdat* such as Dziuba's comment that the notion of 'a single socialist (Soviet) nation' was merely camouflage for an extensive policy of Russification.[57] The closeness of the Ukrainian language and culture to Russian and the association of Russian, with social advancement, made Ukrainians relatively easy targets for Russification.

If anything, therefore, national consciousness in Ukraine and Belarus during the 'era of stagnation' was on the decline. The high degree of integration of eastern Ukrainians at least into the Soviet system and their relative indifference to the national question were evident in polls after the March 1990 republican elections, when Ukrainians were found to be more conservative in their political attitudes than Russians, with trust in the centre to rectify problems and support for the Communist Party stronger than among Russians, while support for complete secession was still weak (at a time when the Ukrainian parliament was still not functioning and the democratic opposition was in the process of becoming a wide-based movement). Ukrainians valued 'order' over 'liberty' (Ukrainians were prized for their discipline in the Soviet armed forces), and were afraid of chaos and spontaneity in society.[58] Material rather than cultural or national issues were seen as more important.[59]

DISSENT AND OPPOSITION

Dissent and opposition in Ukraine under Brezhnev however remained vociferous in relation to other republics, despite relatively harsh treatment.[60] Dissent was however a variegated phenomenon.

During the postwar OUN–UPA period, dissent in Ukraine took three forms: open agitation, clandestine work and lobbying within the national communist faction of the CPU. The clandestine tradition was linked to the nationalist movement of the 1940s, whereas the new civil rights movement of the 1960s was a product of the new cultural revival and post-Stalin thaw. Its characteristics were populism, humanism, high intellectual content and a deliberate desire to work in the open.

Some worked 'within the framework of the system' and espoused national communism, calling for a return to the Leninist nationalities policy that had generated the Ukrainisation of the 1920s.[61] The most prominent example was Ivan Dziuba, the mouthpiece of a section of the establishment from 1963 to 1972. Dziuba's argument in his book *Internationalism or Russification?* selectively quoted Lenin in an idealised manner, as a 'sort of unblemished, omniscient hero' to argue that Stalin and Khrushchev had perverted Leninist nationality policy.[62]

Dziuba was eventually subjected to a campaign of vilification.[63] In March 1972 he was expelled from the Writers' Union of Ukraine, then arrested the following month and sentenced in March 1973 to five years' imprisonment,[64] although he later recanted, which spared him his sentence.[65] In early 1972 when Dziuba's house was searched by the KGB, the complete works of Lenin were confiscated, 'with notes in the margins and phrases underlined'.

The opposite side of the spectrum to Dziuba was represented by Valentyn Moroz,[66] whose writings echoed those of Dmytro Dontsov, 'the Ukrainian Nietzsche', who was the inspiration for the Bandera faction of the OUN. 'What connected Moroz with the Dontsovian-OUN tradition was his philosophical voluntarism, his insistence upon the maintaining of the pure national idea at all costs, his scornful rejection of any pragmatic accommodation to existing conditions, his cult of the strong, heroic, self-sacrificing individual, and, finally, his anti-intellect and advocacy of *oderzhymist'* which means approximately "frenzy" or "holy madness",' Ivan Rudnytsky commented.[67]

But neither Moroz nor Dziuba became representative of the mainstream of Ukrainian dissent – either in the Brezhnev or the Gorbachev era. More typical were groups such as the Ukrainian Helsinki Group (UHG) in the Brezhnev period and the Ukrainian Popular Movement (*Rukh*) in the post-1985 era.[68] Ukrainian dissidents adopted the same legalistic approach as their Russian counterparts, trying to force the state to honour its commitments to the rule of law, and individual and national rights. In the 1970s and mid-1980s the balance between the latter two was about equal, but from 1989–90 onwards increasing emphasis was placed on the national question.

In a study of the national composition of dissidents in Ukraine in the late 1960s and early 1970s, Ukrainians accounted for 77 per cent of the total number, while Russians made up only 0.5 per cent, the remainder being mainly Jews and Crimean Tatars. As a privileged group (in the state and socio-economic elites, and with no lack of publications in Russian) within Ukraine, Russians were less likely to engage in dissent or publish *samizdat* in proportion to their numbers.[69] Their relative passivity in the face of a rising tide of Ukrainian nationalist collective action would be problematical by 1990–1, however.

Open anti-Soviet dissent was always most intense in the Soviet west, and this was always the case in western Ukraine as well.[70] The cities and towns of southern and eastern Ukraine had been heavily Russified and at the time of the Russian revolution were islands of Bolshevik support in Ukraine. Galicia, on the other hand, already a stronghold of nationalism, had, after the local Jews had been exterminated by the Nazis and the Poles deported by the Soviets to Siberia in 1939–41 or to Poland in 1944–7, become the most monoethnic region in Ukraine.[71] In addition, 'the urban base of Party activity, which was so important in establishing Communist rule in east Ukraine, was largely lacking in the West.'[72]

The nationalist guerrilla movement had fought on in Galicia until 1952–4,[73] and western Ukraine always played a disproportionate role in the dissident movements of the Brezhnev era and as the leading initial base for the national revival under Gorbachev. By the 1960s, however, central and eastern Ukrainian dissenters were becoming more numerous, as dissent became more of an urban phenomenon.[74] In Kyiv, the intelligentsia was much stronger than in Galicia, and consequently, the peasant-based populism of the OUN and its various would-be successor groups was followed by the civic values of the Ukrainian Helsinki Group.

The first post-Stalin dissident groups were organised in the late 1950s[75] after the end of the underground UPA war in the early 1950s, although arrests of members of the UPA and the OUN continued as late as the early 1960s.[76] Between the late 1950s and 1970s, the majority of nationalist underground groups were uncovered in western Ukraine, such as Levko Lukianenko's Ukrainian Workers' and Peasants' Union, the Ukrainian National Committee, the United Party for the Liberation of Ukraine and the Ukrainian National Front.

The most radical and best organised was the Ukrainian National Front (UNF), which was established in Ivano-Frankivs'k in the early 1960s, although arrests were made as far away as Donets'k. The majority of members were villagers[77] and Uniate Catholic faithful, within the age group 20–30.[78] The UNF stood for state independence, a democratic form of government and agrarian reforms. It published the *samizdat* journals *Volia i Bat'kivshchyna* (Freedom and Fatherland), 16 issues of which appeared, *Zemlia i volia* (Land and Freedom) and *Mesnyk* (The Avenger), and circulated old OUN–UPA

literature. The UNF also circulated leaflets denouncing the occupation of Ukraine and calling for the punishment of those responsible
for Stalinist crimes in Ukraine.[79] The majority of UNF members were
arrested in the late 1960s, but in the early 1980s new reports were
published in the *samizdat Chronicle of the Catholic Church* in Ukraine
that the UNF was again active in the Ivano-Frankivs'k region.

The Soviet authorities continued to persecute former members of
the OUN and UPA, even in some cases executing them, and maintained a persistent anti-nationalist (and anti-émigré) media campaign,[80] attempting to link the contemporary national and democratic
movement in Ukraine to the OUN and UPA and their alleged collaboration with the Nazis in World War II.[81] The number and extent of
such trials sharply increased in the late 1970s and first half of the
1980s, in some cases continuing until 1987–8.[82] This domestic campaign coincided with a large-scale external campaign against émigré
Ukrainians[83] accusing them of harbouring 'Nazi war criminals', which
also ended at about the same time.[84]

The dissident organisations uncovered in eastern Ukraine tended
to have aims closer to those of Russian democratic movements at the
time.[85] The generation of the 1960s (*shestydesiatnyky*) comprised
poets, actors, writers, artists, publicists, historians and teachers – a
'patriotic opposition'. Their goals were to work within the system
(rather than overthrow it) in pursuit of democracy, humanism, an end
to Russification and in defence of Ukrainian language and culture.
They used methods similar to those in Russia – individual and group
letters, petitions, complaints, unofficial gatherings and *samizdat*.

In the summer of 1965 the first arrests of 100 intellectuals were
made in several cities.[86] The authorities were however surprised by the
degree of solidarity the accused received, producing appeals to party
and state leaders, group petitions demanding full publicity and open
trials, and unauthorised protest meetings.[87] One of the outcomes of
this protest was a petition by Ivan Dziuba, to Petro Shelest, attached
to which was the lengthy document 'Internationalism or
Russification?' Dissident networks continued to spread, and by the
late 1960s *samizdat* was widespread in Ukraine.

The clampdown on Ukrainian dissent in 1972 therefore concentrated on intellectuals in Kyiv, where 'the atmosphere resembled in
many respects that of the Stalinist terror'.[88] By 1970–2, as in 1990–1,
the central state's tolerance of limited dissent and a degree of greater
republican autonomy had only led to more radical demands directed
against the system and the Union. The dilemma on both occasions
faced by the authorities was to either allow it to continue, or use

repression and recentralise. In both 1972 and 1991 the authorities chose repression, but by 1991 the degree of imperial disintegration meant that repression would have had to have been undertaken against thousands, rather than hundreds of people, as in 1972.

The clampdown destroyed the hopes of many dissidents to establish a dialogue with the Soviet Ukrainian authorities and work within the system, casting doubt upon the legalistic approach favoured since the 1960s. Dissent prior to 1972 in Ukraine had been shown to be a 'relatively weak and vulnerable phenomenon lacking a definite political programme, adequate organisation or a strong social base'.[88] Nevertheless, the revived *shestydesiatnyky* would return in 1988–91 to provide intelligentsia leadership for the resergent national movement.

Despite the clampdown, the USSR's largest Helsinki Group (Ukrainian Group for the Promotion of the Implementation of the Helsinki accords, or UHG) was established in Ukraine on 9 November 1976, encouraged by the rise in East–West détente to act as an open public association. By 1980 the UHG had issued a total of 30 declarations and appeals, as well as 18 memorandums and 10 bulletins.[89] Unlike the Moscow group, the UHG defended both civil and national rights, although religious and socio-economic rights were relatively neglected.[90] The UHG was 'a veritable microcosm of Ukrainian dissent and represented an attempt to create a unified structure in which ideological and tactical differences would be submerged'.[92] The initiators of the UHG were nearly all members of the middle-ranking intelligentsia, and it was evenly divided between western and eastern Ukrainians.[93]

An extra ingredient in Ukrainian dissent was the possibility of contagion from Hungary, Poland and Czechoslovakia into the sensitive western Ukraine whenever communist control of central Europe became less certain (1956, 1968 and during the early 1980s). Support for the Hungarian uprising existed in western Ukraine,[94] while the 'Prague Spring's' impact upon the Ukrainian minority in eastern Slovakia may have been an added incentive to send the Warsaw Pact forces to crush it.[95]

Information flowed in the other direction. Events virtually unnoticed in the Soviet press were often published by Poland's Ukrainian-language press.[96] The rise of Solidarity in Poland and the continuation of an underground structure after the declaration of martial law on 13 December 1981 were also a cause for concern to both Kyiv and Moscow.[97] In the view of the ideological secretary of the Ivano-Frankivs'k branch of the CPU, western Ukraine is 'literally in the forefront of ideological confrontation. A border *oblast* is always a special region where one constantly smells the fumes of anti-Soviet fire'.[98]

The increased repression of dissent in the USSR during the late 1970s and early 1980s, drove opposition 'almost entirely underground' with dissidents dropping open tactics, and increasingly using pseudonyms in *samizdat* and statements.[99] The authorities first tested new methods of persecution in Ukraine,[100] for example, charging dissidents with non-political crimes (e.g. homosexuality, theft, narcotics), re-sentencing political prisoners for additional terms[101] and forcing dissidents to recant their views for domestic and foreign audiences.[102]

The UHG, which eventually had 40 members, was effectively out of action by the early 1980s, although it never formally disbanded, as the Moscow Helsinki Group was forced to in September 1981. By then, 22 UHG members were in the Gulag (6 received 15 years each, 3 received 12 years each and 13 received 3–9 years' imprisonment), 2 were forced into internal exile, and 6 were forced to emigrate (they then established an external branch led by Mykola Rudenko), although 3 were released from imprisonment. In 1984–5 four UHG political prisoners – Vasyl Stus,[103] Oleksa Tykhyi, Valerii Marchenko and Iurii Lytvyn – died in the Gulag from conditions of confinement.[104] The popular music composer Volodymyr Ivasiuk was allegedly murdered by the KGB on 12 June 1978, while Mykhailo Melnyk committed suicide after a KGB raid on his home.[105] The deaths of the poet Oleksandr Hryhorenko and priest Vasyl Lutskiv were also ascribed to the KGB in UHG documents.

According to the Moscow Helsinki Group, Ukrainian dissidents by the early 1980s constituted the largest single group of political prisoners.[106] The former Jewish political prisoner, Yakiv Suslenskyi, noted that the harshest sentences were meted out in Ukraine, with Balts or Armenians receiving 3–4 years when a Ukrainian would have received 12 years' imprisonment and exile.[107] In the Gulag camps of Mordovia, Ukrainians reportedly accounted for between 60 and 70 per cent of political prisoners.[108]

A former Ukrainian conscript, V. N. Holembovskyi, who served in the Ministry of Internal Troops (MVD) guard at the Mordovian political camps during 1970–2 recounted his story in December 1991.[109] The prisoners of the Mordovian camps where he served were always described as 'state criminals' and 'Banderites', and included many of the well-known Ukrainian dissidents of the 1960s, such as Levko Lukianenko and Viacheslav Chornovil. Upwards of 1200–1300 prisoners were held in the camp where he served, making furniture for high-ranking Communist Party officials.

In the words of Peter Reddaway, 'the biggest short-term risks of the current policy on dissent would seem to be the development of underground groups that the KGB cannot easily monitor – as we have seen, this is already happening – and a sharp rise in acts of violence (hijackings, assassinations, bombings) which so far have been fairly rare.'[110] In going underground, the dissident movement in Ukraine (both in the Gulag and outside) during the late 1970s and early 1980s had become radicalised and moved from demanding democratisation within a Soviet context to calling for independence.[111] Moreover, the ties that were formed among the camp generation helped them serve as the avant-garde of the national movement, after most were released in 1987.

There is evidence that a small number of nationalists in western Ukraine turned to violence during this period, blowing up gas pipelines and railway lines.[112] In June 1982 Borys Terelia (who had spent 16 years in the Gulag) was killed in a shoot-out with KGB security forces in Transcarpathia,[113] confirmed by the first secretary of the regional branch of the CPU, who accused him of being a 'common criminal'.[114] Terelia 'offered resistance to the militiamen, seriously wounded one of them, refused to surrender to the authorities, and continued firing'.

Iosyf Terelia later claimed in the *samizdat Chronicle of the Catholic Church in Ukraine* that his brother had committed suicide rather than be captured on 10 June 1982 in the village of Poliana, and confirmed that his nationalist group had concluded that peaceful forms of protest in the current climate of repression in Ukraine would be unsuccessful.[115] Six years after his death, an émigré newspaper reported that Borys Terelia had been head of the Security Service of the underground OUN in Galicia and Transcarpathia from 1975–82.[116] A crash of a Soviet military plane carrying political-military officers from the Carpathian military district was also attributed to sabotage.[117]

Religion

Dissent in the USSR was always strongest where national and religious demands were combined, such as in western Ukraine and Lithuania. Ukraine on the eve of the Gorbachev era possessed two-thirds of Russian Orthodox parishes in the USSR, half of which were in western Ukraine.[118] Both the Ukrainian Autocephalous Orthodox (UAOC) and Greek Catholic (UCC) Churches had been destroyed in the 1930s and second half of the 1940s respectively, with most Church property being handed over to the loyal Russian Orthodox Church.[119] Historically, both the Tsarist and Soviet regimes had favoured the Russian Orthodox Church as a 'state church', in particular in Ukraine and Belarus where it was an ally of the imperial authorities.[120]

Religion had managed to maintain a strong influence in Ukraine, though, and Kyiv churches were attended by twice as many young people as in Moscow or even Tbilisi.[121] The UCC survived its forced merger with the Russian Orthodox Church by becoming a 'catacomb' church,[122] although the UAOC did not possess any underground structure in the pre-Gorbachev era in Ukraine, with the first lay pressure group not established in Kyiv until February 1988.[123]

The extensive range of anti-Ukrainian Catholic propaganda testified to the latter's continued vitality.[124] The UCC received an infusion of energy with the election of Pope John Paul II, a Pole who was widely regarded as sympathetic to the plight of Ukrainian Catholics.[125] Consequently, at a time when Soviet repression of dissent in Ukraine was becoming harsher in the early 1980s, the UCC began to increase its activities in western Ukraine, helped by the energetic Iosyf Terelia. Pope John Paul II's support for Ukrainian Catholics and Solidarity made him highly unpopular with the Soviet authorities, and the subject of a widescale counter-propaganda campaign. In western Ukraine 587 commissions promoted Soviet festivals and rites, with atheistic propaganda conducted through more than 3000 lecturers and 7000 agitators. For adults there were 450 atheistic clubs while for children 1600 similar institutions existed. Between 1971 and 1981 over 800 publications in the USSR attacked Catholics.[126]

In September 1982 Iosyf Terelia announced the establishment of the Initiative Committee for the Defence of the Rights of Believers of the Church which restricted itself to one goal: legalisation of the UCC. The Initiative Committee began to publish the *samizdat* information bulletin *The Chronicle of the Catholic Church in Ukraine* in 1984, modelled upon a Lithuanian equivalent of a similar name, after Terelia was released from a one-year prison sentence. *The Chronicle* received wide exposure in the West, and served to publicise the growth and continued vitality of Ukrainian Catholics in the early 1980s.[127] Although links existed between the Initiative Committee and the Ukrainian National Front (both of which were based in Galicia and Transcarpathia), there did not appear to be any links with the UHG or overlap in membership between these two organisations.[128] As already mentioned, the UHG's *samizdat* did not cover religious questions.

After Terelia's expulsion to the West in 1987, the work of the Initiative Committee was taken over by Ivan Hel, released from the Gulag during the amnesty of political prisoners in the same year.[129] Ivan Hel renamed the Initiative Committee the Committee in

Defence of the Ukrainian Catholic Church, and from August 1987 Ukrainian Catholics began to agitate openly in support of legalisation of their Church (see Chapters 4 and 5). The activation of the catacomb Uniate Church in 1982–7, during a period of continued Soviet harassment and repression, served to strengthen the Church for its full emergence in 1989–90 when the political climate was more opportune.

Workers' Groups

Specifically working-class agitation in the USSR arrived much later, the first traces in Ukraine appearing only in 1978. National and religious movements in western Ukraine had always included a large number of workers and peasants, whereas Kyiv-based groups such as the UHG were closer to Russian dissidents groups, in terms of their largely intelligentsia membership and in the subject matter of their *samizdat*.[130]

Strikes and workers' protests occurred more frequently in the Soviet Union's periphery, and such strikes tended to be more violent. Often this was due to simple shortages.[131] In 1962 the strikes and riots in Novocherkassk spread quickly throughout the region to include a large section of the working classes in neighbouring Ukraine.[132]

The poor working conditions and exploitation in the coal mining region of the Donbas in eastern Ukraine were exposed by two Western correspondents who visited the area in December 1980. One of the reporters later described the degree of political control 'exercised right down to the level of each individual worker – deliberately fostering divisions, resentment and dissension bordering on hatred within the working class, sapping its unity and potential cohesion in the face of exploitation.'[133] The difficulty of organising a workers opposition movement in the Donbas was brought home to the reporter.

> The bosses had absolute power to fire, reprimand, dock pay, deny vacation or mete out any combination of punishment they chose. In theory the workers enjoyed full rights to petition through their trade unions for redressing unfair treatment. In practice, workers usually agreed with their bosses. They were afraid to challenge them because they could only lose.[134]

The political prisoner Mykola Pohyba wrote a lengthy open letter to Amnesty International in November 1980 claiming that 'the Soviet

Union is ripe for the founding of independent labour unions' and praising Poland's Solidarity. Official trade unions did not support the workers because they were 'an integral part of the party-state apparatus.'[135] Pohyba labelled the Soviet system 'totalitarian state capitalist.'

Whereas the UHG did not deal with socio-economic questions, the more radical Ukrainian Patriotic Movement called (prior to Solidarity's launch) for workers to establish their own independent trade unions, and advised workers that 'It is your sacred right to struggle against the merciless exploitation of your labour by the state.' Another document of the Ukrainian Patriotic Movement called for support for the miners.[136]

The miners expressed sympathy for the Solidarity movement in Poland but felt helpless to act, worrying that if the USSR 'attacks Poland today, it would be us tomorrow.'[137] Strikes and labour disputes did, however, become more frequent and the authorities paid greater attention to trade unions and workers grievances in 1980–1.[138] In February 1978, the Free Trade Union Association of the Soviet Working People was established by two Donbas miners, Vladimir Klebanov and Aleksei Nikitin.[139] The union as Klebanov was ready to point out, had nothing in common with the dissidents, was not anti-communist and was against Ukrainian national rights.[140]

Despite professing loyalty to communism and asking for support to work within the system (in the same manner as the *shestydesiatnyky*), both Klebanov and Nikitin were arrested and incarcerated in psychiatric hospitals in 1978. Nikitin died of stomach cancer shortly after being released in 1984.[141] Klebanov was not released from compulsory psychiatric confinement until 1988.

Klebanov and Nikitin had been warned by the CPU *oblast* first secretary: 'If you stick your nose into our business, I'll mix coal with your blood and take your body and grind it into fertiliser.'[142] Donbas miners' grievances eventually resulted in the strike explosion of summer 1989, however (see Chapter 5), and later in June 1993.

CONCLUSIONS

The pre-Gorbachev era had shown evidence of every strand of dissent and opposition in Ukraine: religious, nationalist, socio-economic and human rights. All had been severely repressed by the authorities. In terms of the argument of Chapter 1, therefore, although the state had to tolerate a greater degree of dissent than in Stalin's time, in the

Brezhnev and Andropov eras, and especially in Shcherbytskyi's Ukraine, no public space was permitted for different small groups, which were regionally and socially dispersed, to coalesce into a large unified movement capable of challenging the power and legitimacy of the Communist Party.[143]

This would only occur in the second half of Gorbachev's rule, when the Ukrainian national and democratic movement took off and posed a serious threat to Moscow's and the CPU's control over the republic. But it would be the hundreds of politically experienced former Ukrainian political prisoners who would be the footsoldiers in the Gorbachev era. They had, after all, graduated from the 'universities' that the Gulag became, to become hardened activists ready to continue their struggle in the new conditions that existed after 1987 for the ideals that Gorbachev now professed – ideals which they had already held for at least two decades.

When Viacheslav Chornovil, a dissident and political prisoner in pre-Gorbachev days, was asked during the presidential elections held in Ukraine on 1 December 1991 what the difference was between himself and his main rival, Leonid Kravchuk, he replied: 'Nothing. Except that my programme is thirty years old, and Kravchuk's three weeks old.'[144]

4 Gorbachev, Dissent and the New Opposition (1987–8)

On coming to power in 1986, Mikhail Gorbachev had little idea of the extent of the potential nationality problem in the USSR. It was not until the end of the decade that he began to turn his attention to this question after riots in Kazakhstan in 1986, the public outcry over the Chornobyl' nuclear disaster, the return of dissidents from the Gulag the following year, and the growing campaign by the cultural intelligentsia to raise questions of Russification and national revival forced the issue on to the agenda.

Almost immediately after Gorbachev came to power, non-Russians began demanding a return to 'Leninist nationality policy' – as they had during previous periods of 'liberalisation' (such as during the 1920s and 1960s). This included demands for the titular nationality's language in each republic to become the state language, as well as for the Ministry of Education to determine the language of instruction in schools in accordance with the national composition of pupils (rather than by parental choice). In Ukraine and Belarus, where enrolment in native language schools had noticeably declined since 1958–9, the situation was far more urgent, leading to the prioritisation of demands for radical changes in educational and cultural policies. Almost immediately, therefore, leading Ukrainian *literati*, such as Oles Honchar, used the opportunities provided by *glasnost'* to revive the debate of the 1960s.

However, the new CPSU programme adopted in 1986 seemed to assume that the nationality question was resolved – the view, we must remember at the time, of most Western Sovietologists.[1] Its section on the nationality question was half as long as that in the 1961 programme and optimistically proclaimed: 'the nationality question, as inherited from the past, has been successfully resolved in the Soviet

Union.' The programme emphasised the Soviet Union's unitary nature, playing down the importance of the republics. Again optimistically, it concluded: 'A new social and international community of people – the Soviet people (has been) formed ... This development entails, in the remote historical future, the complete unity of nations.'[2]

By the following year it was becoming clear to experts on Soviet nationality policies in Moscow that the situation was not as rosy as the CPSU programme had claimed. It was time for an overhaul of the Brezhnev era nationality policies, Eduard Bagromov, a leading Soviet authority on nationality problems, admitted, because events had clearly moved on.[3] In his speech to the 27th CPSU Congress, Gorbachev admitted that Soviet nationality policies until then had been merely 'upbeat treatises reminiscent of times of complimentary toasts rather than serious scientific studies'.[4]

The most contentious issue immediately became language. One of the most 'successful' results of the Brezhnev era nationality policies was the growth of bilingualism, with Russian becoming *de facto* the second language of the majority of Soviet citizens. The demand that the right of parents to choose the language of instruction of schools be revoked was clearly seen as an attempt to reduce the number of Russian-language schools.

Gorbachev therefore criticised the 'blunders and miscalculations' of his predecessor's nationality policies. But, at the same time, lauded the 'process of the flourishing of nations, their unification, their willing unification', which was guided by the CPSU. In his speech to the 27th CPSU Congress, Gorbachev gave no detailed analysis of the Kazakh riots and no hint of new policies to redress the problems that were already evident, except to call for 'a principled struggle against all manifestations of narrow-mindedness and arrogance, nationalism and chauvinism.'[5] Gorbachev's lack of understanding of the nationality question was evident when he visited the Baltic states in spring 1987 and attempted to convince his hosts that the 'Russian warrior' had come to their rescue, that the Baltic states had welcomed Soviet power with open arms.[6]

Although a reformer on other issues, on nationality questions Gorbachev remained a conservative, relying on the dogmas of the Brezhev era. Gorbachev was, after all, the first CPSU General Secretary who had never previously served in a non-Russian republic and hence initially devoted little attention to the nationality question.

THE VIEW FROM UKRAINE

Zbigniew Rau proposed an ideal-type timetable for 'Four Stages of Our Path out of Socialism' which can serve as a benchmark for assessing the development of informal opposition structures in Ukraine:

> Firstly, the emergence of dissident groups; secondly, the establishment of massive revivification movements; thirdly, the launching of independent political parties; and fourthly, the taking of power in competitive elections by these parties.

From 1987 until late 1988, the first tentative steps towards the reconstitution of a Ukrainian dissident movement were made in the limited political space opened up by Gorbachev's reforms, with Ukrainian dissidents initially returning to the battlelines of the Brezhnev era, from which they had been forcibly removed during the arrest waves of 1972–3 and the late 1970s.

The period was characterised by:

- a redefinition of *glasnost'* and *perestroika* by amnestied political prisoners, although within a general framework of support for Gorbachev's programme;
- the launch of small, unofficial 'fronts, leagues or unions' as embryonic political oppositions, but with little mass support beyond the intelligentsia;
- concentration upon the exposure of 'Stalinist crimes' and the rehabilitation of their victims, and on issues of language and culture, as the state was still prepared to use coercive measures against more overtly political groups;
- the Chornobyl' nuclear accident as a catalyst for an environmental movement; and
- an uneven national 'awakening' gradually spreading from western to central Ukraine.[8]

The amnesty of Soviet prisoners of conscience, a disproportionate number of whom had been Ukrainian (see Chapter 3), during the first half of 1987, breathed new life into the political and cultural debate in Ukraine. Shcherbytskyi's 15-year rule had led to widescale repression of all forms of dissent, an all-embracing campaign of Russification and the placing of cadres loyal to the conservative 'Little Russian' wing of the CPU in every layer of state and government from the village upwards.[9]

Although the Western media constantly speculated about Shcherbytskyi's demise after Gorbachev's rise to power in April 1985, he nevertheless remained in office until September 1989.[10] Neither Shcherbytskyi nor his two successors – Volodymyr Ivashko and Stanislav Hurenko – undertook any purge of the CPU to bring it more in line with the policies of *perestroika* and *glasnost'*. Gorbachev refrained from pushing *perestroika* in Ukraine in the interests of maintaining centralised control and not allowing this most crucial of Soviet republics to take the Baltic road to independence and marginalisation of the CPSU in public life.

Therefore, in terms of Alexander Motyl's typology discussed in Chapter 1, the amount of 'public space' available for oppositional activity was still minimal in Ukraine (and often less than in Moscow), although the growing number of small unofficial groups did their best to organise within it. There seemed little sign of any 'national communism' within the state, or of a possible alliance between the CPU and opposition forces. The Shcherbytskyi regime's founding principle had, after all, been the eradication of such tendencies, as they had developed under Petro Shelest from 1963 to 1972.

This was especially the case after the shock received by the CPU in the March 1989 elections to the all-Union Congress of People's Deputies. Iurii Badzo, in a report prepared for the Ukrainian Helsinki Union (UHU) on the March 1990 elections, stated that Gorbachev 'wanted to maintain political stability in Ukraine at the expense of democracy, at the expense of the Ukrainian national revival.'[11] Until 1990–1, it was informal groups, not the CPU, who were the major engine of change in Ukraine. Leonid Kravchuk, then head of the Supreme Council of Ukraine and former ideology chief of the CPU later admitted: 'I agree that, if it had not been for *Rukh* and other democratic currents we would not have come so far so *fast*.'[12]

UKRAINIAN HELSINKI UNION

The most important informal group, whose influence extended into numerous other independent groups which were formed later, was the Ukrainian Helsinki Union (UHU). The UHU viewed itself as the continuation of Ukrainian Public Group to Promote the Implementation of the Helsinki Accords, which had been established in November 1976, as the latter had never formally disbanded. Indeed, initially *perestroika* and *glasnost'* encouraged dissidents to renew the demands of the *shestydesiatnyky* and Ukrainian Helsinki Group during the 1970s and 1980s. These included democratisation, defence of human rights and resistance to Russification.[13]

Consequently, during this first stage the aims of informal groups were little different from those advanced in the Brezhnev era. The first major Ukrainian *samizdat* document of the Gorbachev era was former prisoner of conscience Viacheslav Chornovil's 'Open Letter' to Gorbachev in August 1987. Open letters such as Chornovil's were significant in that, as 'In the 1960s (especially after Khrushchev's fall), Ukraine believed that direct appeals to the authorities or to Shelest himself would redress injustices and solve problems.' Such appeals and open letters to Moscow became less popular after 1989–90, as the USSR began to disintegrate, and the Ukrainian SSR began to breathe real life into its quasi-state structures.[14]

The open letter to Gorbachev began:

> I am informing you that several Ukrainian journalists and writers, who are presently experiencing a ban on their works and within their profession, including myself in this field, are legally reviving the publication of the socio-political and literary journal the *Ukrainian Herald (Ukraïns'kyi visnyk)* which appeared from 1970 to 1972 under difficult circumstances. This journal conforms to the present stipulation of *glasnost'*.[15]

The *Ukrainian Herald* was relaunched as issue number 7, thereby stressing its continuity with the same publication forcibly closed down 15 years earlier, after Shcherbytskyi had come to power in Ukraine. The UHU officially came into being in March 1988 and the *Ukrainian Herald* became its official organ.[16]

Chornovil went on to define his understanding of *perestroika* and *glasnost'*;

> We, the tip of the iceberg, are the individual representatives ... of those healthy forces which resisted the stagnation and bureaucratisation of Soviet society, and in the non-Russian republics, the great-state chauvinistic policies of de-nationalisation ... So you see, it would have been worth listening to the voices of 'anti-soviets' and 'nationalists' fifteen to twenty years ago.

The beginnings of the UHU were later described in a rather romantic way:

In the darkness of Brezhnevite lawlessness, when many had lost faith, a group of patriots formed themselves, which through the strength of their greatness of spirit and at the cost of their own lives proclaimed to the world and to the rulers of the Kremlin that Ukraine continued to live and fight.

The Gorbachev 'thaw' ignited a conflagration of civic-political acts. People gathered around the movement which rejected the Communist path in the life of nations. In July 1988 a political association called the UHU was formed and it quickly became an all-Ukrainian structural organisation. In less than two years of activity, the UHU acquired widespread political legitimacy not only in Ukraine, but beyond Ukraine's borders as well. The Communist rulers of Ukraine were forced to deal with the UHU leadership, despite the fact that the 'Red press' had continually tried to discredit these leaders.[17]

Levko Lukianenko, a prisoner of conscience for over 26 years, was elected as the new leader of the UHU. From exile in the winter of 1988, Lukianenko wrote in his programmatical essay 'What Next?'[18] that Ukraine was 'crucified, pillaged, Russified and torn', and that 'Restructuring means infinitely more for Ukraine – ultimately the life or death of our nation. The continuation of pre-*perestroika* policies would have meant total assimilation and the destruction of our nationality.'

Claiming the moral higher ground for those leaders of the UHG who had never waivered, Lukianenko argued that the Ukrainian intelligentsia should also be in the forefront of reform:

Not very long ago, during the times of the Brezhnevite-Shcherbytskyi oppression, these people – writers, poets, literary critics, film and theatre artists – squeezed fame and ruin out of themselves. Now they have straightened their crooked spines and are slowly beginning to return to the people with the word of truth.

The former political prisoners who dominated the UHU were later to make common cause with the cultural intelligentsia, through the launch of the Taras Shevchenko Ukrainian Language Society, and the Ukrainian Popular Movement for Restructuring (*Rukh*), thereby broadening the public space available for dissent, as the state could not but take a more tolerant view of the activities of the writers and artists who were often themselves part of the state apparatus.

Lukianenko's arguments, however, still reflected the climate of the times. In his view, Soviet society was divided into three groups. The first represented Gorbachev and the CPSU leadership, the second the Soviet New Class or *nomenklatura* and the third the masses. Supposedly, only the first and third groups were in favour of *perestroika* and it was up to the UHU to act as a link between the two, and support restructuring from below as a 'social group of supporters of *perestroika.*'

Fear among the Ukrainian masses was still a problem, Lukianenko claimed, although it was decreasing: 'The number of people who dare to speak the truth, sign declarations, petitions, protests, participate in rallies and unofficial gatherings, form unofficial groups, and so forth, is growing.'

Although Lukianenko did not disguise his view that independence, 'was the most favourable condition' for Ukraine, nevertheless the priority was 'first of all to defend the rights of citizens and to raise language and cultural issues.' The UHU Declaration of Principles, therefore, which was written by Chornovil and the brothers Mykhailo and Bohdan Horyn and released in the summer of 1988 represented a tactical compromise designed to win broad support from an atomised Ukrainian public still reluctant to support very radical demands.[19]

The Declaration of Principles noted that, unlike the Moscow Helsinki Group, the UHG had never formally disbanded, although arrests had rendered it largely inoperative by 1980. It claimed to have been 'subjected to a more devastating pogrom during the Brezhnev years of stagnation than any other Helsinki group in the USSR'. Four members of the group died in the Gulag under Gorbachev – Oleksa Tykhyi, Iurii Lytvyn, Valerii Marchenko and Vasyl Stus. Others had been forced to emigrate, such as Mykola Rudenko, who became the head of the external branch of the UHU.

The Declaration of Principles claimed that the UHU was not a political opposition party but formally, 'an organisation which activates the masses in order to encourage participation in the government of the country' and a 'federative union of self-governing human rights groups and organisations'. In practice, however, the UHU regarded itself as an unofficial popular front with the intention of uniting a broad range of people in opposition to the CPU. As more unofficial groups began to appear, the UHU conceived of its role as leading such groups into progressively more radical positions by always being one, but only one, step ahead of them in its demands. The UHU was, however, split from the start between supporters of Chornovil, who wished to preserve a loose federal structure for the organisation, and those who were increasingly openly prepared to copy Leninist vanguard tactics.

The Declaration of Principles' 20 sections dealt with political, constitutional, language, education and economic reform. The UHU stood for the transformation of the USSR 'into a confederation of independent states' (a position forced upon a reluctant Gorbachev only after the failed coup in August 1991). While going much further than the demands raised by the UHG of the 1970s, many of the Principles were later included both within the Democratic Bloc election programme to the Supreme Council of Ukraine in March 1990, and enshrined in the July 1990 Declaration of Sovereignty. These included points such as a transfer of power from the CPSU to democratically elected councils, Ukrainianisation, the right to independent Ukrainian diplomatic activity, a market economy, an end to nuclear power, legalisation of banned religious denominations and public control over the law enforcement agencies. These represented a 'minimum' programme which was advanced by most informal groups during the early stages of the evolution of Ukrainian dissent.

Members of the UHU, however, were still subject to severe official harassment, and its activity throughout 1988 was still very much circumscribed.[20] Hence dissidents and the radical intelligentsia increasingly submitted their energies into more overtly cultural groups, which they calculated would be less likely to be repressed.

UKRAINIAN ASSOCIATION OF INDEPENDENT CREATIVE INTELLIGENTSIA

In Chornovil's 'Open Letter to Gorbachev', he also announced the intention of the UHU 'to form our own creative circles independent from the official ones, which enforce a ban upon us, and forming our own associations of persecuted Ukrainian writers, journalists, artists, even though the circulation of our publications may well be limited'. This was a reference to the Ukrainian Association of Independent Creative Intelligentsia (UANTI), launched in October 1987, whose founding document was signed by fourteen well-known former prisoners of conscience.[21]

UANTI would act as an unofficial Writers' and Literary Union because, according to the UANTI Declaration, the official unions, 'do not fully represent the spiritual, literary, cultural and public processes' that are taking place in Ukraine. Stepan Sapeliak, a leading UANTI activist from Kharkiv, stated that the official unions had 'created only a pseudo-culture, modelled upon socialist realism.'[22]

UANTI promised to publish literary periodicals and almanacs, hold art exhibitions and 'support all those who desire to put their talent and civic courage at the service of the good and the spiritual develop-ment of the Ukrainian people, and the national life of Ukraine.' The signatories included seven honorary members of International Pen: Ihor Kalynets, Mykhailo Osadchyi, Mykola Rudenko, Ievhen Sverstiuk, Ivan Svitlychnyi, Iryna Senyk and Viacheslav Chornovil.

One of the first acts of UANTI was to demand the reburial in Ukraine, 'of the bodies of the talented poets and public-cultural figures – Vasyl Stus, Oleksa Tykhyi and Iurii Lytvyn – murdered during the period of stagnation' in a letter signed jointly with the Ukrainian Culturological Club to International PEN in October 1987, which pointed out that, to this very day, the grave of Vasyl Stus 'at the camp cemetery is marked simply as no. 9'. He died during 'the era of stagnation, when spiritual values plummeted catastrophically. A con-sumerist mentality corrupted the souls of an entire generation. Fear made people petty and mean.'[23]

UANTI appealed to both International PEN and the Soviet Ministry of Culture to honour Stus's fiftieth anniversary on 6 January 1988, for Soviet publishing houses to print a selection of his works, and for the KGB to release the works which were confiscated from him in the camps.[24] Since then the official literary press has published the works of Vasyl Stus, and a book of his poetry has appeared.[25]

UANTI held its first congress in L'viv in January 1989, 15 months after it was founded, with 26 participants from throughout Ukraine. By then UANTI had contributed to opening up public debate through its official periodical, *Kafedra* (L'viv), edited by Mykhailo Osadchyi, and other independent literary journals whose editors belonged to UANTI – *Ievshan zillia* (L'viv), edited by Iryna Kalynets, *Karby hir* (Kolomyia), edited by Dmytro Hrynkiv, *Snip* (Kharkiv), edited by Valerii Bondar, and *Porohy* (Dnipropetrovs'k), edited by Ivan Sokulskyi. Members of UANTI were also active within the Taras Shevchenko Ukrainian Language Society and *Tovarystvo Leva*.[26]

UKRAINIAN CULTUROLOGICAL CLUB

The Ukrainian Culturological (literally, the Culture and Ecology) Club was another of the political clubs that was to have an ephemeral existence as a home of convenience for the hedging opposition. It was formed in August 1987 in Kyiv, and according to the weekly *samizdat* bulletin *Express-Chronicle*, held its first meeting on 27 September, where copies of its charter were distributed.[27] The Club was organised mainly by former prisoners of conscience to spread the ideas of democratisation and national revival in the republic's capital. It immediately began to campaign for the release of all remaining prisoners of conscience and for a widening of the discussion surrounding the blank spots in Ukrainian history (in particular, the artificial Ukrainian famine of 1933, a subject which was recognised by the CPU in 1990). Leading individuals in the Club included Serhii Naboka, Leonid Miliavskyi, Oles Shevchenko and Olha Matusevych.[28]

One of the first actions of the Culturological Club was to appeal to UNESCO with the proposal that 1988 be made the 'Year of Vasyl Stus'. In addition, evenings were devoted to Stus and a petition was organised to demand the return of his body for reburial in Ukraine. Other evenings organised by the Club dealt with the millennium of Christianity in Ukraine, the 175th anniversary of the birth of Ukraine's national bard Taras Shevchenko, Ukrainian national figures who had fallen out of favour with the authorities and nuclear power and the environment.

In addition, in May 1988 the Culturological Club held meetings with members of the editorial board of the journal *Iunost'* after which they jointly called for the legalisation of the Ukrainian Catholic Church. Appeals by the Culturological Club were addressed to a West German television station criticising a Soviet official's comparison of the Russian nationalist organisation *Pamiat* with the Culturological Club, and in defence of the venerated Mohyla Academy in Kyiv, which was then being used by the Soviet military.[29]

The authorities responded almost immediately to the activities of the Culturological Club with a harsh press campaign in both *Vechirnii Kyïv* and *Radians'ka Ukraïna*. Although the Culturological Club and its members were described in the traditional pre-Gorbachev manner as 'nationalists' who were exploiting *glasnost'* for their own ends, and entire pages of *Vechirnii Kyïv* were devoted to letters (some of which were favourably disposed, however, towards the Club), the campaign, by all accounts, had the opposite effect to that intended. Instead of arousing the hostility of the republic's population towards the Culturological Club, the articles publicised the Club's activities. *Radians'ka Ukraïna*, in a series of articles between 19 and 21 May 1988, claimed the Culturological Club 'approaches the history of Ukraine, especially its Soviet period, only with black paint in hand'.

The Culturological Club also refused to incorporate into its statute that it upholds 'Marxist Leninist ideology' and 'struggles against Ukrainian bourgeois nationalism'. The Culturological Club was even reputed to have argued that 'Russian great-power chauvinism' is a far worse threat than 'Ukrainian nationalism'.[30]

On 26 April 1988, on the second anniversary of the Chornobyl' nuclear accident, the Culturological Club organised a demonstration in central Kyiv. Members of the Culturological Club held placards which read 'No More Chornobyl's', 'Turn Ukraine into a Nuclear-Free Ukraine' and 'The Ukrainian Culturological Club is Against Nuclear Death.' The authorities used loudspeakers to drown out speeches and arrested 17 people, sentencing Oles Shevchenko to 15 days' imprisonment. Two days later *Prapor komunizmu* claimed that 'a group of extremists, mostly representing the Ukrainian Culturological Club, tried to whip up unrest, interfere with street repairs, and obstruct the flow of traffic.' Only two years later the authorities eventually officially recognised 26 April as Chornobyl' Day, permitting officially sanctioned marches.

The Culturological Club also commemorated the annual Taras Shevchenko anniversary on 22 May 1988, although the authorities tried to upstage it with an official celebration. On 5 June 1988 the Club organised unofficial celebrations to mark the millennium of Christianity in Kievan Rus'. Similar unofficial Clubs devoted to culture and ecology were opened in other Ukrainian cities, including Kharkiv, and eventually became the initiators of more radical independent groups.[31]

Both the radicalisation of the opposition and sections of the public at large led to a decline in the activity of the Culturological Club towards the end of 1988. The opposition movement in Ukraine was moving to a higher second stage in its evolution. Leading figures in the Culturological Club moved into other groups, such as the UHU, the Ukrainian People's Democratic League and the movement for the legalisation of the Ukrainian Autocephalous Orthodox Church.

HROMADA

The unofficial student organisation *Hromada* (Community) named after the cultural societies formed in late-nineteenth-century Ukraine, began at Kyiv University in the spring of 1988, where many of the original members were students in the physics faculty. *Hromada* published a 30-page *samizdat* journal, *Dzvin* (Bell), five issues of which are known to have appeared, and an irregular bulletin – *Chronicle of Opposition*. The activation of students in *Hromada* helped to broaden opposition circles beyond the elder generation of former-political prisoners who controlled the commanding heights of the UHU and the Cultorological Club.

One of the first activities of *Hromada* was the holding of a meeting to call for the refoundation of the Kyiv Mohyla Academy, founded in the seventeenth century but closed in 1917. They, like the Culturological Club, demanded the removal of the military political school from its premises. Close co-operation with the more senior dissidents in the Culturological Club could be seen when Bohdan Horyn read out an appeal to the Nineteenth Communist Party Conference which argued that people should not be solely concerned with the preservation of monuments (like *Hromada*) – but also with the question of whether power should lie with the KGB and *nomenklatura* or with councils' of people's deputies.[32]

In September 1988 members of *Hromada* travelled to Erevan, capital of Armenia, to voice their support for Armenian demands over Nagorno-Karabak'h, while the demonstration in Kyiv attended by 10 000 in November 1988 in support of the formation of a Ukrainian Popular Front and in opposition to nuclear power was also mainly the organisational work of *Hromada*.[33] Members of *Hromada* organised a successful boycott of military instruction classes at Kyiv University during the latter part of 1988, demanding that military education become voluntary. The boycott was suspended after a number of concessions were made – military classes were shortened for most and abolished for second-year students. In late November the boycott was renewed with the demand that all military classes be voluntary and that a leading *Hromada* member – Volodymyr Chemerys – be reinstated.[34]

At first, the instructors refused to discuss the issue, but eventually compromised on a cutback in training and the right not to wear uniforms in class. The action by *Hromada* 'stirred debates at a subsequent university conference involving students, the military and university administration' and showed that 'the long-lost traditions of free thought are being revived in their independent publications and political clubs. And the signs are that their aspirations are beginning to count'.[35]

The third issue of *Dzvin* published an open letter, dated October 1988, from *Hromada* to the plenum of the CPU, arguing that the present republican Party leadership which 'has remained unchanged virtually since 1972' is 'responsible for the stagnation in Ukraine'. Demanding the removal of Shcherbytskyi and others responsible for the catastrophic state of Ukrainian culture and language, *Hromada* argued for a system of republican cost accounting, Ukrainisation of all spheres of life in Ukraine, the formation of Ukrainian military units, the liquidation of party privileges and an end to the construction of new nuclear plants (demands which clearly converged with those of the UHU).[36]

The impact of *Hromada* could best be gauged by the hostile official reaction to it. The local Kyiv University newspaper *Kyivs'kyi universytet* published numerous attacks upon the student group throughout 1988, accusing them of being 'overcome by demagogic nationalistic slogans'. According to *Kyïvs'kyi universytet*, the authorities were not hostile to *Hromada* when it was first launched, thinking it to be another harmless informal student group, but became increasingly concerned when it became more politicised during the course of the year. When finally in November 1988 *Hromada* organised a meeting to discuss the UHU's Declaration of Principles this was the last straw for the authorities, who began to expel some students.[37]

RELIGION

In 1982, three years prior to Gorbachev's ascent to power, members of the illegal Ukrainian Catholic Church formed the Initiative Committee to Defend the Rights and Believers of the Church in Ukraine. The Group began to publish the *samizdat* journal *The Chronicle of the Catholic Church in Ukraine*, 33 issues of which were published during the course of five years. The leading figure behind both the Committee and the *samizdat* journal was Iosyf Terelia, who was deported to the West in 1988.[38]

In August 1987, during the same month that Chornovil wrote his 'Open Letter to Gorbachev', 206 underground bishops, priests, monks, nuns and faithful of the Ukrainian Catholic Church emerged from their catacomb existence and wrote to Pope John Paul.[39] Thereafter, they campaigned through petitions, meetings with the Council for Religious Affairs and statements to government institutions, international bodies, and high-ranking religious figures to legalise their Church, forcibly disbanded by Stalin in 1946.[40]

In the early part of 1988 the Initiative Group was renamed the Committee in Defence of the Ukrainian Catholic Church under Ivan

Hel, and the Chronicle was merged with a new *samvydav* journal entitled *Khrystyians'kyi holos*.[41] This publication ceased after four issues and was replaced by *Vira bat'kiv* (L'viv) and *Dobryi pastyr* (Ivano-Frankivs'k). The strength of Ukrainian religious feeling could be seen when upwards of half a million visitors came to the site of a reported apparition at Hrushiv in western Ukraine on the second anniversary of the Chornobyl' nuclear accident in April 1988.[42]

TOVARYSTVO LEVA

In the spring of 1987, yet another informal group was established in L'viv entitled *Tovarystvo Leva* (The Lion Society). In an undated two page leaflet, entitled *'Tovarystvo Leva.* Who Are We? What Are We Now?' it described itself as an 'independent, community eco-cultural youth organisation which stands on a platform of democracy, the motto of which could be: The revival of a Ukrainian Sovereign State through Culture and Intellect.'

The leaflet described how during the era of stagnation there was moral, national and economic decline in Ukraine, and a rising ecological catastrophe. Together with other informal groups, *Tovarystvo Leva* believed they should support *perestroika* from below: 'Given from above, but in effect begun from below, restructuring pushed forth a large section of conscious society into concrete deeds, in the first place young people.' In L'viv the decline of established youth organisations left a vacuum into which *Tovarystvo Leva* could step to promote 'patriotic, internationalist and aesthetic inculcation of people, especially the youth, arousing feelings of national consciousness' and advance the 'development of the Ukrainian language, struggle for its cleanliness, and inculcate respect for the language and culture of other peoples.'[43]

Tovarystvo Leva was formally established on 19 October 1987[44] by enthusiasts, artists, students, workers and pupils, although individuals had been active since the spring.[45] They began by renovating the Lychakivs'kyi cemetery in L'viv, and then moving on to renovate churches. It took a two-year 'struggle with the conservative authorities and reactionary political system' before it was formally registered, even though it functioned under the auspices of the *Komsomal* at L'viv University, and received limited financial help from the Ministry of Culture.[46]

In the village of Havorechyna, only three old craftsmen remained who could produce traditional Black Ceramics. In a few years the craft would have died out. *Tovarystvo Leva* opened a school to teach the craft in the nearby town of Bilyi Kamin'. During Christmas 1988 and Easter 1989, the society initiated the revival of national traditions such as the *Vertep* play and *Hahilky* dances, not seen in Ukraine for over 40 years. They promoted rock music, amateur theatre groups such as 'Meta' (which performed the play 'Marusia Churai'), exhibitions of the formerly banned novel 'Sobor', the cabaret show 'Ne Zhurys' and folk singers and composers such as Andrii Panchyshyn, Viktor Morozov and Vasyl Zhdankin.[47] In May 1988 *Tovarystvo Leva* organised an ecological expedition entitled 'Dnistr 88' to raise awareness about the pollution of the river.[48] Expeditions have since taken place into eastern Ukraine and as far away as the Sakhalin Islands to raise national consciousness among denationalised Ukrainians outside Ukraine.

Although, in contrast to the Kyiv-based Culturological Club, *Tovarystvo Leva* attempted to concentrate upon non-political issues, in the Soviet context this was very difficult.[49] The authorities refused permission for the use of a hall in L'viv at the very last minute after delegates had arrived from throughout the USSR in October 1988 for the congress of *Tovarystvo Leva*.[50] They were apparently afraid of discussion of the arrest of Ivan Makar and the need for the organisation of a Ukrainian Popular Front. Iryna Kalynets, editor of the independent literary journal *Ievshan zillia*, was a strong supporter of *Tovarystvo Leva* and the journal was rumoured to have been proposed as the organ of the society at one stage. But in April 1989 *Tovarystvo Leva* began publication of the bi-monthly *Postup* 'the first unofficial youth newspaper in Ukraine', with a circulation of 20 000.

THE GREEN WORLD ASSOCIATION (*ZELENII SVIT*)

The Chornobyl' nuclear accident in April 1986 proved to be the catalyst for many informal groups, because it highlighted the lack of Ukrainian sovereignty over the activities of all-Union ministries and enterprises in Ukraine, and on this occasion the callous indifference of Moscow to the republics. In late 1987 the Green World Association was launched as an informal group which immediately came into conflict with the established Ukrainian State Committee for the Protection of Society (USCPS), especially as, once again, it functioned *de facto* as an umbrella organisation for a broad spectrum of the informal opposition, from the poet Ivan Drach, eventual leader of *Rukh*, to Anatolii Lupynis, later leading member of the far right.[51] At this stage, however, the Green World Association was something of a loyalist alternative to the more radical Culturological Club.

In January, the Green World Association chose the writer Serhii Plachynda as its first president, and on 29 March 1988 the Green World Association held a joint conference with the Writers' Union of Ukraine, to express the concern of the association at the Chornobyl' accident, and call for a demonstration on 5 June as 'Environmental Protection Day.'[52] Its demands were: greater *glasnost'* on the state of the environment and food supplies, greater openness from medical staff about radiation sickness, the publication of ecological textbooks and a newspaper, holding of referendums on the building of nuclear power stations and formation of commissions of scientists on the question of the construction or completion of nuclear power stations.

A demonstration planned on 28 June by the radical wing of Green World Association, the *Zelena varta* (Green Guard), did not take place after the leader Anatolii Lupynis was arrested for three hours.[53] In comparison with Green World Association, which concentrated on letters and petitions, *Zelena varta* was more action-orientated. In comparison with Ukraine State Committee for the Protection of Society though, the Green World Association was more radical. Founded in 1946, the Ukraine State Committee for the Protection of Society had millions of members, representing one of the largest organisations in Ukraine, but even its leaders admitted that during the era of stagnation it had fallen into 'formalism' and 'bureaucratism'. In a list of the presidium published in 1986, 14 of the 15 members were ministerial functionaries. 'There are no well-known educated ecologists, writers, journalists, youth representatives or informal ecological organisations', one newspaper reported. Many younger members of the Ukraine State Committee for the Protection of Society were now looking towards the Green World Association as a 'self-governing' group in which they were 'putting all their hopes for the future.'[54]

A member of the Kaniv branch of the Ukraine State Committee for the Protection of Society wondered if the leaders of the organisation agreed with his views that both ecological associations should merge, even if it meant that the Ukraine State Committee for the Protection of Society was renamed 'Green World'. The executive secretary of Green World Association, Sviatoslav Dudko, believed that the work of the Ukraine State Committee for the Protection of Society was 'ineffective' and asked, 'Isn't this the reason why the committee was against our association's foundation – because we meant the end of its quiet life?' Ukraine State Committee for the Protection of Society concentrated upon ecological information to raise awareness, whereas Green World Association, according to Dudko, 'tackled environmental protection problems in a different way: we lay emphasis upon practical efforts to rectify previous mistakes and avert new ones.'[55] Its first major campaigns were to save the historical island of Khortytsia, the Cossack former capitol, and to prevent the construction of new chemical plants in Ukraine.[56]

An important catalyst for increasing the influence of Green World Association was the first large demonstration in Kyiv on 13 November 1988. The demonstration attended by 10 000 people had two main subjects – ecology and the need to organise a Popular Front. Marchers stood in the rain for three hours while speakers denounced the ecological crisis in Ukraine. 'For Ukraine it was just not normal,' one participant later commented.[57]

However, public reaction to the Chornobyl' disaster meant that an environmental movement could not be easily suppressed. Therefore Green World Association became a flag of convenience for many other radicals, while environmental discourse permeated throughout political life, and became a useful shorthand for criticism of Ukraine's lack of control over its own destiny.

FIRST POPULAR FRONTS

In the summer of 1988 simultaneous attempts were made to launch Popular Fronts in L'viv, Kyiv and smaller towns, although the authorities quickly utilised new legislation against unsanctioned meetings and the black-bereted OMON (Special Purpose Militia Detachments) to break up mass meetings.[58] The Democratic Front in Support of Perestroika grew out of such mass meetings held in L'viv and attended by between 20 000 and 50 000 people during June and July 1988, which arose in parallel with similar demonstrations in the Baltic republics.

The main unofficial groups which joined together to launch the would-be Popular Front were the UHU, the Committee in Defence of the Ukrainian Catholic Church, *Tovarystvo Leva* and the *Ridna Mova* Society (the precursor to the *Taras Shevchenko* Ukrainian Language Society). For the first time, however, middle-level CPU functionaries were also beginning to seek common cause with the opposition, such as elements in the L'viv *Komsomol* led by Bohdan Kotyk.[59]

The demonstrators expressed a lack of faith in delegates to the Nineteenth CPU Conference and called for an end to party privileges, the closure of the KGB, greater republican autonomy and release of remaining prisoners of conscience.[60] Some participants held aloft pictures of Gorbachev, whose policies they believed they supported but which were being obstructed by the CPU in Ukraine.[61] To further its end, the Popular Front pledged to stand in elections, ensure the continuation of the democratisation process and influence citizens' commissions and the media.[62]

With increased use of the OMON (in Ukrainian, ZMOP) and with the authorities denying premises to the Popular Front, by August–September monthly meetings by the Ivan Franko monument had dwindled to 3000–4000.[63] The first attempt then to form a Popular Front in Ukraine was thus a relative failure. According to the Russian newspaper, *Sobesednik* (no. 35), the UHU was seeking to 'direct public opinion in L'viv', where it had managed through the creation of the Popular Front to effect, 'a rather strange symbiosis of nationalistic slogans and slogans connected with *perestroika*.' However, the UHU alone could not hope to create a mass organisation when the authorities were still prepared to use coercion to prevent them, and when it was still relatively young.[64]

In Kyiv, a similar attempt had been made to create a 'Popular Union in Support of *Perestroika*' at a meeting in June 1988, attended by 500 people. An initiative committee was established under Alexandr Sheikin, and a later meeting in July featured prominent speakers from the Culturological Club, such as Leonid Miliavskyi.[65] Again, however, middle-level CPU members took part, such as Oleksandr Iemets (later as influential member of the PDRU) from the Higher Military School, and others from the Institute of History. Tentative contacts between the first secretary of the Podil' region, Ivan Salii and the 'informals' were also made. The Kyiv 'Popular Front's' occasional publication *Narodnaia volia* was in Russian, however, indicating that it may have been formed outside the structures of the main Ukrainian dissident groups.[66] (Russian Popular Front groups were also established in L'viv in the winter of 1988, resulting in the Russian-language bulletin *Na polnyi golos*. Its leaders then became founders of the Ukrainian social democratic movement, established in 1989–90.)

However, once again the authorities were not prepared to tolerate an open challenge to their monopoly on power, and the would-be Popular Fronts in Kyiv and L'viv along with similar groups in Vinnytsia and Khmel'nyts'kyi, were stillborn.[67]

Hence, in the winter of 1988–9 a second attempt was made under the alternative leadership of radical elements within the Writers' Union of Ukraine.

INTER-REPUBLICAN LINKS

The UHU was also the initiator of the Co-ordinating Committee of Patriotic Movements of Peoples of the USSR, formed in early June 1988 in L'viv by representatives of national democratic movements from the non-Russian and non-Muslim republics of the USSR.[68] The Co-ordinating Committee represented the most ambitious attempt in the post-Stalin era to form a united bloc against Soviet domination. In September, at a meeting in Riga, they issued a draft statute appeal to the Helsinki review conference dealing with prisoners of conscience, nuclear power and freedom of conscience.[69]

In January 1989, in Vilnius, two further documents were drawn up, a 'Charter of the Captive Peoples of the USSR' and 'An Appeal to the Russian Intelligentsia'. Whereas the 'Appeal', which argued that only a minority of Russians had still come out in favour of non-Russian aspirations, was signed by all four UHU representatives, the 'Charter' was signed by only Ivan Makar and Bohdan Hrytsai. Oles Shevchenko and Mykola Horbal refused to sign the 'Charter' because its demand for Ukrainian independence contradicted the Declaration of Principles of the UHU.[70]

CONCLUSIONS

As yet, therefore, opposition groups were only able to operate on a small scale. Moreover, with the notable exception of the UHU, they were forced to confine themselves to a 'cultural' agenda. With little change evident in the conservative politics of the CPU, Ukraine still seemed one of the most quiescent of the Soviet republics.

5 Consolidation (1988–9)

THE VIEW FROM THE CENTRE

By 1988–9 the nationality question had become increasingly acute in the Soviet Union, but Gorbachev still refused to consider a new union treaty or the transformation of the USSR into a confederation of sovereign states (a demand raised earlier by the non-Russians, but not backed by Gorbachev until after the August 1991 attempted putsch). This period saw the growth of new Popular Fronts throughout the non-Russian republics, criticism of bilingualism, demands for a return to 'Leninist nationality policy', complaints about the role of the Russian 'elder brother' and condemnation of the non-voluntary nature of the Soviet Union.

Gorbachev therefore belatedly conceded: 'we must get down to some very substantive work on nationalities policy. Among all avenues, both in theory and practice.'[1] In the traditional way of Soviet leaders, Gorbachev blamed current problems on his predecessors, specifically the 'era of stagnation'. But he was still short of new ideas. Indeed, Gorbachev's insensitivity to the nationality question could be seen in the fact that the number of Russians within the central organs of Soviet power increased during the latter part of his term in office.[2]

Although Gorbachev claimed that, whereas there had been notable achievements in Soviet nationalities policies there were also 'obvious shortfalls, omissions and difficult connections with the unresolved nature of specific socio-economic issues'. But, he sincerely believed that the introduction of the rule of law, economic sovereignty and the creation of the Congress of Peoples Deputies would defuse the nationality question.

At the 19th Conference of the CPSU the resolution on nationality questions outlined the following facts and policy recommendations:[3]

- the existence of a new community of the Soviet people;
- the correctness of 'Leninist nationality policies', as well as certain 'violations in legality';
- support for 'full-bloodied and dynamic unity within national diversity';

- a proposal to create a new body for nationalities within the Supreme Soviet;
- the CPSU as the 'cementing force behind nationalities';
- the armed forces were a 'genuine school of internationalism'.

THE VIEW FROM UKRAINE

The period in Ukraine from the end of 1988 until the autumn of 1989 was characterised by the following features:

- alliance building: official cultural organisations helped launch a popular front initiative with dissidents, as middle-ranking elements in the *apparat* sought to build bridges with the 'informals';
- the opposition was broadened by the rise of an unofficial workers' movement;
- a myriad of informal groups attempted to mobilise society in the all-Union election campaign of March 1989;
- campaigns were conducted to legalise the Uniate Church and the Ukraine Autocephalous Orthodox Church;
- the CPU was confronted with an increasing challenge to its monopoly over public life.

POPULAR FRONT

After 10 000 had attended the Kyiv demonstration on 13 November 1988 organised by *Hromada*, the Green World Association and various writers, the Kyiv branch of the Writers' Union of Ukraine (WUU) and the Taras Shevchenko Institute of Literature joined forces to form an initiative committee for the launch of a Ukrainian popular front. Whereas in western Ukraine the dissident UHU was playing an important role in the organisation of similar groups and demonstrations, in Kyiv and eastern Ukraine (where the UHU was weaker) official bodies, such as the Writers' Union, played a larger role.

Pavlo Movchan and Viktor Teren originally proposed the idea on 1 November at a meeting of the Party organisation of the Kyiv branch of the Writers' Union.[4] A joint plenum of cultural unions in mid-November resolved to draft a programme. The working group consisted of 20 writers, headed by Ivan Drach. The WUU was immediately accused, however, of trying to form an alternative to the CPU, and threatening to make those who did not speak Ukrainian 'second-class citizens'.[5]

At a plenum of the WUU in December 1988 it was resolved to instruct the initiative group to 'draw up a draft of programme for a Ukrainian Popular Movement in Support of Restructuring'.[6] Leading *literati* would now take the lead, with dissident groups such as the UHU helping in the background with organisational matters. A meeting of supporters of a popular front on 4 December was attended by informal groups (such as the UHU, Ukrainian Language Society, Green World Association and Memorial) and writers.

On 31 January 1989 the initiative group presented the draft programme to the plenum of the WUU. The CPU-dominated press demanded that they insert a clause supporting the 'leading role' of the CPSU. Leonid Kravchuk, then ideological secretary of the CPU, claimed a popular front was unnecessary, as the Communist Party itself was undertaking *perestroika*, and attacked the programme in the media as 'anti-constitutional'. CPU members meanwhile were advised not to joint the front.[7]

The CPU attempted in every conceivable manner to prevent the publication of the draft programme of the Popular Movement (*Rukh*). Ivan Drach even threatened to publish it in *samizdat* if it was not published in an official newspaper. On 13 February, leading writers went to Moscow to appeal to Mikhail Gorbachev, who was forced to make an unscheduled visit to Ukraine on 19 February. The draft programme was eventually published on 16 February in *Literaturna Ukraïna*, the weekly organ of the WUU, the only newspaper which dared to print it.

Although it is not clear if Gorbachev gave the go-ahead to publish the draft programme, his remarks during his visit to Kyiv attacking Ukrainian nationalism meant that the CPU felt its stance vindicated and proceeded to launch an all-out media campaign against *Rukh*. Many unofficial activists were arrested for the duration of Gorbachev's visit.[8] Gorbachev may have been heartened after seeing the draft *Rukh* programme, which supported the continued leading role of the CPU/CPSU in society, but nevertheless his concern at developments in Ukraine made him maintain Volodymyr Shcherbytskyi in power until September, four years into his programme of democratisation, *glasnost'* and *perestroika*.

The launch of *Rukh* was welcomed by the main unofficial group, the UHU. In an appeal it stated: 'It is only in Ukraine that the Party has preserved in full with complete inviolability the Stalinist terrorist method of propaganda'. After the media campaign against the UHU and the Culturological Club, the Popular Movement was next in line. The UHU claimed that 'the democratic initiative of the Ukrainian patriotic intelligentsia' had been answered by 'the old Stalinist method of demoralising society and reducing to nothing the constitutional right to freedom of thought, speech and independent action'.[9]

The draft programme of *Rukh* called for a front of independent groups and the reformist wing of the CPU opposed to the leadership of the party. *Rukh* was a

> demonstration of support for revolutionary restructuring set into motion in our country by the Party. It represents a new coalition of Communists and non-Party members united in a new struggle for a fundamental social renewal in all spheres of public, governmental and economic life in the Ukrainian SSR.

The programme emphasised a continuing commitment to left-liberal ideas, such as 'humanity, peace and progress'. *Rukh* 'recognised the leading role of the Party in a socialist society. The Movement is a unifying link between the programme of restructuring proposed by the Party and the initiative of the broad masses of the people'.[10]

Rukh would assist the CPSU in broadening democratisation. In reality, however, *Rukh* dominated the public debate, keeping the CPU on the defensive, forcing it to move somewhat in the direction of accommodating public opinion. *Rukh* promised to expose all attempts at slowing down democratisation, to improve the environment, to raise living standards, to ensure the establishment of a law-based society and to campaign for republican sovereignty. The Supreme Soviet of Ukraine should control Ukrainian resources 'along the lines of the principles formulated by Lenin on the national question'. The draft programme included sections dealing with sovereignty, human and national rights, social justice, the economy, environment, national question and language policy.

The leadership structure of the CPU (as described in Chapter 3), however, remained impervious to such appeals so long as Shcherbytskyi was at the helm, and hopes for significant co-operation between the opposition and reform-reminded communists had to be repeatedly postponed until at least the spring of 1990. Hence, a growing number of *Rukh* members became increasingly hostile to the CPU, although many CPU members ignored Leonid Kravchuk's original advice against the CPU joining *Rukh*, and links did begin to develop.

COMMUNIST CAMPAIGN AGAINST *RUKH*

After the publication of the draft programme there followed a media campaign orchestrated by the CPU to discredit it. The editor of *Vechirnii Kyiv*, for example, which at that time had a daily circulation in Russian nearly three times higher than that in Ukrainian, stated that two-thirds of the thousands of letters his newspaper had received by the summer were positively inclined towards the draft programme.[11] One of the 3000 letters that *Literaturna Ukraïna* – the newspaper which had published the draft programme – claimed to have received by early March 1989 complained that while all the other newspapers had refused to publish the draft programme they nevertheless began a vicious campaign against it. 'How can one link this to democracy and *glasnost*'?' the author asked.[12]

The newspapers *Radians'ka Ukraïna*, *Pravda Ukraïny* and *Robitnycha hazeta* were the most virulent in their attacks upon *Rukh*.[13] Borys Oliinyk, head of the Ukrainian Cultural Fund, joined in the attack on the draft programme.[14] *Radians'ka Ukraïna* threatened that 'political realities must not be disregarded. We are making history and any haste is inopportune.'[15] The draft programme contained 'too much detail' and 'was worked out without the participation of specialists'. It included a 'great deal of spontaneity and dilettantism'. There was a lack of input from workers, whereas the author's goal was to create a structure 'based on confrontational positions'. 'The question that arises is this: is the movement to be a socialist and internationalist structure or not?'

High-ranking members of the Academy of Sciences wrote in *Pravda Ukraïny* that, as in the Baltic republics, 'their organisation cannot boast of a real contribution to practical achievements in restructuring. But the division along national lines, mutual suspicions and distrust, on the other hand, run quite deep'.[16] There was nothing new, the authors alleged, compared with the documents already drawn up by the CPSU. 'The entire experience of restructuring has clearly shown that in its role as a generator of restructuring ideas and guarantor of their implementation, the party is irreplaceable,' they claimed. The draft programme of *Rukh* restricted the CPSU to being merely a 'generator of ideas'. 'How do the draft's authors conceive of co-operating with the CPSU while bypassing the republic's party organisation?' The call to Ukrainise the education system conflicted with the interests of the '20 million Russian-language speakers' living in Ukraine.

Pravda Ukraïny criticised the leaders of *Rukh* for remaining in the CPU as a violation of party discipline: 'they have to remember that ideology and organisational unity are an inviolable law in our Party's life, that any manifestation of factionalism and grouping is incompatible with adherence to the Marxist-Leninist Party'.[17] Kravchuk asked how leaders of *Rukh* could remain members of the CPU when they regularly criticised it.[18]

The writers were apparently surprised and caught off guard by the fury of the media campaign, which accused them of fomenting civil war, nationalism and separatism and trying to establish an opposition political party.[19] Despite the continuing Ukrainian belief that Moscow and Gorbachev were more progressive and sympathetic to *Rukh* than was the conservative CPU, *Pravda* joined the chorus of attacks by claiming *Rukh* was 'standing above the organs of Soviet power and basically in opposition to the CPSU'.[20] A meeting in April of the Kyiv branch of the WUU passed a message to the central committee of the Communist Party of Ukraine from Dmytro Pavlychko, 'that our tasks are the same: to accelerate *perestroika*'.[21] But at that stage the Communist Party remained interested only in initiatives put forward by itself from above, and not others from below.

The CPU continually claimed that informal groups were busy influencing *Rukh* in a negative manner, especially in western Ukraine where the UHU was said to be especially influential in *Rukh*. *Rukh* was allegedly a vehicle for groups such as the UHU with 'no mass following' to expand their adherents.[22]

In July the Kyiv *oblast* branch of *Rukh* held its conference, and elected the philosopher Myroslav Popovych as its leader. Ivan Drach claimed that *Rukh* already had 200 local groups with 200 000 members in the *oblast*, despite the fact that 'the respective ideological workers have launched an offensive against it'. The media was accusing *Rukh* of being 'extremists', at which Petro Osadchuk quoted the dictionary definition of 'extremists' as a term usually applied 'by reactionaries and reformers to revolutionaries'.[23]

OPPOSITION LEAGUES AND FRONTS

At this stage of development, many oppositional forces in Ukraine were still prepared to act within an all-Union context. Ukrainian representatives attended the founding conference in Moscow of the Democratic Union opposition party in May 1988. One of the demands raised at this conference was the withdrawal of Soviet troops from the areas occupied after the Molotov–Ribbentrop Pact, including western

Ukraine. Iurii Skubko, a Ukrainian member of the Moscow-based *samizdat* journal *Tochka zrennia* and a leading Democratic Union activist, then reported that branches had been established in Kyiv, L'viv and Sumy in Ukraine.[24] Ukrainian representatives also attended the second Democratic Union congress in Riga between 26 and 29 January 1989.[25]

The Ukrainian Democratic Union (UDU) planned to hold its first founding congress on the weekend of 22/23 January 1989 in Kyiv, the anniversary of the declaration of Ukrainian independence in 1918, but the authorities prevented the congress from taking place.[26] In December 1988 a leading member of the UDU, Leonid Miliavskyi, claimed that UDU groups already existed in Kyiv, Dnipropetrovs'k, Odesa, Kharkiv and Rivne with a total of 100 members. They had decided quite early to establish a separate organisation, and not be merely a regional branch of the Russian Democratic Union. In Miliavskyi's view, the most preferable option for Ukraine would be outright state independence. When asked about the difference between it and the UHU, Miliavskyi replied:

> Firstly, we formed our group before the Helsinki Union. So there is no competition. Secondly, we are purely political – an opposition political organisation. It is a federation of human rights groups to which members of the Communist Party and members of the UDU can belong. They have a wider programme, like the Estonian popular front or the Latvian one. It is really an unofficial popular-front because an official one cannot, as yet, be recognised.
>
> We have a purely political programme which is ideologically motivated. The Ukrainian Helsinki Union does not address itself to the Marxist Leninist question, nor to the questions of socialism or capitalism.[27]

The UDU was composed of three factions – liberal democratic, Christian democratic and social democratic – in the same manner as the Russian Democratic Union.[28] In February 1989 the UDU changed its name to the Ukrainian People's Democratic League (UPDL) in order to break completely with the Russian Democratic Union. The programmes of both the UDU and UPDL were similar, although the UPDL adopted a new policy of not allowing separate factions. The UPDL programme, adopted by the Kyiv regional branch of the organisation on 12 February 1989, declared that it was a 'political organisation that united people of different views and beliefs, who stand for the general principles of democracy, humanism and freedom and aims to promote the political, economic and spiritual revival of Ukraine'.[29]

Therefore, the UPDL represented yet another political club, seeking to provide a common shelter for the various informal groups, although it had already moved on to more radical demands. The UPDL planned to develop and propagate alternative programmes, participate in election campaigns, form new branches, publish UPDL newspapers, journals and leaflets, conduct meetings and discussions, hold referenda and opinion polls, strikes and pickets. At the large 22 May 1989 meeting to honour Taras Shevchenko's 175th anniversary in Kyiv members of the UPDL were seen holding placards reading 'Long Live a United, Independent Ukraine!'

The first issue of the UPDL's *Bulletin I (Documents)* in July 1989 included the programme of the League, ratified at the inaugural congress held in June in Riga, an 'Appeal to the Citizens of Ukraine' and 'Resolutions of the fiftieth anniversary of the Molotov–Ribbentrop Pact', as well as condemning attempts by the authorities to incite inter-ethnic hatred in Ukraine. In late July 1989, the UPDL issued leaflets in support of the striking miners and organised a hunger strike in front of the Supreme Soviet of Ukraine in protest at their refusal to introduce legislation on Ukrainian national symbols.[30]

The Ukrainian Christian Democratic Front (UCDF) was formed in November 1988 in Ivano-Frankivs'k *oblast*, western Ukraine.[31] The UCDF was led by two former political prisoners, Vasyl and Petro Sichko. Petro Sichko had served a long sentence for his membership of the Ukrainian nationalist underground during the 1940s, and his entire family had been deported to Siberia. Vasyl Sichko studied journalism at Kyiv University, but was expelled for publishing a *samizdat* journal in the early 1970s. After organising a requiem service on the grave of the young composer Volodymyr Ivasiuk, allegedly murdered by the KGB in 1979, he was sentenced to eight years' imprisonment.

The UCDF hoped to capitalise upon the greater degree of national consciousness, stronger bonds with western Europe and greater proportion of believers to launch a Ukrainian Christian Democratic movement in the Catholic *oblasts* of Galicia (L'viv, Ivano-Frankivs'k, Transcarpathia and Ternopil'), that would be comparable to the Christian Social Union (CSU) in Bavaria. Despite indications of isolated pockets of UCDF support beyond western Ukraine in cities such as Odesa, most UCDF sympathisers were Ukrainian Catholics.[32]

The first inaugural meeting of the UCDF was held in L'viv in a private residence on 13 January 1989, where a programme and statute were ratified.[33] The room was decorated with a large trident and the inscription:

> God hear our pleas. Misfortune is destroying our land. The strength of the nation lies in unity, God grant us unity! God remove the shackles from us, do not let us die in captivity. Send Ukraine her freedom, grant her happiness and good fortune.

The L'viv branch of the UCDF was the most active, organising concerts of formerly banned patriotic songs and poetry, which were attended by several thousand people. Repression against this radical informal group began almost immediately after the UCDF was launched. The inaugural meeting was interrupted for one hour by the militia and KGB, who conducted a search and took the names and addresses of delegates, preventing a prayer service from taking place. However, a central council was elected, consisting of Vasyl Sichko (chairman), Lidiia Chekalska (secretary) and 11 others.

The UCDF's emphasis on raising the national consciousness of the young led them to relaunch *Plast*, the pre-war Ukrainian scout organisation, with Taras Kartyn as its head. The meeting resolved to renew the *Prosvita* (Enlightenment) Society, which had fostered literacy and national consciousness prior to the Soviet occupation of western Ukraine, and Iaroslav Kormeliuk was elected its head. Funds had already been launched to help remaining Ukrainian prisoners of conscience and victims of the Armenian earthquake. Other resolutions adopted included calls for the erection of a monument to the late Ukrainian Catholic Metropolitan Andrii Sheptytskyi and for official commemoration of 22 January (the date of the 1918 declaration of independence) as an annual national holiday. A petition to the Supreme Soviet of Ukraine demanding official registration of the UCDF was given to the KGB and central committee of the CPU for scrutiny. The registration document was even sent to Moscow and then returned to Ivano-Frankivs'k *oblast*. Despite the fact the UCDF did not contravene Soviet law and worked openly, its registration was refused.

The UCDF's draft programme believed that the Communist Party was incapable of solving Ukraine's and society's problems, which only the full recognition and adoption of religious values would allow. It called for a halt to the persecution of all Christian denominations in Ukraine, an end to the study of atheism in schools, conscientious objection on religious grounds and a multi-party system and mixed economy. Other areas which the UCDF programme dealt with were national symbols, rehabilitation of repressed individuals in culture, ecology and nuclear power. The programme was wider and more radical than the other main informal groups active at that time, including the Ukrainian Helsinki Union (UHU). Although both Vasyl and Petro Sichko were originally also members of the UHU, they resigned in the spring of 1989, after disagreeing with the more moderate policies propagated by the UHU.[34]

By the summer of 1989 the UCDF claimed to have 1000 members in western Ukraine, the majority belonging to the younger, more radical, generation. The UCDF developed a more politicised and confrontational attitude towards the authorities than the Committee in Defence of the Ukrainian Catholic Church, believing, unlike the latter, that the Church should be used as a vehicle for politicising believers.

In the autumn of 1989 the UCDF launched the Ukrainian Christian Youth Association, a body aimed primarily at young people between the ages of 16 and 30, headed by Ivan Loi from L'viv.[35] (The *Plast* scout organisation would now be concerned mainly with educational matters with children below the age of 16.) The Association's first statement appealed 'to all patriotic organisations to take an active role in an alternative to totalitarian methods of educating the youth and the rebirth of youth *Plast* traditions and camps, where youngsters could learn their native history, culture and religion, and undergo a beneficial, ethical educational course'.

In a programmatical document entitled 'What to do next?' (an obvious reply to Lukianenko's programme of a similar name), dated May 1989 and presented to the sixth conference of non-Russian national democratic movements in Estonia, Vasyl Sichko proposed a new alliance between the Ukrainian Catholic Church and national-democratic groups, like the UCDF, which had proved successful in the earlier part of this century in Galicia, and gave his reasons for criticism of the less radical UHU. In his view, Gorbachev's reforms and his so-called policies of 'democratisation' were a lie, which the West had foolishly been hoodwinked into believing; the USSR was nothing more than a 'Russian empire', an empire which was 'despotic', 'ill', 'based on falsehoods' and in 'economic ruins'. The reforms introduced by Gorbachev would merely turn the USSR into a law-based, but still despotic, state.[36]

In Sichko's view, the UCDF was the first organisation to stand for the right to full state independence for Ukraine (this was incorrect as the UPDL also stood for secession). The UCDF was therefore attacked not only by the Party, but also by the 'loyal opposition' – members of the UHU who were 'collaborationists' and 'confederalists'.

In an open letter to the Christian Democratic International in October 1989, the UCDF complained of official repression ever since the launch of the organisation. The authorities, refusing to register the UCDF, demanded that it disband of its own accord. The open letter then went on to give numerous examples of repression by the KGB and militia conducted against the UCDF, which might be taken as typical of the authorities' actions in general; disrupting meetings, press attacks on them as 'extremists' and 'terrorists', refusal to allow demonstrations, repeated rearrest on 10- and 15-day terms, beatings by unknown assailants, tapping of telephone lines and censorship of mail, dismissal from work and physical deportation to prevent attendance at meetings.[37]

RELIGION

The revival of religion in Ukraine during 1989 gathered momentum outside Galicia. In January 1989 a lecturer at Kyiv State University's Department of the History and Theory of Atheism, Vladimir Tencher, said, 'As seen by much of our youth, atheism has simply become old-fashioned. It is the view of grandfathers and grandmothers.'[38] In February 1989, the Initiative Committee in Support of a Revival of the Ukrainian Autocephalous Orthodox Church was launched in Kyiv, with support from unofficial groups.[39] (The Ukrainian Autocephalous [or Independent] Orthodox Church had been relaunched after the Bolshevik revolution, but was liquidated in 1930.)[40]

The revival of the UAOC, backed by informal groups such as *Rukh*, UPDL and UHU, in some ways posed more of a threat to the Russian Orthodox Church than the Uniate Church, because of the intimate connection between the unity of the Russian Orthodox Church and the unity of the Soviet state. In 1988 of the 6893 functioning ROC churches in the USSR, 4000 were located in Ukraine, half of them in the western region of the republic (the RSFSR boasted only 2000 churches). Two-thirds of new churches opened under Gorbachev were in Ukraine, while three-quarters of all vocations to the priesthood were from Ukraine.

Therefore, a church schism in Ukraine was a 'mortal danger' to the ROC, and it remained hostile towards both the UAOC and UCC.[41] In May, Metropolitan Filaret, then a high-ranking figure in the ROC and head of the ROC exarchate in Ukraine, said that the UAOC was the 'work of politicos, not church people, who want to exploit it with the aim of taking Ukrainian believers out of the Russian Orthodox Church. But our church, as one knows from history, does everything to unite peoples. That is why she is against autocephaly.'[42]

The Committee for the revival of the UAOC exerted great pressure upon the Russian Orthodox Church to accommodate Ukrainian aspirations in part at least. Consequently, the ROC introduced some cosmetic changes. Priests were allowed to hold services in Ukrainian and no longer in old Church Slavonic (which is closer to Russian). The print-run of *Pravoslavnyi visnyk*, the organ of the Ukrainian exarchate, was increased, and the Odesa seminary was allowed to give instruction in the Ukrainian language.

The Russian Orthodox Church had never restricted itself solely to Russian believers and had acted as an imperial arm of both the Tsarist and Soviet regimes. Even some Russian Orthodox believers in Ukraine and the RSFSR had begun to move towards the émigré ROC because of the subservience of the Moscow Patriarchate to the Communist Party.[43]

The UAOC Committee initially received strong encouragement from the UHU and the Culturological Club. The UHU press service published the appeal of the UAOC Initiative Committee to the Supreme Soviet of Ukraine, All-Union Supreme Soviet and International Christian Community as release number 68. Many Culturological Club activists, such as Serhii Naboka, Oles Shevchenko and Ievhen Sverstiuk, were active supporters of the UAOC and had dared to hold unofficial celebrations of the millenium of East Slavic Christianity in Kyiv in the summer of 1988, when the official celebrations were held in Moscow.

The appeal claimed that the UAOC's historical roots lay in the Ukrainian Orthodoxy usurped by the ROC in 1685. It also eulogised the Church's revival in the 1920s, when 5000 parishes and 4000 priests had been registered in Ukraine. 'But the Russian Orthodox Church does not recognise the very fact of the existence of the UAOC and is incapable of satisfying the religious needs of Ukrainian believers.' The UAOC Committee would therefore petition legislative bodies in the attempt to have UAOC religious communities registered.

Initial contacts between the UAOC and the Ukrainian Catholic Church were friendly, as evidenced by the joint service by Orthodox and Catholics in L'viv on the 175th anniversary of Shevchenko's birth on 26 February 1989. The wholesale collapse of the ROC in western

Ukraine towards the end of 1989, though, faced many priests with a stark choice – either to go over to the Ukrainian Catholic Church, or, if they wish to uphold 'Orthodoxy', to move into the UAOC. Therefore in Galicia, which had no UAOC tradition, a sizeable number of former ROC priests, particularly in the countryside, joined the UAOC; this would later lead to friction over the allocation of buildings (although technically all Church property in the USSR belonged to the state). Eastern and southern Ukraine, which was more Russian-speaking and contained a proportionately smaller number of believers, remained broadly loyal to the ROC, whereas Central Ukraine was a mixture of all Churches: Orthodox, Uniate and even Protestant. Here, the UAOC's strength was concentrated in the urban areas, where the radical intelligentsia were to be found.

Consequently, the revival of the UAOC throughout 1989 took place primarily in western Ukraine. A young leading UAOC priest, Iurii Boiko, admitted, 'You know it's quite a complicated task to restore the UAOC in eastern Ukraine. Particularly here in Kyiv we have much scarcer grounds to revive the UAOC than in western Ukraine'.[44] The security services and CPU were only too happy to help the UAOC establish itself in western Ukraine – while, at the same time, hindering its revival in eastern Ukraine. Father Boiko commented, 'The Russian Orthodox Church considers the UAOC non-existent canonically, therefore any dialogue with us is out of the question.' He quoted a reformist, former ROC prisoner of conscience, Father Iakurin, who had told him that he objected to Ukrainian autocephaly because it would result in the ROC being virtually extinguished in Ukraine.

In August 1989, the parish and priest of the Church of SS Peter and Paul in L'viv seceded from the ROC and became the first UAOC parish (and Metropolitan see) in Ukraine. They called upon the Ukrainian people to support the revival of an Orthodox Church in Ukraine independent of Moscow. They proposed that new religious communities should attempt to gain registration as UAOC, that parishes adopt resolutions stating their refusal to obey the hierarchy of the ROC and to mention Patriarch Demetrius I of Constantinople – not Patriarch Pimen – in their sermons. In statements to the Council for Religious Affairs they called the ROC in Ukraine 'none other than an organ of the spiritual enslavement of the Godfearing Ukrainian nation'.[45] UANTI quickly voiced its support for the emerging UAOC and Mykhailo Osadchyi offered to work on a UAOC information service, calling for the establishment of a Ukrainian patriarchate.

In May 1989 the campaign for the legalisation of the Ukrainian Catholic Church gathered momentum when three bishops and three priests travelled to Moscow to meet Supreme Soviet officials. In protest at their refusal to meet them, all six began a hunger strike, their ranks being later swelled by the arrival of new priests and lay activists from Ukraine. Boris Yeltsin, Oles Honchar and Rostyslav Bratun were persuaded to try to raise the question of the legalisation of the Ukrainian Catholic Church in the Congress of People's Deputies.[46] Roman Fedoriv, editor of the L'viv-based journal *Zhovten'* (since 1990 *Dzvin*) called for the legalisation of both the Ukrainian Catholic and Autocephalous Orthodox Churches at the Congress. On 18 June over 150 000 Ukrainian Catholics throughout western Ukraine held prayer services in response to Cardinal Myroslav Liubachivskyi's call for a worldwide vigil for Ukrainian religious freedom.[47]

ALL-UNION ELECTIONS

During the second stage of the evolution of the opposition in Ukraine the elections to the all-Union Congress of People's Deputies in March 1989 made an important contribution to the mobilisation of public opinion and informal groups. These were, after all, the first semi-free elections in the USSR since the Bolshevik revolution, although the election law compiled and controlled by a state machinery still in the hands of the CPSU reserved one-third of the seats for CPSU organisations, and the nomination of candidates was strictly controlled.

Consequently, on 18 December 1988 the Co-ordinating Committee of the UHU, one of the few informal groups active at that stage, called for a boycott of the elections: 'The Ukrainian Helsinki Union, which if democratic elections were held even today would have realistic chances of victory in a string of electoral districts, is deprived of such a possibility by the new undemocratic laws.'

The UHU believed that their participation would benefit 'only the reactionary forces of society, helping them to create an illusion of legality'. They therefore recommended that the UHU not put forward candidates and not participate in them, that election cards be cancelled and for UHU members to explain their position to the electorate. (Eventually, the UHU supported certain candidates such as Rostyslav Bratun, who endorsed its key policies, for all-Union laws to apply only after ratification by the Supreme Soviet of Ukraine, for

Ukrainian to be the state language, for republican self-financing and sovereignty, and for the closure of nuclear power stations.)[48]

The L'viv *oblast* branch of the UHU attacked the 'naive hope that the election to the so-called Congress of People's Deputies of several more liberal deputies can in some way influence the composition of the Supreme Soviet, the composition and policies of the future government'. Participation would merely 'help the CPU receive a mandate to govern'. They therefore recommended that voters write 'BOYCOTT' across the ballot card, write a statement to this effect to the district election authorities or give the ballot card to the UHU.[49]

Popular candidates, such as Bratun and Ivan Drach in L'viv and Alla Iaroshynska in Zhytomyr, were subjected to a dirty tricks campaign by the CPU to prevent their nomination. Despite Bratun receiving 13 000 signatures on a petition, the backing of work collectives and support of all informal groups (including national minority societies), he was accused by the media and CPU of various sins, including membership of the OUN in his youth. (At the time in question Bratun was only 14.)[50]

Bratun's programme supported sovereignty, political pluralism, an end to nuclear power, Ukrainian as the state language, freedom of conscience, the abolition of all-Union ministries, the depoliticisation of the judiciary and direct elections to the Supreme Soviet. 'There should be a union agreement in which the economic and political rights of republics are clearly outlined in conditions of a genuine democratic federation,' Bratun stated in a leaflet disseminated by *Tovarystvo Leva*, which ended with the words, 'Bratun is struggling for democracy, restructuring and *glasnost'*! Bratun is struggling for the realisation of the resolutions of the nineteenth party conference!' (Of course, informal groups and the CPU interpreted such resolutions in a different manner.)

In Zhytomyr, Alla Iaroshyns'ka was one of five candidates standing, although the only one who was a non-Party member. Her journalistic exposure of housing corruption in the city by the CPU had earned her the wrath of the authorities. Nevertheless, this reputation as a crusading journalist made her highly popular and she won 90 per cent of the vote.[51]

The vast majority of candidates were CPSU members, although Iurii Shemshuchenko, director of the Institute of State and Law, Academy of Sciences in Kyiv, believed that 'there is no contradiction. Of course, every deputy who is a member of the CPSU ... should follow the Party line in a corresponding representative body. At the same time, he should define the interests of his electorate where the majority are non-Party people.'

But the CPU was shocked at the election results many of its candidates received, in particular those running unopposed (a third of all CPSU candidates ran unopposed). In L'viv 36 000 ballot cards were either defaced or were left blank, primarily in protest at candidates running unopposed. In Drohobych, near L'viv, the supposedly moderate first secretary Iaroslav Pohrebniak ran unopposed, after the local UHU had rejected overtures to support him.[52] Pohrebniak claimed, 'The national problem does not exist. The language problem does not exist', and he defined democracy as a system in which 'If one has a certain position and prestige, then the other candidate may withdraw out of a certain respect.' The electorate thought differently and he received less than 12 per cent of the vote.[53]

Shcherbytskyi stood in his home constituency of Dnipropetrovs'k, also unopposed. The official Soviet news agency described 'the main point in his election programme as the Party's all-round concern for the happiness and well-being of the people', and continued: 'the attempts of individuals and groups to use democracy and *glasnost'* to the detriment of the people's friendship and consequently, to the detriment of *perestroika* are therefore totally unacceptable.'[54]

The election results were a shock to the CPU, but instead of addressing the crisis of its own legitimacy, the CPU blamed its setback on the opposition, particularly the UHU, and on excessive press freedom. 'We are still learning the art of democratic judgement and ability to hold a discussion,' Chornovil stated.[55]

Any hint of poor election results was not publicised in the Soviet Ukrainian press. At a plenum of the CPU in May, Shcherbytskyi complained of even army officers, Afghanistan veterans and certain members of the CPSU (supporters of the Democratic Platform and *Rukh*) distancing themselves from the CPU. He called upon the organs of power to 'deal a timely, convincing, open and most decisive rebuff to demagogues and extremists'.[56]

MEMORIAL

In March 1989 the Ukrainian branch of the historical-educational society Memorial was formed, with support from various informal groups and the Cinematographers', Theatre Workers' and Architects' Unions, as well as the Ukrainian Cultural Fund.[57] The initiative group to establish Memorial in Ukraine had been working for six months prior to its inaugural congress on 4 March, in the midst of the election campaign and on the anniversary of Stalin's death, 'but efforts to form a Ukrainian arm of Memorial had long run into stable but potent opposition on high'.[58]

Memorial sought to publicise 'Ukraine's Katyn', a mass grave reputed to contain over 200 000 bodies at Bykivnia near Kyiv, which the authorities had for years tried to blame upon the Nazis.[59] 'Memorial is already a focus for nationalist-orientated groups in the republic', one report stated, with many informal groups in attendance at the congress.[60] In L'viv the UHU was the main organising force behind Memorial.

The congress attracted 500 delegates from 40 cities, together with 300 guests, including such well-known former prisoners of conscience as Stepan Khmara, Bohdan and Mykhailo Horyn, Iaroslov Lesiv and Ivan Hel.[61] The resolution commission at the congress included M. Horyn and Ievhen Proniuk. Memorial, during the congress, 'expressed [its] willingness to cooperate with various movements, ecological, groups, religious and informal organisations; irrespective of what the functionaries think about them'.[62]

Having stressed that although 'Stalin is dead, his followers are still among us', the congress demanded the restoration of traditional place names in Ukraine, free access to KGB and MVD archives, abrogation of the law on rallies and the investigation and punishment of officials involved in repression under Brezhnev, and supported the embryonic *Rukh*. At the rally the following day additional demands were made, such as the legalisation of the Ukrainian Catholic Church, and rehabilitation and compensation for former prisoners of conscience.[63]

THE UKRAINIAN LANGUAGE SOCIETY

The second stage of development of the opposition movement in Ukraine witnessed the establishment of the Taras Shevchenko Ukrainian Language Society, the successor to the *Ridna Mova* Society.[64] As the first large-scale popular movement to escape CPU control, and to pursue specifically national ends, it acted as a *de facto* precursor of *Rukh*, uniting in its ranks many of the future leading lights of the opposition.

The *Ridna Mova* Society had originated in western Ukraine and by the congress already claimed 10 000 members in Galicia.[65] The inaugural congress of the ULS took place in Kyiv between 11 and 12 February 1989, supported by the Writers' Union of Ukraine, the

Institute of Philology and the Academy of Sciences Institute of Literature.[66]

The inaugural congress was attended by 700 participants, including 500 delegates. Informal groups, government officials and members of the creative unions all attended. The opening speech was given by Oles Honchar, later followed by Ivan Dziuba. During the congress Iurii Ielchenko, of the ideology department of the central committee of the CPU, attempted to drive a wedge between the Ukrainian Language Society (which was praised), and *Rukh* (which was condemned). The Ukrainian Language Society resolved, however, to support *Rukh* and become a collective member of it.

The congress recommended that the Ukrainian Language Society publish a newspaper and an information bulletin, prepare a draft programme for Ukrainian as the state language, prepare sociological research on the functioning of the Ukrainian language and publish a Ukrainian edition of the *UNESCO Courier*, a new *Pravopys* (Orthography), an ecological supplement in Ukrainian, Russian and English to *Pravda Ukrainy*, and that Ukrainian television broadcast a programme on the functioning and development of the Ukrainian language.

The delegates criticised the damage inflicted upon the Ukrainian language in recent years, as a 'withdrawal from Leninist nationalist policy'. Shcherbytskyi was heavily criticised, the CPU was condemned for its media campaign against *Rukh* and there were calls for the rehabilitation of those repressed under Brezhnev, such as Vasyl Stus. Ielchenko walked out after his calls not to support *Rukh* were rejected. A minute's silence was held for all those who died under Stalin and Brezhnev. Ivan Kandyba read a greeting from UANTI, while Vasyl Barladianu and Levko Lukianenko spoke from the UHU, and Bohdan Horyn from the UHU was elected to the executive.[67]

The Ukrainian Language Society, in keeping with the climate of the times, argued that '*perestroika* creates the best possible conditions for the people's spiritual resurgence, for granting the Ukrainian language full rights'. It called upon all nationalities in Ukraine to support constitutional protection for the Ukrainian language, its elevation to a state language and prioritisation in everyday functions. Russian should be the means of communication between the nationalities of the USSR, while Ukrainian should be the means of communication within Ukraine. The Ukrainian Language Society promised to become active within election campaigns and support *perestroika*. The Ukrainian Language Society would 'establish the Society's primary organs in localities – at industrial enterprises, schools, newspapers, institutes of higher learning, research and cultural establishments and institutes ...'[68]

The statute of the Ukrainian Language Society described itself as a 'voluntary community organisation which organises its activities in accordance with the constitutions of the Soviet Union and Ukrainian SSR, Soviet laws and its statute'. The Ukrainian Language Society 'supports *perestroika* as initiated by the CPSU and will base its work on principled internationalism, democracy, social pluralism, self-government and *glasnost'* ... ' The Ukrainian Language Society would undertake lectures, festivals, conferences, translation work, publishing, give advice and organise branches to raise awareness and national consciousness.[69]

A pensioner described how during the last three decades use of Ukrainian had fallen, while Russian had increased in cities such as Kyiv: 'People were just ashamed of speaking Ukrainian, using it in practical jokes and anecdotes. I wouldn't like a language to come into or out of fashion. If most people want Ukrainian to be the state language our government should take a relevant decision and make a law.'[70]

By the middle of 1989 Dmytro Pavlychko, elected head of the Ukrainian Language Society, claimed 70 000 members for the Society, which by then had been officially registered. The Ukrainian Language Society avoided confrontation with national minorities, although: 'We emphasise – and people should understand – that if one lives in Ukraine, then one should know the Ukrainian language.' Pavlychko claimed that Gorbachev had supported the Ukrainian Language Society, as had the top levels of the CPU with whom they were 'working harmoniously' and able to 'count upon their support'. It was only on a lower level that the Ukrainian Language Society had problems from 'those who are not behind *perestroika*' he claimed.[71]

Clearly, a pattern was now developing whereby the Kyiv cultural intelligentsia was always foremost in the development of unofficial organisations. As stated in Chapter 2, the growth in the twentieth century of the Ukrainian intellgentsia had been impressive, particularly given the situation in 1917, when most of the leading elements in Kyiv were not identified with the Ukrainian cause. As Krawchenko argues, this gave new possibilities to the processes of indigenous culture formation and reproduction, and to leadership of the national movement.

In this respect, the Ukrainian movement had much in common with the nineteenth-century national revivals described by Hroch.[72] First, isolated, often scholarly, individuals nurture the national idea. However, the second phase, 'the formation period of national consciousness' requires a broad social base, so that elite leadership of the national movement appears as a result of regularised social relations, and not simply through individual choice.[73] Finally, the creation of an organisational base for the national movement allows the elites to take their message to the masses (Krawchenko's argument, and Drobizheva's paradigm of intelligentsia leadership of national movements under *perestroika* described in Chapter 2, are clearly similar to Hroch's).

The fact that the iniators of *Rukh*, Memorial and the Ukrainian Language Society were largely the elite of the Writers' Union of Ukraine, and their foot-soldiers the broader intelligentsia (teachers, those with higher education) fits the paradigm quite well. The cultural intelligentsia obviously had a career interest in resisting the pressure of Russification. The WUU provided a ready-made organisation, and at this stage, Ukrainian cultural elites were allowed a certain autonomy, although Kravchuk had warned writers not to join *Rukh* at the Kyiv Writers' Union of Ukraine plenum on 31 January 1989, and the intelligentsia still found it difficult to contest the state's near-monopoly control of the public sphere.[74]

Hence the mass organisation stage still faced a difficult birth.

6 The Birth of Mass Politics (1989–90)

Are you really not able to understand that soon you will be dealing with a mass social movement?

(Valentyn Moroz, Report from the Beriia Reserve, 1967)

THE VIEW FROM THE CENTRE

The nationality question became increasingly acute after 1989 with massacres of Meshketians in Central Asia, pogroms and ethnic conflict within Azerbaidzhan as well as the centre's clumsy repression of Georgian nationalists. In addition, the elections to the Congress of People's Deputies radicalised demands within the republics, strengthening the activities of the Popular Fronts. In some republics there was already effectively shared power between all-union institutions and the Popular Fronts. In December of that year the Lithuanian branch of the CPSU seceded, causing the first serious fracture in the once monolithic Communist Party. Throughout the non-Russian republics the legitimacy of Communist Party rule was undermined, especially as *glasnost'* revealed previously taboo 'blank spots' in history with Stalin-era mass graves of victims opened up to public scrutiny and condemnation (Bykivnia in Ukraine, Kuropaty in Belarus).

It was only in September 1989 that the central committee of the CPSU devoted a plenum to the subject of the nationality question. Gorbachev admitted that 'unresolved issues have surfaced one after another, errors and deformations that were accumulated over decades have now made themselves felt, and ethnic conflicts have erupted after smouldering for years'.[1] The new Gorbachev line had become a rejection of the fusion[2] concept of the Brezhnev era in favour of a strong centre and strong republics. This would be accomplished through a 'renewed union' where each republic would have wide opportunities for the development of its economy and culture through devolution. The question of how the division of powers would be accomplished between the republics and centre now entered the debate.

103

Gorbachev, however, steadfastly refused to accept the division of the CPSU into national branches or any dropping of the leading role of the CPSU. Nationalism was declared to be incompatible with membership of the CPSU. Gorbachev was therefore initially opposed to the creation of a separate Russian Communist Party but did not oppose the establishment of Russian symbols of statehood (cultural, scientific, economic and academic) which had not existed previously. The Russian language was also made the new 'state language' of the USSR. Nevertheless, Gorbachev finally accepted the need to replace the 1922 Union Treaty in order to overcome arguments made in the non-Russian republics that the USSR was a non-voluntary creation.[3]

CPSU plenums proved to be disappointing as they failed to elaborate a new set of policies, thereby opening up the field to the Popular Fronts and national communists to agitate for their own proposals. Gorbachev accepted that the republics needed to be given greater decision-making powers, rejected border changes and called for action against violent separatists. But what was an offer was 'either too little and too late to meet heightened demands or, in the case of republican state languages and republican economic autonomy, for example, merely a belated and not necessarily wholehearted endorsement of initiatives taken in the republics'.[4]

The plenum was followed in July 1989 by Gorbachev's first broadcast to the Soviet people on the nationalities question. While rejecting separatism Gorbachev accepted the need for a 'profound transformation in the Soviet federation' and promoted the benefits of the Union.[5] Gorbachev's calls for actions against separatists led to the adoption of amendments to the article in the Soviet legal code 'On Criminal Liability for State Crimes' – amendments which were more repressive than article 70 which had been used to imprison dissidents in the pre-Gorbachev era.

The CPSU's new draft platform on the nationalities question called for a radical overhaul of centre–periphery relations, with each republic retaining its independence (*samostoyatelnost*). The draft platform outlined the following priorities:[6]

- the transformation of the federation;
- greater rights for the republics;
- equal rights for all ethnic groups;
- the establishment of conditions for the free development of national cultures and languages;
- greater guarantees against ethnic discrimination;

- greater attention to ideological work on the nationalities question;
- rejection of the federalisation of the armed forces and the CPSU;
- the centre would define all-union principles and policies, maintain control over security policy and co-ordinate the economic, scientific and cultural spheres;

Clearly therefore, the draft platform fell far short of converting the USSR into a genuine confederation of sovereign states, a demand that the republics had been demanding since 1988–9. Many of them would soon drop this demand in favour of independence after failing to obtain any support for confederation from Gorbachev prior to 1990.

THE VIEW FROM UKRAINE

The period between the autumn of 1989 and autumn of the following year, marked the crucial period of transition in Ukraine, during which small, isolated groups were transformed into larger alliances, and a powerful opposition was formed.

The non-Russians had not been in a position to rebel in the pre-Gorbachev era, because 'As long as the public sphere is occupied and more importantly, as long as the KGB remains intact, the deprivatisation of anti-state attitudes will be problematical, anti-state collectives and elites will be unlikely to mobilise, alliances between workers and intellectuals will not materialise and rebellions, revolts and insurrections will be well-nigh impossible'.[7]

All these obstacles began to dissolve in 1989–90, although in Ukraine, unlike the Baltic republics, the state retained sufficient powers to delay the formation of a true multi-party system and embryonic civil society until after the republican elections of March 1990. Hence the CPU was initially dominant in the new parliament as well.

The most significant features of the pre-election period were:

- the end of the 'Brezhnev era' in Ukraine with Shcherbytskyi's resignation;
- the failure of the CPU to crush *Rukh* in its infancy;
- the beginnings of a working-class movement in Ukraine after the strikes of July 1989; and
- the legalisation of the Ukrainian Catholic Church.

The key point in this stage was September 1989 when three important events occurred: the resignation of Shcherbytskyi, mass meetings
of Ukrainian Catholics and the inaugural congress of *Rukh*.

SHCHERBYTSKYI REPLACED BY 'REFORMER'

In September 1989 Volodymyr Shcherbytskyi was replaced as first secretary of the CPU by Volodymyr Ivashko. Although born in Poltava,
Ivashko had been the first secretary of the Dnipropetrovs'k *oblast*
CPU, the same region from where Shcherbytskyi (and Brezhnev) had
originated. In January 1988 he had become a member of the
politiburo of the central committee of the CPU, and in March 1989
was elected as a deputy to the USSR Supreme Soviet.[8]

Although there was little evidence to back the claim, the Western
press, which had speculated for many years over Shcherbytskyi's
demise, now wrote that Ivashko was 'a protégé of Gorbachev' and
'considered a relative moderate in the Communist Party'.[9] His election to the post of first secretary of the CPU was a 'victory for *perestroika*'.[10] Yet Ivashko was a former political adviser to the
Soviet-backed communist regime in Afghanistan.[11]

In the view of the CPU, 'democratisation' of Soviet society was to be
undertaken by transferring communist control from the Communist
Party to the state structure. Hence in Ukraine, Ivashko was eager to
combine the two posts of first secretary of the CPU and chairman of
the Supreme Council of Ukraine, which he achieved by 4 June 1990,
replacing Valentyna Shevchenko as chairman of the Supreme Council.
However, little more than a month later, Ivashko gladly dropped his
two Ukrainian positions to accept Gorbachev's offer of a position in
Moscow as deputy general secretary of the CPSU.

Gorbachev probably judged that he was just conservative enough to
satisfy the more moderate conservatives in the Party, while appearing
just reformist enough not to frighten the more moderate reformists,
one report claimed.[12] In other words, Ivashko was a committed communist, but also a realist, balancing between conservatism and reform
– like Gorbachev.

Ivashko's resignation from the post of chairman of the Supreme
Council of Ukraine showed that he did not regard it as an important
position, and also reflected Gorbachev's continued lack of tact and
understanding of the nationality question. Ironically, Ivashko turned
out to have made a poor career move, as Mykhailo Horyn (head of

the *Rukh* secretariat) prophesied: 'only a man who does not think about his future can abandon the post of president [sic] of a 52 million-strong nation to become deputy chairman of a party which is dying on its feet'.[13]

Ivashko, for example, stated on Soviet television[14] after his defection to Moscow that he was 'a staunch supporter of *perestroika*' and warned, 'we must in no way allow a split in the party' or 'push our republic and country over the cliff with non-constructive criticism and confrontation in society'.[15]

Only a month after taking up the position of deputy general secretary of the CPSU, Ivashko, with Oleg Shenin, central committee secretary responsible for cadres, began circulating instructions, later leaked, to central committee departments actively to support the beleaguered communists in Lithuania.[16] He proposed that a military unit under KGB command be established to protect the pro-Moscow CPSU and demanded that communists employed in the KGB, MVD and Prosecutor's Office organise 'legal proceedings against the leaders of various nationalist and anti-Soviet formations'. In August 1991, Ivashko also neglected to condemn the attempted coup.

However, despite his personal views, the long-term logic towards the creation of 'national communism' outlined in Chapter 1 had already forced Ivashko to make crucial concessions to the opposition in the Supreme Council.

NATIONAL SYMBOLS

As the embryonic *Rukh* began to develop its organisational capacity, it increasingly sought to challenge official interpretations of Ukrainian history, and to replace them with more specifically national myths and symbols, which would help to solidify national consciousness and assist in the organisation of collective action.

Rukh, the UHU and other 'informals', for example, opposed the official celebrations of the 280th anniversary of the Battle of Poltava on 6–9 July 1989. Official Soviet historiography had always interpreted Poltava, when Peter I's armies defeated Charles XII's Swedes and the Ukrainian Cossacks under Hetman Ivan Mazepa, as marking the final stage in the mutually beneficial 'reunification' of Russians, Belarusians and Ukrainians, but *Rukh* wished to reclaim it as a specifically nationalist uprising, nobly defeated. In particular, the desire of various all-Union groups, such as *Rossiia molodaia* (Young Russia – affiliated to *Pamiat*) to come to Ukraine for the celebrations was widely condemned.

At the inaugural congress of the Kyiv branch of *Rukh* on 1 July 1989, the leading writer Ivan Drach stated:

> The relations between the closest and most kindred peoples (Ukrainians and Russians) have never been idyllic, although our home-grown scribblers tried hard to present things in this way in their quasi-ethnography ... It is well known that Peter I and Menshikov annihilated thousands of Ukrainians for the so-called treachery of Mazepa ... What would happen if we, in order to boost Ukrainian patriotism, organised a trip along the route traced by Hetman Petro Sahydachnyi who, jointly with the Poles, captured Moscow in 1616? I am sure they would break our legs in the first *oblast* of the RSFSR we had to cross, and they would be absolutely right to do so.[17]

Although the 'informals' were not yet strong enough to prevent the official ceremonies taking place, a counter-demonstration was organised, and the overt siding of the authorities with Russian chauvinists helped to push disillusioned semi-official groups towards the ranks of the ex-dissidents.

On 6 May 1989 the central committee of the CPU published a Resolution regarding the 'reunification' of western Ukraine with Soviet Ukraine 50 years earlier, which was published in all the major Soviet Ukrainian newspapers and journals, and announced a programme of celebrations including a special joint meeting of the central committee of the CPU and Supreme Council of Ukraine, and meetings with, 'those who took part in the revolutionary-liberationary struggle for socialist construction', veterans of World War II and western Ukrainian CPU and cultural activists.[18] A documentary film would be released, there would be 'Days of Culture, Art, Exhibitions' with wide-ranging exhibitions in museums, clubs and galleries. A republican academic conference would be organised, a new 'Historical Outline of the Communist Party of West Ukraine' (the Communist Party of inter-war Galicia and Volhynia') would be published, together with the collected works of well-known activists of the Communist Party of West Ukraine (CPWU).[19]

The Resolution was notable for its lack of reference to Stalin, or of the repression against the local population that occurred after the 'liberation'. Only the last, short paragraph added that a commission attached to the Politburo of the central committee of the CPU would be looking into the question of rehabilitating members of the CPWU who had died during the Stalin era.

The problems surrounding Soviet legitimacy in all the areas occupied as a consequence of the Molotov–Ribbentrop Pact were ignored. In the words of Professor Norman Davies, a historian of Poland:

> If the Baltic states can now reclaim their independence on the grounds that they were victims of Soviet aggression, so too can all the other lands affected by the protocols of the Pact – eastern Finland (Karelia), eastern Poland (Belarus and Ukraine) and eastern Romania (Moldavia). So too, indeed, can all the non-Russian republics of the Soviet Union, every single one of which was incorporated by force either in 1918–21, in 1939–40 or in 1944–5.[20]

On the other hand, *samizdat* writings noted that 'liberation' brought with it mass repression, deportation and executions of political prisoners.[21] According to Viacheslav Chornovil,

> Exactly how did Ukrainian history benefit by turning away from a mild Polish occupation, under which western Ukraine at least had some possibilities of democratic decision-making and cultural development, to the terrible occupation by Stalin? And can we forget that the Ukrainian lands were gathered together not for the good of the people, but in order to widen, under the pretext of reunification, the Russian empire?[22]

The UHU was also concerned to stress that the nationalist alternative to the Communist Party of Western Ukraine (which itself was disbanded on the orders of Stalin by the Comintern in 1938), the Organisation of Ukrainian Nationalists (OUN), had played a positive role in protecting Ukrainians from 'Polish national and social oppression', and in its later struggle against both German and Soviet occupation.

As early as winter 1987, the *samizdat* journal *Ukrainian Herald* had published the secret protocols of the Molotov–Ribbentrop Pact.[23] The accompanying editorial had argued that the secret protocols could not form the basis for the 'reunification' of Ukrainian lands.

The Ukrainian People's Democratic League, a more radical group than the UHU, issued a statement about the 'reunification' of western Ukraine at its inaugural congress in Riga, between 24 and 25 June 1989. In their view, 'With the occupation of the regions of western

Ukraine this was the final act in the occupation of Ukraine begun in 1918'. They proceeded to demand that a commission be established by the Congress of People's Deputies to examine the Molotov–Ribbentrop Pact, in order that all the documents be published, that it hold 'public hearings' which would discuss and 'denounce this deceitful Pact'.[24]

In early June, Viacheslav Chornovil discussed the reasoning behind the opposition's decision to celebrate the anniversaries on 23 August and 17 September as acts of occupation – not 'liberation' or 'reunification'. He believed that the real anniversary to be celebrated each year was 22 January 1919, when the Ukrainian People's Republic had united with the West Ukrainian People's Republic briefly to form a united Ukrainian independent state.[25]

On 23 August in Kyiv's Central Stadium a 2000-strong meeting organised by the Ukrainian People's Democratic League (UPDL) and the UHU to condemn the Molotov–Ribbentrop pact was violently broken up by the authorities, when the demonstrators refused to agree to a demand from the authorities that they take down their Ukrainian national flags. In L'viv 4000 people attended a rally against the pact, where Bohdan Horyn (head of the L'viv *oblast* UHU) and Volodymyr Iavorskyi spoke. In Kharkiv riot police occupied the city centre to prevent a demonstration.

Oles Shevchenko, head of the Kyiv branch of the UHU, said in his speech: 'There cannot be an independent Ukraine, without an independent Lithuania, Latvia and Estonia.' Another member of the UHU, Serhii Naboka, editor of the UHU newsletter *Holos vidrodzhennia* (Voice of Rebirth) warned against inciting inter-ethnic conflicts. Ivan Hel, the head of the Committee in Defence of Ukraine Catholic Church, meanwhile announced that on 17 September that there would be a march and special mass in L'viv to deliberately coincide with the Communist Party-sponsored 'reunification' anniversary.[26]

On 21 January 1990, *Rukh*'s organisational ability reached a high-point when 750 000 formed a human chain from Kyiv to L'viv and Ivano-Frankivs'k to celebrate the 1919 anniversary.[27] This was to have a major impact on the election campaign, and, as the evidence of popular support for the opposition accumulated, helped put the CPU on the defensive.

Only a minority was receptive to this new nationalist historiography, however. The working class in particular remained largely immune. The revisionist intelligentsia could not reach a mass audience until the resources of the state, the mass media especially, begun to sing the same tune in early 1991.

INDEPENDENT TRADE UNIONS[28]

Towards the end of 1989 the opposition was broadened by the first stirrings of a working-class movement, although links with intelligentsia-led organisations, such as the embryonic *Rukh*, were initially very poor. Signs of working-class discontent had long been apparent. In 1988, *Robitnycha hazeta* had carried workers' complaints that they had not noticed any *perestroika* at their enterprises. Readers of the newspaper demanded 'action at all levels. Not to wait for new instructions'.[29] In Kharkiv a bi-weekly newspaper *Kharkivs'ki profspilky* (Kharkiv Trade Unions) had been initiated by Vitaliy Korotych, an all-Union deputy and editor of *Ogonëk* in September 1989 to promote democratisation, and trade union reform.[30]

But the problems of organising an all-Ukrainian independent workers movement modelled upon Solidarity were due primarily to the uneven level of national consciousness in Ukraine. Iurii Zhyzhko, then a UHU activist, wrote in 1990: 'It is not surprising that beyond the large academic centres in Ukraine, a wide section of society is thoroughly indifferent to and distrustful of political demands – even partly towards the national revival.'[31] Zhyzhko continued:

> As events have shown, workers have exhibited solidarity in protests against the Party apparatus, but not yet all workers connect their employment and societal poverty to the social system and Communist ideology, because not all have been convinced of the idea of Ukrainian state independence. The simple citizen is directed by a salami psychology, he resembles a hypnotised rabbit not ready to undertake independent steps and always glancing at the almighty state.[32]

Vladimir Klebanov, who in 1977 had organised the Free Trade Union Association of the Soviet Working People (which suffered repression from the authorities and was subsequently broken up), remained committed to an all-Union agenda, as opposed to a specifically Ukrainian one. Speaking during December 1989, Klebanov voiced his personal opposition to Ukrainian independence, stated his preference for Russian as the state language of Ukraine and said he believed most workers in the Donbas were negatively disposed towards *Rukh*.[33] Workers had been 'fooled by Communist propaganda' and 'the majority of workers are afraid of politics'.[34] A miner at the *Rukh* congress in September lamented: 'We drank before, they pushed bottles in front of us. Enough! We need to learn. Organise us lectures. Only not "schools of young Communists" – we need legal, economic and political knowledge.'[35]

From 18 to 24 July 1989, the Donbas miners were on strike, as part of the first (publicised) mass all-Union industrial action since the 1920s.[36] At its height, 141 out of 273 pits were on strike.[37] The strikes quickly spread to the more nationally minded miners of western Ukraine, who introduced more political demands, such as democratic elections and the removal of the local CPU leadership, and called for the creation of independent trade unions along the lines of Solidarity.

In the main, however, demands remained strictly economic. The miners sought a pay rise, longer holidays, the recognition of certain diseases specific to miners, improved housing, increased soap quotas, priority food supplies, a profit-sharing scheme, a minimum wage and many other things.[38] On the other hand, they also demanded the 'prohibition of the establishment of co-operatives and the disbandment of existing medical and food co-operatives'.[39]

Opinion polls showed that 62 per cent of miners rejected specifically political demands, although the long-term potential for radicalisation was shown by the fact that 72 per cent would consider broadening their struggle to include political aims, if their original demands were not met.[40]

Petro Pohrezhnyi, deputy head of the Donbas Strike Committee, told the *Rukh* congress in September 1989 that they lacked any information about *Rukh*, because the Communist Party-controlled press was attempting to divide workers and the intelligentsia. 'Well, it is not our fault that we do not know our symbols and the history of the Ukrainian people,' he said. Answering claims that the summer 1989 miners' strikes were purely economic, he said: 'Comrades! Do not think that our strike is purely economic. It is also political. We are undertaking restructuring from below.'[41]

The miners were very distrustful of officials, the media and 'outsiders', including the emissaries of opposition groups from Kyiv or Galicia. When an official told the striking miners, 'Go to work and everything will be done. I give you my honest word as a Communist,' they jeered him.[42]

A strike leader told the Tass news agency (17 July 1989) that 'At the outset, when we elected a strike committee, a man arrived from L'viv. He introduced himself as a member of the UHU and gave us leaflets, of an apparently instigatory and provocative character.' Another leaflet was prepared by the Ukrainian People's Democratic League, and ended with the words:

Put forward not only social and economic demands, but also political demands! Change your strike into a struggle against the exploiters – the party bureaucracy. Demand economic and political sovereignty for the Ukrainian republic ... Without political freedom there cannot be economic freedom![43]

Such overtures were largely rebuffed.

The miners did not directly criticise Gorbachev at this stage, choosing to blame the local Communist Party instead for the problems, and claiming to support the more rapid development of *perestroika*.[44] Gorbachev himself was ambivalent, both riding the tiger of unrest and attacking the strikes as organised by 'people hostile to the socialist system'.[45]

In the period after the strikes, a large number of new trade unions and strike committees began to be formed. However, the lack of any sense of working-class solidarity in Ukraine was soon reflected in the growth of a large number of overlapping and/or rival organisations, often doomed to only an ephemeral existence.

In August, at a meeting in Horlivka in the Donbas, the miners formed the Regional Union of Donbas Strike Committees, representatives of which later attended the *Rukh* congress. Plans for a second wave of strikes commencing on 1 October were only cancelled after Gorbachev's direct appeal on television the day before.

During the summer an Association of Illegally Dismissed Workers was established in Kharkiv, with 200 members. Up to 10 000 in the *oblast* had allegedly been dismissed from work.[46]

On 26 November in Donets'k a constituent assembly of the *Vilni profspilky Ukraïny* (Free Trade Unions of Ukraine) was held, and Volodymyr Stemasova, head of the miners' strike committee, became its head. *Rukh* and the UHU attended the founding congress as guests.[47]

In October the Independent Workers Union was established in Kharkiv. The main supporter of this move was Valerii Semyvolos, the head of the Kharkiv *oblast* branch of the UHU. The ultimate aim of the Independent Workers Union was to launch a Council of Independent Trade Unions of Ukraine.

The Independent Workers Union promised to 'defend political, economic and social rights of workers from the authoritarian rule of administrative, enterprise, state and Party bureaucracy'. The Independent Workers Union stood for workers' democracy, profit-sharing, the right to strike for both economic and political demands, private initiative in industry, alternative and direct elections. The Independent Workers Union agreed to 'co-operate with any public organisation, but will not recognise the leading role of any public political organisation' (a clear reference to the CPSU).[48]

Between 10 and 11 February 1990 in Kharkiv a congress of strike committees and independent workers' groups decided to launch the first all-Ukrainian free trade union *Iednist'* (Unity). Unity sought to counteract the already worrying centrifugal tendencies in the working-class movement, although, for example, the independent but all-Union *Sotsprof* with a base in the Donbas refused to take part.

The congress was sponsored by both *Rukh* and the UHU, who worked together closely in Kharkiv, and this could be seen in the combination of both political and socio-economic demands in Unity's programme.[49] The participants laid flowers at Shevchenko's monument and attended an *oblast Rukh* meeting. A co-ordinating committee of 35 was elected, 7 of whom were to act as the executive, including Khmara and Semyvolos, the head.

The congress ratified a workers' statute and passed a list of resolutions, which called for an end to repression and the release of all prisoners of conscience. Unity appealed for recognition to the International Labour Organisation. Unity's long-term aim was to struggle for a law-based state in a politically and economically independent Ukrainian republic. It would help to foster a civil society, democratic structures and the political and cultural rights of workers.[50]

In an appeal to the working classes of Ukraine, Unity stated that in the struggle against informal groups, 'the party bureaucracy has moved to propagate inter-ethnic, inter-religious and inter-class conflicts. The ancient principle – divide and rule – works for them even today'. Unity called for the unification of the working classes against the CPSU and for Ukrainian sovereignty, 'regardless of one's position in the national, religious or social structure'.

In March 1990 the *Solidarni profspilky Ukraïny* (Solidarity Trade Unions of Ukraine) was launched in Kyiv, its main organiser being Aleksander Sheikin. The Solidarity Trade Unions of Ukraine was an outgrowth of the Workers' Society formed in November 1989 by 40 enterprises in Kyiv. Solidarity Trade Unions of Ukraine united 26 unions from the Donbas, Cherkasy, Mariupol' and elsewhere. Unlike the official unions, the Solidarity Trade Unions of Ukraine would defend workers' interests and allow its branches complete autonomy. It applied to join the International Confederation of Free Trade Unions, and in August 1990 began to establish a newspaper entitled *Volia*.[51]

1. (*top left*) Ukrainian Cossack, Summer 1990.

2. (*top right*) Demonstration outside KGB headquarters in L'viv, Summer 1990.

3. (*below*) Young men and women take an oath of allegiance to an independent Ukraine, Summer 1990, Kryvyi Rih.

4. (*left*) Pre-election rally in Kyiv, February 1990.

5. (*below*) Ukrainians wearing the uniforms of the 1917–20 'Sich Sharpshooters' in Kyiv, January 1990.

6. Mass demonstration by 100 000 people in Kyiv on 30 September 1990 against the signing of Gorbachev's Union Treaty.

7. Members of the 'People's Council' lead demonstration in Kyiv, Autumn 1990.

8. Celebration of the 500th anniversary of the 'Days of Cossack Glory', in Dnipropetrovs'k (Sicheslav), Autumn 1990.

9. Levko Lukianenko addresses a rally in the forest of Bykivnia near Kyiv, where, , according to 'Memorial', up to 240 000 Ukrainian victims of the NKVD lay buried, May 1989.

10. Ivan Drach addresses rally in support of Lithuania's declaration of independence, Kyiv, March 1990.

11a. (*above*) Searching for a lost relative, 7 May 1989.

11b. (*left*) Human bones uncovered at the Bykivnia site, April 1989.

12. Radical MP, Stepan Khmara, speaking at the Supreme Council of Ukraine before his arrest in November 1990.

13. (*left*) Viacheslav Chornovil. Ex-dissident, (former) chairman of L'viv *oblast* council and leading challenger to Leonid Kravchuk in the December 1991 presidential elections.

14. (*right*) Levko Lukianenko, leader of the Ukrainian Helsinki Union–Ukrainian Republican Party, 1988.

15. Leading ex-political prisoners, now all deputies, on the day of the Ukrainian Declaration of Sovereignty, 16 July 1990.

16. The catacomb Ukrainian Catholic Church holds a service in the woods, Ivano-Frankivs'k, Christmas 1989.

17. (*above left*) Patriarch Mstyslav, (formerly) leader of the Ukrainian Autocephalous Orthodox Church.

18. (*top right*) The Second *Rukh* Congress October 1990, Kyiv.

19. (*bottom right*) Opposition figures carry the coffins of leading Ukrainian dissidents from the Brezhnev era – Oleksa Tykhyi, Vasyl Stus and Valerii Marchenko – who died in the Gulag, for reburial in Kyiv.

20. Ukrainian Catholic hunger strikers in Moscow, August 1989.

21. 250 000 crowd demanding the legalisation of the Ukrainian Catholic Church, L'viv, September 1989.

22. (*left*) Demonstration being broken up by riot police outside the Ukrainian parliament, Kyiv, October 1990.

23. (*below*) Student hunger strike, 'Independence Square', Kyiv, October 1990.

24a. (*top*) and 24b (*above left*) The first dismantling in the USSR of the statue of V. I. Lenin in L'viv, September 1990.

25. (*above right*) Ukrainian miner protests against ecological damage to Ukraine, Kyiv, October 1990.

26. May 1990: Dnipropetrovs'k Afghan veterans beat up *Rukh* activists whilst militia look on.

27. Kyiv, Summer 1991. Poster reads 'Kravchuk, do not fool around with the Ukrainian people. Luhans'k demands freedom for Ukraine!'

A member of the Solidarity Trade Unions of Ukraine, Nadiia Iatsenko, described how only independent trade unions and citizens' committees (see Chapter 7) as 'organs of self-government' could promote Ukrainian aspirations. Workers had to ditch the 'concentration camp complex' and 'not wait for the blessing of Muscovite benefactors' to undertake something on their behalf. Polish Solidarity, she reminded her readers, which by then was the Polish government and introducing economic reform, also began from humble beginnings similar to those of Solidarity Trade Unions of Ukraine.[52]

In L'viv the unprovoked attacks against peaceful demonstrators on 1 October 1989 led to the formation of a radical strike committee by the UHU.[53] As Mayor of L'viv, Kotyk admitted, 'the UHU are at the helm of the strike committee.'[54] Appeals and letters to the authorities after similar violent actions by the infamous 'Black Berets', the Special Purpose Militia Detachments called ZMOP in Ukrainian (in Russian OMON) in August 1988 and March 1989 had fallen on deaf ears. As Chornovil commented, 'they wanted to provoke the imposition of martial law, but provoked the formation of a strike committee.'[55]

Whereas *Rukh* was hesitant about supporting radical workers' action in L'viv, unofficial groups such as the UHU had no qualms. The strike committee's bulletin *L'vivs'kyi visnyk* was helped technically by the UHU. Levko Lukianenko believed that 'the Communist stronghold is the old factory managers, who have unlimited control over the workers. If we privatise the economy and free it from Communist control, we shall free the working class from Communist control too'.[56] Consequently, the UHU, and its successor the Ukrainian Republican Party, consciously began to copy the traditional communist tactics of organising both territorial and workplace cells, in order to counteract CPU domination of the workplace.

Three days later, L'viv experienced a two-hour strike and meeting attended by 30 000 people in protest at the OMON action. Strike committees were founded in each enterprise and institution to utilise the political strike (economic strikes were illegal). The L'viv strike committee was led by a Russian, Valerii Furmanov, and his deputy was Stepan Khmara. A general strike organised on 27 October was not backed by *Rukh*, which demanded that the strike committee consult with it before launching such actions. Furmanov replied 'Some misunderstandings or disorganisation during the strike is altogether unsurprising; well, we don't have any experience of this kind of work. The political consciousness of the masses is only awakening – it needs time.[57]

In early December, L'viv hosted a meeting of strike committees, unofficial workers' groups and other organisations with the aim of forming an all-republican strike committee that would also enable the co-ordination of actions during the forthcoming election campaign. The Kharkiv-based Independent Workers' Union, Poltava-based Independent Workers' Union and miners' strike committees from Chervonohrad and Horlivka attended.[58]

The L'viv strike committee organised demonstrations in L'viv against the deployment of Ukrainian conscripts in the Caucasus in January and in support of Lithuanian independence in March 1990.[59]

The radicalisation of public opinion in Ukraine was reflected in the miners' more political demands, when a second wave of strikes and mass demonstrations rocked the Donbas in June and July 1990.[60] The miners now demanded the resignation of the Ukrainian government, liquidation of CPU cells and the nationalisation of CPU property, reflecting their complete lack of faith in Gorbachev and the Communist Party after the latter's failure to fulfil the promises of 1989.

As the Donbas strike committee stated, 'The only thing the party and the people who run the mines are interested in is filling production quotas and their own stomachs. Last year we shook the government and we have reminded them again how we feel. The miners will not accept this for much longer. I think there could be bad trouble in the mines.'[61]

The miners, now grouped together in the Union of Strike Committees of the Donbas, however, still seemed better able to express what they did not want – as opposed to what they wanted to replace it with. They rarely referred to the Supreme Council and talked more of vague notions of 'workers' control', although the radicalisation of the public and greater contact between the miners and intelligentsia was gradually having an impact.[62] One independent union leader for the miners said, 'Ukraine is very rich. It has enormous potential. The Donbas workers will support sovereignty and independence for Ukraine if it makes economic sense.'[63] The parliamentary Peoples' Council issued an appeal in support of the striking miners which stated: 'The way out of the crisis situation is possible only on the basis of a real peoples' government and state sovereignty for Ukraine. The People's Council calls upon miners to support our parliamentary struggle for the adoption by the Supreme Council of complete sovereignty and a decree on the government.'[64] The working-class movement was therefore beginning to have an indirect effect. Their actions helped to pressure Communist deputies, for example into voting for the Declaration of Sovereignty (see Chapter 7).[65]

At this stage of its development, however, the labour movement in Ukraine was still highly fragmented, reflecting working-class distrust of any form of political organisation, and the fact that 70 years of working-class atomisation and organisational passivity under communism made mobilisation very difficult. In contrast to Poland in the Solidarity era, the formation of links between the working class and intelligentsia remained problematical.

POPULAR MOVEMENT OF UKRAINE (*RUKH*)

The inaugural congress of *Rukh* took place on 8–10 September in Kyiv, attended by 1100 delegates,[66] 85 per cent of whom were ethnic Ukrainian. Seventy-two per cent had higher education, but only 10 per cent were workers and a mere 2.5 per cent collective farmers. Only 228 were members of the CPSU. Approximately half the delegates were from western Ukraine, 35 per cent came from the eight central *oblasts* and only 15 per cent from eastern and southern Ukraine. Ninety per cent of deputies were male, and 58 per cent between the ages of 25 and 45.

A poll of delegates' priorities showed most support for political and cultural, rather than simply economic aims (seeking 'to promote democratisation and the expansion of *glasnost'* was supported by 75 per cent, 'the development of Ukrainian culture and language' by 73 per cent, but 'the solving of pressing economic problems' by only 46 per cent).[67] *Rukh* members approached economics as something to be solved through tackling political issues, which reflected *Rukh*'s nature as a movement of the intelligentsia of western and central Ukraine, without Solidarity-style working-class participation. Hence a potential gulf already existed between *Rukh* and the population at large, whose priorities remained conservative and practical.

The congress included nearly 100 national minority representatives, including Russians, Jews and Poles, who rejected the notion of a Baltic-style Inter-Front. The miners' movement was represented at the congress by Petro Pobrezhnyi, who argued for the removal of Shcherbytskyi, for an alliance with *Rukh* and for republican sovereignty, but expressed reservations about the use of Ukrainian national symbols.

Guests from Solidarity, such as Adam Michnik, gave loudly applauded speeches calling for Ukrainian–Polish solidarity, but only called for a 'democratic' and 'free Ukraine', falling short of calling for an 'independent Ukraine' – which might have been too provocative to Moscow.[68]

The radical wing of *Rukh*, however, represented by the UHU, with much influence in western Ukraine, used the occasion to promote calls for Ukrainian secession from the USSR. Lukianenko's speech, which called upon *Rukh* members 'to abolish this empire as the greatest evil of present-day life', was the only one from the congress not published in *Literaturna Ukraïna*.[69] The 'extremist wing of the movement has long been formally established' in L'viv, one newspaper claimed; while these delegates 'set the tone in the discussion', which included numerous speeches against socialism, the CPSU and Lenin and openly calling for *Rukh* to take power.[70]

Chornovil argued that the essential theses of the UHU Declaration of Principles were now included in the new *Rukh* programme. Criticising the attempts by the CPU to drive a wedge between the UHU and *Rukh*, Chornovil said:

> The fact that a Lukianenko or a Chornovil see Ukraine as an independent democratic country in the future, while Drach and Iavorivskyi aspire to broaden sovereignty within a recognised Union structure, or that the former support political pluralism, while the latter see merely the liberalisation of the Party to which they belong, does not yet constitute sufficient grounds for disunity. The mission of the Popular Movement of Ukraine is precisely to unify all the people who care about the fate of Ukraine.[71]

The congress approved a new programme for *Rukh* which supported the calls for the 'radical renewal of society' proclaimed at the Twenty-Seventh Congress of the CPSU, the Nineteenth All-Union CPSU conference and the Congress of People's Deputies. More than eighteen months before Gorbachev agreed to contemplate the idea, the *Rukh* programme called for 'the creation of a sovereign Ukrainian state which will build its relations with the other republics of the USSR on the basis of a new Union treaty'. A 'radical transformation in the Soviet federation' would ensure Ukrainian sovereignty, it stated.[72]

Rukh still saw itself as a vehicle to implement *perestroika* in Ukraine, with its main goals being 'democratisation and a humane society'. *Rukh* would co-operate with the CPU, the government and other organisations, but also put forward candidates in elections, propose new legislation, use public pressure and influence, conferences, publications, pickets, demonstrations and open letters to the press. It would promote the rebirth of Ukrainian national customs, and monitor compliance with human rights agreements.

The congress adopted many resolutions on subjects such as economic sovereignty, the ecological situation, elections, support for the Crimean Tatars, the legalisation of Ukrainian churches, national symbols, the Ukrainian diaspora, and publishing.[73] A powerful resolution condemned anti-Semitism.[74] Another asked Russians living in Ukraine for support.[75] Myroslav Popovych condemned the slogan 'Ukraine for Ukrainians!' touted by some marginal nationalist groups, because 'Ukraine is a common home to everybody living there.'[76]

When Kravchuk claimed that although, 'They are our opponents, we hope to win them over by arguments', in fact it was elements within the CPU that were won over gradually by *Rukh* (with Kravchuk himself eventually adopting the bulk of the *Rukh* programme in the 1 December 1991 presidential campaign).[77] Much of *Rukh*'s programme would be included in Ukraine's Declaration of Sovereignty, adopted only ten months later.

The poet Ivan Drach (a member of the CPSU) was elected head of *Rukh*, with Serhii Koniev from Dniprodzerzhyns'k as his deputy. Mykhailo Horyn, a former prisoner of conscience and high-ranking member of UHU, was elected to head the secretariat.

In his speech to the congress Kravchuk claimed that the CPU would like to see in *Rukh* an ally in restructuring. But, he warned, 'All those who have once embarked upon their political path in search of an answer to "Who's to blame?" have lost their political direction. I would like *Rukh* to take this under consideration.' Kravchuk opposed the 'dismemberment of the USSR', but stood for sovereignty and improving the 'Soviet socialist federation'.[78] However, he also promised that *Rukh* would be allowed to publish its own paper and would be registered in time for its candidates to stand in the republican elections due in March 1990 (although this did not in the end happen until 14 February, too late for *Rukh* to participate).

COMMUNIST CRITICISM

There was still little sign of the CPU seeking to build bridges with *Rukh*. The official media remained implacably hostile after the *Rukh* congress, arguing that the congress did not represent the social composition of Ukraine, when, for example, only 125 of the 1100 delegates were workers and peasants.[79] The lack of live television coverage was blamed by state television and radio upon *Rukh*'s refusal to grant them accreditation, which 'was not in the style of *glasnost'* and pluralism, not in the spirit of *perestroika'*.[80] The congress was portrayed as dominated by the 'activities of various informal associations of reactionaries and of an extremist persuasion who use *perestroika* slogans as a blind resort to gross violation of public order and flouting of the law'.[81]

The CPU, meanwhile, attempted to organise anti-*Rukh* meetings in Kyiv and L'viv, where 'military school students dressed up in civilian clothes are brought to the stadium to speak against *Rukh* as civilians'.[82]

The central committee of the *Komsomol* criticised it for being increasingly influenced by 'anti-socialist groups', who were making *Rukh* more anti-communist. The *Komsomol* resolved to only 'support healthy forces in *Rukh'* and to struggle against 'anti-socialist elements, expansion of anti-Soviet and nationalist ideas'. Serhii Vovchenko, secretary of the central committee of the *Komsomol*, argued that they 'must work within *Rukh*, help its orientation towards positive activity, further strengthening within it healthy forces'.[83] The central committee of the *Komsomol*, however, was to change course in April 1990, with its L'viv branch defecting wholesale to the opposition as the renamed Democratic Union of L'viv Youth.[84] (Although as late as January 1991 a plenum of the Poltava *oblast Komsomol* adopted a resolution denying members the right to join *Rukh*.)[85]

Further cracks in CPU unity appeared when the UHU, which was the focus of numerous attacks in the official press ever since it was launched in March 1988, was invited to 'round-table constructive talks' with the local CPU committee in L'viv, the most nationally conscious region of Ukraine, with the greatest number of unofficial groups and demonstrations.[86]

Bohdan Volkov, the first secretary of the L'viv city CPU, met leading figures from the UHU, Chornovil (editor of the *samizdat* journal *Ukrainian Herald*), Mykhailo and Bohdan Horyn (head of the L'viv *oblast* UHU). The aim of the discussion was simply to make contact with members of the group with a view to understanding their positions. The talks were not intended to follow a specific theme.

According to *Robitnycha hazeta*, the three leading members of the UHU (who did not attend in an official capacity) put forward fairly radical demands: 'The [republic's] budget should be set not from above – but should originate from below and work its way upwards; there should be a fair medium of exchange between different regions; profits for republican enterprises should be reinvested within the same republic and there should be a move away from central power to local authorities.' The article reported that Chornovil put forward the idea that Ukraine's regional diversity should be recognised in a devolution of economic and administrative power to regions such as Volhynia and Galicia, as in the USA.[87]

The article claimed (untruthfully) that during the discussions, the UHU representatives emphasised that, in contrast to Sajudis (the Lithuanian popular front), the UHU had not put forward the question of Ukraine's secession from the USSR.[88]

Robitnycha hazeta also claimed that the UHU stood for 'the reconstruction of the Union from an authoritarian state to a federal one'. Volkov spoke at great length about the preparations to the forthcoming republican elections and asked the participants for their opinions. Mykhailo Horyn replied by saying that existing political structures ought to be preserved. However, such bodies ought to be filled with 'true statesmen, who would completely dedicate themselves to the service of the people and would take part in parliamentary work on a professional level'. Horyn added that there would be UHU representatives among future candidates to the Congress of Peoples' Deputies.

Robitnycha hazeta quoted Horyn as speaking out sharply against rumours circulating in L'viv, allegedly from the UHU, that it was anti-Russian and was preparing a pogrom against them and other minorities. 'The security services should catch every person, who wanted to provoke conflicts on the basis of nationality. This is a very dangerous game. We cannot and have no right to allow a situation to develop similar to that in Karabakh and Fergana,' said Horyn.[89]

The article admitted that the attitude of the security forces towards the UHU was often not conducive towards calming down the political tension in L'viv. The article also reported the feelings expressed by the UHU representatives towards the signing of the Ribbentrop–Molotov pact. Whilst the unification of all Ukrainian lands was welcome, Stalin brought with it mass terror, which at first was allegedly directed against Communists, they believed.

The L'viv city CPU had, under pressure of public opinion in western Ukraine, initiated discussions with individuals of the UHU, but this had neither the blessing of Kyiv, Moscow nor even the Executive Committee of the UHU; the head of which, at the time, was on a visit to Western Europe. As argued in Chapter 1, the CPU would eventually have to seek common political ground with the opposition, in order to rebuild its authority, but this would only begin to happen on a mass scale in 1991.

Rukh's nature as a broad church often meant arguments, splits and defections for the authorities to publicise. Tensions with east Ukraine were highlighted in late September in Kharkiv, when 15 members of *Rukh* resigned because of the alleged 'anti-democratic nature of several of the principles in its programme and charter', and announced their intention to establish a rival Popular Front.[90] According to Vladimir Grinev (later to become deputy chairman of the Supreme Council of Ukraine and a presidential candidate in December 1991), after the inaugural congress of *Rukh,* '*Rukh*'s self-appointed leaders showed their separatist intent, lack of a clear-cut stance in the relations with the Party, as well as authoritarian views and a wish to suppress dissident views within the movement ... Instead of arguing over national colours, we call for real action.'[91] Delegates from the Voroshylovohrad (Luhans'k) strike committee also resigned, but were ready to return provided *Rukh* distanced itself from 'every-thing nationalist and extremist'.[92]

UKRAINIAN LANGUAGES LAW

On 28 October 1989 the Supreme Council of Ukraine adopted a Languages Law after much deliberation and debate, and in response to similar measures adopted in other republics. The Law proposed the gradual increased use of Ukrainian over a number of years in all spheres of life, including the state, government, media and education. Ukrainian was now the state language, but the free use of all languages was guaranteed, and 'the languages of international co-operation in the Ukrainian SSR are Ukrainian, Russian and other languages. The Ukrainian SSR guarantees the free use of the Russian language as the language of international co-operation of the peoples of the USSR'. Therefore, Russian was to be the language of 'interrelations between republican and local state, party and public bodies, enterprises, establishments and organisations and all-Union bodies'. In addition, in areas of compact settlement of national minorities their language could be used alongside Ukrainian. 'Public humiliation or contempt, deliberate distortion of the state or other languages' was proscribed by law.[93]

The Supreme Council resolved to introduce the Languages Law over a period of ten years, and therefore charged the Council of Ministers with working out and adopting by 1 July 1990 a 'state programme for the development of the Ukrainian language and other national languages in the Ukrainian SSR in the period up to the year 2000'.[94]

The Languages Law was introduced prior to the first semi-free republican elections in March 1990, and therefore at a time when the

Ukrainian parliament was still dominated completely by appointees from the Shcherbytskyi era. It is therefore ironic indeed that the Languages Law was described as necessary because of 'deviation from the Leninist principles of nationalities policy', precisely the same argument as used by Ivan Dziuba in the 1960s (see Chapter 3).[95] Those that now lamented the limitations imposed upon the Ukrainian language were, after all, the very same people who had threatened Dziuba with imprisonment and subjected Ukrainian to a severe policy of Russification during Ukraine's 'era of stagnation' (1972–89).

The Languages Law was therefore criticised by nationalists because of the weakness of its provisions concerning the revival of Ukrainian, and because of the role of Russian as an intermediary between nationalities in Ukraine, arguing that Ukrainian should have this role. (Some deputies, particularly from southern and eastern Ukraine, had in fact called for both Russian and Ukrainian to become the state languages of the republic.)[96] On the other hand, the mildness of the law, particularly in comparison with those adopted in the Baltic republics, was one factor in limiting the emergence of ethnic tensions in Ukraine.[97]

RELIGION

September 1989 marked the launch of a mass Ukrainian Catholic movement for legislation prior to the planned Vatican meeting between Pope John Paul II and Gorbachev. On 17 September in L'viv, in a demonstration deliberately organised to coincide with the fiftieth anniversary of the Molotov–Ribbentrop Pact, an estimated 150 000 people demanded the relegalisation of the Church. In the evening L'viv residents turned out their lights and placed candles in their windows in commemoration of those repressed after the Soviet occupation of western Ukraine in 1939–41. The rally broke the 1931 record when 120 000 had gathered in L'viv[98] and coincided with an important ground-breaking article in the Moscow-based reformist magazine *Ogonëk* supporting the Galicians' demands.[99]

The rally, organised by the Committee in Defence of the Ukrainian Catholics Church, was addressed by its head, Ivan Hel, and independent activists such as Viacheslav Chornovil. Chornovil said in his speech that 'a decisive step has been taken toward the rebirth of the Ukrainian Church ... After today I am certain we will be successful when the Pope meets Mr Gorbachev in Rome.'[100] Cardinal Liubachivskyi stated that the rally 'sends a message to the Soviet government: legalise our Church ... Our people in Ukraine proved this through their demonstration on 17 September and we in the West will continue to give them our support.'[101]

Meanwhile, the UAOC Initiative Committee began to publish a *samizdat* newspaper in September 1989 entitled *Pravoslav'ia, nasha vira*, the editors of which were Mykola Budnyk, Mykhailo Orfeniuk and Oleksandr Tkachuk. The first issue included material on Metropolitan Vasyl Lypkivskyi, who established the UAOC after the 1917 revolution; the February 1989 appeal of the Initiative Committee; and an interview with the poet and *Rukh* supporter, Pavlo Movchan.

A major breakthrough for the UAOC was the emergence from retirement of Bishop Ioan of Zhytomyr, who had previously served in the Russian Orthodox Church to become *de facto* head of the UAOC in Ukraine. At a press conference after a meeting of the Holy Synod of an alarmed ROC hierarchy in November, Ioan was 'excommunicated' for 'his schismatic activities' and because he 'had subjected the souls of believers to temptation'.[102]

The UAOC, however, continued to expand. A petition of 10 000 was collected in Volhynia by November, calling for the UAOC to be given the Cathedral in Luts'k. Volhynia, according to one appeal, was always a 'bastion' of the UAOC and Orthodox Brotherhood and it called upon believers to support Bishop Ioan and 'return to the bosom of their native UAOC'.[103] In early December 1989, a meeting of UAOC parishes in Kyiv resolved to establish a UAOC Brotherhood (a tradition which had existed in Ukraine in the fifteenth and sixteenth centuries) to act as a lay group support mechanism for the UAOC and help to foster the spread of religious culture. The UAOC organisation 'Sisters of St Princess Olha' was also established.

Conflict between the UAOC and the Ukrainian Catholic Church in western Ukraine continued meanwhile, with the UAOC caught between the hostility of both the Ukraine Catholic Church and the Russian Orthodox Church. In Galicia the UAOC was often supported by the Communist Party, to prevent the spread of the Ukrainian Catholic Church, whereas the communists continued to support the ROC in eastern Ukraine. For many in the Ukraine Catholic Church, the UAOC in Galicia was an 'intermediate stage' between the ROC and Ukraine Catholic Church, and in future the UAOC and Ukrainian Catholic Church would merge.[104]

Chornovil, head of the UHU press service, attempted to reconcile the two sides. The UAOC should, in his view, accept priests into their ranks only if they fulfilled a number of conditions, including condemning the 1685–6 subordination of the Kyiv metropolitanate to Moscow and the destruction of the UAOC during the Great Terror, and supporting the separation of Church and state and the rehabilitation of Metropolitan Vasyl Lypkivskyi. New UAOC priests should sign their names under these points, Chornovil stated.[105]

During the latter part of 1989 and early 1990 the Soviet press was full of accusations and complaints from the Russian Orthodox Church alleging violence and hostility by Ukrainian Catholics in western Ukraine.[106] The ROC attacked *Rukh* and other informal groups for supporting the actions of Ukrainian Catholics. An open letter was drafted to the Pope from the 'Committee in Defence of the Ukrainian Orthodox Church'.[107] People were agreeing to become Ukrainian Catholics only after 'threats of physical violence', the ROC claimed. The ROC clamoured for the imposition of a 'state of emergency' in western Ukraine and the return of Church property to the ROC. A monk from the Pochaïv monastery in Ternopil *oblast* was reported as saying that the Orthodox Church in western Ukraine 'is faced with a dilemma, either to go underground or to use force against the Uniates'.[108] The local authorities, afraid of the forthcoming elections, were accused of turning a blind eye to the occupation of churches.

By December 1989, 600 Ukrainian Catholic parishes had applied for registration, with over 200 ROC priests defecting to the Ukrainian Catholic Church.[109] An investigation by a Vatican delegation found no evidence of the use of violence in the seizure of churches, despite claims to the contrary by the ROC in the central Soviet press.

The meeting of Pope John Paul and Gorbachev in Rome on 1 December 1989 was used to announce the registration of Ukrainian Catholic parishes in western Ukraine, and the first synod of the Ukrainian Catholic Church since 1945 was held in January 1990, which proceeded to denounce and condemn the 'so-called L'viv synod of 1946' which 'reunified' the Ukrainian Catholic Church with the Russian Orthodox Church.

The 1 December statement envisaged 'the assignment of ... buildings to religious communities ... in accordance with established procedures'. As these were not trusted by the Ukrainian Catholic Church, according to Ivan Hel, the settlement 'does not provide a real legal basis for the Church'.[110] A tripartite commission was therefore set up to negotiate between the ROC, the Vatican and the Ukrainian Catholic Church, but broke down after the Ukrainian Catholic Church walked out, primarily because the ROC refused to accept the illegality of the 1946 Synod or to accept the legality of the Ukrainian Catholic Church as a Church with a hierarchy, and not as parish communities.[111]

In September, when the tripartite talks resumed, the ROC walked out owing to the continuing dispute over the St George's Cathedral complex in L'viv.[112]

In a statement released in March 1990 the hierarchy of the Ukrainian Catholic Church put forward a number of conditions to be met before dialogue could be resumed: the 1946 illegal dissolution (the so-called 'L'viv Sobor') should be regarded as 'uncanonical'; all Church property should be returned and all the clergy of the Ukrainian Catholic Church who were repressed should be rehabilitated; the Ukrainian Catholic Church should have full rights as a church and be allowed to remain in contact with the Vatican; Cardinal Liubachivskyi should be allowed to visit L'viv (an event eventually scheduled for late March 1991); the Metropolitanate of Halych should be raised to the status of a Patriarchate; and printing activities should be freed of restraint.[113]

Once most local councils in Galicia passed into opposition control after the March 1990 elections, the Ukrainian Catholic Church obtained most of what it had been demanding.

By the early part of 1990 the Ukrainian Autocephalous Orthodox Church (UAOC) had seven archbishops and over 200 priests. The Russian Orthodox Church remained on the defensive and, at a synod in February, the formation of 'autonomous' Ukrainian and Belorussian Orthodox Churches was announced.[114] But despite numerous cosmetic changes to the Russian Orthodox Church in Ukraine, little fundamentally changed. An open letter from first- and second-year seminarians in Kyiv in late June complained of an 'atmosphere of terror' against sympathisers of the UAOC and the Ukrainian Catholic Church.[115] Despite Ukrainian being proclaimed the state language and the existence of an autonomous Ukrainian exarchate, all seminary disciplines were still conducted in Russian. The seminarians resigned and left to join the UAOC and the Ukrainian Catholic Church, 'where we are convinced that better human and Christian conduct will be forthcoming and be more democratic towards us'.

In early June in Kyiv the UAOC held its first *Sobor* (ecumenical council) for five decades.[116] Metropolitan Mstyslav, head of the UAOC in the USA, was refused a visa to attend, but 547 delegates, after a religious service in St Sophia Cathedral and the laying of flowers at Shevchenko's monument, held their *Sobor* without him. The excommunication of Bishop Ioan was condemned and Metropolitan Mstyslav was elevated to the rank of Patriarch. In October Patriarch Mstyslav was finally allowed to travel to Ukraine, where he visited numerous regions and attended the second *Rukh* congress, after the UAOC was formally registered on 1 October.

On the last day of the second *Rukh* congress, on 28 October 1990, Patriarch Aleksii of the ROC visited Kyiv, which resulted in mass protests at what was seen as a provocative visit.[117] When he attempted to address believers in Volhynia in Ukrainian, 'it was a praiseworthy but unsuccessful act'. Patriarch Aleksii was driven around Ukraine in the old official car formerly used by Shcherbytskyi. The incident surrounding the visit prompted leading academics in the USA and Canada to join with leaders of *Rukh* in demanding the return of St Sophia Cathedral to the UAOC.[118]

The situation of the ROC in Ukraine was critical, but it continued to refuse to discuss anything with the UAOC, maintaining an 'irreconcilable attitude to the very idea of autocephaly'.[119] Metropolitan Filaret, who had compromised himself in the eyes of Ukrainian believers, remained the key obstacle to change.

CONCLUSIONS

The first signs of emergent civil society were now visible in Ukraine. The steady growth in support for informal organisations left many opposition leaders confident that they would progress inexorably to command a natural majority. The Ukrainian elections of 1990, however, showed that this was not the case, and that the opposition would need the additional strength of national communist defectors from the established order if it was to achieve its agenda.

7 1990: Ukrainian Elections and the Rise of a Multi-Party System

The all-Union elections of March 1989 were followed by elections for a new Ukrainian parliament, or Supreme Council, in March 1990. 1990 was therefore characterised by:

- further partial mobilisation of the population during the election campaign;
- the authorities successfully delaying the formation of a multi-party system, and the first signs of an independent civil society in Ukraine until after the elections; and
- (despite this) the formation of an opposition in the Supreme Council after the elections, and the beginnings of significant parliamentary politics.

REPUBLICAN ELECTIONS

In August 1989 the draft election law was published.[1] It envisaged quotas for public organisations as in the recent all-Union elections, although the *Komsomol* refused to take the twenty seats allocated to it.[2] The Supreme Council was to have one chamber, and its number of seats was to be reduced from 650 to 450. Most controversially, however, candidate nomination was to be controlled by district election commissions, created by local *oblast* (i.e. CPU-controlled) executive committees. Groups of 200 electors had first to nominate candidates, but any such nomination could be vetoed by the local district election commission.

The reaction from the new independent groups was very critical, in particular from the newly established Club of People's Deputies, the Ukrainian branch of the reformist Inter-Regional Group in the all-Union Supreme Soviet. (Of the 262 Ukrainian deputies to the all-

Union body, nearly 70 were reputed to be supporters and sympathisers of *Rukh*.)[3]

In August 1989 an open letter signed by 38 all-Union deputies[4]
threatened: 'In the event that respective organs of power will not take
into account alternative projects – to call for a boycott of the elections,
including also strikes', and proposed an alternative law entitled 'On
Elections to the Organs of Popular Rule'.[5]

The alternative election law attacked the allocation of 25 per cent
of seats to communist organisations, proposed that only 'one person,
one vote' should be the basis for the elections, demanded more candidates than seats, direct proportional elections to the Supreme Council
and to the presidency, and argued against the electoral commission's
influence on the registration of candidates. After the publication of
the alternative election law, one newspaper claimed to have received
60 000 proposals and comments 'which repudiated the act of the
group of USSR People's Deputies aimed at replacing broad dialogue
and constructive discussion ... by the fuelling of tension and psychological pressure'.[6] But the Deputies countered by saying they had 'felt
strong support from below'.[7]

At the inaugural congress of *Rukh*, the Deputies Club issued an open
letter to Gorbachev demanding that Shcherbytskyi should go. They
agreed that tension was rising in Ukraine, but blamed this upon the
republican Party apparatus, 'which is leading not to a consolidation of
all healthy forces, but to confrontation'. The removal of Shcherbytskyi,
they argued, would restore faith in socialism and *perestroika* because
public confidence in the top leadership of the CPU had plummeted.[8]

At a meeting in Kyiv on 18 November, the Democratic Bloc was
formed as a coalition of 40 independent groups to fight the elections
on a common platform.[9] Two-thirds of the programme was a negative
appraisal of the situation in Ukraine, which stated that after nearly
five years of Gorbachev's rule *perestroika* had failed. The elections
would decide if Ukraine would be free and sovereign or 'politically,
economically, culturally, a province of the central authorities'. The
Democratic Bloc called for 'real political and economic sovereignty
for Ukraine', economic and political pluralism, a new constitution,
national rebirth, freedom of conscience and an end to nuclear power,
and legal and political guarantees 'to prevent a return to the Stalinism
and neo-Stalinism of the Brezhnev-Suslov eras'.

The programme appealed for a negative vote against the CPU and
the ruination it had brought upon Ukraine. There was little in terms of

a concrete counter-programme. Other leading independent activists also issued their own individual programmes. Oles Shevchenko, Levko Lukianenko and Viacheslav Chornovil of the UHU still stressed sovereignty – and not independence – in their programmes, with Chornovil proposing the radical reorganisation of Ukraine along federal lines.[10] The leading radical Stepan Khmara, also from the UHU, was one of the few candidates who at this stage argued for complete independence.[11] *Tovarystvo Leva* supported Ihor Hryniv, second secretary of the *Komsomol* in L'viv and head of the regional branch of Memorial, in a programme based upon the Democratic Bloc's call for complete republican sovereignty. All of the issues raised and proposed by the Democratic Bloc ultimately made their way into the Declaration of Sovereignty in July 1990.

The election campaign began in earnest during January and February 1990, after the highly successful human chain from L'viv to Kyiv organised by *Rukh* on 21 January. Numerous rallies were organised throughout Ukraine, even in the de-nationalised Donbas where an openly anti-communist mood was increasingly dominant, as in many similar urban areas in the RSFSR.

After a round-table at the newspaper *Vechirnii Kyiv* on 15 February 1990 a rally was called in Kyiv entitled 'Time for Unity – not Discord!'[12] The Democratic Bloc and UHU issued a number of appeals condemning anti-Semitism and attempts by unspecified sources to incite inter-ethnic strife.[13] In L'viv the Democratic Bloc was allegedly overshadowed by more radical groups, such as the strike committee. Pickets held aloft portraits of the leader of the wartime OUN, Stepan Bandera; there were calls for punishment of those who had ordered the use of OMON militia on 1 October 1989 against demonstrators and for 'occupation troops' to go home.[14] Oleh Vitovych, later a leader of the radical Association of Independent Ukrainian Youth was quoted as saying, 'every Communist was, is and will be the hated enemy of all Ukrainians'.

The Democratic Bloc had many popular candidates, including well-known writers, intellectuals and former prisoners of conscience.[15] But the refusal of the authorities to register *Rukh* until February, after the deadline for registering candidates had passed (which broke the promise made by Kravchuk at the inaugural congress of *Rukh*), together with the refusal on a local level in many areas to recognise candidates from Green World Association and the Ukrainian Language Society, meant that the elections were not wholly free.[16] Of Ukraine's 33 000 polling stations, 20 000 lacked supervisors. The state's monopoly over the mass circulation media confined publicity for the opposition programme to small, independent publications. According to *Vechirnii Kyiv*, 75 per cent of the ballot in the elections were tainted in the above fashion.[17] Often the Party-controlled electoral committees refused to investigate violations of the electoral law, even though M. O. Lytvyn, secretary of the Central Electoral Commission, eventually received 800 complaints.[18]

Eighty-five per cent of the candidates were members of the CPSU (although this included many leaders of *Rukh*). Many CPU candidates stood in rural areas, where the electorate was conservative and more easily manipulated, or utilised conscripts to bump up their vote (such as Ivashko in Kyiv *oblast*).

In the first round on 4 March, 84.69 per cent voted, whilst 78.80 per cent participated in the run-off elections.[19] The results, despite the evidence of manipulation,[20] were in some respects a disappointment for the Democratic Bloc (DB), even though they managed to obtain between 25 and 30 per cent of the seats.[21] In the three *oblasts* of Galicia (L'viv, Ivano-Frankivs'k and Ternopil') the DB obtained 43 out of the 47 seats, in Volyn and Rivne 11 of the 19, but in Chernivtsi and Transcarpathia (where independents won 11 of the 19 seats) fared badly. In central Ukraine the DB obtained 50 per cent of the seats, including 16 of the 22 in Kyiv. In eastern and southern Ukraine, with the exception of the cities of Donets'k and Kharkiv, the DB fared poorly.

However, a closer look at eastern Ukraine and Kharkiv showed that 28 out of the 40 DB candidates were successful, but only 2 out of 16 in southern Ukraine, indicating that in the east the DB's problems may have been more those of obstruction than of a lack of support.[22] The relatively high number of uncommitted deputies from eastern Ukraine – 32 out of 122 – showed that the population was prepared to vote against the CPU establishment, if not ready to accept the cultural programme of the Ukrainian national democrats. Eight Democratic Bloc deputies came from Donets'k, and 'it is upon this unity (of national democrats and workers) that rests the further fate (of Ukraine)', argued *Tovarystva Leva*.[23] Southern Ukraine was still 'an oasis of stagnation in Ukraine'.

Of the 442 deputies elected in March 1990, 373 were Communist Party members. The CPU obtained between 25 and 30 per cent of its seats from rural constituencies. Seats in the big towns, however, were split roughly equally – 50 going to the CPU, 36 to the uncommitted and 66 to the DB.[24]

The social composition of the new parliament was 95 from the CPU apparatus (CPU first secretaries and the like), 60 from the state apparatus (ministers, bureaucrats), 67 from the industrial apparatus (managers, experts), 44 from the agricultural apparatus (collective farm chairmen, directors of the agro-industrial complex), 14 from the armed forces, 19 from the official trade unions and allied institutions, 27 were working class, 16 unknown and 102 from the intelligentsia.

Sixty-five per cent of DB deputies were from the intelligentsia and 85 per cent of the eventual hard-line CPU group were from the command-administrative apparatus – a clear and obvious divide. A surprisingly high proportion of the managerial and economic elite (24 out of 67) were uncommitted, however. Of the deputies, 331 were Ukrainian (73 per cent) and 99 were Russian (22 per cent), with 20 from other nationalities. This almost exactly mirrored the composition of the population as a whole in Ukraine. Only 13 women were elected.

Local elections were held at the same time. These resulted in the DB breaking the CPU's local monopoly on power. The DB gained absolute control in the three Galician *oblast* councils and in many urban areas. Chornovil became the high-profile leader of L'viv *oblast* council, and was later the main initiator behind the formation of the Association of Democratic Councils and Democratic Blocs in Dniprodzerzhyns'k on 28–29 July 1990. Thus, for the first time, the opposition had a foothold in the state, and some control over the institutional resources at its command.

The elections signalled the end of the CPU monopoly over political life in Ukraine, and therefore represented a watershed in the development of the opposition. Ievhen Proniuk, a leading UHU member who failed to be elected in Kyiv due to alleged malpractice, believed that the campaign had awoken the 'political and national consciousness' of key sections of the public. Public opinion had clearly been radicalised, and anti-Communist sympathies had risen, while many CPU members began to distance themselves from the conservative leadership of their party.

The DB, however, could not yet command a natural majority in Ukraine, which still rested with the CPU because of its strength in small towns, rural areas (outside Galicia) and southern and eastern Ukraine, but the opposition had nevertheless set the agenda for the elections, and its programme ultimately became the basis for the Declaration of Sovereignty. The opposition would force the pace of change in the new Supreme Council.

The retreat to the countryside and the loss of most big cities was a crucial psychological and political blow for the CPU: psychological because the CPU claimed legitimacy for its 'leading role' in society in virtue of its function in the vanguard of urban progressive forces, and political because urban centres were now the crucial arena of political struggle, but were now dominated by the DB or by the 'uncommitted' – candidates from the technocratic and managerial elite, who were later to become an important swing group in the Supreme Council.

LOCAL COUNCILS

A statement released by the first session of the L'viv *oblast* council, which elected Chornovil as head, described the *oblast* as an 'island of freedom' which intends to 'end the totalitarian system' and 'the usurpation of power by the Communist Party'. The *oblast* saw itself on the right path 'for the fulfilment of the eternal vision of our nation for an independent, democratic Ukrainian state'. According to one report, 'Everything is in turmoil ... L'viv today is seething with political passions, the clash of ambitions, the struggle of ideas and characters, stripped of parliamentary niceties'.[25]

The first decrees of the Galician councils sought to replace Soviet with Ukrainian national symbols, increase the size of peasant plots and close down communist cells in factories and institutions. Later resolutions adopted by the L'viv *oblast* council included depoliticising the militia, legalising the Ukrainian Catholic Church (Ivan Hel, chairman of the Committee in Defence of the Ukrainian Catholic Church, was elected as Chornovil's deputy) and returning its property, (all officials, such as Mayor Kotyk, were now sworn in by taking an oath on the Bible), taking local manufacturing out from under the control of central ministries, registering informal groups and attempting to take over official CPU newspapers, such as *Vil'na Ukraïna*.

The early sessions were broadcast live to crowds outside, and when a huge bill was deliberately presented to the council to attempt to cut these live proceedings, an appeal for donations from the public brought in millions of roubles within days.

On 17 April 1990 the Central Committee of the CPU, Council of Ministers and Supreme Council of Ukraine issued a threatening statement denouncing the 'destructive elements' which had taken control of councils in western Ukraine.[26] In quoting the statement, *Izvestiia* claimed that 'a wide-scale campaign to discredit the Communist Party has been devised, and psychological pressure on Communists is increasing: they are threatened with dismissal from work and are being forced to leave the CPSU. Practical steps are being taken for the removal from enterprises, institutions and educational institutions of party and *Komsomol* organisations'.[27]

Stanislav Hurenko would later compare the fate of communists in western Ukraine to those in the Baltic republics, where the 'democrats' were 'violating the Constitution and Soviet laws with impudence and impunity. Their actions are ostentatious, defiant and provocative. They are clearly provoking a sharp retaliatory action'.[28] Coming just less than a month after the military repression in Lithuania and Latvia, this was clearly a warning by Hurenko that the same action could be undertaken in western Ukraine.

A further warning came in mid-April 1990 when the first secretary of the L'viv *oblast* CPU, Pohrebniak, was replaced by the more hardline V. Sekretariuk. *Pravda* claimed that under Pohrebniak, the Democratic Bloc had operated, 'under conditions of the *oblast* Party committee's 'ideological neutrality' … This is why Party members found themselves without a rudder and sails, as it were, in a raging sea of public passions'.[29] This merely served to strengthen nationalism and led to election defeat.

In such circumstances Chornovil, despite the initial euphoria of his election, found it difficult to undertake wholesale change, particularly given a partial economic blockade against western Ukraine. In other words, he faced the classic dilemma of holding office without power.[30] The opposition was still hamstrung whilst the central state (both in Kyiv and in Moscow) remained strong and under conservative control. Chornovil found his local popularity slipping by mid-1991.

Similarly in Kyiv after weeks of inconclusive wrangling and two dozen unsuccessful attempts in which no candidate achieved a majority, the Kyiv City Council finally elected A. Nazarchuk, from the Democratic Centre Group (allied to *Rukh*) as mayor. In his acceptance speech Nazarchuk stated that his goal was, 'to see Ukraine independent both politically and economically'. O. Mosiiuk, a senior *Rukh* member, was elected as his deputy. The council was unable to achieve much more than symbolic change, however. In a centralised state, power has always been concentrated at the top, but increasingly that would mean Kyiv rather than Moscow, particularly as the new Ukrainian parliament began to assert itself.

PARLIAMENTARY POLITICS

During the first session of the new Supreme Council from May to August 1990 factions began to be established. However, it should be borne in mind that, because Ukrainian political culture was still in an embryonic stage of development, and because non-communist political parties were formed only after the elections, the Ukrainian Supreme Council did not yet have a classic parliamentary system, with a mature system of party discipline. Factions lacked unity, their memberships overlapped (deputies could belong to up to two fractions) and, although they may well have met as a caucus, the decisions of such caucuses tended to be recommendatory rather than binding. Even the CPU group, initially monolithic, had become fractious and undisciplined by 1991.

In June, the radical wing of the opposition formed the *Nezalezhnist'* group of 22 deputies, dominated by the UHU.[31] The formation of a People's Council was also announced in *Literaturna Ukraïna* in June, based on the Democratic Bloc. By the summer, after the addition of some independents and the Democratic Platform of the CPU, it claimed 115–33 members.[32] The head of the People's Council was Ihor Iukhnovskyi, a *Rukh* supporter and member of the CPSU until December 1990. His deputies were Levko Lukianenko, Oleksandr Iemets and Dmytro Pavlychko, with Les Taniuk as secretary.

The People's Council was soon opposed by the hardline CPU group 'For the Soviet Sovereignty of Ukraine', created on 1 June and led by Oleksandr Moroz (but more commonly known as the 'Group of 239' after the size of the conservative majority).

The People's Council's apparent minority position was bolstered by four main factors, however. First, the People's Council's deputies were more committed and regular attenders at the Supreme Council than the Communists. This gave the former disproportionate influence on the key (legislative drafting) committees of the chamber, and on the 27-man Presidium, composed of the chairman of the Supreme Council and the heads of the above committees, which issues decrees on behalf of the Supreme Council when the latter is not sitting. Many CPU deputies, on the other hand, tended to be occupied with their other jobs in the *apparat*, and were probably guilty of underestimating the newfound importance of the legislature, accustomed as they were to a political system where real power lay elsewhere. A total of 63 CPU deputies were absent at the Twenty-Eighth CPSU Congress in Moscow during the crucial sittings of the Supreme Council leading up to the Declaration of Sovereignty.

The decision to allow the opposition the chairmanship of certain key committees was in fact taken under Ivashko in May. These included the Human Rights committee under Oleksandr Iemets (of the Democratic Platform), the Culture and Spiritual Revival

Committee under Les Taniuk, Foreign Affairs under Dymytro Pavlychko (*Rukh,* and later the Democratic Party), Chornobyl' under Volodymyr Iavorivskyi (also Democratic Party), Education and Science under Iukhnovskyi, and Economic Reform under Volodymyr Pylypchuk. In addition, the deputy chairman of the Council, an ex-officio member of the Presidium, Vladimir Grinev, belonged to the Democratic Platform.

Hence, the opposition carried disproportionate weight on the influential Presidium, where it was later to form crucial links with more moderate members of the CPU.

Second, the CPU was put on the defensive by the 'Ivashko affair'. It will be recalled from Chapter 6 that, having only just been appointed chairman of the Supreme Council on 4 June 1990 (a vote boycotted by the People's Council because he maintained his position as first secretary of the CPU), Ivashko suddenly cut his ties to Ukraine, and accepted a job in Moscow as number two to Gorbachev in the CPSU on 11 July.[33] (He was replaced by a diumvirate consisting of Stanislav Hurenko as first secretary of the CPU and Leonid Kravchuk as chairman of the Supreme Council.)

Third, the People's Council had by now succeeded in establishing a sphere of acceptable opposition activity in civil society, as the CPU's ability and/or willingness to apply coercion declined, and for the first time had a foothold in the state system. Unable to take power itself, it pursued a two-pronged strategy of pressuring the reform-minded elements on the CPU, and the 'uncommitted', to take state-building measures on its behalf, while at the same time supporting a rising tide of public protest, which gradually undermined the confidence of CPU elites and undermined their will to resist. The first big public demonstrations of 1989 continued through the 21 January 'human chain', and were to culminate in the 'October Events' of 1990.

Fourth, external events, particularly the election of Yeltsin and the RSFSR's Declaration of Sovereignty on 11 June 1990, and the surprisingly hostile reaction by the Ukrainian public to the Ryzhkov government's price reform of 24 May, helped to slowly edge the CPU, under Ivashko's rather uncertain interregnum, towards the positions previously espoused by *Rukh.*

Under pressure from the Democratic Bloc, the CPU had already incorporated sovereignty for Ukraine within a 'renewed Soviet federation' into its platform for the March elections.[34] This position was endorsed by the plenum of the central committee of the CPU in April 1990.[35] But, as with so much during the last few years in the USSR and Ukraine, the understanding by the CPU of sovereignty and that by the opposition was quite different. The CPU believed declaring sovereignty was a step towards adopting a new Union treaty, and instructed its deputies to 'actively participate' in preparing one. The opposition, on the other hand, looked at the issue of sovereignty as a means in itself, or as a step on the path to independence. Serhii Koniev, deputy head of *Rukh*, said, 'It's the beginning of independence'; whereas, Ivan Pliushch, first deputy chairman of the Supreme Council, was reported as saying on 16 July, 'Today is a celebration – a day of the declaration of sovereignty of Ukraine within the confines of a renewed Soviet federation'.[36]

The major achievement of the first session of the Supreme Council was the Declaration of Sovereignty, adopted by 355 votes to 4 on 16 July as an amalgam of the five different alternatives that had been circulated by the factions.[37] The Declaration was more radical than observers had expected, although it was more a statement of intent, rather than a legally binding document, and the majority of those who spoke at the session stressed that the concept of sovereignty should not be directed towards secession from the USSR'.[38] The Declaration claimed the 'exclusive right of the Supreme Council of Ukraine' to 'speak on behalf of the Ukrainian people', and the 'supremacy of its constitution and laws on its territory'. Ukraine was economically sovereign, could create a separate currency and banking system, its borders were invioable, and it had the right to create separate armed forces. Military service should only be on the territory of Ukraine.

However, many radical demands were not met. The Declaration referred throughout to the 'Ukrainian SSR' rather than 'Ukraine'; the notion of dual citizenship of the Ukrainian SSR and the USSR had been opposed by many on the People's Council; the Ukrainian SSR only had 'the right to' form its own armed forces (a compromise reached between the People's Council and Communists); and the final clause stated that 'the principles of the Declaration on the Sovereignty of Ukraine are to be used in the preparation of a new Union treaty'.[39]

The session also passed several laws of similar intent, such as the 'Law on the Economic Independence of the Ukrainian SSR' on its last day – 3 August – and measures to limit military service to Ukrainian territory.[40]

THE REPUBLICANS: UKRAINE'S FIRST OPPOSITION PARTY

After the elections, the process of forming fully fledged political parties began in earnest, once the February 1990 CPSU plenum had opened the way for the abolition of Article 6 from the USSR and Ukrainian SSR constitutions, which had formerly given the Communist Party's monopoly of power legal status.

The inaugural congress of the Ukrainian Helsinki Union (UHU) had originally been scheduled for November 1989. The UHU's earlier 'popular front' function had now clearly passed to *Rukh*, and the UHU's leaders felt it could now fulfil its vanguard function more effectively as a political party – a party whose clear commitment to independence would help to push *Rukh* in the same direction. The repeated postponement of the congress, primarily because the organisation placed all its efforts into helping to launch *Rukh* and to push its candidates in the election campaign (eleven of whom became Deputies), was criticised by the more radical members of the UHU. They argued that 'The Declaration of Principles had already long ago lost its radical edge' and the UHU 'had stopped being in the avant-garde of the socio-political processes in Ukraine', and was losing members to more radical parties such as the Ukrainian Christian Democrats Party.[41]

The UHU finally held its inaugural congress on 29–30 April 1990, attended by 381 delegates representing 2300 members, 190 centres of activity, and 28 branches (including 2 outside Ukraine in the USSR); 351 delegates were Ukrainian: 157 were workers, 99 intelligentsia, and 26 were students, pensioners or the unemployed.[42] At this stage in the development of the Ukrainian opposition, the UHU was effectively the only party with an all-republican structure, although half its members still came from Galicia. (The membership figures given at the party's second congress on 1–2 June 1991 were 55 per cent from Galicia, 6.2 per cent Volhynia 5.6 per cent Transcarpathia and Chernivtsi, 22 per cent Central Ukraine (15.9 per cent Left Bank, 6.1 per cent Right), 7.3 per cent from the East, 3.6 per cent from the South – were probably similar to those of 1990.)[43] The UHU could capitalise on its well-known leaders, who had the moral authority of long prison terms behind them, and enjoyed by far the largest number of independent publications.

The UHU was renamed the Ukrainian Republican Party (URP) at the congress, Levko Lukianenko was re-elected Chairman, and Stepan Khmara and Hryhorii Hrebeniuk (from Donets'k) the two vice-chairmen.

The Republican Party adopted a radical programme which stood finally for complete independence, and claimed that 'Russian imperialism and chauvinism were and remain the biggest danger to the existence of the Ukrainian nation'.[44] The Republican Party stood for the adoption of a new constitution, a parliamentary republic, depoliticisation of the judiciary, military and security services, nationalisation of CPSU property, priority of ecological over economic concerns, a Ukrainian state bank and private banks, and a Ukrainian currency. It argued that the 'Union treaty (of 1922) is invalid because it was signed by an illegal government'.

There was, however, some criticism at the congress of the party's preoccupation with the national issue, and its lack of discussion of socio-economic problems, especially by the 1970s dissident Leonid Pliushch, now an exile member of the UHU in Paris.[45]

Chornovil, who issued a declaration of dissent signed by 11 other delegates, also attacked Lukianenko's conception of the party as a vanguard nationalist group with tight internal discipline, modelled on the democratic centralism of their CP opponents (as the party still had to operate semi-underground), which he saw as a betrayal of the UHU's original federalist structure and human rights priorities.[46] 'We are creating a highly centralised organisation of the Bolshevik–Fascist type,' he claimed at the congress.[47] Consequently, he kept his distance from the new party.

Arguments over the Republican Party's attitude to the Supreme Council also soon came out into the open, echoing the basic issue in wider opposition circles about whether to seek alliances with national communists. Lukianenko believed in participating in parliament's structures, and had put himself forward, symbolically, as a successor to Ivashko in July, but in August the more radical Khmara called the Supreme Council 'not a parliament, but a proto-parliament', to be regarded as a tribunal to publicise the views of the opposition and influence legislation. Khmara believed 'real power at the moment lies in the hands of the CPSU apparatus. This will remain the case until there is a change of forces in the Supreme Council'.[48] He was soon calling for the Republican Party, and the People's Council as a whole, to withdraw.

The Republican Party's radical faction had been strengthened in the wake of the congress, partly because Lukianenko, in attempting to balance West and East Ukraine by the appointment of Khmara and Hrebeniuk as his deputies, had actually chosen two ultra-radicals, around whom a nationalist faction began to coalesce. Their ally Roman Koval, a member of the Republican Party secretariat, argued that the Republican Party lacked a 'clear-cut programme of action', and should pursue a more aggressive strategy of blocking the activities of the communist majority in the Supreme Council and seeking to remove communists from local councils. The younger members of the

Republican Party were becoming increasingly impatient with their older leaders, many of whom were deputies and more ready to co-operate with the CPU. Serhii Zhyzhko characteristically believed that the Republican Party should stop just 'talking about the struggle and begin to struggle'.[49]

Koval believed that by the winter of 1990 the season of meetings had ended, hence the need to search for new methods and means for struggle. The Republican Party 'sees as positive the path of destabil-isation' which awakens the 'yearning for struggle in new layers of the population'.[50] The Republican Party should push for the KGB to be abolished, but should seek to expand its influence in the militia by 'enlightenment work, based in the first place upon a reawakening of national self-awareness, making clear to them the criminal activities of the CPSU/CPU whom they unfortunately defend'.

In November 1990 Koval argued that the People's Council, Association of Democratic Councils and leaders of main opposition groups should 'work out a joint strategy and form the necessary struc-ture, a shadow Council of Ministers, which can at any moment be ready to take over the reins of power in Ukraine'. In other words, frus-tration at the slow pace of reform and the inability of the opposition to gain a majority were attracting radical elements within the Republican Party to the Trotskyist strategy of 'dual power' first pro-posed by radical groups in the summer of 1990 (see below). Instead of seeking alliances with reformist-minded elements in the state, they were prepared to promote alternative structures of power to challenge the authority of the state.[51]

MULTI-PARTY POLITICS: THE EMERGENCE OF A RIGHT WING

The radicalisation of the Republican Party was partly due to the emergence of other competitor right-wing parties in 1990. They also arose because of disillusion with *perestroika* and the continued con-servatism of the CPU. Many were also financed by radical émigré parties, particularly the Banderite OUNr, which was anxious to construct a right wing nationalist movement in its own image.[52] Such parties were soon displaying all the classic symptoms of a 'vicious circle of sectarianism', as a large number of small parties, barely different to one another, but nevertheless strenuously competitive, began to appear.[53]

Such parties tended to lack a material base in terms of members and resources (although some received support from the diaspora), and hence were forced to escalate their aggressiveness and exaggerate the uniqueness of the party's profile in order to sharpen its image, and maintain members' loyalty by providing them with a strong sense of purpose and identity. This, in turn, alienates other organisations, further cutting the party off from resource-building activities, leading to a further escalation in its aggressiveness ... and so on.

Hence, right-wing parties soon began to make a lot of noise, and were usually prominent in street demonstrations, but the importance of these was declining, as the centre of activity moved into Parliament, and the moderate nationalists sought to find and ally with reformers in the CPU. The extreme nationalists' politics, therefore, were largely self-limiting, particularly as they adopted the kind of radicalism that only had a tradition of support in Galicia. Beyond Galicia the activities of the radicals were eagerly seized on by the CPU to discredit the opposition as a whole.

One such was the Ukrainian Democratic Peasants' Party formed in March 1990 to mobilise the Ukrainian peasantry. An appeal signed by 21 people 'To the peasants, workers and intelligentsia of Ukraine' was partly worded as follows:

> The peasants and those whose fate is tied with the village have remained the most socially unprotected stratum of society. For their hard work they receive the lowest remuneration. Their standard of living is the least regulated, and children of peasants form the lowest percentage of students at institutes of higher education. The peasant has the lowest level of medical care and the least possibility of spiritual and cultural development.
>
> Peasants! Who is defending your interests?
>
> To a certain extent – nobody. For this reason it is time to form an organisation which knows the life of the peasant and of the village intelligentsia, their problems and their questions and is prepared to defend without compromise their interests.
>
> The Ukrainian Democratic Peasants Party can become such an organisation, which will put general human values above class values and which will work towards the renewal of national agriculture and various forms of economic systems and ownership.[53]

Its priorities were the revival of the Ukrainian village and its national traditions, arresting the demographic decline of the Ukrainian nation, and ending the colonial exploitation of Ukraine and its agricultural sector in particular. Although its first congress in Kyiv on 9 June 1990 was addressed by moderates such as the head of the People's Council, Iukhnovskyi, Ivan Zaiets, and others, by the time of its second congress in February 1991 it was more firmly under the control of its radical leader, the well-known writer Serhii Plachynda.[55]

The UDPP found it difficult to expand its influence beyond Western Ukraine, but its popularity there was sufficient for the CPU to organise a rival 'Ukrainian Peasant Union', as an attempt at forming a 'Peasant Inter-Front'.[56]

Another Galician-based conservative party, the Ukrainian Christian Democratic Front (UCDF) mentioned in Chapter 5, attempted to consolidate its position after what amounted to the legalisation of the Ukrainian Catholic Church in the winter of 1989 and spring of 1990, and the clean sweep for the opposition in Galicia in the March 1990 elections. The UCDF had displayed its radicalism by defying the law to urge a boycott of the elections in a statement issued in February 1990. 'No genuine elections can take place as long as Ukraine is an occupied territory'. The UCDF refused to nominate candidates to the 'occupational parliament', because: 'To participate in these elections … would be tantamount to betraying the interests of the Ukrainian nation'.[57]

The second congress of the UCDF was held on 21–22 April 1990 in L'viv, attended by 200 delegates, each representing on average 10 members, with another 206 guests (the first congress had far fewer delegates). Two Ukrainian Catholic priests, the Rev. Iaroslav Lesiv and the Rev. Petro Zeleniuk, began the congress with a prayer service. The congress was greeted by the chairman of the Lithuanian Christian Democratic Party and a statement was read out from the Christian Democratic International. Other Ukrainian political parties, Ukrainian deputies and guests from Donets'k, Odesa, Georgia, Leningrad and Moscow also gave their greetings. The congress heard a report by the head of the UCDF, Vasyl Sichko, and adopted a new programme and statute for the Ukrainian Christian Democratic Party, as the UCDF decided to rename itself.[58]

'It is also important to note that the majority of both delegates and guests were young people, which is witness to the popularity of the movement among the youth,' one report stressed.[59] Vasyl Sichko was re-elected chairman of the UCDP.

A day after the congress ended on April 23, the Co-ordinating Council of Christian Democratic Organisations of (Soviet) Captive

Nations held a conference in L'viv. The resolutions criticised the introduction of a presidential form of leadership in the USSR, stated that
they would 'search out dialogue and co-operation with those Christian
organisations in Russia which recognise the right of each nation to
self-determination', thanked the Christian Democratic International
for supporting Lithuania and called for 'brotherly relations with our
neighbours in Central Europe'. The statement was signed by the
UCDP, Georgian National Democratic Party, Georgian Christian
Democratic Association, Lithuanian Christian Democratic Union,
National Union of Lithuanian Youth and Estonian Christian Union.

The second congress of the UCDF and formation of the Ukrainian
Christian Democratic Party coincided with the launch of the newspaper of the UCDP – *Voskresinnia* (Resurrection). The first issue contained an appeal to the Ukrainian nation, extracts from the statute
and programme, a report of the first Central European Christian
Democratic conference in Budapest in March 1990 and extracts from
the Bible for children.

Despite the UCDP's early promise, and Galicia being a natural base
for a Christian Democratic movement, the party was soon paralysed by
the sectarianism that plagued other right-wing parties, and in 1991
effectively split.[60] Having helped to radicalise public opinion and speed
up the retreat of the state from high totalitarianism, the UCDP like
many other parties found it more difficult to put down long-term roots
as an independent civil society struggled to establish itself in Ukraine.

INTEGRAL NATIONALISTS

A further group of right wing parties more consciously sought to echo
the interwar Ukrainian nationalism of Dmytro Dontsov and the OUN,
until now taboo.[61] These were the parties closest to the OUNr,
although the latter tended to shift its support from one to another, as
none would serve as a simple puppet.

The Ukrainian National Party was established as the first non-
communist political party in Ukraine as early as October 1989 by
Hryhorii Prykhodko, a former prisoner of conscience and critic of the
UHU. The UNP adopted as its programme a 'maximalist' position,
refusing to participate in any official structures as 'those of the occu-
pying power', copying the rejectionist tactics previously employed by
the radical Citizens Committees in Estonia and the campaign for a
'National Congress' in Georgia. The UNP's programme demanded

the withdrawal of occupation troops from Ukraine, independence, Ukrainian armed forces (the UNP was one of the first groups to propose this), the establishment of a provisional government in Ukraine after the convocation of a Congress of Citizens owing their allegiance to the Ukrainian People's Republic of 1917, the abrogation of the 1922 Union treaty that formed the USSR and recognition by the West of the colonial status of Ukraine.[62] It also supported 'the right to bear arms' as the best guarantee of liberty.[63]

The UNP claimed 'principled differences' with the Republican Party, because the latter was supposedly prepared to compromise with the 'colonial government'. The smalls size of the UNP was not a drawback, Prykhodko, claimed, 'in today's situation the important question is not numbers, but the purity of an idea, its elite aims. Only the CPSU can brag about numbers today'.[64] The UNP then became the main initiator of the Inter-Party Assembly (IPA) which was launched in the Summer of 1990 by radical groups who refused to take part in the Supreme Council of Ukraine and criticised *Rukh* for being 'collaborationist' and too moderate.

The main purpose of the IPA was to register citizens of the Ukrainian People's Republic. When 50 per cent of the population were registered, the IPA would call a Citizens' Congress to elect a government which would declare independence. By the end of 1990, 1 million had been registered within a period of six months. The IPA also supported widespread strike action and the Kyiv strike committee was based in the Assembly's offices.

Although the list of groups participating in the Assembly was long, only two – the UNP and Ukrainian People's Democratic Party – were sizeable political parties.[65] It soon fell victim to the fissiparous tendencies described above. At the third session of the IPA in December 1990, the UNP and Prykhodko walked out (and the UPDP soon followed) after disagreements with the majority of participants who criticised their undemocratic behaviour. It is noticeable that not only the UCDP, but also the Federation for Ukrainian State Independence (the successor to the Ukrainian National Front of the 1960s and 1970s, with some of the strongest links with the OUNr) – despite all their similar ideological positions (their differences being more of a personal nature coupled with competition for domination of the integral nationalist wing of the political spectrum in Ukraine) – refused to cooperate with the IPA.

The IPA eventually came under the control of its best organised element, the Ukrainian National Union. Although ultra-radical, it remained the most active and most visible political force to the right of the Republican Party, particularly after the 5000 strong paramilitary 'Ukrainian Self-Defence Forces' were set up under its auspices in the Autumn of 1991. Its leaders, such as Viktor Melnyk, openly compare their party's situation with that of the Nazis in Weimar Germany, hoping that his party's fortunes could be similarly transformed by economic decline.

The Federation for Ukrainian State Independence was established in April 1990 in L'viv and was led by another former prisoner of conscience Ivan Kandyba, who had been imprisoned with Lukianenko as a member of the Ukrainian Workers' and Peasants' Union of 1958–61. Although calling for only peaceful methods to achieve independence, the Federation was based upon the structure of the OUN of the 1940s, as was the National Front during the 1960s and 1970s in which leading members of FUSI had been involved. Kandyba refused to have any dealings with the UNP, despite being asked on numerous occasions.[66] The Federation's programme explicitly called for 'the building of an Ukrainian state within its ethnographic borders'.[67]

YOUTH GROUPS

Numerous independent youth groups were also established during this period, and tended to share the same problems of sectarianism and fissiparity as the right-wing parties.

These included student and youth organisations – the Ukrainian Students' Union in eastern Ukraine and the Student Brotherhood in western Ukraine. The Ukrainian Students' Union was established between 8 and 10 December 1989 at a congress in Kyiv University, attended by delegates from throughout Central and Eastern Ukraine. The programme of the Ukrainian Students' Union included making military education voluntary, the removal of Marxist-Leninist courses from higher education, the introduction of Ukrainian history courses, religious freedom of conscience and demands for the political and economic sovereignty of Ukraine.[68]

The Student Brotherhood was launched at an inaugural congress in L'viv on 25 May 1989, although it traced its origins back to November 1988.[69] (The major impetus for the launch of Student Brotherhood had been the repressive actions undertaken by the authorities in L'viv, in particular in March 1989.)[71] The programme of Student Brotherhood aimed to protect the social needs of students and help form a 'democratic national intelligentsia'. The Student Brotherhood 'was against all violations of social, political, national and religious rights of students and youth. It supported the raising of national and political consciousness and development of a democratic way of thinking'.[71]

On 20 and 21 February 1990 student groups organised strikes to press their demands, which included a minimum grant, guaranteed living quarters, and an end to Marxist-Leninist instruction, the political repression of students and military education.[72] The strikes also aimed to draw the attention of the Ministry of Higher Education, USSR and Ukrainian people's deputies and to attempt to awaken students out of their passivity.[73] Besides the above demands, the strikers demanded the abolition of *Komsomol* committees in Higher Education and the repeal of article 6 of the Ukrainian SSR constitution on the 'leading role' of the CPU.

The strikes were followed by the congress held between 23 and 25 February 1990 in L'viv that launched the Confederation of Student Organisations of Ukraine, an umbrella group uniting the Ukraine Students' Union and Student Brotherhood. Its programme reflected the radicalisation of the student movement in Ukraine, demanding the introduction of religious holidays, national symbols, the raising of national consciousness among students and young people, the closure of nuclear power stations and punishment for those responsible for the Chornobyl' disaster.[74] The Confederation also called for Ukrainian independence and claimed that 'student problems, as well as those relating to all young people, are the result of the subjugated status of Ukraine and the totalitarian socialist system of economics. We believe that the political, economic, social and legal problems can only be resolved through democratic methods and the parliamentary way.' The Confederation also stood for the closure of Communist Party and *Komsomol* cells in enterprises, offices, education and the media.

A year later, on 30 and 31 March 1991, the Student Brotherhood and Ukrainian Students' Union formally amalgamated into one organisation, the Union of Ukrainian Students.[75] The authorities' response, even at this late stage, was to attempt the old method of forming a group with a similar name entitled the Socialist Union of Ukrainian Students.[76] Not all members of the Ukraine Students Union agreed with the merger into the Union of Ukrainian Students, though, and a section led by Oles Donii, a leading organiser of the October 1990 student hunger strikes maintained a separate organisation.[77]

The Association of Independent Ukrainian Youth (SNUM) was initially organised by the Ukrainian Helsinki Union as its youth wing, but it soon evolved into a completely separate formation.[78] SNUM held its inaugural congress in Ivano-Frankivs'k on 26 and 27 May 1990, attended by 205 delegates representing an estimated 2000 members.[79] The congress was marred by disputes between radicals and moderates, the former eventually splitting off only six months later to form at first 'SNUM-nationalists' and then the Ukrainian Nationalist Union (UNU). SNUM-n and UNU joined the Ukrainian Inter-Party Assembly, and later came to dominate it by default as other groups left.

The programme of SNUM stated that 'it is a political civic youth organisation with co-operates with the progressive democratic forces in Ukraine and strives for political, economic and social sovereignty as a step towards complete state independence'.[80] It counterposed itself to the *Komsomol*, which educated 'youth as a reserve for the Communist Party of Ukraine and aspires to implant in them only communist ideas'. This had led to 'the persistent education of youth in the spirit of so-called atheism, national nihilism, slavish submissiveness and careerism' which, in turn, had, 'resulted in spiritual degeneration and apathy'.[81]

However, it soon developed into a mirror image of its rival. A former member of SNUM, Iryna Tymochko, wrote that 'Upon leaving the Association I achieved liberty ... there is a need for more goods, less hostility, less careerism, which, unfortunately, exists among members of the Association. And in the first place there is a need to love one's country, and not oneself, she wrote.[82] Bohdan Horyn, the head of the L'viv *oblast* Republican Party, stated in an interview that because SNUM had refused to be 'guided' by the older generation it had declined over the years since its foundation.[83] Its ultra-radicalism certainly soon led to falling membership and the alienation of mainstream public opinion.

For some, however, even SNUM was too moderate; for example, the Association of Ukrainian Youth, established in Kharkiv and then Kyiv and Donets'k, from the outset declared its allegiance to integral nationalism, in competition with the 'democratic' SNUM.[84] The Organisation of Democratic Ukrainian Youth was the youth branch of the émigré Ukrainian Revolutionary Democratic party, which began to establish branches in eastern Ukraine.[85]

Other youth groups established included *Plast* scouts, which had existed in pre-war Western Ukraine as an organisation to which the Galician Ukrainian intelligentsia and middle class had sent their children both in Poland and in the diaspora. It held its inaugural congress in L'viv on 16 December 1989.[86] At its second congress Oleh Pokalchuk, the well-known young folk singer, was elected head.[87]

As mentioned in Chapter 6, the L'viv *Komsomol* in 1990 broke its ties with the CPU, and renamed itself the Democratic Union of L'viv Youth. Unlike the other groups, it remained in possession of significant institutional resources, with a membership of maybe 22 000 (although this was far less than in its *Komsomol* days). The L'viv *Komsomol* newspaper *Lenins'ka molod* also defected to the L'viv Union and renamed itself in early 1990 *Moloda Halychyna.* The L'viv Union was allied to and influential within *Tovarystvo Leva* (publisher of *Postup* and later *Post-Postup*) and the Ukrainian Youth Fund (attached to the *oblast* council).[88]

OTHER INFORMAL GROUPS

The pre-war Union of Ukrainian Women was relaunched in Galicia,[89] and three human rights groups were also established during this period – Helsinki-90, the Union of Former Political Prisoners and the All-Ukrainian Society of the Repressed.[90] In September the Committee of Soldiers' Mothers of Ukraine was formed under Liudmyla Trukhmanova, in order to campaign against the draft, and in favour of military service on Ukrainian territory only.

UKRAINIAN POPULAR MOVEMENT (*RUKH*)

When the second 'All-Ukrainian Assembly' of *Rukh* gathered in Kyiv between 25 and 28 October 1990, a majority of delegates considered its programme outdated, as its major points had already been achieved in the Declaration of Sovereignty and *de facto* growth of a multi-party system in Ukraine.

Data on the social composition of *Rukh*'s Second Congress showed that its membership closely resembled that of Solidarity in Poland. Both were 'crisis-generated anti-partocratic movements' possessing charismatic leaders. The average age of both *Rukh* and Solidarity was 35, and each focused on 'abstract values and principles of justice, dignity, democracy, equality and freedom', with national symbols playing an important role in the movement's life.[91]

However, while Poland is relatively homogeneous ethnically, Ukraine is not, and *Rukh*'s monoethnic nature (95 per cent of delegates were Ukrainian) and disproportionate base in western Ukraine (48 per cent of delegates) and in the cultural intelligentsia was to prove problematical in 1990–1. *Rukh*'s increasing radicalisation meant that, despite considerable growth (it now had 632 828 members)[92] it could not mobilise the population to the same degree as the Baltic popular fronts (*Rukh*'s membership at its first congress represented 0.5 per cent of the population, compared with 3 per cent in the Estonian popular front at the same stage).[93] It attracted as many negative opinions as positive,[94] and it began to alienate centrist and non-Ukrainian elements as it moved from a generally democratic to a more specifically national programme.

The opening speech of Ivan Drach, the head of *Rukh*, for example, sounded a radical note.[95] Although *Rukh* rejected any 'seizure of power', and would continue to seek alliances with reformist elements in the CPU, any return by the *apparat* to the methods of the past would, he declared, be met by 'extra-parliamentary means', which included, 'strikes, meetings, demonstrations, pickets, petitions, the refusal to pay taxes, the refusal to deliver agricultural and industrial produce which is unlawfully expropriated by the party-state ... and non-payment for communal services'.

Rukh's new programme demanded 'the state independence of Ukraine' and 'the creation through non-violent means of a democratic republic', and rejected any Union treaty or confederation as simply 'a new noose ... for the oppressed nations', which would merely safeguard the monopoly of the CPSU.[96] As one *Rukh* activist put it, 'we have understood that the only way out of the crisis is also out of the Soviet Union', because the 'way to integration is through disintegration'.[97] *Rukh* had to move forward, as many of the planks in its original programme had been endorsed by the CPU. *Radio Moscow* commented that '*Rukh* has now become generally speaking, an association of anti-Party forces', 'the nucleus of the official opposition in the Supreme Council of Ukraine'.[98]

The congress ratified a decision taken earlier by the *Rukh* Grand Council, to drop the words 'for *perestroika*' from the title of the organisation. In the words of Volodymyr Muliava, '*Rukh* has risen to a new rung in its evolution, namely from the popular movement for *perestroika* to the popular movement of Ukraine for independence'.[99] Membership in *Rukh* was denied to those who belonged to a political party whose principal base lay outside Ukraine – a clear reference to the CPSU/CPU.

Rukh's position on the national question was now more radical. Its original February 1989 programme had envisaged national–cultural autonomy and local administration for national minorities, but now

Rukh only promised the former.[100] A Council of Nationalities was established, but it rarely met.

That said, *Rukh* leaders, mindful of the mistakes made by Baltic nationalists vis-à-vis their Russian minorities, alienated by seemingly threatening language and citizenship laws, to become a susceptible audience for populist 'Interfronts', always tried to concentrate on territorial, as opposed to ethnic, conceptions of nationalism. This helped to minimise ethnic tensions in Ukraine.

A discordant note was again set by the speech of Chornovil, who condemned ill-prepared strikes that relied too heavily upon workers in Western Ukraine (to strike in Western Ukraine when the councils are in democratic hands was 'counter-revolutionary'). *Rukh*, he believed, should act as the cradle for the emergence of political parties, whereas the Association of Democratic Councils and Blocs should be the kernel for the development of democratic state structures.[101]

MULTI-PARTY POLITICS: THE EMERGENCE OF CENTRE–LEFT PARTIES

During the second half of 1990, the political spectrum was further expanded by the establishment of five new centrist or centre-left political parties. This was in response to the radicalisation of *Rukh* and the Republican Party, and, from the Autumn of 1990, the CPU. Such parties sought to occupy what they saw as a vanishing centre ground, and maintain the old strategy of seeking alliances with CPU reformers. They also saw *Rukh*, the Republican Party and the rightist parties as too narrowly based in Galician extremism, and sought instead to act as bridges between east and west Ukraine.

Their numerical strength, particularly in the Supreme Council, soon began to outweigh that of the marginalised ultra-radicals, and, once elements in the CPU also returned to the centre ground after spring 1991, the national communist-opposition alliance could finally began to take shape.

Social Democrats

Social democracy has a well-established tradition in Ukraine, going back to the Revolutionary Ukrainian Party/Ukrainian Social Democratic Workers' Party of Volodymyr Vynnychenko and Symon Petliura, active in Greater Ukraine from 1900 to 1920, and the West Ukrainian Social Democratic Party of 1899–1939.[102]

Therefore, towards the end of 1988 social democratic groups with an all-Union perspective had been formed in a number of Ukrainian cities. In L'viv one such group, led by a Russian, Ievgenii Patrakeev, began to publish a *samizdat* bulletin entitled *Na polnyi golos* and its members were active in local initiative committees to establish Popular Fronts in the city.[103] On 4 and 5 February 1989 in Leningrad the second all-Union conference of social democratic groups took place with 39 delegates from 14 cities. At this conference 10 groups united to form the Social Democratic Confederation, including the Social Democratic Federation of Ukraine (Kyiv) and the Association of Social Democrats (L'viv).

Ukrainian social democratic groups, primarily in L'viv and Kyiv, did not establish an independent profile until late 1989 when a programme was released in Russian.[104] Ukrainian social democrats tended to stress the retention of the welfare aspects of the Soviet system, mindful of a potential working-class constituency in central and eastern Ukraine. Consequently, the programme devoted little space to the national question, a criticism levelled against it by Ukrainian national activists.

However, in May 1990 the inaugural congress of Ukrainian social democrats led to a 'left' and 'right' split. The larger, rightist group felt itself closer to western European social democracy on socio-economic questions, but was relatively willing to place more emphasis on the national question. Its programme declared that 'Although historically, Social Democracy is linked to the teachings of Marx, we resolutely abandon the ideological doctrine of Marxism as a philosophy tainted with utopianism and violence ... and do not support the traditional socialist idea of restructuring society.'[105] It took the name the Ukrainian Social Democratic Party, while the 'left' faction, which was less willing to cut its ties with the traditional ideas of the Second International, became the United Ukrainian Social Democratic Party.[106]

The former moved quickly rightwards on economic questions, as it came to feel the urgency of radical market reform, but at its conference on 24 and 25 November 1990 condemned the 'national ultra-radicalism' gaining ground in *Rukh*.[107]

Green Party

The draft programme of the Green Party was published in April, and a manifesto in May 1990, but these were not ratified until the inaugural congress of the Greens on 28 September 1990.[108] The Green

Party was established on the basis of the Green World Association, and would strive for the all-round renewal of Ukrainian society. The party dropped the former's 'eco-socialism', and based itself on a general humanism instead, totally rejecting all 'anti-humanistic theories and the practice of bolshevism, national socialism and totalitarianism'.[109] The Greens were, however, increasingly radicalised, as they came to believe that root-and-branch overhaul of the economic system was the only way to deal with its disastrous ecological side-effects.

The guiding principles of the Greens were 'pacificism, active community activity, non-violence and direct democracy'. The Greens were for independence and against a new Union treaty, and announced their disillusion with the prospects for reform within the CPSU. 'We are certain that the solution of ecological problems in Ukraine is impossible in the event of the maintenance of the totalitarian–bureaucratic regime and colonial status of our native land. That is why the Green Party stands against tying Ukraine to a central-imperial Union treaty', the congress appeal stated. The Greens would struggle to unify people, 'in the struggle for an independent, democratic, ecologically free, non-nuclear Ukraine'.[110] Iurii Shcherbak, head of the Green World Association, said that he saw the Greens 'as an integral component of a strong left-centre bloc of democratic forces'.[111]

The party lacked any representation in the Supreme Council, as its candidates had been prevented from standing in the 1990 elections, but its long history of activism, and the public reaction to Chornobyl' and other environmental disasters usually placed them at, or near, the top of public opinion polls.[112] In 1991 Shcherbak became environment minister.

The Party of Democratic Revival

The small liberal wing of the CPU, part of the all-Union Democratic Platform, announced its intention to break away from the party on 27 July 1990, after the disappointments of the Twenty-Eighth Congress of the CPSU and CPU, taking 28 deputies of the Supreme Council of Ukraine with it.[113] The party, under the provisional name of the 'Party of Democratic Accord' also began to attract non-party centrists, and those disillusioned with *Rukh*'s growing radicalism, such as the original head of *Rukh* in Kyiv, and *Rukh*'s spokesman in the televised debates of 1989, the philosopher Myroslav Popovych.

The party contained many parliamentary 'grandees' who maintained their links with CPU circles, such as second deputy chairman Vladimir

Grinev and Oleksandr Iemets, head of the Commission on Human Rights, while its sympathisers included Iukhnovskyi and Pylypchuk. By the time of the party's second congress on 15 and 16 June 1991, it claimed a 36-strong faction in the Supreme Council (20 members and 16 supporters).[114] Hence it is often compared to Shevardnadze's and Yakovlev's 'Movement for Democratic Reform' in Russia.

The party's strongholds were among the reformist *apparat* and technical intelligentsia of East and Central (mainly Left-Bank), Ukraine. The party's largest organisations were in Donets'k, Luhans'k, Kyiv and Kharkiv, with pockets of support in L'viv. Eight of its deputies were from Donets'k, and seven from Kharkiv. it contained a rough balance of Ukrainian and Russian speakers, with the latter feeling increasingly alienated by *Rukh*'s national radicalism. Therefore, the party was to play a crucial role, after it joined the People's Council in summer 1990, as a bridge between *Rukh* and the Russian-speaking radicals of eastern Ukraine, and can be credited with playing a key part in persuading potentially separatist Russian elites in Ukraine to throw in their lot with the independence movement. Because of its Russian element, the party stressed the importance of maintaining practical links with Russia, and it was the driving force behind the creation of the inter-republican 'Democratic Congress' on 26 and 27 January 1991 (see Chapter 8).

At its inaugural congress on 1 and 2 December 1990, the party was renamed the Party of Democratic Revival of Ukraine (PDRU), and announced it had 2340 members in 23 *oblasts'* (except Transcarpathia and Zhytomyr). Twenty-five per cent of the members were still in the CPSU, but any members of the CPSU could only attend as 'guests'.[115] The party's social profile was confirmed by the fact that 208 delegates (or 64.2 per cent) were '*sluzhbovtsi*' (i.e. white-collar) and 55 (17 per cent) were scientific workers; 268 (82.7 per cent) had higher education and 77 (23.7 per cent) were deputies at one level or another.[116]

The congress highlighted two tendencies within the party – liberal and social democratic, reflecting the difference between libertarians such as Popovych, and east Ukrainians, such as Volodymyr Filenko, who had only recently cut their ties with the CPU, and were aware of the importance of socio-economic issues in the east.

The congress therefore stressed economic and practical issues in a clear attempt to target the urban population of eastern Ukraine.[117] The congress, however was also critical of the CPU's recent atavistic lapse into authoritarianism (see Chapter 8),[118] and instead of the proposed new Union treaty suggested a 'Commonwealth of Republics'.[119]

The party also pursued a strategy of using its former links with the CPU 'to deepen ... the divergences between sovereign and imperial communist [that is, between national communists and pro-centre hardliners], and show Communist Party members the path towards integration in the civil, political, cultural and economic life of an independent, democratic Ukraine'.[120] It was described as having 'a strong potential to become one of the primary forces in a possible wide-encompassing centre coalition: social democrats, liberals, PDRU, Greens and the Democratic Party of Ukraine. In the transition period from totalitarianism to democracy the formation of such an influential centre would be very important'.[121] After the August 1991 attempted coup, the PDRU was to initiate the formation of just such a centrist grouping, *Nova Ukraïna* (New Ukraine).

The Democratic Party

On 15 and 16 December 1990, the Democratic Party of Ukraine was launched by those leading members of *Rukh* and former members of the CPSU, such as Ivan Drach and Dmytro Pavlychko, who had been the original driving force behind the alliance between the Writers' Union of Ukraine and dissidents formed in the winter of 1988–9. Iurii Badzo, a former prisoner of conscience, was elected the leader of the new party, with Pavlychko deputy chairman and parliamentary leader.

The party's roots lay in the attempt by Drach and Pavlychko to turn *Rukh* into a full-scale political party, announced in early March 1990 in *Literaturna Ukraïna* but then rejected by the Grand Council of *Rukh* at Khust later in the same month. The rationale for this move, and the subsequent decision to form the Democratic Party, was to distance *Rukh* from the increasingly radical tactics of the Republican Party, and continue the strategy of seeking alliances with the CPU, while at the same time attempting to transfer *Rukh*'s popularity to a new political party.

The original draft programme written by Badzo as long ago as April 1989 had envisaged a 'Ukrainian Party of Democratic Socialism and State Independence', reflecting Badzo's Eurocommunist roots, and the fact that the party's origins lay with the CPU elite in the Writers' Union of Ukraine. The larger manifesto and draft programme published in May and November 1990 stated that the party 'continues the traditions of Ukrainian Social Democracy ... and will strive to ensure that Ukrainian society, on its path to economic and political freedom, does not repeat the experience of primary capitalist accumulation with its acute social antagonisms and unchecked egoistic private ownership'.[122]

The party was therefore more centrist than the Republican Party on socio-economic questions, and viewed the Republican Party's neo-Bolshevik discipline and largely working class membership with distaste (and was therefore closer to the PDRU or Ukrainian Social Democrat's in its social base or methods of working). But, as the party of the Ukrainian-speaking cultural intelligentsia, it shared the Republican Party's views on the national question.

The much delayed December congress was attended by 523 delegates representing 2763 members and, reflecting the general radicalisation through 1990 of the cultural intelligentsia that was the party's bedrock, ratified a programme calling for independence and a market economy. Sixty-six delegates were workers, and 370 members of the cultural intelligentsia, teachers, scientists and the like.[123]

The party claimed as its central idea the notion of balance between left and right, between the rights of individuals and the rights of the nation or state, between east and west Ukraine. When the party was registered in June 1991, its membership figures were more evenly spread than the Republican Party (concentrated in Galicia and Kyiv), or the PDRU (concentrated in central and eastern Ukraine), but, reflecting its nature as the party of the Ukrainian intelligentsia, were still biased towards the west and the Right Bank (33.6 per cent were in Galicia, 4.8 per cent Volhynia-Polissia, 6.3 per cent Transcarpathia and Chernivtsi, 35.6 per cent central Ukraine (19.1 per cent Left Bank, 16.5 per cent Right), 12.4 per cent in eastern Ukraine, and 6.9 per cent in the south).[124]

The party claimed a faction of 22–26 in the Supreme Council, although eight of these were from L'viv alone.[125] At the congress Dymtro Pavlychko attacked both the 'dictatorship of one-party Bolshevism ... and Nietzschean nationalism',[126] while Badzo stressed the party's sympathy with *Rukh* 'not simply as a bloc of oppositional, but of *democratic* oppositional forces'.[127] Badzo also argued that, because the CPU 'was far from being an organisation of the like-minded, but was created artificially ... not like a party, more like a social class',[128] it was important 'not to drive Kravchuk and his supporters towards Hurenko [by then Kravchuk represented 'national communism' and Hurenko conservatism and the centre] but to seek the division between them and widen it'.[129]

The year 1991, however, saw a growing rapprochement between the Democrats and the Republicans, because of their common radical stand on the national question. If the Republicans represented mainly ex-dissidents, and the Democrats the cultural intelligentsia, the prospects for a cooperative division of labour between them were good once the Republicans had shed its ultra-radical element.

CONCLUSIONS

The period after the March 1990 republican elections saw the development of a embryonic multi-party system, both inside and outside parliament with four basic groupings.

First, the CPU and United Social Democratic Party on the left; second, the Democratic Party, PDRU, Liberal Democratic Party, Greens and People's Party in the centre and centre left; third, a centre right consisted of the Republicans, Peasant Democrats and Christian Democrats, and People's Democratic Party and finally, the far right comprised the Ukrainian National Party, the Federation for Ukrainian State Independence, and the Inter-Party Assembly (after August 1991 the Ukrainian National Assembly).[130]

However, despite the consolidation of a wide spectrum of political opinion, the Ukrainian party system of 1991 remained in many crucial respects underdeveloped. Although the Republican Party had 8879 members at its Second Congress in June 1991, most other parties struggled to attract the 3000 members necessary for official registration (reduced to 300 in September 1991). The total membership of all non-communist political parties in 1991 was only 35 000–40 000, out of a population of nearly 52 million (the CPU, by contrast, claimed 2.9 million members at its December 1990 congress).[131]

Nearly all political parties still lacked organisational or social roots, and only had a regional base, although this was to be expected during the period when civil or public society was still in the early phase of reconstruction. Programmes tended to be simply declaratory and repetitive, and exhibited a considerable overlap in philosophy. Party discipline in the Supreme Council and local councils was weak or nonexistent. Most parties were in fact little more than personality-based factions, as parties were still in the stage of defining themselves by their anti-communism, rather than developing a more positive self-image.[132] Many parties had created overly diffuse and decentralised organisations in the idealistic initial enthusiasm, but soon had to create more streamlined and efficient structures, as the former's ineffectiveness became apparent.

The PDRU reduced its number of joint heads from seven to three, and established a ruling presidium at its second conference on 29–30 June 1991.[133] The Social Democrats' second congress on 26 and 27 October 1991 established the new post of party leader and more clearly delineated the spheres of competence of the party's leading organs.[134] The Greens, originally only a federation of political clubs, introduced a governing political council and secretariat in December 1991. Even the Democratic Party felt compelled to devolve power from its larger national council of 83 to a smaller working council and Presidium.[135]

Although the parties helped to fill the developing ideological vacuum with the nationalist agenda, organisationally they were still no match for the resource of the state. Unable to take power on their own, they were still awaiting the emergence of the national communists.

8 Stalemate and the Rise of National Communism (1990–1)

THE VIEW FROM THE CENTRE

By 1990 Gorbachev understood that maintaining the Soviet nationality policies of his predecessors with only minor alterations was no
longer acceptable to the ruling elites of the Soviet republics. The three
Baltic republics of Lithuania, Latvia and Estonia, together with
Armenia and Georgia, had already declared independence. The
March 1990 elections had empowered new and more democratic parliaments within the 15 republics as well as given access to state
resources and the media to anti-communist and democratic groups. A
'war of laws' began between the newly elected republican parliaments
and the centre, followed by declarations of sovereignty in the summer
and autumn.

1990 also witnessed the emergence of Boris Yeltsin in the centre.
Yeltsin was to form his own power base within the Russian Supreme
Soviet from which he progressively challenged Gorbachev and the
Soviet centre. Yeltsin championed the right of Russia also to possess
its own attributes of statehood and sought allies among the other
republican leaders against Gorbachev. The rise of the Communist
Party of the Russian Federation that year ensured that Yeltsin was
able to cut his ties to it ahead of Kravchuk in neighbouring Ukraine.
The Russian Communist Party remained a conservative, anti-
reformist institution in total opposition to Gorbachev's *perestroika*
(as well as Yeltsin's post-Soviet reforms). Yeltsin's opposition to
Gorbachev came from the opposite end of the political spectrum,
accusing Gorbachev of not being reformist enough.

Russia became an important ally of the non-Russian republics who
pressed for the USSR to be transformed into a confederation, in contrast to what Gorbachev offered ('renewed federation'). Russia signed
bilateral agreements with the other republics, including with Ukraine
in November 1990, which recognised existing borders. Any new Union

Treaty should be built on these bilateral treaties, the republican leaders argued. Gorbachev, who had rejected a new Union Treaty in September 1989, realised six months later that the USSR would not survive without one. In June 1990 a working group was therefore established to draw up a new Union Treaty, the first draft of which was presented in November of that same year.

The draft Union Treaty quickly ran into problems. A multi-tiered federation, with some republics backing confederal and others federal ties, would be a recipe for chaos. If Gorbachev had not opposed a new Union Treaty between 1988 and 1989 the majority of the republics would have settled for this minimalist position. As it was, Gorbachev's refusal to consider restructuring centre–periphery relations led inevitably to the radicalisation of demands by both Popular Fronts and national communists after 1990. The majority of the republics would no longer accept a cosmetic re-working of the USSR; to them the 1922 Union Treaty had never been voluntary and the state had never been a genuine federation. From the late 1920s Soviet republics had far less power than American states or Swiss cantons. By mid-1990, therefore, what Gorbachev was offering was too little, too late. The bulk of the Soviet republics, particularly the two key ones – Russia and Ukraine – would only accept a renewed USSR in the form of a confederation of sovereign states built from the bottom up on the basis of bilateral treaties.[1]

In April 1990 the Supreme Soviet adopted a new law 'On the Procedure for Dealing With Matters Connected With the Secession of a Union Republic from the USSR'. The process would take up to six years. Autonomous republics could decide to remain within the USSR and therefore the seceding republic could lose territory. Secession had to be backed by a referendum where two thirds had to approve the decision. If it failed another referendum could not be held for five years. If the vote was less than two thirds a second referendum could not be held until after ten years.[2] The law was therefore immediately dubbed a law 'Against Secession', geared primarily to holding back the Baltic and Trans-Caucasian republics from pushing for independence.

THE VIEW FROM UKRAINE

From the autumn of 1990, it became increasingly clear that the CPU was losing its previous unity, and that the long-desired alliance between the opposition and reform-minded elements in the CPU was at last taking shape, as the logic of 'national communism' outlined in Chapter 1 finally began to unfold. However, from the summer of 1990 until August 1991, this tendency would be interwoven with a counter-attack against the opposition by conservative elements within the CPU, co-ordinated with similar moves by Moscow hardliners (and to a certain extent orchestrated by them).

As the opposition was not strong enough to take power on its own and was increasingly weakened by growing radicalisation and different-iation within its ranks, an uncertain period of stalemate, both between the two wings of the CPU and between the CPU and the opposition, lasted until August 1991. Then the CPU hardliners discredited them-selves by their support for the coup and left the path clear for an alliance between the national communists and the nationalists.

Hence, although the predicted rise of national communism within the CPU was initially obscured by an uncertain transition period of 'dual power' – of competition between the two wings of the CPU, and between the institutions of Party and state – it is important to bear in mind that the national communist wing of the CPU had already been promoting state building measures in alliance with the People's Council throughout the third session of the Supreme Council from February to July. The failed coup only accelerated this process, rather than beginning it.

STUDENT HUNGER STRIKES AND REACTION

The first session of the new Supreme Council from May to August 1990 had been marked by partial victories for the opposition People's Council, and had seen the CPU on the defensive since its Twenty-Eighth Congress in June 1990.[3] The diumvirate elected to replace Ivashko, Leonid Kravchuk as chairman of the Supreme Council and Stanislav Hurenko as first secretary of the CPU, seems originally therefore to have been intended to lay the foundations for a counter-attack against *Rukh* and the People's Council. Kravchuk's initial elec-tion as Chairman of the Supreme Council on 23 July 1990 was boycotted by the People's Council, which at the time only remem-bered him for his leadership of the media assault on *Rukh* as CPU ideology secretary in 1988–9. Consequently, they issued a public state-ment relinquishing 'responsibility for the activities of the newly elected chairman of the Supreme Council of the Ukrainian SSR'.[4]

There was certainly little doubt that Hurenko at least was a dour traditionalist. In his view, 'What is particularly worrying is the continuing underestimation of the danger of anti-communism and the absence of even the slightest attempt at countering its increasing onslaught'. Having 'sustained a furious onslaught from anti-communist propaganda in a state of ideologial demobilisation', the CPU should now reassert itself again, he argued.[5]

Hence, after a lull in the summer, the second session of the Supreme Council from October to December 1990 was marked by growing tension and confrontation. A 200 000-strong mass demonstration in Kyiv on 30 September was timed to coincide with the session's opening, and was followed by a general strike (albeit patchily supported) on 1 October.

When things appeared to be calming down, up to 150 students, organised by L'viv's Student Brotherhood and Kyiv's Ukrainian Students' Union, began hunger strikes in Kyiv that were to last from 2 to 16 October.[6] The students demanded the resignation of Prime Minister Masol, new parliamentary elections on a multi-party basis, military service to be on Ukrainian territory only and the nationalisation of CPU and *Komsomol* property, and adamantly opposed the signing of any Union treaty (seeking to bind the authorities to a statement already made by the Presidium of the Supreme Council on 30 September that Ukraine would not sign any Union treaty until it had revised its own constitution).[7] Unlike the spring student strikes, the hunger strikes attracted widespread popular support and appeared to catch the authorities (and the People's Council, apart from the radical wing of the Republican Party) unawares.

Divisions within the *apparat* were obvious once the hunger strikers were not dispersed in the traditional fashion, and after several days of rising tension, and increasingly large public demonstrations, the authorities conceded an agreement on 17 October that met most of the students' demands. Although a section within the *apparat* was prepared to implement the accord, and Prime Minister Masol was replaced by Vitold Fokin on 23 October, others viewed it merely as a device to end the strikes, and the period from November onwards was marked by a series of measures designed to restore CPU control.[8] Clearly the time was not ripe for the national communists to come to the fore, as too many within the CPU had their eye on the trend in the opposite direction in Moscow. Moreover, in retrospect the People's Council, despite issuing a call for Polish-style round-table talks, was not sufficiently organised to take advantage of the opportunity to enforce wholesale change.[9]

When the Supreme Council reconvened on 13 November, the CPU forced through limitations on the right of public demonstration during workdays, and reduced the necessary quorum for Supreme Council business from two-thirds of the deputies to a half, thereby depriving the 120 or so People's Council deputies of their power to stop proceedings by simply leaving the chamber.

Ukraine was also, of course, subject to the more hardline measures coming from Moscow during this period, such as extra powers for the KGB and militia patrols on the streets, and conservatives forces were clearly in the ascendent during the second phase of the Twenty-Eighth Congress of the CPU in Kyiv on 13 and 14 December.[10] The conservatives were also disturbed by the campaign spreading from Galicia to Kyiv for the rehabilitation of the nationalist movements of the 1940s, the Ukrainian Insurgent Army (UPA) and the Organisation of Ukrainian Nationalists (OUN). In an opinion poll conducted in the summer of 1991 in L'viv *oblast*, 95.8 per cent viewed the UPA and OUN as a historically positive phenomenon.[11]

In April 1991 an All-Ukrainian Brotherhood of Veterans of the UPA and OUN was launched in L'viv to propagate Ukrainian military traditions and halt criminal actions against Ukrainian defectors from the Soviet armed forces.[12] The Veterans organisation also sought to rehabilitate the UPA and OUN, and erect memorials, called for the release of political prisoners, and, not surprisingly, opposed the Union treaty.

Although Ukraine did not suffer from the use of military force in the winter of 1990–1 in the same way as the Baltic states did, there were several disturbing incidents that led to an escalation of tension. In December 1990 and June 1991 three nationalist monuments to Stepan Bandera and Ievhen Konovalets (leaders of the OUN), and to the SS Galicia Division (a Ukrainian force trained by the Germans in World War II) were blown up. According to Ihor Derkach, member of the parliamentary commission on military and security affairs, this was the work of the same KGB 'Alpha' anti-terrorist unit based in Moscow used in the assault on the TV tower in Vilnius in January 1991. The day after the Lenin monument was removed in Ivano-Frankivs'k on 10 October 1990, a hand grenade was thrown inside the city council building. At the scene a note was left which said it was 'Revenge for Lenin' and signed by *'Pamiat'*.[13]

The destruction of the monuments was apparently organised by Moscow. A copy of a letter dated 13 December 1990 from the Soviet Ministry of Defence to military officers in L'viv *oblast* called upon them to 'increase the combat readiness of troops' in response to 'the provocations' of 'destructive and nationalist elements' in western Ukraine.[14]

The letter told officers to 'earnestly counter' the erection of monuments to 'fascists', which were to be 'liquidated' wherever possible. On 7 December 1990 the Kyiv military garrison received orders of General Varennikov 'to place under military defence Soviet monuments where this is called for', and to destroy 'fascist monuments'. In the same month a Communist Party of Ukraine plenum called for the prevention of the erection of monuments to nationalist heroes.

THE KHMARA AFFAIR AND THE NEW RIGHT

The most celebrated instance of reaction came on 7 November, when the radical deputy and joint deputy leader of the Republican Party, Stepan Khmara, who had presented a draft law calling for the nationalisation of CPU property in October, was set up on charges of assault. The 239 (plus one) hardline CPU deputies then voted to strip him of his parliamentary immunity on 17 November, leading to his subsequent arrest in the parliament building itself.

By targeting Khmara, the CPU hoped to split the opposition, not all of whom were prepared to join in the campaign for his release, and associate themselves with his radical politics. Hence the affair was dragged out until the aftermath of the August attempted coup, with Khmara spending two long terms in prison, leaving moderates in the Republican Party from speaking out against him and his policies while he remained something of a popular hero.

The conservative counter-attack served to promote its mirror image – a more militant and oppositional right-wing nationalism. However, the rise of such groups soon led to tensions with those People's Council moderates seeking to encourage the emergence of a national communist group with whom alliance-building would be possible.

The theoretical conference of the Republican Party held on 23–24 February 1991 in Kyiv demonstrated the growth of such radical nationalism among the party's young members, who tended to support Khmara, and were calling for the party to adopt a mythologised version of the OUN's ideology, or of Dontsov's elitist nationalism.[15] The party's radicals had close links with the Inter-Party Assembly and other radical groups,[16] who were becoming increasingly noisy, if not necessarily increasingly influential, through the early part of 1991.[17] The émigré OUNr had been supporting such groups financially, and by supplying the works of authors such as Dontsov and Bandera in order to promote their own radical brand of nationalism.[18]

The Republican Party's leadership shared the desire of the rest of the opposition to co-operate with the national communists, especially in times of rising reaction, whereas for the young radicals this represented weakness and compromise. Ukraine was simply a colony that required liberation, and those who, by participating in its structures 'help to perpetuate the colonial status of Ukraine, are an enemy of the Republican Party, and an enemy of Ukraine'.[19] Such views led to a series of bitter disputes between Koval and the Republican Party's parliamentary moderates, represented by Oles Shevchenko, and rampant factionalism on the Republican Party's secretariat.[20]

In the run-up to the party's second congress on 1–2 June, the radicals – Koval, Hrebeniuk, Zhyzhko, Iavorskyi and others – were all purged. The party also forbade joint membership of the Republican Party and Inter-Party Assembly.[21] However, although support at the congress for Khmara's brand of radicalism was confined to 15 per cent of the delegates, the leadership felt compelled to retain him as Lukianenko's deputy, given his continued persecution and consequent popularity.[22] As a result, the Republican Party would continue to be sidetracked by the Hydra-like return of its radical element, despite the growing desire of Lukianenko and the Horyn brothers to co-operate with the national communists.[23]

PARTY ALLIANCES

The Republican Party was not alone in its problems. The CPU's attempts to divide and rule the opposition had some success, as the climatic October had failed to result in outright defeat for the CPU, the euphoria of the mass meetings of 1990 had dissipated, and the opposition's ability to organise collective action had declined. *Rukh's* second congress had failed to deal with the threat that the newly created political parties posed to its umbrella function, and increasingly the parties tended to pursue their own line, as *Rukh* faded into the background.

Rukh had tried to devise a system of collective membership for political parties to counter this threat, but none of the major parties had taken up the offer. The Republican Party wished to preserve its distinctive profile, while at the same time using 'entryist' tactics to promote its interests within *Rukh*. The PDRU and Social Democrats saw themselves as centrists and distrusted *Rukh*'s growing nationalism, and the Democratic Party did not join because of similar fears expressed by delegates from eastern Ukraine at its founding conference.[24]

Attempts at merger or coalition between the parties floundered, despite the fairly minimal ideological distance separating them. Cooperation at a local level encouraged the Democratic Party, PDRU and Social Democrats to talk of merger, but such overtures were eventually rebuffed by the Democratic Party because of the others' supposed indifference to the national question.[25] The Democratic Party's own attempt to unite all nationally minded parties in a coalition entitled 'Independent Democratic Ukraine' collapsed on 10 June 1991, as Drach saw it as a rival to *Rukh*, and Lukianenko again wished to preserve the Republican Party's distinctive face.[26]

In November 1990, a Committee of Public Accord was formed in L'viv by nearly all parties, to support Chornovil's council in the face of the CPU's counterattack. In effect, it usurped many of the functions of *Rukh*, but the example was not copied elsewhere in Ukraine.[27]

Hence, all attempts to transcend the problems created by weak and fissiparous political parties failed. Parties were more successful, however, in forging foreign links.

The PDRU was the main Ukrainian initiator of the 'Democratic Congress' of 46 opposition groups from 10 republics (mainly also centre-left groups, such as the United Democratic Party of Belorussia [Belarus], and the Russian Republican Party and Social Democrats), formed in Kharkiv on 26–27 January 1991.[28] The congress promoted the idea of a commonwealth of sovereign states, which the PDRU and its Russian allies then placed before their respective parliaments. The PDRU, therefore, claims the credit for first promoting the notion of a 'CIS' that was eventually adopted for the dismantling of the USSR in December 1991. The congress was also designed to promote good Ukrainian–Russian relations, as the Ukrainian centrists had long advocated.[29]

More radical groups had begun meeting as early as January 1988, as the 'Co-ordinating Committee of the Patriotic Movements of the Peoples of the USSR'.[30] Ukrainian delegates were mainly from the UHU, and helped to establish the Co-ordinating Committee as an international lobby for individual and national rights, and to promote mutual understanding among the republics and a common front against the centre.

The Ukrainian Greens also established links with their counterparts in other republics at meetings in Kyiv on 4 July, and in Tbilisi on 9 September 1991.[31]

DIVISIONS IN THE CPU

However, despite the apparent supremacy of the conservatives within the CPU, the bifurcation of the CPU leadership was beginning to have its effect. Divisions between the hardline and pro-Moscow approach represented by Hurenko and the embryonic national communism of Kravchuk began to surface in the aftermath of the January 1991 events in Luthuania and Latvia. The Presidium of the Supreme Council issued a statement condemning the events, stating that it 'supports legally elected state executive organs of the Republics ... [and] ... considers inadmissible the use of military force on the territory of any Republic for the solving of internal and inter-ethnic conflicts without the approval of the legitimate authorities of the Republic'. Whereas the CPU central committee adopted a resolution condemning the 'provocative campaign, conducted by national-separatists and extremist forces' in Lithuania.[32] Hurenko on 4 February called for solidarity with 'our party comrades who are being persecuted in this region [the Baltics] in a most flagrant, uncivilised and dangerous way ... [We should] offer them political and moral support'.[33]

Kravchuk, meanwhile, had since its first meeting on 1 November 1990, headed a 59-man committee of experts established after the 17 October accord with the students to draw up a project of constitutional reform. Divisions over its deliberations surfaced at the CPU plenum in February 1991.[34] According to Hurenko, 'We and Kravchuk have different points of view concerning the realisation of sovereignty. Leonid Markarovych's speech shocked many at the last plenum of the central committee of the CPU.'[35] Kravchuk, on the other hand, defending Parliament from the Party, said 'Many [Communists] have not parted with the illusion that it is not a [Supreme Council] session in which they are participating, but a Party plenum'.[36]

When the committee's plans were presented to the Supreme Council on 14 May, it became clear that Kravchuk intended to proceed with state-building measures, that is to give genuine content to the July 1990 Declaration of Sovereignty, which at the time had been little more than a statement of intent. This would also allow Ukraine to stall on signing Gorbachev's Union treaty, claiming that determining its own constitutional status had to be logically prior to deciding its constitutional relations with other republics.

THE MARCH 1991 REFERENDUM, THE UNION TREATY AND THE RISE OF KRAVCHUK

The first results of the developing centrist alliance between 'national communists' and the majority in the People's Council came in the run-up to the 17 March 1991 referendum called by Gorbachev on the future of the Union. The old 'Group of 239' was only able to muster 135 votes for the presentation of Gorbachev's question ('Do you consider it necessary to preserve the USSR as a renewed federation of equal sovereign republics, in which human rights and the freedoms of all nationalities will be fully guaranteed?') on its own. Radical proposals in the Supreme Council of Ukraine for a boycott or a ballot on outright independence also failed to gain a majority.

On 27 February Kravchuk secured a 277–32 vote to present Gorbachev's question simultaneously with a second, specifically Ukrainian, question. ('Do you agree that Ukraine should be part of a Union of Soviet Sovereign States on the basis of the Declaration of State Sovereignty of Ukraine?')[37] The opposition-controlled Councils in the three Galician *oblasts* later added a third question. ('Do you want Ukraine to become an independent state which independently decides its domestic and foreign policies, and which guarantees equal rights to all of its citizens, regardless of their national or religious allegiance?')

The 70.5 per cent support for Gorbachev's question was not unexpected, but the Ukrainian question received an even higher 80.2 per cent, and 88.4 per cent voted for independence in Galicia. As all the questions were basically contradictory, it was possible for all political forces in Ukraine to interpret the results as they saw fit. The interpretation that mattered, however, was Kravchuk's. He ignored the first and third ballots, and used the second (plus the October 1990 student agreement) to support his line of negotiating a commonwealth of sovereign states, but only once Ukrainian sovereignty had been achieved. Ukraine had first to constitute itself as a legal subject capable of signing such a treaty.

The February–July Supreme Council session would indeed discuss much constitutional reform, but at a pace which gave Ukraine the power to procrastinate on the Union treaty as it deemed necessary.

The referendum in fact largely confirmed the balance of political forces in Ukraine first revealed in the March 1990 elections. The conservative and pro-Union forces were stronger in the south and east, and in small-town Ukraine and the countryside, whereas radical nationalism dominated in Galicia (spilling over into Volhynia), Kyiv and some other urban centres. (See Table 8.1.)

Public opinion in Ukraine remained more conservative than in many other republics (the Balts, Georgians, Armenians and Moldovans boycotted the vote altogether), while the opposition had found it difficult to improve on its 1990 results without access to the mass media, which remained largely under CPU control.

After Gorbachev used the March referendum to begin the Union treaty process at the Novo-Ogariovo meeting on 23 April, Kravchuk had to perform a difficult balancing act (Ihor Iukhnovskyi had voiced the suspicion in March that Kravchuk was saying one thing in Moscow and another at home in Kyiv).[36] The domestic pressures on him were considerable. The Republican Party was demanding outright independence, and even the relatively moderate PDRU was insisting on a '9 and 0' formula, rather than a '9 and 1'; that is nine republics could form a union as equal partners, but there must be no centre.[39] Significantly, Kravchuk had organised a meeting in Kyiv on 18 April between the leaders of Ukraine, the RSFSR, Belarus, Uzbekistan and Kazakhstan to organise a common front in defence of this position, and avoid being bounced by Gorbachev.[40]

Kravchuk, if not duplicitous, was certainly seeking a middle course, but a middle course that split the difference between Gorbachev's demand for a renewed federation with 'a strong centre and strong republics' and strong domestic pressures. These left him insisting that

> if we wish to preserve the Union it can only be as a union of sovereign states. ... We are adopting a clearly radical position. Our aim is not to destroy the Soviet Union, but we don't want to see it once again become a formal union of 'sovereign states' where powerless governments and powerless parliaments would once again be required to rubber-stamp dictates from the centre.[41]

In the face of a call by the Republican Party for a general strike, and student threats to renew hunger strikes if any Union treaty was signed, 345 deputies voted on 27 June to delay any consideration of the Treaty until 15 September, when the Supreme Council of Ukraine was due to reassemble.[42] This represented a victory for the line

Table 8.1   Results of the 17 March 1991 referendum in Ukraine (per cent)

Oblast	Union question	Republican question	Galician question
Galicia			
L'viv	16.4	30.1	90
Ivano-Frankivs'k	18.2	52.1	90
Ternopil'	9.3	35.2	85.3
Volhynia			
Rivne	54.2	79.6	
Volyn'	53.7	78	
Other West			
Transcarpathia	60.1	69.5	
Chernivtsi	80.8	83.2	
Left Bank			
Kyiv (city)	44.6	77.8	
Kyiv (*oblast*)	66.9	84.6	
Kharkiv	75.8	83.8	
Poltava	78.8	88.7	
Sumy	78.8	87.1	
Chernihiv	83.3	90.3	
Right Bank			
Kirovohrad	82.4	89.5	
Cherkasy	77.3	88.8	
Vinnytsia	81.2	89.2	
Zhytomyr	81.7	88.4	
Khmel'nyts'kyi	87.8	87.9	
East			
Donets'k	84.8	88.2	
Luhans'k	86.3	88.9	
Zaporizhzhia	79.8	86.8	
Dnipropetrovs'k	77.5	85.1	
South			
Mykolaïv	85.2	87.7	
Kherson	81.4	87.4	
Odesa	82.15	84.5	
Crimea	87.6	84.7	
Total	70.5	80.18	88.43

83 per cent of those eligible to vote took part.

Source: Electoral Commission, official results.

pursued by Kravchuk and the deputy chairman of the Supreme Council, Ivan Pliushch, over Hurenko's desire to lock Ukraine into the treaty at an early stage.

Kravchuk was able to take this line because the previously mono-lithic unity of the hardline CPU 'Group of 239' in the Supreme Council began to disintegrate in Spring 1991, and a centrist alliance started to replace it as the dominant force. (Of the 450 deputies elected in 1990, 373 had been members of the CPSU/CPU, but this numerical dominance was much reduced by later defections and the *de facto* existence of a large bloc of independents. The term 'Group of 239' had therefore referred to the hardcore CPU majority revealed in controversial votes such as the 17 November 1990 decision to wave Stepan Khmara's parliamentary immunity.)[43] By June 1991, Kravchuk could claim that 'in practical terms ... this group [the '239'] no longer exists. In essence, it has liquidated itself'.[44]

The increasing bifurcation of the CPU was also apparent beyond the Supreme Council. On 15 June an open letter from CPU dissidents styling themselves 'Initiative Group-91' appeared in *Ternopil' Vechirnii*. It attacked the party as 'the main obstacle to democracy and social progress ... [and] to the independence of Ukraine' and called 'for the split of the Communist Party of Ukraine from the CPSU, for its complete independence, and for its transformation into a Social Democratic parliamentary party'.[45] The growing climate of disillusion with the party had reportedly reduced its ranks from 3.5 to 2.5 million, with many more not paying their dues.[46] On the other hand, Hurenko was still defending 'the socialist choice' and attacking the opposition for 'always nudging Kravchuk' away from Communist orthodoxy.[47]

NATIONAL COMMUNISM

There were several reasons for this development. Before 1990, power had clearly been concentrated in the hands of the CPU central com-mittee-ministerial nexus. (In so far as any real power had been devolved to Ukraine – see Chapter 1.) A formal separation of powers had existed, but the legislature and courts had a purely decorative role. The old system was not replaced overnight in March 1990, but slowly gave way to an institutional pluralism, in which party, minister-ial, legislative and eventually presidential structures competed for influence, without any of them being hegemonic. (This inevitably also meant a highly chaotic and inefficient system of government.)

A crucial fault-line then developed within the CPU majority, between those who belonged primarily to the party *apparat* and those who belonged to state or economic institutions, with the latter group, as argued in Chapter 1, being more susceptible to 'national communism'.

According to Mark Beissinger, the behaviour of republican elites in the former Soviet Union can be analysed in terms of three alternative rational-technical, patronage and authority-building models.[48] All three, under given conditions, would predict growing tendencies towards national communism, particularly among state officials. Rational-technical theory would argue that the system of *nomenklatura* – the selection of leadership cadres according to ideologial loyalties – had to be increasingly supplemented by the co-optation of specialist elites for efficiency reasons. The system is then progressively subject to the priority of technical over political objectives, and even the importation of nationalist ideologies, in so far as rational-technical elites will reflect the culture of the society from which they are drawn. Such technocrats will then seek to gain personal control over their own activities, given that they will tend to assume that such areas should be regulated by their own professional competence, rather than by political interference from above.

Given the absence of professional organisations or true pressure groups in the former USSR, the only way to make such an assertion of professional independence was through Union-republican structures, rather than at the lower level of individual enterprises and institutions. Additionally, as the Soviet economy and ministry system descended into utter chaos in 1990–1, it became rational for rational-technical elites to seek to escape from the all-Union system as part of an elementary exercise in crisis management. Some may have sought to evade past traditions of vertical control altogether. Some may have hoped to re-establish subsidies, and the inter-enterprise exchanges without which the Soviet economy could not function at a republican level. Some thought that a sovereign Ukrainian government would be easier to influence and control.

As the Soviet economy began to slow, and eventually to shrink in 1990–1, it also became rational for local elites to seek an expanded role for local political institutions, in order to compete more effectively in a zero-sum struggle over diminishing resources.[49] Such Ukrainian elites were represented in the Supreme Council of Ukraine by the 67 members of the 'industrial *apparat*', i.e. mainly enterprise managers; the 44 members of the 'agricultural *apparat*', or mainly collective farm chairmen; and the 16 members of the 'institutions *apparat*', that is representatives of scientific or cultural institutions.[50] Increasingly through spring 1991, this group supported aggressive state-building measures, which it perceived as likely to serve its own interest. Key figures in this group were Vasyl' Ievtukhov, head of the so-called 'industrial faction', Leonid Kuchma, head of the Pivdenmash rocket factory, and Volodymyr Slednev, director of a metallurgy complex in Donets'k.[51] Thus, for example, the vote to establish a national Ukrainian bank in April 1991, on a platform of establishing a Ukrainian currency, and the June declaration of control over all Soviet enterprises on Ukrainian territory were measures first and foremost promoted by the 'industrial faction'.

Patronage, or patron–client networks, could logically strengthen either integrative or centrifugal forces, depending on whether the most important circles of patronage existed at a republican or an all-Union level. Traditionally, Ukrainians' status as 'younger brothers' meant that considerable channels of opportunity were open to them at an all-Union level. This was often a deliberate tactic to ensure the loyalty of Ukrainians to the imperial system, and also to remove many of the more active and ambitious elements from Ukrainian territory.[52] Ivashko's departure to Moscow in July 1990 exemplifies this trend.

Although the upper reaches of the CPSU became increasingly Russified under Gorbachev, it largely remained true that a majority of CPU party officials continued to see their career progression in an all-Union context.[53] Few in the CPU central committee sought to cut ties with Moscow in the manner of the Lithuanian CP. The 1990 CPU programme stated that, 'while assigning importance to the widening of the independence of the Communist Party of Ukraine, we at the same time consider that it must be dialectically unified with the strengthened international, principled and organisational unity of the CPSU'.[54]

However, the all-Union logic that continued to dominate in party structures was of decreasing importance in state or economic structures. As argued in Chapter 1, the logic of 'national communism' was primarily one of the incubation of nationally-minded elites in *state* structures, who then sought to gain power over their own societies whenever the imperial centre contracted. The elections of 1990, and the declining authority of central ministries (and their simple inability to deliver resources), further encouraged this increasing separation of party and state. State institutions sought to invest themselves with the power they had lacked in the past – and enterprises increasingly came to rely on horizontal supply links between themselves, rather than on traditional vertical lines of authority.

As Kravchuk became an increasingly aggressive spokesman for Ukrainian interests, others hitched themselves to his bandwagon, such as his deputy as Supreme Council chairman, Leonid Pliushch, and other powerful figures on the Presidium, including Mykola Khomenko, head of the parliamentary secretariat, Anatolii Chypurnyi, of the agriculture committee, Vasyl Riabokon of the deputies' ethics committee, and (at a later stage) Anatolii Matvienko of the youth committee. Such allies, along with the People's Council representatives, gave Kravchuk a majority on the Presidium, while Khomenko and Pliushch were especially useful in helping Kravchuk manipulate what was after all a very inexperienced parliament.

Most importantly, however, authority-building strategies led to national communism. Competitive republican elections in conditions where alternative focal points for organisation, such as class, were not available (see Chapter 1), meant that authority-seeking republican elites had to ground their appeals in the myths and symbols of populist nationalism. Thus, by mid-1991, it was Kravchuk, as much as the opposition, who was reviving the cultural discourse of national moral patrimony, in preparation for his presidential bid in the autumn.

In July 1991, for example, Kravchuk referred in a speech at the Palace of Culture to the present day as Ukraine's *third* attempt to establish national independence in the modern era (after Khmelnytskyi in 1648, and the hitherto officially reviled Ukrainian People's Republic of 1917–21.)[55] On 18 June *Radio Kyiv* announced that 16 July would be celebrated as a public holiday and Ukraine's Day of *Independence* (not just sovereignty), replacing 'USSR Constitution Day'.

The logic of national communism was thus playing itself out. The failure of the centre to recentralise while this was perhaps still possible, in 1990 or early 1991, meant that centrifugal forces were close to attaining critical mass. Moreover, the failure to overthrow the governments of the Baltic republics in January, and the second big wave of Ukrainian miners' strikes in March 1991, and the apparent rapprochement of the national movement and the working class that followed, had reduced the CPU's options and made a conservative programme less feasible.

STATE-BUILDING MEASURES

Meanwhile, the Supreme Council, although not yet prepared to fully overhaul the constitution, took the initial decision on 21 May to establish a presidential form of government for the republic, whose name, state symbols, and exact form of administration were to be decided by referendum, as was the question of whether the future state would maintain its 'socialist choice' (the referendum plans were subsequently overtaken by the August events.)[56] Clearly, an executive presidency would be used to strengthen the position of Kravchuk, but the People's Council also supported such moves in so far as Kravchuk was beginning to adopt their policies, and because they saw a more powerful presidency as the best means of circumventing the hardliners in the CPU (previously the president had only chaired the Presidium, real power lying elsewhere with the first secretary of the CPU).

A federal form of government within Ukraine was rejected, and local councils were to be transformed by having their elected chairmen function simultaneously as presidential plenipotentiaries. The Law on the Presidency eventually adopted on 5 July gave the President the power to issue decrees and to reorganise the government (Article 7), although not to dissolve the Supreme Council of Ukraine, or veto its laws (Article 5). The President could not 'be a people's deputy, or occupy any [other] position in state organs or social organisations' [i.e. political parties] (Article 2).[57] The first such Executive President would be chosen in direct elections on 1 December.

The new President would be able to take a more active role in pushing for additional state-building measures to those already adopted. By July, more than thirty[58] laws had already been passed to give substance to the Declaration of Sovereignty, including the May streamlining of the Ukrainian government, the nationalisation of the metallurgy and coal-mining industries in June, the election of Volodymyr Matviienko as chairman of a newly created Ukrainian National Bank in June on a platform of introducing a Ukrainian currency, and the June declarations asserting control over all Soviet enterprises on Ukrainian territory and claiming for the Ukrainian government the sole right to levy taxes on its territory.

At this stage, however, such declarations often had only symbolic affect, as shown by the fact that similar, but more effective, measures were passed in the wake of the failed August coup.

Ukraine also sought to expand its sovereignty by a series of bilateral agreements with other Soviet republics (most importantly, with the

RSFSR on 19 November 1990)[59] and neighbouring states, including Hungary in September and Poland in October 1990.[60]

Ukrainian economic policy had also become increasingly nationalist and protectionist since the adoption of the 'Pylypchuk-Fokin programme' on 1 October 1990. This introduced a system of coupons (paid with salaries) that had to be used in parallel to roubles for the purchase of most goods and services. This was designed to prevent Ukrainian products leaving Ukraine, as was the introduction of a licence system on 10 April 1991 for the 'export' of all consumer goods. In the summer, the government introduced measures to prevent the sale of grain to other republics and introduced patrols on the republic's borders to enforce the measures (although never in sufficient numbers.)[61]

MOVES TOWARDS A CENTRIST COALITION

The other side to the equation concerning the possibility of a centrist alliance was the People's Council. The March 1990 elections had given the opposition a foothold in power for the first time, and in retrospect created the first real opportunity for co-operation with reform-minded elements in the CPU. (Such a combination was less feasible when the opposition was confined to the streets.) Practical co-operation within the unicameral Supreme Council of Ukraine, where deputies are seated alphabetically and by region, also had its effect.

At the same time, the best strategy for the People's Council itself seemed to be the pursuit of an alliance with 'national communists' in the CPU. The People's Council itself was by 1991 divided into four main groups, consisting of the 36 members and supporters of the Party of Democratic Revival (PDRU), the 26 claimed by the Democratic Party,[62] the radical *Nezalezhnist'* group dominated by the Republican Party's 11 deputies, and the rest as nominal independents.[63] The radicals, however, were often marginalised, or in disarray. The Khmara affair had forced the Republican Party into an isolated position in his defence. The Inter-Party Assembly had begun to splinter, with many of its founder members leaving, and the radical nationalist movement in general developing extreme fissiparous tendencies. On the other hand, the defection of the PDRU from the CPU in mid-1990 had both strengthened the position of the centrists on the People's Council, and provided it with valuable leadership and a crucial bridge to the national communists with whom the PDRU had been closely associated.

Moreover, the results of the 1990 republican elections, largely confirmed by the March 1991 referendum (see above), indicated that opposition forces did not yet enjoy a natural electoral majority, even if a trend in their favour was detectable. The People's Council, therefore, pursued a strategy of pushing Kravchuk to take state-building measures on its behalf. In this respect, the continued campaign of public demonstrations, resumed again on a large scale in spring 1991 (people remained more passive in winter in Ukraine), helped to maintain the psychological pressure on the CPU, as did the strike wave in March.[64] No one demonstration was ever crucial in itself, but their cumulative effect was to indicate to potential 'national communists' that the key to any future authority-building strategy would be the co-optation of national myths and symbols.

'INTERFRONTS' AND MINERS' STRIKES

Conservative communists in the Baltic republics had based their survival strategies on creating 'interfronts' to drive a wedge between indigenous intelligentsias with programmes of national cultural and linguistic revival, and a largely Russian working class of recent immigration, susceptible to populist appeals concerning the threat of nativisation and factory closure. The social structure of Ukraine, however, as indicated in Chapter 2, was not fertile ground for such a policy (74 per cent of the working class was Ukrainian as early as 1970, and Russians and Ukrainians were much closer linguistically and culturally than Russians and Balts).[65] Ukraine's Russians, even when in-migrants, were joining a Russian community with deep historical roots in Ukraine rather than being settlers in a hostile community, as in the Baltics and Moldova (the Crimea is an exception here, hence later problems).

Attempts were nevertheless repeatedly made to establish a Ukrainian interfront, and to play up minority or Russian discontents, particularly in Crimea, and Transcarpathia.[66] Anti-*Rukh* rallies were organised in Kyiv on 12 and 20 November.[67] However, such efforts had limited success. The 1989 Ukrainian Languages Law was as yet a paper tiger, and fears of 'Ukrainisation' difficult to stimulate. Most importantly, the Baltic interfronts were established to oppose governments already dominated by nationalists, whereas in Ukraine the national communists seemed likely to keep power themselves. It was therefore illogical for all but hardline communists to support such populist movements. Interfronts only began to take off after the autumn of 1991 and the Ukrainian Declaration of Independence and banning of the CPU, when they seemed the only way for many *local* elites to ensure their survival.

The miners' strikes of March 1991 had in fact revealed a level of political radicalisation wholly absent in 1989. If anything, their demands were over-politicised and unrealistic: the resignation of Gorbachev, the dissolution of the all-Union Congress of People's Deputies and the granting of constitutional status to Ukraine's Declaration of Sovereignty over and above their economic demands.[68] Such radicalisation indicated that the most organised sections of the working class were not yet promising material for a populist appeal.

The strikes themselves, however, were a relative failure, revealing a lack of organisation and co-ordination with the broader opposition movement.[69] As in 1989–90, working class living conditions were sufficiently appalling to persistently create outbreaks of unrest, but a lack of social cohesion always meant that the organisations thrown up by the unrest soon went into decline, or began to splinter. Ukraine is not mono-ethnic, and lacked the Catholic Church that had underpinned Solidarity in Poland.

The strikes' disorganisation, however, led to a post-mortem round table of union and opposition leaders at Pavlohrad in May[70] and the subsequent inaugural congress of the 'All-Ukrainian Union of Workers' Solidarity' (VOST) in Kyiv on 21–23 June.[71] Three hundred and thirteen delegates claiming to represent 1–3 million Ukrainian workers,[72] adopted a highly radical platform, and elected the Donets'k miner Oleksandr Ivashchenko as leader.[73] VOST self-consciously styled itself on Poland's Solidarity movement, and formed a 'Consultative Council' of political advisers, dominated by radicals such as Stepan Khmara and Larysa Skoryk, in the hope that the long period when the intelligentsia-led national movement and the unions developed largely in isolation was coming to an end.

However, the moderates on the People's Council maintained their distance from the workers' movement, as they courted the CPU's 'national communists', while council leaders such as Chornovil continued to condemn strikes as a 'stab in the back to democracy'.[74] VOST's alliance with radicals (from the Republican Party, and even Inter-Party Assembly) was therefore something of a blind alley, and an obstacle to the organisation's further growth. VOST was as much a street-based protest movement as a workplace trades union. Tensions also remained in the Donbas with the all-Union 'Independent Miners Union', denounced by Skoryk as 'clearly a new imperial connivance'.[75] The official trades unions, although discredited, also proved difficult to displace, given their control over many welfare benefits, sanatoria and so on.

CONCLUSION

Hence on the eve of the August coup attempt, the national communists were clearly gathering strength. The possibilities for a conservative counterattack had been weakened by the half hearted assault on the Baltic republics in January, the continuing decline of the imperial centre, and the apparent *rapprochement* between the opposition and the working class. In retrospect it is clear that the coup attempt came too late. The slippage of power to the republics, and their leaderships' reorientation towards their own national electorates had gone too far.

9 From Soviet to Independent Ukraine: The Coup and Aftermath

THE VIEW FROM THE CENTRE

The first draft of the new Union Treaty was heavily criticised for devolving too little power from the centre to the republics. Only nine republics participated in its discussion. Gorbachev hoped to speed up the adoption of a new Union Treaty by holding the referendum on a 'renewed federation' in March 1991. Of the nine republics which had participated in the new Union Treaty discussions, Ukraine and Azerbaidzhan added a second question in the March 1991 referendum calling for a 'renewed confederation'. The three Baltic states had declared independence and refused to recognise the new law on secession. Georgia and Armenia agreed to hold referendums on independence in March and September 1991 while Moldova refused to participate in the Union Treaty discussions.

Despite the outcome of the March 1991 referendum the republics steadfastly stuck to their demands for a Soviet confederation. By May 1991 the republics were being termed 'sovereign states' while Gorbachev dropped his earlier insistence that autonomous republics be granted the same status as republics in the new Union Treaty. Those outside the new Union Treaty though would be subject to *de facto* economic blockade and pressure, especially *vis-à-vis* energy supplies. The republics, however, ensured that the new Soviet confederation would be built from the bottom up through proposals advanced by the republics.

The August 1991 putsch changed the balance of power between the centre and periphery completely. Yeltsin, after defeating Gorbachev, allied Russia with the Soviet centre in a last ditch attempt to save the Union (in contrast to his alliance with the republics against the centre prior to August 1991). Yeltsin assumed that Russia would, of course, 'naturally' rule the USSR through a new confederation.

The new draft Union Treaty therefore began to look increasingly unpalatable to the non-Russians who interpreted the defeat of the August 1991 putsch differently: 'To the Russians, it meant a historic "democratic defeat" of the communists. To non-Russians, it signified an open Russian hegemony over the nations of the multi-national country in which they all lived.'[1]

The main problem remained Ukraine. It had declared independence and was gearing up to a referendum, which many Russians, Gorbachev especially, could not believe would obtain 50 per cent of the vote, let alone two-thirds. They pinned their hopes on eastern-southern Ukraine and the Crimea. Both Gorbachev and Yeltsin, therefore, badly misjudged the domestic evolution of events within Ukraine after August 1991.

The new Union Treaty was to be signed on 25 November 1991 by Russia, Belarus, Kazakhstan and the four Central republics as well as the Soviet centre. But there still remained considerable disagreement between Yeltsin and Gorbachev over whether the new Union of Sovereign States would be a loose union or a new state. The signing ceremony was therefore postponed to give a chance to the republican parliaments to discuss the issue further. The demand for a confederation would have made Gorbachev, or any Soviet president, into a *de facto* puppet of the republics. The republics therefore demanded their own citizenship, control over their own territory and governments but accepted integrated armed forces. The republics would become sovereign subjects of international law. Those that refused to join the new Union of Sovereign States would be regarded as having seceded and liable to follow the law on secession adopted earlier that year.[2]

The Ukrainian referendum result of 90 per cent in favour of secession on 1 December 1991 sealed the fate of the USSR.[3] Nevertheless, even after the creation of the Commonwealth of Independent States (CIS) on 7–8 December 1991 Yeltsin still believed that Ukraine would opt to remain in a CIS confederation. As Yeltsin said five years later: 'Yes, I was very much upset, because I did not want the Union to fall apart ... to say at that time that I wished for disintegration is not, and, I repeat not, the case.' As for the CIS accords, Yeltsin regarded them, as, 'a sort of attempt to salvage at least something you know. We had to prevent the republics running away from each other for good.'[4] Ukraine and Russia, or to be more precise Kravchuk and Yeltsin, therefore entered the post-Soviet era with vastly different interpretations of what the CIS was meant to be – a mechanism for 'civilised divorce' or the Union of Sovereign States minus the Soviet centre, but dominated by Russia.

THE VIEW FROM UKRAINE

From 19 to 21 August Ukraine was rocked by the *coup d'état* that was designed to forestall the Union treaty, which Ukraine had ironically already indicated it would not yet be a party to. Although the People's Council and nearly all political parties immediately condemned the coup, Kravchuk equivocated, and it seemed for a time that the 'national communists' were reverting to type. However, in the aftermath of the coup's failure and the collapse of the old imperial centre, the logic of national communism reasserted itself with a vengeance, and virtually the entire CPU threw in its lot with the opposition, as the only way to save their skins. This resulted in Ukraine's Declaration of Ukrainian Independence by 346 votes to 1, and the adoption of a range of other radical measures from 24 August onwards.

Not all in the CPU were, of course, sufficiently flexible to make the necessary political mutations, resulting in the creation of a Socialist Party of Ukraine, in opposition to the national communist-nationalist alliance.

THE COUP IN UKRAINE

Kravchuk was first informed of the coup at 6.30 on the morning of 19 August by General Chichevatov, commander of the Kyiv military district.[5] Kravchuk later claimed to have phoned Yeltsin on his way to the Supreme Council, and agreed that neither would recognise the junta, but this was not made public at the time.[6] At 9 a.m. Kravchuk, along with Hurenko, met with the junta's representative, General Varennikov, who threatened the extension of the state of emergency to Ukraine if there was any resistance to the junta. Kravchuk had refused Varennikov's request to meet in the central committee of the CPU, saying that real power in Ukraine lay with the Supreme Council, and reportedly resisted pressure to commit himself to the junta.[7] At 11 a.m., however, a delegation from the People's Council was rebuffed by Kravchuk, when it asked him to condemn the coup.[8]

Meanwhile, *Rukh* and most political parties had rushed out statements condemning the plotters. The Democratic Party called on the population to 'be prepared for an all-Ukrainian strike and other acts of civil disobedience', the Republican Party for 'all party organisations to organise open party meetings in the streets, squares and factories', and condemned the attempt 'to start a civil war in the republics'. The PDRU more soberly called 'on all citizens of Ukraine to maintain calm ... [and] not to engage in any provocation'.[9] *Rukh*'s call for a general strike was even published in *Vechirnii Kyïv* on the 20th. In western Ukraine a 'people's guard' (*L'vivs'ka varta*) which had been used to steward *Rukh* demonstrations, had already drawn up plans to launch a mass political strike, defend postal, telephone and local-authority buildings, and blockade train stations, airports and import-ant roads in the event of martial law.[10]

On Ukrainian television at 4 p.m., Kravchuk appealed for Ukrainians to be 'calm and patient', but, while stressing that the state of emergency did not apply in Ukraine, he neither condemned nor condoned the coup.[11] On Soviet television that evening, his statement that 'what has happened was bound to happen' was more compromis-ing, although he later claimed that his remarks were censored.

During a 'turbulent and fruitless' meeting of the Presidium from 6 to 9 p.m., Kravchuk blocked attempts by Iukhnovskyi, Taniuk, Iemets, Pavlychko and Iavorivskyi both to condemn the plotters and to call an emergency session of the Supreme Council.[12] According to deputy Serhii Holovatyi, meanwhile, Ievhen Marchuk and then Deputy Prime Minister Vitalii Masyk along with various Presidium members had set up the necessary structures to implement the junta's orders in Ukraine.[13] Ukraine's press published all the junta's decla-rations, and Iukhnovskyi later listed all those who had collaborated with the junta at a local level.[14]

On the 20th the deadlock continued as Kravchuk continued to wait on news from Moscow. After an all-day meeting, 15 out of 25 members of the Presidium voted for a statement which stressed that the Ukrainian constitution remained in force and restated Ukraine's defence of her sovereignty, but stopped short of actually opposing the junta. Kravchuk had again prevaricated on the calling of an emer-gency session of Parliament (and stonewalled again when visited by Grinev, Iemets and Iukhnovskyi at 3 a.m. at the height of the events outside the Moscow White House), and prevented Iavorivskyi's state-ment of support for Yeltsin from even being discussed.[15] The national communists on the Presidium, in other words, were inching back towards the People's Council, but were still waiting to see how the chips would fall in Moscow.

Rukh and the political parties, which had already met in the Writers' Union building on the 19th, formed a coalition for an 'Independent Democratic Ukraine' and at 6 p.m. called for an all-Ukrainian strike to begin at noon the next day (although the opposition's ability to organise one was never put to the test).

Kravchuk only came off the fence on the 21st, when it was clear the coup was failing, and after the necessary 150 signatures had been collected to force his hand and call an emergency session of the Supreme Council. (The signatories included 57 non-Party deputies, and 30 members of the CPU, indicating that national communists like Salii and Ievtukhov were beginning to raise their heads again.)[16] Kravchuk contacted Yury Lukianov, chairman of the Moscow Supreme Soviet, condemned the unconstitutionality of the coup, and demanded the return of Gorbachev to Moscow. On television, Kravchuk stated 'the so-called emergency committee ... no longer exists ... and actually never existed. This was a deviation from the democratic process, from the constitution and the legal process.'[17]

The People's Council now had the initiative, and on Thursday the 22nd the Presidium voted 15–11 to call the emergency session on the 24th, and in the working group set up to prepare an agenda leading opposition figures, such as Taniuk and Iemets, were prominent.[18] The People's Council asked for a demonstration outside parliament in support of their agenda on the 24th.[19]

DECLARATION OF INDEPENDENCE

On 24 August, Kravchuk survived calls for his departure by resigning from his positions in the CPSU/CPU (and from the Party altogether on the 27th) and moving swiftly to support the opposition's agenda. Even before the key notes, he was talking of his desire to see Ukraine 'turned into a truly independent sovereign state'.[20]

The resignation of 20 further national communist deputies from the CPU deprived the 'Group of 239' of the voting majority they had hitherto possessed (half the total of 450 deputies), and with the CPU discredited and in disarray, the majority traded support for Ukrainian independence for the maximum possible salvation of CPU influence.

Most importantly, by 346 votes to 1 (Albert Korneev' a Russian member of the CPU from Donets'k) the Supreme Council voted to declare Ukrainian independence. The Act stated that 'In view of the deadly threat posed to our country on the night of 18–19 August, and continuing the thousand year old tradition of state-building in Ukraine ... the Supreme Council solemnly proclaims the Independence of Ukraine ... The territory of Ukraine is indivisible and inviolable. From now on only the Constitution and laws of Ukraine will be in force on its territory'.[21] This Declaration of Independence was subject to a referendum to be held on 1 December, the same day as the presidential elections already scheduled.

By 331 votes to 10, the Supreme Council also voted to remove political parties from the KGB, Ministry of Internal Affairs, and Prosecutor's Office, and 321 voted to remove parties from all state structures, television and radio, and enterprises 'at the discretion of work collectives'.[22] By 256 to 13 all armed forces on Ukrainian territory were to pass under Ukrainian control, and a Minister of Defence was to be created,[23] and 328 voted to introduce a Ukrainian currency.[24] Kravchuk's *volte-face* was rewarded by granting him emergency powers, with opposition members such as Ivan Zaiets and Mykola Porovskyi openly stating that such measures were conditional on Kravchuk using them for the further building of Ukrainian statehood.[25]

Just as interesting, however, were the measures that failed to get a majority. A more radical proposal for sweeping compulsory removal of political parties from all state organs and enterprises failed, with only 217 votes, and a call to prevent the destruction of incriminating documents received only by 177.[26]

Events continued to move rapidly. As evidence accumulated concerning the CPU's complicity in the coup, and Russia banned the Communist Party outright, the CPU had its assets frozen by the Presidium on the 25th, was 'suspended' on the 26th and was banned on the 30th. Moroz, who on the 24th had announced that if the Central Committee 'did not declare the autonomy of Ukraine's Communists, I will take the responsibility onto myself to organise a Ukrainian Communist party',[27] officially dissolved the CPU majority in the Supreme Council on 4 September.

The vote for secession left Ukraine independent – but still primarily under national communist control. The exceptions were areas controlled by democratic councils, in particular western Ukraine, where the old structures had been progressively dismantled since the victory of the Democratic Bloc in the March 1990 elections.

The attempt to isolate Ukraine from anti-communist, democratic influences emanating from the RSFSR, as well as the radicalisation of public opinion and the contrast between Kravchuk's and Yeltsin's actions both during and after the coup, now made national communism the only feasible survival option for the CPU.

Ironically, the CPU was now less interested in any Union treaty with Yeltsin's democratic RSFSR (or that proposed by Gorbachev at the USSR Supreme Soviet). The only way, they believed, that they could maintain power and some degree of influence, even after the CPU was suspended, would be by going it alone. This danger – 'the possibility of the Albanian variant in Ukraine: the CPU having a majority in Parliament and remaining the most reactionary force that will attempt to "build" Communism in a separate state'[28] – had long been considered dangerous by some of the opposition. On the 24th, Taras Stetskiv had warned against 'Ukraine becoming a game reserve of Communism'.[29] Iukhnovskyi had outlined Ukraine's dilemma – either to press for independence first and foremost, or to copy Yeltsin and place decommunisation at the top of the agenda.[30]

Most members of the opposition had clearly shown their preference for the former route, though the PDRU's liberals preferred the latter. As argued throughout this book, the nationalists had always needed an alliance with the national communists to secure their aims. With the majority of, or at least the commanding heights of, the ex-CPU now in the national communist camp, nearly all political forces in Ukraine were working towards independence, and this was likely to prove an unstoppable force. An atavistic minority however remained.

THE COMMUNISTS' SUCCESSORS

The Supreme Council Presidium banned the CPU on 30 August, despite the Central Committee of the CPU attempting to forestall the decision by declaring the autonomy of the party on the 26th.[31] Its considerable assets were frozen, until a decree on 20 December transferred all of its property to the state.[32] However, Oleksandr Moroz, following his declaration of intent on 24 August, established an organising committee for a successor party as early as 18 September, under 'the working name of the Party of Social Progress'.[33]

After a series of regional conferences, the party was reborn as the Socialist Party of Ukraine (SPU) on 26 October in Kyiv.[34] Moroz was elected leader, and claimed a membership of 60 000, making the party again the largest in Ukraine (in reality, this was closer to 30 000 but the next largest, the Republican Party, still had only 10 000 members.). Although over 100 Supreme Council deputies still supported hard-left positions only those were prepared to join the Socialists openly.[35] Moroz however deliberately did not ask senior figures from the old CPU onto the SPU's leading organs. He sought a new image for the party, and, in any case, most of the old establishment was now support-ing Kravchuk.

Instead, the party represented middle-ranking apparatchiks con-cerned for their privileges, as well as a hard-core atavistic element such as Professor Viktor Orlov of the Higher Party School, 'who is remembered for stating at one of the plenums of Ukraine's Communist Party that he was ready to take up a Kalashnikov machinegun to protect the system'.[36] Only 42 of the 287 delegates were under 35.[37] Moroz steered the Congress away from calls to boycott the December referendum and presidential election, and to declare the SPU the legal successor to the CPU.

His strategy was instead to copy the Polish Communist party, and create an economically populist party to capitalise on the inevitable hardship and unemployment created by economic reforms. By the new year, the SPU was already denouncing 'speculation' and posing as the defender of the common man.[38] As the economic situation contin-ued to worsen, there was every sign that such a strategy could bring considerable success, especially as the national communist-nationalist alliance preferred to concentrate on defence and state-building mea-sures, rather than on practical economic reforms.

The SPU's statute, although declaring itself a parliamentary party, retained certain Communist Party practices by talking only of the right to 'unite in platforms', but not to form fractions within the party, and proposing that party cells be formed in workplaces, as well as on the territorial principle.[39]

On 25 January 1992 a rural equivalent to the SPU, the Peasants' Party, was formed in Kherson by representatives of the collective farm *nomenklatura*, and the agro-industrial complex, one of whom, Serhii Dovhan', was elected leader.[40] The Minister of Agriculture, Oleksandr Tkachenko, was a member of the council, and the party's guiding force (Tkachenko's alliance with Morov could be seen in his pro-motion to the post of deputy chairman to the Ukrainian parliament after March 1994). The party was established to oppose Plachynda's radical Ukrainian Peasants' Democratic party and preserve the rural privileges of the old *apparat*, although not necessarily by obstructing land privatisation, as its members were the most likely purchasers.

RED ENTREPRENEURS

Whereas some former communists joined the SPU, others transferred capital into joint and business ventures. According to evidence given to the parliamentary commission on the nationalisation of the property of the CPU and *Komsomol*, from January to August 1991 the central committee of the CPU passed 19 935 000 roubles to its local branches in order to establish small and joint ventures, stock exchanges and other economic spheres of activity.[41] Again, civil society was still too weak. Few 'new' businessmen were genuinely new. Most came from the old *apparat*, as only they had the capital and the contacts to take advantage of new opportunities.

Much of the money was deposited in and/or used to open co-operatives, banks, small enterprises and commercial associations. The commercial bank '*Ukrinbank*', for example, had over 40 million roubles on deposit from the CPU. The parliamentary commission found 37 examples of the CPU organising small enterprises to the tune of nearly 9 million roubles. Often the CPU would finance the starting capital for brokers' offices in the regional commodity exchanges. The CPU also invested funds into foreign trade associations, such as 'Zhoda'.

The purpose of this was to launder CPU funds into commercial and business ventures in order to both control the newly emerging private sector and hide the large amount of funds creamed over the years from the state. As the former first secretary of the L'viv *oblast* CPU, Sekretariuk, told his members: 'as long as there's an *apparat*, there's a Party'.[42] Often former high-ranking members of the CPU would become directors of factories, or presidents of banks and foreign trade associations, claiming that they had resigned from the CPU, but, in reality, continuing secretly to pay their membership dues.[43]

Two business lobbies, the Congress of Business Circles of Ukraine formed in September 1991[44] (which aspired to become a Ukrainian equivalent of the Confederation of British Industry) and the Ukrainian League of Businesses with Foreign Capital formed on 16 November,[45] had strong links with the old *apparat*, and helped fund the Kravchuk presidential campaign.

The more radical parties therefore, such as the Republican Party were soon attacking '*nomenklatura* privatisation' and the *apparat*'s renewed 'control of the national wealth'.[46] Despite the Republican Party's (and *Rukh*'s) supposed free market ideology, their populist economic rhetoric began to echo that of the SPU. This was especially true of radical right parties.

Disillusion with the slow pace of economic reform and continued *nomenklatura* domination of industry led to the formation of the PDRU-business group 'New Ukraine' as a liberal economic reform lobby and potential 'shadow cabinet' in January, however.[47] Fifty-eight deputies had signed 'new Ukraine's' founding statement by 15 March 1992.[48] Whilst the nationalists in the Republican and Democratic parties, and the *Rukh* leadership (Chornovil excepted) moved closer to support Kravchuk after his 1 December victory (see below), the 'New Ukraine' lobby kept its distance and remained in opposition to the national communists. New Ukraine would become the basis for Leonid Kuchma's 'Party of Power' after he defeated Kravchuk in the summer 1994 presidential elections.

STATE-BUILDING MEASURES

The dominance of the nationalist-national communist alliance was apparent after the Supreme Council reassembled on 4 September, and during its fourth (autumn) session, and set about giving substance to the Declaration of Independence. Outside observers were surprised at the priority given to military and state-building measures over economic reforms, largely delayed until Spring 1992, but Ukraine's leaders were only following Lenin's dictum that the first task in a revolutionary situation is to secure power. Moreover, Kravchuk and the former opposition both subscribed to the view that Ukraine's independence bid in 1917–20 had failed because of the lack of adequate armed forces. Ukraine's new elites had first to secure Ukraine's statehood in order to take control over their own society, and therefore concentrated on measures to this effect, including a Law on State Frontiers on 5 November,[49] and a draft Citizenship Law.[50]

Because the process of creating an independent state was largely controlled by the national communists, the new state was often simply built on the old. Many institutions were simply renamed. For example, the KGB became the 'National Security Service of Ukraine' on 20 September (later the 'National' was dropped).[51] The new head appointed on 6 November, Marchuk, was the old deputy head.[52] The Supreme Council's Committees on Reform of the Security Service, and Defence and State Security, vetted positions in the new service, but the shortage of qualified staff meant that a large proportion came from the old service.

In a similar fashion, the *Komsomol* metamorphosed at its Twenty-Seventh Congress on 21 September into the 'Union of Youth Organisations of Ukraine'.[53] (The *Komsomol*'s contacts with disaffected youth had, however, already led to it distancing itself from the old regime.)

Ukrainian newspapers also changed names, if not character. *Leninskoe znamia* turned into *Narodna armiia* (People's Army) on 12 October, and became the official organ of the new Ukrainian Ministry of Defence, while the CPU stalwart *Radians'ka Ukraïna* became *Demokratychna Ukraïna* on 8 October.

On national symbols, Kravchuk's national communists had to tread a careful path. On the one hand, they were now forced to steal the clothes of the former opposition, in order to create a new national ideology that would legitimate their right to govern. On the other hand, Kravchuk was well aware of the fragile nature of the young state, and was prepared to go slow on the adoption of potentially divisive symbols until the election and referendum campaigns were over. On 17 September, all references to Ukraine's 'socialist choice' were expunged from the constitution, but only 265 voted to fly the blue-and-yellow flag over the Supreme Council building on 4 September,[54] and the adoption of the flag, trident, and national hymn 'Ukraine has not yet died' as the sole official state symbols had to wait until the new year.[55] Even then, 72 voted against the trident, and 70 were against the flag, or abstained.[56] Three-quarters of these were Russian-speaking members of parliament.

There was as yet, however, little constitutional reform to replace the chaotic 'institutional pluralism' described in Chapter 7. Creeping Presidentialism gathered pace after 1 December, but there was still no proper cabinet system of professionalised civil service to replace CPU discipline as a backbone for the state system. In any case, Ukraine's new leaders were unlikely to pay much attention to supplanting the old CPU *apparat* with a professionalised bureaucracy, as the former was the central component of their power base. The new elite was also reluctant to devolve much of its newly won power to institutions such as the National Bank, soon embroiled in political controversy.[57]

In order to build a nation-state however, security issues were of supreme importance.

SECURITY POLICY

The concentration on security measures in Autumn 1991 also reflected a two year campaign for the establishment of Ukrainian armed forces, however. Radical right groups, such as the Ukrainian National Party, had begun to raise the issue as early as autumn 1989, but military disputes only became part of mainstream politics in 1990 with rising controversy over the draft and the use of Soviet troops in nationalist hot-spots outside Ukraine. As stated in Chapter 7, the July 1990 Declaration of Sovereignty had given Ukraine 'the right' to form armed forces. The Supreme Council also responded to controversy over the draft and the campaigning of the Committees of Soldiers' Mothers with a resolution on 30 July 1990 calling on local conscripts to do their service only on Ukraine soil, and a call on 10 October for all conscripts to be returned to Ukraine by 1 December. But, 'unfortunately the mechanism for fulfilling these decrees was not made. The decision remained on paper'.[58]

At two congresses on 27–28 July and 1–2 November 1991, the Union of Officers of Ukraine (UOU) was formed.[59] Having seemed a radical, marginal group in July (the UOU was close to the Republican Party), the November gathering was addressed by the new Ukrainian Minister of Defence. By then, the UOU claimed 25 000 members, and was being consulted on all key legislation, as Ukraine struggled to win the loyalties of those troops deployed on its territory.

The emergency session of the Supreme Council on 24 August 1991 began the process of creating a legal framework for the formation of Ukrainian Armed Forces, as described above.[60] It was swiftly followed by the appointment of Konstantin Morozov, a Russian, to the newly created position of Minister of Defence on 3 September.[61] On 7 September the Presidium responded to rumours of military hardware disappearing to Russia with a decree banning the redeployment of troops and equipment. On 10 September the decree 'On Military Formations of Ukraine' placed all interior troops of the Ministry of Interior, and border troops, their weapons, technology and administrative staff under Ukrainian jurisdiction.[62]

The Cabinet of Ministers decided on 8 October to launch a Ukrainian National Army over the course of two years, with a provisional strength of 450 000 troops. This figure was arrived at simply by taking a supposed European average of 0.8 per cent of the population for the size of a suitable armed force.[63]

A National Guard was established on 4 November, and its commander named as Colonel Volodymyr Kukharets.[64] The first units were 6000-strong, and drawn from Ministry of Interior troops already stationed in Ukraine. A force of 30 000 was envisaged by April 1992, to be armed with requisitioned Ministry of Interior equipment.[65]

After the Supreme Soviet took control of all border guards stationed in Ukraine on 23 October, the Law on State Frontiers of 4 November gave them something to police. The guards, under the command of Valery Hubenko, were to patrol Ukraine's land, sea, air, river and 'economic' frontiers, together with 12 miles of territorial waters.[66]

On 6 December, the Law on Armed Forces and Law on the Defence of Ukraine were passed. Kravchuk then made himself Commander-in-Chief of Ukrainian forces in one of his first decrees on 12 December, which announced the formation of Ukrainian Armed Forces on the basis of the troops of the three Soviet military districts covering Ukrainian territory (Kyiv, Odesa and Transcarpathian), plus the Black Sea Fleet, and 'other military formations deployed on Ukrainian territory', but excepting the strategic forces by then belonging to the CIS.[67] A voluntary oath of loyalty was also prepared for the above troops to swear 'never to betray the Ukrainian people', and administered after 3 January 1992.

Ukraine thus consistently pursued the control of the forces on its territory as its rightful 'inheritance'. However, this obviously led to problems with Russia, as outlined below. Ukraine's right to form its own armed forces was disputed by those who placed a broad interpretation on the notion of CIS control of 'strategic forces', by those who thought that Russia should be the sole inheritor of USSR Armed Forces by right, and by those who simply disliked the idea of Ukraine as a well-armed neighbour.

The one great exception to Ukraine's desire to build a militarily strong state was nuclear weapons. The 1986 Chornobyl' disaster left Ukrainian public opinion profoundly anti-nuclear, and this sentiment had been embodied in the 1990 Declaration of Sovereignty, which committed Ukraine 'not to accept, not to produce and not to acquire nuclear weapons'. This was then reaffirmed by a Declaration of Ukraine's non-nuclear status on 24 October 1991.[68] Ukraine eventually removed all tactical nuclear weapons for destruction by summer 1992, and all strategic weapons by June 1996.

Although *realpolitik* may have indicated that it was irrational for Ukraine to abandon such strategic bargaining chips for no concrete return, only the far right objected at the time. Iurii Shukhevych, leader of the Ukrainian National Assembly (as the Inter-Party Assembly had restyled itself from September 1991), argued in October that nuclear weapons were 'a guarantee of respect' and a defence against 'the territorial pretensions of Russia'.[69] Such pressure was, however, for the time more than counterbalanced by the prestigious Green Party, whose renewed call for Ukraine to respect its non-nuclear commitments in September was echoed by nearly all political parties.[70] The

growing conflict with Russia however would mean that other nationalists, led by the Republicans and Democrats, were close to Shukhevych's
position by Spring 1992.

UKRAINE, RUSSIA AND THE UNION

Ukraine's defence ambitions and independence drive, therefore,
brought it into increasing conflict, first with the old USSR, and then
with Russia.

Ukraine had signed a bilateral agreement with Russia, recognising
each others' sovereignty and inviable borders, as early as 19 November
1990.[71] However, comments by Yeltsin's press secretary in the aftermath of Ukraine's Declaration of Independence that implied Russian
territorial pretensions on the Russian-speaking areas of eastern and
southern Ukraine instantly poisoned the atmosphere. The row was
temporarily defused by a Russian delegation's hastily arranged trip to
Kyiv on 28–29 August, but proved easy to rekindle. The Ukrainian-
Russian border, hotly disputed even under Soviet rule in the 1920s,
had never sharply delineated spheres of influence, and the pressure to
intervene in each other's affairs would remain.

As far as relations with the old centre were concerned, it was clear
from an internal perspective, particularly if one looked at the campaign for the 1 December votes, that Ukraine was heading for full
independence. The fact that Ukraine did not yet make a clean break
with the Union, and continued to toy with some of the ideas emanating from the centre had more to do with the practical difficulties of
disengagement, than with any serious hesitation on Ukraine's part.

Moreover, despite some nationalists voicing the opinion that the
referendum was unnecessary,[72] Kravchuk understood that large sections of Ukrainian society still had to be prepared for the idea of independence, and that forcing the issue would make such groups easy
prey for separatist forces. Kravchuk was also fairly confident that
enough of the old power structures remained to ensure victory after a
careful period of manipulation.

Ukraine therefore blew hot and cold over at least maintaining its
economic links with the old Union. Despite Gorbachev trying to force
the pace on a treaty of economic union, Ukraine sent only observers
to the signing ceremony in Moscow on 18 October. Pliushch argued
that horizontal ties between the republics were more important for
Ukraine, while Kravchuk firmly stated his opposition to the resurrection of traditional vertical channels of control.[73]

Prime Minister Vitold Fokin, on the other hand, as the ex-head of Ukraine's *Gosplan*, was much keener on the concept of maintaining a single economic space. His threats to resign, plus Russian insistence on linking the treaty to a promise to reiterate the November 1990 agreement and respect Ukrainian borders on 6 November,[74] forced the Supreme Council to approve initialling, but not signing, the treaty on the same day, although the People's Council voted against.[75] However, 26 qualifications were added, while Ukraine maintained both that its obligations were contingent on the 1 December result, and that it saw the accord purely instrumentally, as an 'exit towards international co-operation' and as a means of securing international credits.[76] Ukraine had accordingly agreed joint responsibility for the USSR's debt on 28 October.

Ukraine's qualified agreement was probably also a device to forestall pressure towards renewed political union. On 25 October, the Supreme Council resolved against any further participation in interrepublican structures that threatened Ukrainian sovereignty. Henceforth, Ukrainians only attended the USSR Supreme Soviet as 'observers'.[77] Kravchuk was stalling, refusing to consider any new political arrangements until after the 1 December vote, which he hoped would then bury the Union.

Once armed with a 90.3 per cent vote in favour of independence (see below), Kravchuk was able to use the Minsk meeting on 7 and 8 December to trade Ukraine's desire to see the end of the empire for Yeltsin's wish to get rid of Gorbachev by the creation of a Commonwealth of Independent States (CIS) to replace the USSR (Kravchuk claimed the idea had been hatched as long ago as 15 November).[78] Although the former centre was now impotent, it still monopolised the attention of the West, and from Ukraine's perspective, the CIS originally seemed the ideal device to somehow emerge from under its carapace.

The new accord pleased the West, and ditched Gorbachev and the old Union, while its anodyne documents did not restrain Ukraine with any significant obligations. It announced that henceforth 'the USSR as a subject of international law and geopolitical reality ceases its existence'.[79] From the Ukrainian perspective, the republics, rather than the CIS itself, would be its successor states, although the retention of the rouble as a common currency and CIS control over 'strategic' military forces (including all nuclear weapons) was envisaged by the Minsk and Alma-Ata agreements.

In any case, despite ratifying the agreement with 288 votes, the Supreme Soviet added 13 crucial amendments, stressing that 'Ukraine will form its own Armed Forces on the basis of the Armed Forces of the former USSR deployed on its territory', and Ukraine's right to adopt its own currency.[80] Similarly, the Alma Ata accords that completed the CIS's creation on 21 December did not threaten Ukrainian priorities, as the attempt to resurrect an all-CIS conventional armed force was defeated.[81]

Nearly all political forces in Ukraine saw the CIS as instrumental, as a happy solution to the dilemma of 'either Gorbchev, or a civilised form for the collapse of the Union'.[82] By January, when it threatened to become something more, the Republican and Democratic Parties were already calling for Ukraine's departure from the CIS.[83]

This was because the one serious disadvantage for Ukraine of the CIS was that, by removing the centre, Ukraine now stood in direct confrontation with Russia. Firstly, even on the Ukrainian interpretation of the CIS as nothing more than a holding arrangement between successor states, the logic of imperial disentanglement implied a struggle over the division of the resources of the now non-existent centre. Secondly, it soon became clear that it was in Russia's interest to follow a twin-track policy of declaring itself the legal successor to the USSR and/or granting the CIS statehood, and then blurring the two concepts to its own advantage. This was also bound to lead to conflict with Ukraine, as the latter would loose its expected inheritance to the extent to which the USSR's assets (foreign embassies, the Black Sea Fleet)[84] were declared to be 'strategic' and under CIS control.

Kravchuk therefore erred at the Alma-Ata when he conceded the principle of Russia inheriting the USSR's seat on the UN Security Council. Although the PDRU remained in favour of the accord, Ukrainian nationalists were soon arguing that 'it is becoming obvious that, under the abbreviation CIS certain forces are planning the reanimation of the Russian empire'.[85]

REFERENDUM AND PRESIDENTIAL CAMPAIGNS

In order to secure control over their own society, the national communists also had to secure a favourable vote for independence. The fact that both the independence vote and the election of the first Ukrainian executive President were to be held simultaneously on 1 December 1991 was a further factor forcing the old opposition and the national communists into the same camp. Kravchuk's pursuit of office soon became indistinguishable from his advocacy of independence, and therefore the People's Council and the political parties found it difficult to oppose him, as he had stolen their clothes. Many in fact supported him. The fact that all significant political forces in Ukraine supported independence, even at the last moment the SPU,[86] meant that the eventual 90.3 per cent vote was perhaps not that surprising.

Ninety-five candidates for the presidency were whittled down by 1 November to a final seven (six after the Agriculture Minister Tkachenko withdrew in favour of Kravchuk) by requiring all candidates to collect 100 000 signatures in order to stand. Kravchuk was the only candidate of the former CPU, and had no challenger to his left.

The People's Council, however, was split between five candidates. Ukraine's political parties faced a classic Rational Choice dilemma. As they were organisationally weak and not yet well known to the public, it was individually rational for each to put forward a candidate to promote the party's face, but of course collectively disastrous when they all did so.[87] Only the two best-organised parties managed to collect 100 000 signatures, the Republican Party because of its tight internal discipline (for Lukianenko), and the PDRU because of its relatively strong intelligentsia support (for Iukhnovskyi as its official candidate, and for Grinev as a Russian-speaking wild card). The leader of the tiny People's Party, Leopold Taburianskyi, secured his candidature with the help of the resources of his 'Olimp' co-operative.

Rukh's official candidate was Chornovil. However, given the Republican Party's entryism, key figures in the *apparat*, Drach included, and *Rukh*'s Political Council (led by the Republican Party's Mykhailo Horyn) supported Lukianenko. *Rukh*'s disunity was exacerbated by the decision on 1 September by *Rukh*'s Grand Council to allow local branches to campaign for any democratic candidate.[88] The Donets'k branch ended up supporting Kravchuk.[89]

The far right candidate from the Inter-Party Assembly (now the Ukrainian National Assembly), Iurii Shukhevych, the Greens' Shcherbak and the Democratic Party's Pylypchuk fell short of the necessary number of registration signatures required. The SPU's supported Kravchuk; the United Social Democrats, the Russian Kadets, the eastern branches of the PDRU and some of the Donbas strike committees Grinev; the SDPU Chornovil; and the Ukrainian Language Society (now called 'Prosvita') and Union of Ukrainian Students Lukianenko.[90]

The key to the campaign, however, was Kravchuk's candidature, and the mass media barrage in favour of independence and the new national ideology that accompanied it. The media were still in the hands of national communists, as the People's Council had failed in its bid to remove the television and radio boss Mykola Okhmakevych for complicity in the coup on 17 September. (In other words, the national communists had a clear understanding of where their power lay.) Despite the Supreme Council's resolution on 9 October that all candidates should have equal access to the mass media,[91] Les Taniuk, an ally of Chornovil's, claimed that 62 per cent of airtime went to Kravchuk (and initially Tkachenko).

The state no longer had a formal monopoly of the press, as papers like *Vechirnii Kyïv* (Kyiv's evening paper) had been communicating an independent message for some time, and where the opposition had controlled the local councils since 1990 it had converted council-supported papers into opposition organs, such as *Za vil'nu Ukraïna* (For a Free Ukraine) in L'viv, or the DPU paper *Volia* in Ternopil'. However, the government press received preferential treatment in the supply of paper.[92] *Vechirnii Kyïv* was only a double broadsheet at the most, for example.

The government's dominance of the mass media, however, was now being used to push an entirely one-sided national message. Even the official Supreme Council Appeal to the People talked of independence as 'an objective requirement ... the dream of our fathers and grandfathers', and stated 'Any other path, apart from independence, does not exist for Ukraine.'[93] The All-Ukrainian (and all-confessional) Religious Forum in Kyiv on 20 November, and the equivalent All-Ukrainian Inter-Ethnic Congress in Odesa on 16 and 17 November, were carefully stage-managed to bridge the religious and ethnic divides, and produce declarations in support of independence.[94] Kravchuk drew support across the board, eventually triumphing with 61.6 per cent of the vote. Like the early Gorbachev, he was successful in appearing as all things to all men, and bridging the many divisions that threatened the unity of the young state. However, the overall voting patterns and distribution of opposition and CPU strengths showed a remarkable similarity to those of 1990 and March 1991, as shown in Table 9.1.

Kravchuk won 13.3 per cent in Galicia, 52.4 per cent in Volhynia-Polissia, 52.2 per cent in Transcarpathia and Chernivtsi, 66.1 per cent in the Left Bank, 73.3 per cent in the more rural Right Bank, 72.4 per cent in the East and 66.7 per cent in the south.[95] (Some of Kravchuk's natural support in the east and south was taken by the Russian-speaking Grinev, who called for a federalised Ukraine with increased autonomy for

Table 9.1   Results of the presidential elections of 1 December 1991 (per cent)

Oblast	Grinev	Kravchuk	Lukianenko	Taburianskyi	Chornovil	Iukhnovskyi
Galicia						
L'viv	0.83	11.58	4.70	0.16	75.86	4.43
Ternopil'	0.43	16.79	19.6	0.18	57.45	3.19
Ivano-Frankivs'k	0.55	13.70	11.63	0.14	67.10	3.32
Volhynia						
Rivne	0.80	53.07	13.38	0.43	25.55	3.57
Volyn'	0.83	51.85	8.90	0.34	31.39	3.25
Other West						
Transcarpathia	1.32	58.03	4.98	0.39	27.58	2.83
Chernivtsi	1.42	43.56	4.40	0.42	42.67	1.97
Left Bank						
Kyiv (city)	3.54	56.13	6.36	0.54	26.71	3.52
Kyiv (*oblast*)	1.68	65.99	5.62	0.48	21.23	1.51
Kharkiv	10.90	60.85	2.08	0.44	19.66	0.97
Poltava	2.46	75.05	4.21	0.61	13.63	1.26
Sumy	2.53	72.35	3.88	0.52	14.73	1.81
Chernihiv	1.46	74.15	6.69	0.40	12.34	0.90
Right Bank						
Kirovohrad	1.65	74.77	3.54	0.55	13.55	1.06
Cherkasy	1.36	67.14	1.96	0.38	25.03	0.98
Vinnytsia	1.39	72.34	3.25	0.36	18.25	1.62
Zhytomyr	1.12	77.59	3.30	0.35	13.97	1.05
Khmel'nyts'kyi	1.19	75.46	3.25	0.42	15.40	1.65
East						
Donets'k	10.98	71.47	3.11	0.71	9.69	0.93
Luhans'k	6.75	76.23	2.01	0.52	9.94	0.74
Dnipropetrovs'k	3.20	69.74	2.47	1.85	18.15	1.21
Zaporozhzhia	3.87	74.73	3.07	0.65	12.98	1.32
South						
Mykolaïv	5.63	72.33	2.26	0.39	15.06	0.69
Kherson	3.27	70.23	2.23	0.54	18.13	0.97
Odesa	8.38	70.69	2.77	0.52	12.83	1.13
Crimean ASSR	9.43	56.68	1.93	0.86	5.03	0.90
Sevastopol' city	8.38	54.68	1.80	0.84	10.93	0.89
Black Sea Fleet	6.00	74.40	4.00	1.50	23.00	1.10
Total	4.17	61.59	4.49	0.57	23.3	1.69

84.2% of those eligible to vote turned out.
Totals do not always add up to 100 per cent because of spoiled ballots (although such figures were not provided directly by the Electoral Commission).

Source: Electoral Commission, official results.

Russian-speaking areas, and polled 10.9 per cent in Kharkiv, 11 per cent in Donets'k, 8.4 per cent in Odesa and 9.4 per cent in Crimea).

Kravchuk's national communist coalition was strongest in the countryside, where the control of collective farm chairmen remained almost feudal, in small-town Ukraine, and among the less-educated and lower social groups where the government's control of the mass media had most effect. Non-Ukrainians were more likely to support him than the more nationalist candidates. The old *apparat*, and the official trade unions, still saw him as one of their own, and supported him as the best guarantor of their privileges.[96]

According to opinion poll evidence, Kravchuk was supported by 34.6 per cent of managers and specialists (the low figure is explained by the poll using the percentage of all in the group, rather than of those who actually voted), 31.1 per cent of employees and non-specialists, 31.3 per cent of qualified workers, 38.8 per cent of workers with few qualifications, 38.1 per cent of peasants, 36.5 per cent of pensioners and 22.6 per cent of students.[97] Those with higher education gave 39.7 per cent support to Kravchuk, those with middle education 41.8 per cent and those with middle or uncompleted education 45.0 per cent.[98] In one early poll, 39.9 per cent of Ukrainians chose Kravchuk, 16.5 per cent Chornovil and 4.4 per cent Lukianenko, whereas the figures for Russians were 34 per cent, 9.3 per cent and 1.1 per cent respectively.[99] The data for selected *oblasts* by *raion* showed that Kravchuk's score in the countryside was usually 10–30 per cent higher than in the *oblast'* centre.[100] (Interestingly, one poll showed that 43.8 per cent evaluated Kravchuk's role in the coup more or less positively, and only 25.3 per cent more or less negatively, showing both how successfully he had wrapped himself in the flag since then, and the conservatism of Ukrainian public opinion in general.)[101]

The leading challenger Chornovil's 23 per cent, and the support for the other three People's Council candidates (leaving out the wild card Grinev) was a mirror image to Kravchuk's, and again was remarkably similar to the March 1990 and 1991 results. The opposition's stronghold were in Galicia, Kyiv and other central urban centres. The polls mentioned above showed 10.4 per cent of managers and specialists supporting Chornovil, 6.3 per cent of employees, 9.8 per cent of qualified workers, 7.8 per cent of the low-qualified, 8.5 per cent of peasants (given the strength of rural nationalism in the west), 9.4 per cent of students and 5.9 per cent of pensioners.[102] Eleven per cent of those with higher education supported Chornovil, 11.2 per cent of those with middle or specialised education, 7.2 per cent of those with middle and 7.9 per cent of those with incomplete or middle.[103] The pattern of intelligentsia support was more pronounced for the urbane Iukhnovskyi, but less so for the more populist Lukianenko.

As shown in Table 9.2, support for independence was almost universal. The total vote of 90.3 per cent, on a 84.2 per cent turnout, exceeded all expectations, although it was in line with the rising trend of support displayed throughout the autumn. Even Crimea voted 54.2 per cent in favour. Although support sagged as expected in the south and east, it was as high as 85.4 per cent in Odesa and 83.9 per cent in Luhans'k. Poll evidence showed more men (72 per cent) than women (58 per cent) in favour (again, these figures are percentages of the total group, not of those who voted).[104] Among the under-35s support was 68 per cent; among those aged 36–55, 67 per cent; and in the over 55s, 57 per cent. Seventy-three per cent of specialists supported independence, 73 per cent of students, 73 per cent of those employed in education, 67 per cent of workers, but only 58 per cent of those employed in agriculture, and 56 per cent of pensioners. Those with higher education gave 75 per cent support to independence, as against 63 per cent for those with only middle education and 57 per cent for those with incomplete or middle.

The inhabitants of larger towns gave 68 per cent support, those in medium-sized towns 66 per cent, those in the villages 58 per cent. Sixty-eight per cent of Ukrainians, 55 per cent of Russians and 46 per cent of other minorities were in favour. Finally, a very high 87 per cent of both UAOC and UCC believers voted in favour, but only 60 per cent of ROC (now the Ukrainian Orthodox Church) believers.

The conservative nature of public opinion and the dominance of practical concerns was well demonstrated. Nationalist cultural priorities came well behind economic worries. In a typical poll, 78.6 per cent gave 'escape from economic crisis' top priority, 62.4 per cent 'stabilisation of the economy and a better standard of living', 60.3 per cent ecological improvement, 54.9 per cent an 'effective struggle with crime', but only 21.2 per cent listed 'the cultural rebirth of Ukraine', and only 18.3 per cent 'the securing of the political sovereignty of the republic'.[105]

In other words, the most socially mobilised sections of the population showed highest support for independence, as predicted by Krawchenko. The gulf between the intelligentsia and the mass of the population remained large, however, both in terms of values and priorities, and in terms of the organisational ability of the intelligentsia. The state was still the predominant factor in political communication; the free press and autonomous social institutions of a civil society were only just beginning to emerge. However, the state had usurped the intelligentsia's national ideology to fill the vacuum left by the collapse of communism and promoted it with a vengeance. Moreover, it

Table 9.2   Support for independence in the 1 December 1991 referendum
(per cent)

Oblast	'Yes' vote	'No' vote
Galicia		
L'viv	97.45	1.86
Ternopil'	98.70	0.78
Ivano-Frankivs'k	98.42	1.03
Volhynia		
Rivne	96.80	2.56
Volyn'	96.32	2.29
Other West		
Transcarpathia	92.59	4.49
Chernivtsi	92.78	4.13
Left Bank		
Kyiv (city)	92.67	5.28
Kyiv (*oblast*)	95.52	2.87
Kharkiv	86.33	10.43
Poltava	94.93	3.67
Sumy	92.61	4.90
Chernihiv	93.74	4.10
Right Bank		
Kirovohrad	93.88	4.38
Cherkasy	96.03	2.76
Vinnytsia	95.43	3.03
Zhytomyr	95.06	3.58
Khmel'nyts'kyi	96.30	2.62
East		
Donets'k	83.90	12.58
Luhans'k	83.86	13.41
Zaporizhzhia	90.66	7.34
Dnipropetrovs'k	90.36	7.71
South		
Mykolaïv	89.45	8.17
Kherson	90.13	7.20
Odesa	85.38	11.60
Crimean ASSR	54.19	42.22
Sevastopol' city	57.07	39.39
Black Sea Fleet	75.00	–
Total	90.32	7.58

Source: Electoral Commission, official results.

had adapted it to the task of preserving power in Ukraine's fragile and multifaceted society, and probably made a better job of maintaining cohesion along the path to independence than the nationalists would have done.

The gap between the 25–33 per cent support for the Democratic Bloc/*Rukh* in 1990–91 and the 90.3 per cent vote for Independence was clearly due to the addition of the resources (communicative, coercive and material) of the state.[106] The majority so easily assembled soon began to appear fragile, however, especially given Ukraine's minority problems.

REGIONALISM IN UKRAINE

As argued in Chapter 2, Ukraine is a multi-ethnic state whose divergent regions have different historical and cultural traditions. The passing of the 1990 Declaration of Sovereignty and 1991 Declaration of Independence forced Ukraine's minorities to show more concern for their future, a development exacerbated by many local ex-CPU elites stirring up minority grievances as a means of holding on to power after the banning of the CPU on 30 August.[107]

The Supreme Council's response to developing problems with minorities and separatist pressures was ambiguous. On the one hand, it passed the conciliatory 'Declaration of Rights of Nationalities of Ukraine' on 1 November 1991, whose seven articles promised full minority rights, and promised that in 'territorial units, where a certain nationality lives compactly, their language may function on an equal footing with the state language' (i.e. Ukrainian), while 'the Ukrainian state guaranteed to its citizens the right to freely use the Russian language'.[108] The Supreme Council and *Rukh* were also the joint sponsors of the first All-Ukrainian Inter-Ethnic Congress held on 16 and 17 November in Odesa. A thousand delegates representing 150 ethnic organisations endorsed Ukrainian independence on a multi-ethnic basis.[109]

On the other hand, however, the Supreme Council of Ukraine passed on 11 October a law criminalising 'appeals and other activities aimed at the violation of the territorial integrity of Ukraine', with punishments of up to three years' imprisonment, or fines up to 100 000 roubles. The nationalist Republican and Democratic parties were soon clamouring for its application, and other firm action against 'separatists'.[110]

The Crimea

The Crimean peninsula's population in 1989 was 67 per cent Russian, 26 per cent Ukrainian (47 per cent of whom are Russian-speaking) and 7 per cent others. Schooling and the mass media are almost entirely in Russian, which was adopted as the local state language in 1991. The Crimea was only added to Ukraine in 1954, and many of its inhabitants are post-war settlers from Russia. In addition, many of the 269 000 Crimean Tatars, deported by Stalin in 1944 for alleged collaboration with the Germans (when they made up some 19 per cent of the Crimea's 1 million or so population),[111] began to return in increasing numbers after the USSR Supreme Soviet started their rehabilitation in 1989.

The Tatars had been demonstrating for a return to their ancestral lands since 1987. After much procrastination, the USSR Supreme Soviet passed a resolution on 14 November 1989 condemning their unlawful expulsion, and on 24 July 1991 the USSR Council of Ministers approved a decree 'Concerning the Organisation of the Return of the Crimean Tatars and Guarantees for their Arrangements'. However, their return has been consistently impeded by the Crimean Supreme Soviet, which has effectively banned the resettlement of Tatars in the prosperous southern coastal, Simferopol', and Bakhchysarai regions, and has sought to play on the fears of post-war settlers that they will loose their property to the Tatars.[112] After a meeting between the Tatars and Kravchuk in September 1990 a special commission of the Supreme Council was established, and eventually began limited state funding of resettlement.[113]

Frustration at the slow pace of return (less than 300 000 by 1991) led to the OKND (Organisation of the Crimean–Tatar National Movement), led by Mustafa Jemilev, replacing the conformist NDKT (National Movement of the Crimean Tatars) as the most vocal representatives of the Tatars. On 26–30 June 1991 in Simferopil', the former elected a *Medzhlis*, or Supreme Tatar Assembly, which on 28 June passed the 'Declaration of Sovereignty of the Crimean Tatar People', Article 1 of which states that the 'Crimea is the national territory of the Crimean–Tatar people, on which they alone possess the right to self-determination'.[114] The *Medzhlis* therefore boycotted the Crimean Supreme Soviet, evoking the memory of the short-lived Tatar republic of 1917 instead. It also sought to mobilise the support of the 5 million or so Tatar diaspora, especially in Turkey.

The strengthening of Ukraine's nationalist movement and the Tatar challenge simultaneously threatened the power of the local CPU leadership, led by Nikolai Bagrov, and, at the same time, allowed them to play on fears of enforced Ukrainisation/Tatarisation in an attempt to preserve their position. They had much to hang on to, as a high proportion of the CPU's assets – sanatoria, dachas and the like – were on Crimean territory, as was the former Soviet Black Sea Fleet Headquarters in Sevastopol'.

On 12 November 1990 the Crimean *oblast* Soviet condemned the 1954 transfer to Ukraine from the RSFSR, and in a referendum organised by Bagrov on 20 January 1991, 93 per cent (on a 80 per cent turnout, with the Tatars boycotting) voted to restore the Crimea's status as an Autonomous Soviet Socialist Republic (within the Ukrainian SSR).[115] On 12 February the Supreme Council of Ukraine passed a 'Law on the Renewal of the Crimean ASSR', and on 26 June by 303 (mainly Communist) votes confirmed Crimea's new status as a constituent part of the Ukrainian SSR, but with a separate constitution. The draft version of the Crimean ASSR constitution adopted in Sevastopol' on 22 July 1991 rejected the presidential form of government chosen for Ukraine as a whole, and established Russian as the state language.

During the coup of 19–21 August 1991, when President Gorbachev was held in the Crimea, the local elite showed its conservative colours. Only two members of the 13-strong Presidium of the Crimean Soviet supported a motion to condemn the plotters, with one abstaining.[116] In the backlash after the coup's failure, Bagrov sacrificed many of his colleagues on 29 August 1991, when most of the Crimean Presidium resigned, but ensured his own survival. The still-dominant communists, however, reacted to the 30 August decision by the Kyiv Supreme Council of Ukraine to nationalise CPU property by declaring Crimean state sovereignty on 2 September, and by passing the 'Law on the Organs of State Power' of Crimea on 10 September 1991.[117]

Moreover, the 'Republican Movement of Crimea' (headed by Crimean deputy, Iurii Meshkov), the 'Russian Society of Crimea' (headed by Anatolii Los), the 'Citizens' Forum of Crimea' and the 'Organisation of the 20 January' founded on 5 October[118] began campaigning for a referendum to annul the 1954 decision, and transfer Crimea to the RSFSR. Their campaign was financed by the economic association 'Impeks-55 Crimea', formed with CPU funds.

The democratic or pro-Ukrainian opposition in Crimea, on the other hand, was decidedly weak, although 28 local deputies announced the formation of a Democratic Bloc on 28 April.[119] Even the Citizens' Forum of Crimea, headed by Ukrainian SSR deputy Volodymyr Sevastianov, which on 22 September called for the dissolution of the

Crimean Soviet, multi-party elections, and a multi-ethnic state, with full rights for Crimean Tatars, still supported Crimea's potential separation from the Ukrainian SSR. The 'Democratic Crimea' group united all-Ukrainian groups such as *Rukh* and the Republican Party, but its influence was minimal.

Kravchuk attended the crucial session of the Crimean Soviet on 23–25 October, persuading it to side-step the question of a referendum, provoking a walkout by Meshkov, and his commencement of a hunger strike outside the building. It must be presumed that Kravchuk promised not to threaten the power of the local elite, if they, in turn, refrained from supporting separatist agitation. Kravchuk was soon under fire from nationalists in Kyiv for offering too little stick and too much carrot, and for feeding Bagrov's appetite for further concessions. Meshkov's supporters, having collected a petition of 30 000 and the support of 66 deputies, soon persuaded the Crimean Supreme Soviet to backtrack on 5 November, and call another emergency session on the 22nd, when, as expected, a local referendum law was duly adopted, paving the way for a potential future vote on secession.

In the 1 December referendum, Ukrainian independence secured a surprisingly high majority of 54.2 per cent in Crimea (57.1 per cent in Sevastopol'), on a turnout of 67.5 per cent (63.7 per cent in Sevastopol'). However, Ukraine's designs on the Black Sea Fleet after January 1992 seemed to tilt the balance of power again in the separatists' direction, as Russia was drawn openly in to the struggle (a delegation of deputies from the RSFSR, members of the Democratic Party and Christian Democratic Movement of Russia, had first arrived in Crimea on 19 and 20 October 1991 to support separatist agitation) and sought to make it clear that Ukraine could have the fleet or the Crimea, but not both.[120]

The vote by the RSFSR Supreme Soviet on 23 January 1992 to instruct its committees to re-examine the 1954 decision dramatically raised the stakes, and threatened Ukraine with a conflict it seemed at the time likely to lose. The 1 December vote had probably reflected Crimeans' judgement that short-term living standards were likely to be higher in Ukraine than in Russia, but Ukraine had yet to establish the cultural ties with Crimea that would guarantee its long-term loyalty. Crucially, Crimea remained isolated from the new national message promoted by the Kyiv media. The press was Russian-language, and Ukrainian television was often jammed. Kravchuk's policy of accommodation with local elites seemed not to work in the Crimean case, when Bagrov could also court Russia as an alternative sponsor.

Transcarpathia

Minority problems also exist in Transcarpathia at the other end of Ukraine.[121] Officially, its population of 1.2 million in 1989 was 78 per cent Ukrainian, 13 per cent Hungarian, 4 per cent Russian and 5 per cent others. However, many of the 1 million or so Ukrainians have in the past considered themselves ethnically distinct Ruthenians or Rusyns, and there have been some signs of this tendency re-emerging, albeit at the urging of the local Communist Party, since 1989. An international scientific conference in Uzhhorod on 17 April 1991 on 'The Traditions of the Regional Culture of Rusyns – Ukrainians in Transcarpathia and the Diaspora' heard claims by the Canadian professor Paul Robert Magocsi and others that, despite similarities of language and religious traditions (the local religion is Uniate Catholic, as in Galicia), the Rusyns' subjective sense of separateness should be considered sufficient grounds in itself for their identification as a separate Slav ethnie (a claim hotly contested by Ukrainian nationalists). The Hungarian consulate in Kyiv claimed that the Transcarpathian population in fact consisted of 200 000 Hungarians, 800 000 Rusyns, and 125 000 Ukrainians proper.[122] The region was added to Ukraine by a Soviet-Czechoslovak treaty of 1945, having previously belonged to Hungary until 1918, and Czechoslovakia until 1938, although it enjoyed brief quasi-independence as the Republic of Carpatho-Ukraine until the Hungarian invasion in 1939. The Society of Carpatho-Rusyns (SCR) was originally established as a cultural-educational society in the *oblast'* capital of Uzhhorod on 17 February 1990, but on 29 September 1990 it published a declaration demanding 'the return of the status of an autonomous republic to Transcarpathia *oblast'*. The local CPU, led by Mykhailo Voloshchuk, supported the SCR, as a way of building a local power base after Ukrainian nationalists took power in Galicia in spring 1990 and cut the Transcarpathian Communists off from the rest of the Soviet Union. It also campaigned for Transcarpathia to become a 'free economic zone', to take advantage of links with Central Europe and increased their freedom of manoeuvre as '*nomenklatura* capitalists'. (The Minister for Foreign Trade, Vitalii Kravchenko, announced in November 1991 that Transcarpathia, Mariupol, and Odesa would enjoy such status.)[123]

On the other hand, the local Hungarian minority, represented since February 1989 by the Hungarian Cultural Association of Transcarpathia and with 18 deputies on the *oblast'* Soviet, had relatively good relations with the Ukrainians, although these began to worsen after the more politicised Hungarian Democratic Alliance of Ukraine was set up in October 1991 to campaign for autonomy.

As in the Crimea and Chernivtsi, outside forces were accused of fomenting agitation. Since 1990, the extremist Czechoslovak Republican party demanded the return of Transcarpathia, and the Slovak government hosted the World Congress of Rusyns in Medzilaborce on 23 April 1991.[124] However, the Czechoslovak government rejected a call by the SCR on 23 December 1991 to annul the 1945 treaty,[125] and on 25 May 1992 a Ukrainian-Czechoslovak treaty committed both parties to renouncing territorial claims on each other.

The local CPU, discredited by support for the August coup, attempted to save its position by proroguing the *oblast'* Soviet that gathered on 30 August until 27 September, and by passing various populist measures, including additional places for local students at Uzhhorod and Mukachiv universities. On the 27th, with rival groups of Rusyns and Ukrainians demonstrating outside, a motion of confidence in Voloshchuk received 57 votes, 4 short of the necessary majority, and a motion for his removal was defeated 53–51.[126]

However, the attempt to further prorogue the session until 1 October provoked hunger strikes in the square outside the Soviet by local deputies and students, and confrontations with the local OMON. After the students called for a political strike throughout the *oblast'* on 30 September, Voloshchuk and his deputy Iurii Vorobets bowed to the inevitable and resigned. The hunger strikers won partial victory on their other demands. Free, multi-party, elections in Transcarpathia were to be held before 30 March 1992, and a commission was promised to look into the events of 19–21 August and 27–30 September 1991.

On 1 December 1991, 92.6 per cent of Transcarpathians voted to support Ukrainian independence on a turnout of 82.9 per cent; 78 per cent, meanwhile, voted in a second ballot for the status of 'a special self-governing administrative territory' within Ukraine[127] (the phrasing having been carefully moderated by Kravchuk from the SCR's original demands) and a corresponding law was drawn up by the following February.[128] Meanwhile, in the Berehove region on the Hungarian border, 81.4 per cent supported the Hungarian Democratic Alliance's call for the formation of a Magyar 'national district'.[129]

Transcarpathia differs from Crimea in its relative closeness to Central European political culture and because separatist forces are balanced by a strong local Ukrainian national movement. Slovakian independence would lessen the pull from the West, but if the area fulfills its potential for tourism and as an economic crossroads, the locals may be reluctant to share their new wealth with Kyiv. Kyiv, meanwhile, mindful of the mistakes made in Crimea, may be reluctant to deliver on promises of autonomy.

The Donbas

The two Ukrainian *oblasts'* in the Donbas (15 per cent of which is inside the RSFSR), Donets'k and Luhans'k (formerly Voroshylovhrad) are heavily industrialised and Russified. Forty-four per cent of the Donets'k population was Russian in 1989, 45 per cent in Luhans'k. Moreover, 34 per cent of Donbas Ukrainians gave Russians as their mother tongue (in 1989). Much of the area's industry is non-economic and environmentally hazardous, and is therefore likely to be threatened with closure by a young and impecunious Ukrainian state.

Consequently, relations between the Ukrainian national movement and the area's radical trade unions, formed after the miners' strikes of 1989 and 1991, have always been difficult. As in Transcarpathia, conservative local Communists had been pressing for a regional 'free economic zone' in 1990–1, but then discredited themselves by support for the August putschists. Attempts to form a Baltic-style 'Interfront' had never previously gained much momentum,[130] but after the banning of the CPU, local Communists such as Iurii Smirnov, head of Donets'k *oblast'* Soviet, sought to revive similar organisations as an alternative local power base. The revived SPU also provided support.

Such groups included the 'United Society for the Protection of the Russian Language Population of the Donbas', formed in Mariupol, on 15 September 1991. Despite a split at the congress, the Society issued demands for a federal Ukrainian state, with the Donbas having its own legislative institutions and militia, and the right to use Russian as the local state language. At the Donets'k *oblast'* Soviet, an organising committee for a referendum on the re-establishment of the Donets'k-Kryvyi Rih Republic, that had a brief existence after February 1918, was set up on 24 September under the leadership of USSR deputy, Oleksandr Boiko, and the Ukrainian deputies Albert Korneev (the only man to vote against Ukrainian Independence in August) and Aleksandr Chyrodeev.

A close ally of Smirnov's, Boiko was also the chief instigator of the 'Democratic Movement of the Donbas', formed at a meeting of delegates from Donets'k, Mariupol', Makiivka, Ienakiievo and Shakhtars'k in Luhans'k on 5 October. It attacked Ukraine's Declaration of Independence for 'ignoring the will of the people', called for a renewed Union treaty and 'single economic space', and for an autonomous Donbas within a federal Ukraine.

Demands for federalisation and local state status for the Russian language were supported by the Russian-speaking Vladimir Grinev, one of the leaders of the PDRU, who campaigned hard for the Presidency in the Donbas, capturing 11 per cent in Donets'k and 6.8 per cent in Luhans'k (compared with 4.2 per cent in Ukraine as a whole). However, the key meeting of the Donets'k *oblast'* Soviet on 8–11 October showed strong opposition to such changes from the local *Rukh* (although it has formally split in Donets'k), and other nationalist parties, such as the local Republican Party under Maria Oliinyk, both inside the chamber and in demonstrations outside. Consequently, the session moderated its tone. On 25 October 1991 in Donets'k, Boiko organised a joint assembly of Peoples' Deputies from local Soviets throughout eastern and southern Ukraine (in imitation of the Galician Assembly) and renewed calls both for a federated Ukraine, and for Ukraine to sign a new Union treaty.

Kravchuk, meanwhile, was calling for Ukrainian unity. As in the Crimea, the relative quiescence of separatist forces in the Donbas was undoubtedly predicted on the assumption that Kravchuk would win in December and leave existing local elites be. Despite the separatist actions of the former CPU at a local level, the great virtue of Kravchuk's national communism was that its *raison d'être*, the adoption of a national ideology to retain elite privilege, encouraged potentially fractious regional elites into an accommodation with the centre. This strategy seems to have worked in the short run, with the Donbas seemingly integrated more smoothly into the young state than the Crimea, and the pull from impecunious Russia less strong. The independence votes in Donets'k and Luhans'k on 1 December were accordingly surprisingly high, at 84 per cent (turnout 76.7 per cent) and 83.9 per cent (turnout 80.7 per cent) respectively.

However, Ukraine still had a long-term problem with incorporating the Russian population of the Donbas, Odesa and elsewhere. As *Rukh* became more of a specifically nationalist movement in 1990–1, and less of a movement for democracy in general, the Russian population became dangerously passive, unlikely to participate in collective action organised around Ukrainian myths and symbols. The Donbas became the centre of radical left political forces from winter 1992–3.

Despite the best efforts of the PDRU and Ukrainian Social Democrats to involve Russians in the political process, and Kravchuk's appointment of Russians to key posts, such as Grinev and Morozov, the Minister of Defence, the Russian population increasingly had to face problems of ethnological disorientation. In the past, Russians had seen themselves as part of Russia and/or the USSR, but their cultural framework became tainted with the discredited symbols of empire. Unless they developed an alternative capacity to imagine themselves as 'Russians of Ukraine' they were likely to develop a complex of ethnic discomfort or inferiority, and became fertile ground for populists seeking to over-compensate for the traumas of ethnic transition, and campaign against the oppression of 'Russian culture'. Again, Kravchuk had been surprisingly successful in coping with such transitional problems. The symbolism that he had sought to revive from the past was that of the multinational Cossacks, and Ukrainian humanists such as Hrushevs'kyi[131] not that of the more particularist history of Galicia and the OUN.

The Donbas is not the Crimea, but the loyalty of the local Russians, and those who live in smaller numbers around Kharkiv and in southern Ukraine had yet to be tested in a serious conflict between Ukraine and Russia.

Chernivtsi

The Western *oblast'* of Chernivtsi, made up of North Bukovyna and Bessarabia, plus the district of Hertsa, was joined to the Ukrainian SSR in 1940 as a result of the Nazi-Soviet pact and Stalin's division of former Moldovan lands. Chernivtsi's population in 1989 was 71 per cent Ukrainian, 11 per cent Romanian, 9 per cent Moldovan and 9 per cent Russian and others. In 1990–1, both Moldova and Romania condemned the pact and made revanchist claims on Chernivtsi, and on the province of Southern Bessarabia (part of Odesa *oblast'* since 1954) which was incorporated into Ukraine at the same time.

The local *oblast'* council was quick to nationalise CPU property on 25 August and conceded to Romanian and Moldovan demonstrators on 17 September 1991 that in areas of 'compact settlement', (mainly the Hlyboka region) the Romanian language and national symbols could be used alongside the Ukrainian.[132] On the other hand, the council declared on 3 November 1991 (the anniversary of the abortive attempt by local Ukrainians to join Northern Bukovyna to the Ukrainian National Republic in 1918 before invasion by Romania) a public holiday, and this seems to have been welcomed by the local Ukrainian population.[133]

Meanwhile on 28 November 1991 the Romanian parliament welcomed the forthcoming Ukrainian votes, but stated that it would not recognise the results on the territories claimed by Romania, and urged other states to take the same line. This caused Ukrainian Foreign Minister Anatolii Zlenko to turn back at the border, cancelling a planned trip to Romania which should have resulted in the signing of a treaty of Romanian–Ukrainian friendship, and the establishment of diplomatic relations between the two countries. Romania also condemned attempts by the self-styled 'Dnister Republic' (part of the Ukrainian SSR until 1940) to break away from Moldova, particularly after the virtual military coup designed to prevent the holding of Moldovan Presidential elections east of the Dnister on 6–8 December 1991.

Romania, in turn, was accused of fanning anti-Ukrainian sentiment among the 166 000 Bulgarians and 27 000 Gagauz (Christian Turks) of Odesa *oblast'*, who mainly live in the Bolhrad *raion* of Southern Bessarabia. Such agitation resulted in the question, 'Do you find it necessary to form in the Bolhrad *raion* a Bulgarian national *okruh* within Ukraine, where people of different nationalities would have the freedom to freely develop their languages, culture and traditions?' being added to the 1 December ballot, and receiving 73 per cent support.

The 'Christian Democratic Alliance of Romanians in Ukraine' formed in Chernivtsi on 26 November as 'a national movement for the protection of the legitimate rights and freedoms of Romanians in northern Bukovyna and other parts of Ukraine' called on Romanians to boycott the 1 December polls in support of the Romanian parliament's position. However, 92.8 per cent of the population eventually voted for Ukrainian independence, and the turnout was a relatively high 87.7 per cent. The boycott made a small impact in some Romanian areas. 89.3 per cent voted for the area to be given a 'special economic status'.[134]

Romania's historical claims and the general unravelling of the Nazi-Soviet pact clearly destabilised the situation in the area. However, even if the 20 per cent Romanian-Moldovan minority proves receptive to Romanian propaganda, it is up against a strong local Ukrainian tradition and Chernivtsi's experience of inter-war rule by Romania, including the attempt at forced Romanianisation from 1924 on, which was much harsher than Transcarpathia's in relatively liberal, and prosperous, Czechoslovakia. The Romanian/Moldovan minority is too small to dominate the politics of the *oblast'* in the manner of the Russians in Crimea, but the issue is sufficiently poisonous for Romanian revanchism to be second only to the Russian problem as a threat to Ukraine's national security interests. It is noteworthy that by 1990 Ukraine had signed treaties with all of its neighbours apart from Russia and Romania. These were only to be signed eventually in May and June 1997 respectively.

'Dnister Republic', Moldova

The portion of Moldova east of the River Dnister was part of the Ukrainian SSR until 1940, and its 742 000 population is 29 per cent Ukrainian and 26 per cent Russian.[135] It also contains much of Moldova's heavy industry. After Moldovan nationalists swept to power in 1990 and began to restore ties with Romania, separatist inclinations on the left bank grew rapidly, although it was initially oriented to Russia or the USSR rather than Ukraine, especially as without schools or cultural facilities under the USSR the local Ukrainians are in practice highly denationalised.

In September 1990, the 'Dnister SSR' was proclaimed, and its leaders established a network of paramilitary forces and a 'Joint Council of Work Collectives' to enforce their rule in the area. In 1991, they also benefited from the assistance of Cossack mercenaries and the local forces of the USSR's 14th Army (its head, Gennadii Iakovlev, became Dnistran 'Defence Minister' on 13 December 1991).[136]

The self-styled republic's leaders, mainly hangovers from the highly conservative local Communist Party, welcomed the August 1991 coup, and its promise of a return to the 'good old days'. Correspondingly, in the wake of the coup's collapse and the Declarations of Independence by both Ukraine and Moldova, the area declared its independence on 25 August, while at the same time calling to be a part of a reconstituted USSR.[137] Armed conflicts with Moldovan forces became increasingly common as the Dnister leaders attempted to consolidate their hold on government buildings and the mainly Moldovan countryside. In late November, the situation became critical, in the run-up to rival presidential polls in the two zones.

By now the geopolitical situation had changed, however. Ukrainian independence had cut the 'Dnister republic' off from the rest of the USSR, and Ukraine was dragged into the conflict. The first reason for this was that the Dnister leaders now began to appeal to their newly discovered 'brother Ukrainians' for support. An 'Appeal to the People of Ukraine' was published in the Ukrainian press in October, and on 7 December the inaugural congress of the Union of Ukrainians of the Dnister region took place in the regional capitol of Tyraspol' under the leadership of Oleksandr But.[138]

Second, the Dnistrans developed links with other separatist and ex-communist circles in nearby Odesa. A delegation from the Odesa city council had visited the area on 2 October, and the prospect of a united separatist front from the Dnister to Crimea was of obvious concern to Kyiv.[139] Moreover, Odesa *oblast'* had to cope with 50 000 refugees by the spring of 1992.

Third, it was widely reported that Romania was becoming more openly supportive of Moldova, both diplomatically and militarily, pro-voking further escalation of the conflict.[140] Fourth, radical national-ists in Kyiv began openly to call for support for 'fellow Ukrainians'. Up to 200 UNSO paramilitaries went to join in the fighting in Spring 1992.[141]

Consequently, Ukraine stepped in with a rather plaintive appeal for calm and an offer of mediation in December, although it preferred to keep its distance from an unstable area that threatened Ukraine's hard-won reputation as an oasis of ethnic calm.[142]

Despite suggestions that Ukraine could arrange a swap deal with Romania and/or Moldova, surrendering Chernivtsi and Southern Bessarabia in return for the Left Bank, Romania did not really have a winning position in either area. Rather the problem for Ukraine con-cerns firstly Russia's continued role as a patron in a region far from its borders, and the dangerous precedent of Russian intervention in support of its stranded diaspora, and secondly the risk that nationalist pressure at home could drag it into the conflict.

CONCLUSION

The future for ethnic relations in Ukraine seems delicately poised. Ukraine's leaders, by making skilful use of territorial rather than ethnic nationalism and by soft-pedalling on Ukrainisation, have thus far avoided creating the centrifugal forces that many predicted would overwhelm the young state. However, although the PDRU and the Ukrainian Social Democrats called for a federalised Ukraine, the system is likely to remain unitary and inflexible to minority needs, especially because of the prominence of local ex-communist elites in leading separatist agitation.

Furthermore the legacy of past Russification will surely mean growing nationalist pressure to redress the undoubted current under-provision for Ukrainian language, schools and culture, particularly by strengthening the 1989 Languages Law. Consequent fears of Ukrainianisation, whether justified or not, would provide fertile ground for populist minority leaders, as was seen in the 1994 elections.

10 Conclusions

The thesis of this book has been the notion that, as the Republican Party's (by then honorary) leader Lukianenko was prepared to admit at the party's Third Congress on 1–2 May 1992, 'the glittering victory of 92 per cent [*sic*] of the votes [in the 1 December referendum] became possible only because both nationalists and communists agitated for independence'.[1]

In terms of the analysis presented in Chapter 1, the initial leadership for the national movement from 1987 to the winter of 1988 had to be provided by the dissidents returning from the camps, as the coercive power of the state was still sufficient to dissuade all but the bravest from public opposition activity. Hence the politics of the period strongly resembled that of the 1970s, with tiny numbers of opposition activists pursuing a human rights agenda against a state reluctant to make any real concessions on its monopoly of public life. From the winter of 1988 onwards the dissidents were then joined by the Kyiv-based cultural elite, whilst the membership of the informal groups that sprung up in 1988–90 drew heavily on the lower ranks of the intelligentsia.

According to Krawchenko, this predominance of the intelligentsia reflected the silent social revolution that had transformed the largely leaderless and socially inarticulate Ukrainian peasant mass of 1917 into a 'modernised' and urbanised society, with the most 'mobilised' sections of such a society in the vanguard of the national movement. This is not to argue that the Ukrainian peasantry lacked national consciousness, or was incapable of political organisation. The historical record speaks otherwise. Although peasant nationalism can be mobilised if appropriate institutions and elites exist (such as village teachers or clerics), urban societies, with large working class and intelligentsia groups and modern means of social communication, are governed by a different set of stimuli and have different capacities for organisation and action.

For Krawchenko, the key difference is that modernisation produced a national intelligentsia, that was then politicised by the 'cultural division of labour' that restricted its development. Whereas we have sought to argue that socio-economic explanations alone are insufficient, and that the key feature of the modern era, especially in the Soviet context, is the vast power of the state, which therefore ought to be the starting point in the chain of analysis rather than its conclusion.

The socio-economic approach can certainly shed light on the differences between the late 1980s national movement and that of the 1910s, 1920s, 1940s, or even the 1960s, but the timing of each upsurge of oppositional activity is more easily explained by periods of state tolerance and repression than as the by-product of subterranean processes of socio-economic change. As the state loosened its control over society, oppositional activity could increase, and vice versa. Whilst Shcherbytskyi remained in power, however, it was much more difficult to create a Ukrainian version of the Popular Fronts already established in the Baltic republics in 1988–9.

The predominance of the cultural intelligentsia was also a natural consequence of the importance to Ukrainian nationalism of the language question and the preservation of historical memory (where Church issues were more prominent, priests and religious activists played a more active role, as in Galicia). Moreover, the Ukrainian Writers' Union provided a ready made centre for opposition activity.

The game between the authorities and the intelligentsia was admittedly not entirely one-sided. The organisations established by the intelligentsia during this period, Memorial, the Ukrainian Language Society and eventually *Rukh*, helped to formulate a nationalist agenda, pressurise the state, and widen the space for available political activity, but the state still remained relatively immune from the pressure for change.

During the transitional Ivashko period from September 1989 to the Summer of 1990, *Rukh* was prevented from full participation in the crucial republican elections of March 1990, but the post-election period marked a key turning point, as opposition was legitimised, and Ukraine's embyronic civil society struggled to be born. The various elections and referenda of 1990–1 showed however that the opposition's support had more or less stagnated at the 25–33 per cent gained (as the Democratic Bloc) that March.[2] This limited figure reflected the inherited historical peculiarities of Ukraine described in Chapter 2, and also the inability of the intelligentsia to mobilise more than a minority of the population when faced with a still hostile state, as argued in Chapter 1. Although the state was no longer coercing the opposition, it remained difficult for the opposition to communicate its message beyond its core support.

Public demonstrations became increasingly common after 1989, and the opposition was able to air its views first through *samizdat* and then through such newspapers as *Za vil' nu Ukraïnu* and *Vechirnii Kyïv* but they could not promote the national message as effectively as the mass media. Hence Ukraine lagged behind the Baltic republics in 1988–90, but caught up very quickly once the national communists turned the mass media over to the national cause after mid-1991.

In 1990–1 the effects of imperial decline were being felt in Ukraine just as in the rest of the Union. As the centre lost its grip, the logic of national communism increasingly took hold of the republican communist parties in the periphery. Its late arrival in Ukraine could largely be explained by the hangover from the Shcherbytskyi period (see Chapter 3), but not by anything more fundamental. Hence, the final emergence of Kravchuk as the leading spokesman for the national communists in spring 1991 was only to be expected. With the collapse of the Soviet Empire, its material resources, coercive capabilities and legitimacy system, the national communists quickly realised that the manipulation of popular nationalism was their best hope of retaining power.[3]

By then, the opposing forces, that of the imperial centre and their allies in Ukraine, led by Hurenko, were perhaps still strong enough to brake developments in Ukraine. But the Baltic events in January 1991 and the failure of August's attempted coup demonstrated that it was too late to save the empire as a whole.

Krawchenko would argue that without socio-economic analysis, there is nothing to explain why the fault-lines of imperial collapse should necessarily be national. That would have to be explained by the long term processes of social change prior to the 1980s that had 'nationalised' the state from within.

Given alternative evidence about the relative weakness of Ukrainian national consciousness before 1991, our hypothesis has been instead that it is the post-*perestroika* period that was crucial. It was the collapse of central institutions and the survival strategies of republican elites that created national communism, and that it was the national communists' jumping onto the opposition bandwagon that finally created sufficient momentum towards independence. There would certainly have been a Ukrainian national movement without the national communists, but it would have been much weaker.

Once Kravchuk's wing of the party added its weight to the independence struggle, its control of the resources of the state transformed *Rukh*'s 25–33 per cent popular support into the 90.3 per cent vote on 1 December 1991. This decisive transformation reflected the fact that the local state, although nowhere near as hegemonic as in its near-totalitarian heyday, was still the decisive political force in Ukraine, given that the rival institutions of civil society were so weak and embryonic. In any case, the state and those independent voices that had by then developed were for the moment pulling in the same direction.

Although it is impossible to speculate how far Ukraine might have moved towards independence without the national communists, the top-down campaign by the state from 1991 onwards to rehabilitate and revive Ukrainian cultural nationality had more rapid effect than the cultural intelligentsia could have hoped to have achieved through their own efforts from below. Ukrainian independence was achieved by an alliance between oppositional and state elites, described by Tilly as a common precondition for revolution, but the latter were ultimately decisive.

The long-term future of the national communist group is another question. As of early 1992, their great strength lay in their near-complete control of the resources of the state, material, coercive and institutional. Their great weakness was that they operated in an ideological vacuum, parasitic on the nationalists' ideology and agenda. Having achieved power, the national communists still had to build a strong modern Ukrainian nation-state and overcome the problems listed in Chapter 2. The question of privatisation and the move to a market economy still had to be faced. Both issues would severely test the unity of the national communist camp, and test how far it had transcended its past.

Notes and References

1 Theories of Nationalism and the Soviet Ukrainian Context

1. Of many possible bibliographies, those in Anthony D. Smith, *Theories of Nationalism* (London: Holmes and Meier, 1983) and his more recent *National Identity* (London: Penguin, 1991) are comprehensive.
2. Alexander J. Motyl, *Sovietology, Rationality, Nationality; Coming to Grips with Nationalism in the USSR* (New York: Columbia University Press, 1990). Lubomyr Hajda and Mark Beissinger (eds), *The Nationalities Factor in Soviet Politics and Society* (Boulder, Col.: Westview Press in co-operation with the Harvard University Russian Research Centre, 1990), especially ch. 13. Alexander J. Motyl helps remedy this deficit in *Thinking Theoretically about Soviet Nationalities: Theory, History and Comparison in the Study of the USSR* (New York: Columbia University Press, 1992).
3. For example, such textbook classics as Jerry F. Hough, *The Soviet Union and Social Science Theory* (Cambridge, Mass.: Harvard University Press, 1977); Stephen White, *Political Culture and Soviet Politics* (London: Macmillan, 1979); T. H. Rigby, Archie Brown and Peter Reddaway, *Authority, Power and Policy in the USSR* (London: Macmillan, 1980); and Seweryn Bialer, *Stalin's Successors: Leadership, Change and Stability in the USSR* (Cambridge: Cambridge University Press, 1980).
4. Of the many works of Anthony D. Smith, the following are quoted from: (ed.), *Nationalist Movements* (London: Macmillan, 1976); *Theories of Nationalism* (London: Holmes and Meier, 1983); *The Ethnic Origin Of Nations* (Oxford: Basil Blackwell, 1986); 'The Myth of the "Modern Nation" and the Myths of Nations', *Ethnic and Racial Studies*, vol. 11, no. 1 (January 1988) pp. 1–26; and *National Identity* (London: Penguin, 1991).
5. Smith, 1976, p. 1.
6. Smith, 1988, pp. 9–10. Compare the slightly different wording in 1991, p. 14.
7. Smith, 1986, p. 215.
8. Smith, 1991; or Miroslav Hroch, *Social Preconditions of National Revival in Europe* (Cambridge: Cambridge University Press, 1985).
9. Teresa Rakowska-Harmstone, 'The Dialectics of Nationalism in the USSR', *Problems of Communism*, vol. 23, nos 5–6 (May–June 1974) pp. 1–22; 'The Study of Ethnic Politics in the USSR', in George W. Simmonds (ed.), *Nationalism in the Soviet Union and East Europe* (Detroit: University of Detroit Press, 1975) pp. 20–36; 'Integration and Ethnic Nationalism in the Soviet Union; Aspects, Trends and

Problems', in Carl A. Linden and Dimitri K. Simes (eds), *Nationalities and Nationalism in the USSR: a Soviet Dilemma* (Washington D.C.: Center for Strategic and International Studies, Georgetown University, 1977) pp. 31–39; 'Minority Nationalism Today: An Overview', in Robert Conquest (ed.), *The Last Empire: Nationality and the Soviet Future* (Stanford: Hoover Institution Press, 1986) pp. 235–64.

10. Bohdan Krawchenko, 'The Impact of Industrialisation on the Social Structure of Ukraine', *Canadian Slavonic Papers*, vol. xxii, no. 3 (September 1980) pp. 338–57; 'The Social Structure of Ukraine at the Turn of the Twentieth Century', *East European Quarterly*, vol. xvi, no. 2 (June 1982) pp. 171–81; (with J. Carter) 'Dissidents in Ukraine Before 1972: A Summary Statistical Profile', *Journal of Ukrainian Studies*, vol. 8, no. 2 (Winter 1983) pp. 85–8; (ed.) *Ukraine After Shelest* (Edmonton, Canadian Institute of Ukrainian Studies, University of Alberta, 1983), especially his 'Ethno-Demographic Trends in Ukraine in the 1970s', pp. 101–19; 'Changes in the National and Social Composition of the Communist Party of Ukraine From the Revolution to 1976', *Journal of Ukrainian Studies*, vol. 9, no. 1 (Summer 1984) pp. 33–54; 'The Working Class and the Nationality Question in the UkSSR', *Soviet Nationalities Survey*, vol. 1, nos 9–10 (September–October 1984); (especially) *Social Change and National Consciousness in Twentieth-Century Ukraine* (Oxford: St Antony's/Macmillan, 1985); 'The Social Structure of the Ukraine in 1917', *Harvard Ukrainian Studies*, vol. XIV, nos 1/2 (June 1990) pp. 97–112; 'National Memory in Ukraine : The Role of the Blue and Yellow Flag', *Journal of Ukrainian Studies*, vol. 15, no. 1 (Summer 1990) pp. 1–21.

11. See Karl W. Deutsch, 'Social Mobility and Political Development', *American Political Science Review*, vol. LV, no. 3 (September 1961) pp. 493–514; *Nationalism and Social Communication*, 2nd edn (Cambridge, Mass.: MIT Press, 1966).

12. On such official concepts, see Walker Connor, *The National Question in Marxist–Leninist Theory and Strategy* (Princeton: Princeton University Press, 1984) ch. 8, pp. 199–253.

13. See, for example, E. J. Hobsbawm, *Nations and Nationalism Since 1780* (Cambridge: Cambridge University Press, 1990).

14. Samuel P. Huntingdon, *Political Order in Changing Societies* (New Haven: Yale University Press, 1968) p. 4.

15. John A. Armstrong, 'The Ethnic Scene in the Soviet Union: The View of the Dictatorship', in Erich Goldhagen (ed.), *Ethnic Minorities in the Soviet Union* (New York: Praeger, 1986) pp. 3–49. See also Armstrong's reflections in 'The Soviet Ethnic Scene: A Quarter Century Later', *Journal of Soviet Nationalities*, vol. 1, no. 1 (Spring 1990) pp. 66–75, and the accompanying commentaries.

16. Rakowska-Harmstone, 1977, p. 33.

17. Rakowska-Harmstone, 1977, p. 38.

18. Rakowska-Harmstone, 1977, p. 31.

19. For Krawchenko, see above. Wsevolod Isajiw, 'Urban Migration and Social Change in Contemporary Soviet Ukraine', *Canadian Slavonic Papers*, vol. xxii, no. 1 (March 1980) pp. 58–86.

20. Michael Hechter *Internal Colonialism: The Celtic Fringe in British National Development, 1536–1966* (London: Routledge & Kegan Paul, 1975). See also the special issue of *Ethnic and Racial Studies* on 'Internal Colonialism', vol. 2, no. 3 (July 1979).
21. Paul Brass, 'Ethnicity and Nationality Formation', *Ethnicity*, no. 3 (September 1976) pp. 225–41.
22. Krawchenko, 1983, p. 113. Similar arguments can be found in Ernest Gellner, *Nations and Nationalism* (Oxford: Blackwell, 1983), and Benedict Anderson, *Imagined Communities: Reflections on the Origins and Spread of Nationalism* (London: Verso, 1983).
23. See Ivan L. Rudnytsky, 'Observations on the Problem of "Historical" and "Non-Historical" Nations', in his *Essays in Modern Ukrainian History* (Edmonton: Canadian Institute of Ukrainian Studies, 1987) pp. 37–48.
24. Krawchenko, 1990, p. 106; and 1982, p. 175.
25. Krawchenko, 1990, pp. 100 and 111; and 1985, table 1.5, p. 44. The figures refer to 1897, but Krawchenko, 1990, argues that little had changed by 1917.
26. See Orest Subtelny's comprehensive *Ukraine: A History* (Toronto, University of Toronto Press, 1988) chs 18 and 19. The Ukrainian version is *Ukraïna: Istoriia* (Kyiv: Lybid; 1991).
27. See David Saunders' review article, 'Modern Ukrainian History (II)', *European History Quarterly*, vol. 21 (1991) pp. 81–95, for a discussion of 'Little Russianism', and a survey of some of the recent literature on this period, Subtelny included. Paul Robert Magocsi, 'The Ukrainian National Revival: A New Analytical Framework', *Canadian Review of Studies in Nationalism*, vol. XVI, nos 1–2 (1989) pp. 45–62, also argues that the 'Little Russian' mentality was widespread.
28. Krawchenko, 1985, p. 21. For a view basically supportive of Krawchenko, see Steven Guthier, 'The Popular Basis of Ukrainian Nationalism in 1917', *Slavic Review*, vol. 38, no. 1 (March 1979), and his conclusion that 'The Ukrainian revolution failed not through the lack of a popular base, but through the organisational problems and resource deficiencies arising from its overwhelmingly peasant constituency', p. 47.
     Geoff Ely, on the other hand, argues that political conjunctures were more responsible for the national movement's defeat. See his 'Remapping the Nation: War, Revolutionary Upheaval and State Formation in Eastern Europe, 1914–1923', in Peter J. Potichnyj and Howard Aster (eds), *Ukrainian–Jewish Relations in Historical Perspective* (Edmonton: Canadian Institute of Ukrainian Studies, 1988) pp. 205–46. Motyl, 1990, ch. 7, takes a similar view. Rudolf A. Mark's 'Social Questions and National Revolution: The Ukrainian National Republic in 1919–20', *Harvard Ukrainian Studies*, vol. XIV, nos 1/2 (June 1990) pp. 113–31 argues that party divisions and a lack of popular support were to blame.
29. Ibid., p. 113. The concept of assimilation and whether all of the 37.4 million Ukrainian SSR inhabitants who gave their nationality as Ukrainian in the 1989 census can in fact be considered nationally conscious Ukrainians is considered in Chapter 2 below. For a view more pessimistic than Krawchenko's, see Mikhail Guboglo, 'Demography and

Language in the Capitals of the Union', *Journal of Soviet Nationalities*, vol. 1, no. 4 (Winter 1990–1) pp. 1–11.

30. Krawchenko, 1985, p. 253.
31. *Ukraïns'ka RSR u tsyfrakh: 1990* (Kyiv: Tekhnika, 1991), p. 23.
32. Interestingly, Soviet research has also admitted this possibility. See Iu. V. Arutiunian and Iu. V. Bromlei (eds), *Sotsial'no-kul'turnyi oblik sovet-skikh natsii: Po rezul'tatam etnosotsiologicheskogo issledovaniia* (Moscow: Nauka, 1986).
33. Isajiw, 1980, pp. 60–3.
34. Ivan Dziuba, *Internationalism or Russification?* (London: Weidenfeld & Nicolson, 1968). Complaints about Russian privilege certainly featured prominently in the *samizdat* of the period. See Chapter 3.
35. Motyl, 1987, pp. 103–4. See also the description of the Ukrainian dis-sidents of the 1960s in Vyacheslav Chornovil, *The Chornovil Papers* (New York: McGraw-Hill, 1968).
36. See Krawchenko, 1980.
37. Krawchenko, 1985, p. 3.
38. Alexander J. Motyl, 1990, and *Will The Non-Russians Rebel? State, Ethnicity and Stability in the USSR* (Ithaca: Cornell University Press, 1987). See also his 'The Sobering of Gorbachev: Nationality, Restructuring and the West' in Seweryn Bialer (ed.), *Politics, Society and Nationality Inside Gorbachev's Russia* (Boulder: Westview Press, 1989), pp. 149–73; 'Empire or Stability? The Case for Soviet Dissolution', *World Policy Journal*, vol. VIII, no. 3 (Summer 1991) pp. 499–524; 'Helping Gorbachev or Helping the Nationalities: The Unreformable Soviet Federation and the West', in A. Kagedan (ed.), *Ethnicity and the Soviet Future: Aspects of Centre–Republic Relations in the USSR* (Ottawa: Norman Paterson School of International Affairs, Carleton University, 1991) pp. 133–50; and 'Totalitarian Collapse, Imperial Disintegration, and the Rise of the Soviet West: Implications for the West' in Michael Mandelbaum (ed.), *The Rise of Nations in the Soviet Union* (New York: Council on Foreign Relations Press, 1991) pp. 44–63. Although dealing with the USSR in general, Motyl's work focuses on Ukraine.
39. Motyl, Summer 1991, p. 509. Emphasis in original.
40. Charles Tilly, 'Does Modernisation Breed Revolution?', *Comparative Politics*, vol. 5, no. 3 (April 1973) pp. 425–47. See also Motyl, 1987, pp. 131–4; and 1990, pp. 157–9.
41. Motyl, 1987, ch. 7.
42. Motyl, 1987, pp. 16–17.
43. For a recent survey of rational choice theory and literature, see Patrick Dunleavy, *Democracy, Bureaucracy and Public Choice: Economic Explanations in Political Science* (London: Harvester Wheatsheaf, 1991). See also Charles Tilly, *From Mobilisation to Revolution* (New York: Random House, 1978) p. 7.
44. Motyl, 1987, ch. 1.
45. Examples might include the purge of Babaev in Turkmenistan in 1958, Kalberzins in Latvia in 1959 and the Ukrainian leader Shelest in 1972.
46. O. Bauer, *Die Nationalitätenfrage und die Sozialdemokratie* (Vienna, 1907). On 1920s Ukraine, see George Liber, *Soviet Nationality Policy,*

Urban Growth, and Identity Change in the Ukrainian SSR, 1923–1934 (Cambridge: Cambridge University Press, 1992); and James E. Mace, *Communism and the Dilemmas of National Liberation: National Communism in Soviet Ukraine, 1918–1933* (Cambridge, Mass.: Harvard University Press, 1983).

47. Motyl, 1990, chs 5 and 6. Cf. Steven L. Burg, 'Nationality Elites and Political Change in the Soviet Union', in Hajda and Beissinger, 1990, pp. 24–42.

48. For general overviews of the Soviet Union's nationalities problems, see Bohdan Nahaylo and Victor Swoboda's largely historical *Soviet Disunion: A History of the Nationalities Problem in the USSR* (London: Hamish Hamilton, 1990); or Gregory Gleason's straightforward introduction *Federalism And Nationalism: The Struggle for Republican Rights in the USSR* (Boulder, Col.: Westview Press, 1990).

49. See Motyl, 1990, especially chs 5 and 6; Burg in Hajda and Beissinger, 1990, or Gleason, 1990, especially ch. 5.

50. See, for example, Steven L. Burg again, 1990; or Mark Beissinger's excellent study of UkSSR and RSFSR elites in 'Ethnicity, the Personnel Weapon, and Neo-Imperial Integration: Ukrainian and RSFSR Provincial Party Officials Compared', *Studies in Comparative Communism*, vol. xxi, no. 1 (Spring 1988) pp. 71–85. John A. Armstrong's classic work, *The Soviet Bureaucratic Elite. Case Study of the Ukrainian Apparatus* (New York: Praeger, 1959) describes the local oligarchy in the Ukrainian SSR. On the concepts of 'penetration', 'participation', 'distribution' and 'legitimacy' crises see Leonard Binder (ed.), *Crises and Sequences in Political Development* (Princeton: Princeton University Press, 1971).

51. Motyl, in Mandelbaum (ed.), 1991, p. 47.

52. Mancur Olson, *The Logic of Collective Action* (Cambridge, Mass.: Harvard University Press, 1965).

53. See Olson's own analysis, 'The Logic of Collective Action in Soviet-type Societies', *Journal of Soviet Nationalities*, vol. 1, no. 2 (Summer 1990) pp. 8–27.

54. Mayar N. Zald and John D. McCarthy (eds), *The Dynamics of Social Movements: Resource Mobilisation, Social Control and Tactics* (Cambridge, Mass.: Winthrop Publishers, 1979) p. 14.

55. For some public choice approaches to the phenomenon of nationalism, see Susan Olzak, 'Contemporary Ethnic Mobilisation', *Annual Review of Sociology*, vol. 9 (1983) pp. 355–74; Ronald Rogowski, 'Causes and Varieties of Nationalism: a Rationalist Account', in Edward Tiryakan and Ronald Rogowski (eds), *New Nationalisms of the Developed West* (London: Allen & Unwin, 1985) pp. 87–108; Hudson Meadwell, 'Ethnic Mobilisation and Collective Choice Theory', *Comparative Political Studies*, vol. 22, no. 2 (July 1989) pp. 139–54; and J. Craig Jenkins, 'Resource Mobilisation Theory and the Study of Social Movements', *Annual Review of Sociology*, no. 9 (1983), pp. 527–53 for the general importance of culture.

56. J. Craig Jenkins, 1983, p. 538.

57. Rachel Walker, *Language and the Politics of Identity in the USSR*. Paper presented to the 75th Anniversary Conference of the School of Slavonic

and East European Studies, London, December 1990, pp. 2–3. See also her 'The Relevance of Ideology', ch. 6 in Ronald J. Hill and Jan Zielowka (eds), *Restructuring Eastern Europe: Towards a New European Order* (Cheltenham: Edward Elgar, 1990).

58. George Schöpflin, 'National Identity in the Soviet Union and East Central Europe', *Ethnic and Racial Studies* Special issue on 'National Identity in Eastern Europe and the Soviet Union', vol. 14, no. 1 (January 1991) p. 11.

59. See Timothy Garton Ash, 'Reform or Revolution?' in *The Uses of Adversity: Essays on the Fate of Central Europe* (Cambridge: Granta/Penguin, 1989) pp. 218–30; and Václav Havel, 'The Power of the Powerless', *Living in Truth* (London: Faber & Faber, 1987) pp. 36–122 on the pursuit of post-communist civil society.

60. Tilly, 1973, p. 438; and 1978, ch. 7, on 'multiple sovereignty'; and Motyl, 1990, pp. 103–4.

61. Grzegorz Ekiert, 'Democratic Processes in East Central Europe: A Theoretical Reconsideration', *British Journal of Political Science* vol. 21, pt 3 (July 1991), especially pp. 229 and 301. Although focusing on east central Europe, the arguments also apply to the Soviet Union.

62. C. M. Drobizheva, 'The Role of the Intelligentsia in Developing National Consciousness among the Peoples of the USSR under Perestroika', *Ethnic and Racial Studies*, vol. 14, no. 1 (January 1991) pp. 87–99.

63. Johan Galtung, 'A Structural Theory of Imperialism', *Journal of Peace Research*, vol. 7, no. 2 (1971) p. 81.

64. Kenneth C. Farmer, *Ukrainian Nationalism in the Post-Stalin Era: Myths, Symbols and Ideology in Soviet Nationality Policy* (The Hague: Martinus Nijhoff, 1980); and 'Politics and Culture in the Ukraine in the Post-Stalin Era', *The Annals of the Ukrainian Academy of Arts and Sciences in the US*, vol. XIV, nos 37–8 (1978–80) pp. 180–208.

65. On the difference between the two sorts of national development, see Anthony D. Smith, 1991; or H. Kohn, *The Idea of Nationalism* (New York: Macmillan, 1967).

66. Anthony D. Smith, 1991, p. viii and p. 163.

67. Chew Sock Fan, 'On the Incompatibility of Ethnic and National Loyalties: Reframing the Issue', *Canadian Review of Studies in Nationalism*, vol. XIII, no. 1 (Spring 1986) pp. 1–11.

2 Strengths and Weaknesses of the National Movement

1. S. N. Eisenstadt, *The Political Systems of Empires* (New York: The Free Press, 1963). See also M. W. Doyle, *Empires* (Ithaca, N.Y.: Cornell University Press, 1986). A suitable biography of literature on imperialism can be found in Wolfgang J. Mommsen, *Theories of Imperialism* (London: Weidenfeld and Nicolson, 1981).

2. The sources used here are *Natsional'nyi sostav naseleniia SSSR, po dannykh vsesoiuznoi perepisi naseleniia 1989 g.* (Moscow: Finansy I statistika, 1991); V. I. Naulko, *Razvitie mezhetnicheskikh sviazei na*

Ukraine (Kyiv: Naukova Dumka, 1975); *Ukraïns'ka RSR u tsyfrakh*: 1990 (Derzhavnyi komitet Ukraïns'koï RSR po statystytsi) (Kyiv: 'Tekhnika', 1991); and *Natsional'ni vidnosyny na Ukraïni: Zapytannia i vidpovidi* (Kyiv: Ukraïna, 1991).

3. The name change is a result of the Moldovan desire to re-Latinise their alphabet after 1989.

4. The Starodub region north of Chernihiv was also part of Ukraine under the terms of the Treaty of Brest–Litovsk in 1918. The Treaty also gave to Ukraine the old Tsarist *gubernias* (provinces) of Chelm and Podlachia, now in Poland and Belarus. On the Kuban', see V. Ivanys, *Borot'ba Kubani za nezalezhnist'* (Munich: Ukrainian Technical-Economic Institute, 1958).

5. President Kravchuk, in his inauguration speech on 5 December 1991, promised to defend the interest of 'Ukrainians abroad'. See *Ukrainian Reporter*, no. 22, December 1991. A Congress of Ukrainians of the former USSR was held in Kyiv on 22–23 January 1992.

6. Mikhail Guboglo, 'Demography and Language in the Capitals of the Union', *Journal of Soviet Nationalities*, vol. 1, no. 4 (Winter 1990–1) pp. 8, 21, 13 and 18.

7. See Bohdan Nahaylo, 'Concern Voiced About Six Million Ukrainians Condemned to "Denationalization"', *Radio Liberty Research*, RL 92/88, 9 March 1988; and Ivan Dziuba, *Internationalism or Russification?* (London: Weidenfeld and Nicolson, 1968) p. 109 and throughout.

8. Different estimates can be found in Orest Subtelny, *Ukraine: a History* (Toronto: University of Toronto Press, 1988) and in *Natsional'ni vidnosyny*, p. 7. The problem in giving precise estimates derives from the manner in which the various populations' calculations of the costs and benefits associated with a declaration of a given national status has changed.

9. On Polish–Ukrainian relations in general, see Peter J. Potichnyj (ed.), *Poland and Ukraine: Past and Present* (Edmonton: Canadian Institute of Ukrainian Studies, 1980). On Operation 'Vistula', see T. A. Olszanski, 'All About "Operation Wisla"', *The Ukrainian Quarterly*, vol. XLVII, no. 3 (Fall 1991) pp. 249–62.

10. See Orest Subtelny, *Ukrainians in North America* (Toronto: University of Toronto Press, 1991).

11. *Natsional'ni vidnosyny* ..., 1991, p. 7. See also Subtelny, 1988, chs. 27 and 28; and Armstrong, 1990, ch. 13, which also contain brief accounts of émigré history and politics.

12. W. R. Petryshyn (ed.), *Changing Realities: Social Trends Among Ukrainian Canadians* (Edmonton: Canadian Institute of Ukrainian Studies, 1980). See also Myron B. Kuropas, *The Ukrainian Americans: Roots and Aspirations, 1884–1954* (Toronto: University of Toronto Press, 1991). On the politics of the diaspora, see Taras Kuzio, 'Panorama politychnykh partii ta orhanizatsii ukraïns'koï emihratsii', *Za vil'nu Ukraïnu*, 3 October 1991.

13. *Natsional'nyi sostav*, 1991, p. 78 (figures rounded off to the nearest 10 000). Also, 269 000 Crimean Tatars, expelled by Stalin in 1944 for alleged collaboration with the Germans, are now returning in increasing numbers.

14. Krawchenko, 1982, p. 103; and 1985. See also the essays by Szporluk and Woroby on post-war urbanisation in Ukraine in Ivan L. Rudnytsky (ed.), *Rethinking Ukrainian History* (Edmonton: Canadian Institute of Ukrainian Studies, 1981).
15. Krawchenko, 1984(b).
16. 'The Demography of Ukraine', *Politics of Soviet Economic Reform*, vol. 1, no. 5, 1 November 1991, p. 4. Anderson and B. Silver, 'Some Factors in the Linguistic and Ethnic Russification of Soviet Nationalities: Is Everyone Becoming Russian? in Hajda and Beissinger, 1990, pp. 95–130 consider that the rate of assimilation of Ukrainians is surprisingly low, although they only cover the period from 1959–70.
17. All information on Russians in Ukraine is derived from Dmitrii Vydrin, formerly of the Kyiv Institute of Social Sciences and Political Management.
18. Iaroslav Dashkevych, a radical L'viv historian, claims that the 1989 census was tainted by a variety of administrative and social pressures towards Russification, and out of the alleged 11 million 'Russians' recorded in Ukraine, a minimum of 3.5 million are Ukrainians whilst another 1.5 million are other minorities who classified themselves as 'Russians'. See his article on national minorities in Ukraine in *Derzhavnist*, no. 3, 1991, pp. 24–7.
19. On the Russians in contemporary Ukraine, see Krawchenko, especially 1983, 1984(a) and (b) and 1985; and Isajiw, 1980. Also useful is Roman Szporluk, 'Russians in Ukraine and Problems of Ukrainian Identity in the USSR', in Peter J. Potichnyj (ed.), *Ukraine in the 1970s* (Oakville, Ontario: Mosaic Press, 1975) pp. 195–218.
20. See Chapter 1.
21. See Roman Solchanyk, 'Ukraine and Russia: Before and After the Coup', *Report on the USSR*, RL 346/91, 27 September 1991.
22. In 1989, only 23.2 per cent of Germans, 48.5 per cent of Belarusians and 18.5 per cent of Greeks in Ukraine knew their native language as their first or second language; 84.4 per cent of Poles knew Ukrainian, and 66.5 per cent Russian, whereas the Rusyns were not classed as an ethnic group. In the third category, 95.6 per cent of Hungarians, 84.4 per cent of Moldovans, 62.3 per cent of Romanians, 69.5 per cent of Bulgarians and 93.5 per cent of Crimean Tatars knew their mother tongue. T. M. Rudnyts'ka, 'Natsionalni hrupy i movni protsesy v Ukraïni', *Filosofs'ka i sotsiolochichna dumka*, 1991 no. 5, pp. 145–55.
23. V. I. Naulko, 1975, Table 4, p. 64. The 1926 figure is the author's own estimate for the number of Poles then residing within what became the post-1945 boundaries of the Ukrainian SSR, using the Polish census of 1931.
24. Kristopher Gasior, 'Poles in the Soviet Union', *Report on the USSR*, RL 521/90, 28 December 1990, p. 12. See also P. J. Potichnyi (ed.), *Poland and Ukraine: Past and Present* (Edmonton: Canadian Institute of Ukrainian Studies, 1980).
25. Volodymyr Kubijovyč (ed.) *Encyclopedia of Ukraine*, vol. II (Toronto: University of Toronto Press, 1988) pp. 385–93, which cites the figure of 2.245 million Jews on Tsarist territories in 1897, and 2.68 million overall on the territories of what was the Ukrainian SSR. Krawchenko's calcu-

lation for Jews in Tsarist Ukraine in 1897 is 1.908 million (8.1 per cent of the population), Krawchenko, 1985, Table 5.1, p. 173. On the Jews in Ukraine, see Zvi Gitelman, 'The Social and Political Role of the Jews in Ukraine', in Potichnyj (ed.), *Ukraine in the 1970s*, pp. 167–86; Potichnyj and Aster, 1988 (n. 34, ch. 1); the same authors' *Jewish–Ukrainian Relations: Two Solitudes* (Oakville: Mosaic Press, 1983); *Ukraine and Jews. A Symposium* (New York: The Ukrainian Congress Committee of America, 1966); and Roman Solchanyk, 'Ukrainian–Jewish Relations: An Interview with Oleksandr Buratovs'kyi', *Report on the USSR*, RL 34/91, 18 January, 1991.

26. See Taras Hunczak, *Symon Petliura and the Jews: A Reappraisal* (Toronto: Ukrainian Historical Association, 1985); and Soloman I. Goldeman, *Jewish National Autonomy in Ukraine, 1917–20* (Chicago: Ukrainian Research and Information Institute, 1968).

27. Kubijovyč, vol. II, 1988, pp. 43–7.

28. *Natsional'ni vidnosyny ...*, 1991, p. 25.

29. See Paul Robert Magosci, *The Shaping of a National Identity: Subcarpathian Rus'* 1848–1948 (Cambridge, Mass: Harvard University Press, 1978); and *The Rusyn'–Ukrainians of Czechoslovakia: A Historical Survey* (Vienna: Wilhelm Braumuller, 1983).

30. Ibid., pp. 36–7; and Kubijovyč, vol. II, 1988, pp. 274–5.

31. P. R. Magocsi, 1978, p. 272.

32. I. L. Rudnytsky, 'Carpatho-Ukraine: A People in Search of their History', *Essays in Modern Ukrainian History* (Edmonton: Canadian Institute of Ukrainian Studies, 1987) p. 368.

33. On these territories, see I. M. Nowosiwsky, *Bukovinian Ukrainians: A Historical Background. Their Self-Determination in 1918* (New York: The Shevchenko Scientific Society, 1970); and Vladimir Socor, 'Moldovian Lands Between Romania and Ukraine: the Historical and Political Geography', *Report On the USSR*, RL 473/90, 16 November 1990. On the Romanian declaration of 24 June 1991 see V. Socor, 'Annexation of Bessarabia and Northern Bukovina Condemned by Romania', RL 256/91, 19 July 1991. The Moldovan parliament made a similar condemnation on 23 June 1990.

34. *Natsional'ni vidnosyny na Ukraïni*, 1991, pp. 32–5.

35. *TASS*, 19 June 1991.

36. For Crimean politics in 1990 and early 1991, see Kathleen Mihalisko, 'The Other Side of Separatism: Crimea Votes for Autonomy', *Report on the USSR*, RL 60/91, 1 February 1991; and R. Solchanyk, 'Centrifugal Movements in Ukraine on the Eve of Independence', RL 408/91, 29 November 1991.

37. *Natsional'ni vidnosyny na Ukraïni*, 1991, p. 15.

38. Ibid., pp. 15–16.

39. Kubijovyč, 1988, vol. II, pp. 95–7.

40. *Natsional'nyi sostav*, 1991. See Jan T. Gross, *Revolution from Abroad: The Soviet Conquest of Poland's Western Ukraine and Western Belorussia* (Princeton: Princeton University Press, 1988).

41. Kharkiv, or Slobids'ka Ukraine, could either be included in the Left Bank, because of its traditional position as a key meeting point of

Ukrainian and Russian culture, or in Eastern Ukraine, because of its similar level of industrialisation.

42. *Natsional'nyi sostav*, 1991.
43. Krawchenko, 1983, for a breakdown of ethnicity and language by region. Cf. Roman Szporluk, 'Urbanisation in Ukraine since the Second World War', in I. L. Rudnytsky (ed.), *Rethinking Ukrainian History* (Edmonton: Canadian Institute of Ukrainian Studies, 1981). pp. 180–202.
44. David Marples, *Ukraine Under Perestroika: Ecology, Economics and the Workers' Revolt* (London: Macmillan, 1991).
45. *Chislennost' i sostav naseleniia SSSR (Po dannykh vsesoiuznoi perepisi naseleniia 1979 g.)* (Moscow: Finansy I statistika, 1984) p. 12. The figures refer to 1979, and are rounded to the nearest percentage point.
46. See Paul Robert Magocsi, *Galicia: A Historical Survey and Bibliographical Guide* (Toronto: University of Toronto Press, 1983) on Galician historiography.
47. The classic work on war-time nationalism is John A. Armstrong, *Ukrainian Nationalism*, 3rd edn (Englewood, Col.: Ukrainian Academic Press, 1990) (first edition published by Columbia University Press, 1963), although the author, writing originally in the 1950s, did not have the opportunity to research post-war beliefs and sentiments.
48. Szporluk in Rudnytsky, 1981, p. 198.
49. Guboglo, 1990–1, table 3, p. 7.
50. On the difference between 'ethnic' and 'territorial' nationalism, see Anthony D. Smith, *Theories of Nationalism* (London: Holmes and Meier, 1983) ch. 9.
51. Armstrong, 1990, chs IX–XII. See also L. Shankovs'kyi, *Pokhidni hrupy OUN* (Munich: Ukraïns'kyi Samostiinyk, 1958). The competition between integral and democratic nationalism led to a second split in the exile OUN in 1954, with only Stepan Bandera remaining faithful to Dontsov's ideas. See also n. 12 above.
52. On Autocephalous Orthodoxy in the Ukraine, see Frank E. Sysyn, 'The Ukrainian Orthodox Question in the USSR', *Religion in Communist Lands*, vol. 11, no. 3 (Winter 1983) pp. 251–63. Vasyl Markus, 'Religion and Nationalism in Ukraine', in Pedro Ramet (ed.), *Religion and Nationalism in Soviet and East European Politics* (Durham, N.C.: Duke University Press, 1984) pp. 59–81 looks at religion in general.
53. Bodhan R. Bociurkiw, 'The Ukrainian Catholic Church in the USSR Under Gorbachev', *Problems of Communism*, vol. XXXIX, nos. 11–12 (November–December, 1990) pp. 1–19 is a useful survey, concentrating mainly on the postwar period.
54. With regard to social change in twentieth-century Ukraine, the works of Krawchenko cited in Chapter 1 provide excellent background information. See also Motyl, 1987, ch. 4; Isajiw, 1980; Szporluk in Potichnyj (ed.), 1975; and in Rudnytsky (ed.), 1981.
55. Krawchenko, 1985, p. 181.
56. *Ukrains'ka RSR u tsyfrakh*, 1991, p. 22.
57. Ibid., p. 33.
58. Ibid., p. 36.

59. L. M. Drobizheva, 'The Role of the Intelligentsia in Developing National Consciousness Among the Peoples of the USSR under Perestroika', *Ethnic and Racial Studies*, vol. 14, no. 1 (January 1991) p. 92.
60. See E. and J. Winiecki, *The Structural Legacy of the Soviet-Type Economy* (London: The Centre for Research into Communist Economies, 1992).
61. J. A. Armstrong, 1990; see note 40 above. See also Peter J. Potichnyj and Yevhen Shtendera (eds), *Political Thought of the Ukrainian Underground, 1943–1951* (Edmonton: Canadian Institute of Ukrainian Studies, 1986).
62. Robert Conquest, *The Harvest of Sorrow: Soviet Collectivization and the Terror-Famine* (London: Hutchinson, 1986).
63. On the concept of 'internal colonialism' see Chapter 1. On its application to Ukraine, see the following works by Ivan S. Koropeckyj (ed.), *The Ukraine within the USSR: An Economic Balance Sheet* (London: Praeger, 1977); 'A Century of Moscow-Ukraine Economic Relations: An Interpretation', *Harvard Ukrainian Studies* vol. V, no. 4 (December 1981) pp. 467–96; *Development in the Shadow: Studies in Ukrainian Economics* (Edmonton: Canadian Institute of Ukrainian Studies Press, 1990); and (ed.) *Ukrainian Economic History: Interpretative Essays* (Cambridge, Mass.: Harvard University Press, 1991).

    See also Anna Briscoe. *Internal Colonialism in the USSR: The Case of the Soviet Ukraine*, thesis submitted to the faculty of Graduate Studies, Edmonton, University of Alberta Fall 1986. Marples, 1991, and Gennady Ozornoy, 'The Ukrainian Economy in the 1970s', in Bohdan Krawchenko (ed.), *Ukraine After Shelest* (Edmonton: Canadian Institute of Ukranian Studies Press, 1983) pp. 73–100, are also useful in this context.
64. The notion of an 'internal colony' arguably in fact makes more sense within the political allocation of resources of a command economy, rather than in Hechter's original hunting-ground of Western Europe. The command-administrative system's monopoly on political and economic power is clearly reserved to itself and denied to regions, but in a market capitalist economy no 'region' is deprived of autonomous powers, as the allocative mechanism is impersonal in the first place.
65. M. Dolishnii, 'Rehional'ni problemi ekonomichnoho i sotsial'noho rozvytku Ukraïny', *Ekonomika Radians'koï Ukraïny*, 1991, no. 5, pp. 12–22.
66. *Radio Kyiv*, 27 June 1991.
67. Marples, 1991, ch. 1. See also his 'Ukraine's Economic Prospects', *Report on the USSR*, RL 357/91, 4 October 1991; 'The Prospects for an Independent Ukraine', RL 173/90, 13 April 1990; and 'The Economic Outlook for Ukraine in 1990', RL 80/90, 16 February 1990. Similar points are made by John Tedstrom, 'The Economic Costs and Benefits of Independence for Ukraine', RL 500/90, 7 December 1990.
68. Mykhailo Volobuiev, 'Do problemy Ukraïns'koï ekonomiky', *Dokumenty Ukraïns'koho komunizmu* (New York: Prolog, 1962) pp. 132–230.
69. Koropeckyj, 1981, pp. 469–74.
70. David Marples, *Ukraine under Perestroika*, 1991, especially ch. 4.
71. David Marples, *The Social Impact of the Chornobyl' Disaster* (London: Macmillan, 1988).

72. Motyl, 1987, ch. 3.
73. Koropeckyj, 1981, p. 487.
74. Johan Galtung, 'A Structural Theory of Imperialism', *Journal of Peace Research*, vol. 7, no. 2 (1971) pp. 81–117.

3   Ukraine on the Eve of the Gorbachev Era

1. Borys Lewytzkyj, *Politics and Society in Soviet Ukraine, 1953–1980* (Edmonton: Canadian Institute of Ukrainian Studies, 1984) p. 166.
2. On Shcherbytskyi, see Yaroslav Bilinsky, 'Shcherbytsky, Ukraine and Kremlin Politics', *Problems of Communism*, vol. XXXII, no. 4 (July/August 1983) pp. 1–26; Roman Solchanyk, 'Politics and the National Question in the Post-Shelest Period', in Bohdan Krawchenko (ed.), *Ukraine After Shelest* (Edmonton: Canadian Institute of Ukrainian Studies, 1983) pp. 1–29; Bohdan Harasymiw, 'Political Patronage and Perestroika: Changes in Communist Party Leadership in Ukraine Under Gorbachov and Shcherbytsky', in R. M. Bahry (ed.), *Echoes of Glasnost' in Soviet Ukraine* (North York, Ontario: Captus Press, 1989) pp. 28–39.
3. On Shelest, see Grey Hodnett, 'Ukrainian Politics and the Purge of Shelest' (paper presented at the annual meeting of the Midwest Slavic Conference, Ann Arbor, 5–7 May 1977); which is partly summarised in the more widely available 'The Views of Petro Shelest', *Annals of the Ukranian Academy of Arts and Sciences in the United States*, vol. 14, nos 37–8 (1978–80) pp. 209–43; Jaroslaw Pelenski, 'Shelest and His Period in Soviet Ukraine (1963, 1972): A Revival of Controlled Ukrainian Autonomism', in Peter J. Potichnyj (ed.), *Ukraine in the 1970s* (Oakville, Ontario: Mosaic Press, 1975) pp. 283–305; Y. Bilinsky, 'Mykola Skrypnyk and Petro Shelest: an Essay on the Persistence and Limits of Ukrainian National Communism', in J. R. Azrael (ed.), *Soviet Nationality Politics and Practices* (New York: Praeger, 197) pp. 105–43; Lowell Tillett, 'Ukrainian Nationalism and the Fall of Shelest', *Slavic Review*, vol. XXXIV, no. 4 (Winter 1975) pp. 752–68 mainly considers Shelest's heretical book *Ukraïno, nasha radians'ka* (Kyiv: Politvydav Ukraïny, 1970).
4. Works covering both Shelest and Shcherbytskyi include Lewytzkyj, 1984; his 'The Ruling Party Organs of Ukraine', and Yaroslav Bilinsky, 'The Communist Party of Ukraine After 1966', both in Peter J. Potichnyj (ed.), *Ukraine in the 1970s* (Oakville, Ontario: Mosaic Press, 1975); Mark Beissinger, 'Ethnicity, the Personnel Weapon, and Neo-imperial Integration: Ukrainian and RSFSR Provincial Party Officials Compared', *Studies in Comparative Communism*, vol. XXI, no. 1 (Spring 1988) pp. 71–85; Bohdan Harasymiw, 'Political Mobility in Soviet Ukraine', *Canadian Slavonic Papers*, vol. XXVI, nos 2–3 (June–September 1984) pp. 160–81.
5. *Storinky istoriï Kompartiï Ukraïny: Zapytannia i vidpovidi* (Kyiv: Lybid', 1990) pp. 484–5; and Bohdan Krawchenko, 'Changes in the National and Social Composition of the Communist Party of Ukraine From the

Revolution to 1976', *Journal of Ukrainian Studies*, vol. 9, no. 1 (Summer 1984) pp. 33–54.

6. *Storinky* ..., pp. 482–3. As of 1 January each year, except for 1918 (July). The figures include both full and candidate members. Krawchenko, 1984, gives marginally different figures for 1918 (5000 in October; p. 36), 1922 (56 000; p. 36), and 1940 (680 000; p. 45). However, the 1940 figure and others are not necessarily from 1 January.

7. *Vechirnii Kyïv*, 17 June 1991 cited a decline in CPU membership to 2.5 million. See *Ukranian Reporter*, vol. 1, no. 14 (August 1991).

8. Krawchenko, 1984, p. 49.

9. Despite official disinformation (and some Western analysis) at the time, that Shelest was removed for his hardline foreign policy views, no one would now dispute that Shelest's defence of Ukrainian autonomy, plus his association with the old Moscow circles around Khrushchev and Pidhornyi, were the real reasons for his dismissal. See the works cited in n. 3 above.

10. *Komunist Ukraïny*, no. 4 (April 1973) translated in *Digest of the Soviet Ukranian Press*, May 1973, pp. 1–6. All of the relevant documents are also published in *Za shcho usunuly Shelesta?* (Munich: Suchasnist', 1973). Compare Shcherbytskyi's *Radians'ka Ukraïna* (Kyiv: Politvydav Ukraïny, 1978) to Shelest's book.

11. There are clear similarities between Shelest's and Gorbachev's idealisation of Lenin and denunciations of Brezhnevism. See the former's interviews in *Sil's'ki vist:* 19 January 1989; *Argumenty i fakty*, no. 2, 1989, pp. 14–20; *Kyiv*, no. 10,1989, pp. 90–110; and *Radians'ka Ukraïna*, 29 March 1990. Some of these are discussed in Bohdan Nahaylo, 'Disgraced Ukrainian Party Leader Petro Shelest Reappears After Fifteen Years – a Slap in the Face for Shcherbytsky?', *Radio Liberty Research*, RL 293/88 (29 July 1988); 'Shelest Confirms He Was Ousted For Nationalism', RL 40/89; Alexandr Rahr, 'Shelest Remembers', RL 41/89; *Report on the USSR* (27 January 1989) September 1989. See also P. E. Shelest, ... *Dane Sudymyi Budete. Dnevnikovyie Zapysy*, *Vosprominaniya Chlena Politburo TSK KPSS* (Moscow: Edition, 1995).

12. Jaroslav Pelenski, 'Shelest and his Period ...', 1975, p. 299.

13. Grey Hodnett, 'Ukrainian Politics', 1977, p. 34. (Underlining in original.)

14. Mark Beissinger, 'Ethnicity ...', 1988, p. 79. See also Radio Liberty, *Arkhiv samizdata*, no. 1002.

15. See the collections edited by I. Koshelivets', *Panorama nainovishoï literatury v URSR* (New York: Prolog, 1963 and Munich: Suchasnist', 1974); *Suchasna literatura v URSR* (New York: Prolog, 1964); as well as B. Kravtsiv, *Shistdesiat' poetiv shistdesiatykh rokiv* (New York: Prolog, 1967). See also J. Pelenski, 'Recent Ukrainian Writing', *Survey*, vol. 59, no. 2 (April 1966) pp. 102–17; and George Luckyj, 'Turmoil in the Ukraine', *Problems of Communism*, vol. XVII (July–August 1968) pp. 14–20.

16. Hodnett, 1977, p. 41. See also B. Krawchenko, 1985, p. 177.

17. Ibid., pp. 42–3. See also Krawchenko, p. 227; and A. Biscoe, *Internal Colonialism in the USSR: The Case of Soviet Ukraine*, M.A. thesis, University of Alberta, 1986.

18. *Literaturna Ukraïna* 17 November, 1966.

19. Pelenski, p. 286.
20. See Lewytzkyj, p. 116.
21. Y. Bilinsky, 'The Communist Party of Ukraine After 1966' in Peter J. Potichnyj (ed.), *Ukraine in the Seventies* (Oakville, Ontario: Mosaic Press, 1975) p. 251.
22. Identified by Shelest as his main opponent in Moscow. See note 11 above.
23. See *Molod' Dnipropetrovs'ka v borot'bi proty rusyfikatsiï* (Munich: Suchasnist', 1971).
24. R. Solchanyk, 'Controversial Ukrainian Novel to be Reissued – in Moscow', *Radio Liberty Research*, RL 201/86 (21 May 1986). The novel was republished in Kyiv by Dnipro Publishers in 1989.
25. Originally published in *Vitchyzna*, no. 1, 1968 and then in Kyiv by Dnipro publishers 1968. See also Oles Honchar, *Sobor–Roman* (South Bound Brook, N.J.: Ukranian Orthodox Memorial Church, USA, 1968) and *The Cathedral* (Washington: St Sophia Religious Association of Ukrainian Catholics, 1989).
26. Hodnett, 1977, p. 62.
27. Bilinsky, 1975, p. 249. See also W. Dushnyk (ed.), *Ukraine in a Changing World* (New York: Ukrainian Congress Committee of America, 1977). The central committee of the CPU first heard of Shelest's removal on *Radio Kyiv*. See Bilinsky, pp. 239–40.
28. Translated and edited by O. Saciuk and B. Yasen, *The Ukrainian Herald*, no. 7–8 (Baltimore, Md.: Smoloskyp Publishers, 1976) pp. 126–7. The compiler of this issue was Stepan Khmara (pseudonym Maksym Sahaidak).
29. Ibid., pp. 61–71.
30. Krawchenko, 1984, p. 54.
31. Hodnett, 1977, pp. 67–8. See also Solchanyk in Krawchenko (ed.), 1983.
32. Ibid., pp. 71 and 77.
33. Beissinger, 1988, p. 82.
34. Dominique Arel, 'The State of Ukrainian-Language Schools in Ukraine', unpublished MS in the possession of the authors.
35. Y. Bilinsky, 'Shcherbytsky, Ukraine and Kremlin Politics', *Problems of Communism*, vol. XXXII, no. 4 (July–August 1983) p. 6.
36. Pelenski, p. 252.
37. See, for example, Roman Solchanyk, 'The Perils of Prognostication'; and 'Shcherbytsky: A Long Time Going', in *Soviet Analyst*, 5 March 1986 and 25 March 1987, respectively.
38. R. Solchanyk, 'Ukraine's Ideology Chief Purged', *Soviet Analyst*, 30 August 1979.
39. Solchanyk, in Krawchenko, 1984, pp. 10–19.
40. See David R. Marples, *The Social Impact of the Chornobyl' Disaster* (London: Macmillan/St Antony's, 1988).
41. Harasymiw, in Bahry (ed.), pp. 28–39.
42. Roman Solchanyk, 'Shcherbytsky Discusses "Style and Methods of Leadership"', *Radio Liberty Research*, RL 311/84 (17 August 1984); 'Shcherbytsky Files a Report in Pravda', RL 378/86 (1 October 1986); 'Shcherbytsky Indulges in a Measure of Self-Criticism', RL 166/87 (4 May 1987).

43. Cf. Armstrong's more overtly sociological approach to the notion of 'younger brothers', discussed in Chapter 2.

44. Roman Solchanyk, 'Ukrainian Regional Bosses Virtually Untouched by Gorbachev Purge', *Radio Liberty Research*, RL 52/86 (23 June 1986); 'Overview of the 27th Congress of the Communist Party of Ukraine', RL 85/86 (19 February 1986); Bohdan Nahaylo, 'Ukrainian Party Plenum: Stagnation Wins Out Over Talk of Restructuring', RL 481/88 (25 October 1988).

45. See T. Kuzio, 'Leonid Kravchuk: Patriot or Placeman?' *Soviet Analyst*, 19 June 1991; and 'An Independent Ukraine – But Still Communist?', *Soviet Analyst* 28 August 1991.

46. See Mary McAuley, 'Party Recruitment and the Nationalities of the USSR: A Study in Centre-Republican Relationships', *British Journal of Political Science*, vol. II part (1981) pp. 461–87.

47. Grey Hodnett, Ukrainian Politics ..., 1977, p. 73.

48. Krawchenko, 1984, p. 250.

49. *Socialism: Theory and Practice*, March 1979, p. 129.

50. S. Bloembergen, 'The Union Republics: How Much Autonomy?', *Problems of Communism*, vol. XVI, no. 5 (September–October 1967) p. 35.

51. T. Rakowska-Harmstone, 'The Dialectics of Nationalism in the USSR', *Problems of Communism* vol. XXIV, no. 3 (May–June 1974) p. 14; and Armstrong, p. 32.

52. See R. Solchanyk, 'Russian Language and Soviet Politics', *Soviet Studies* vol. XXXIV, no. 1 (2 January 1982) pp. 23–42.

53. *Financial Times*, 5 October 1982; R. Solchanyk, 'Kiev's 1500th Anniversary and Soviet Nationality Policy', *Radio Liberty Research*, RL 186/82 (5 May 1982) and O. Pritsak, 'Za kulisamy proholoshennia 1500-littia Kyieva, *Suchasnist'*, September 1981, pp. 46–54.

54. See R. Solchanyk, 'Moulding "The Soviet People": The Role of Ukrainians and Belorussians', *Journal of Ukrainian Studies*, vol. 8, no. 1 (Summer 1983) p. 13.

55. R. Solchanyk, 'The Ukraine and Ukrainians in the USSR: Nationality and Language Aspects of the Census of 1979', *Radio Liberty Research*, RL 100/80 (11 March 1980). See also his 'Language Politics in the Ukraine', in I. T. Kreindler, *Sociolinguistic Perspectives on Soviet National Languages* (Berlin: Mouton de Gruyter, 1985) pp. 57–108; and 'Discrimination on the Basis of National and Cultural Identity', a brief submitted to participating states in the Cultural Forum, Conference on Security and Cooperation in Europe, 15 October–25 November 1985, Budapest (Toronto: World Congress of Free Ukrainians, 1985).

56. Krawchenko, 1985, p. 251. See also I. S. Koropeckyj, 1979, p. 150.

57. Dziuba's book *Internationalism or Russification?* was published by Suchasnist' (in 1968 in Ukrainian and in 1973 in Russian). The English editions were published by London: Weidenfeld and Nicolson, 1968 and 1970; and New York: Mosaic Press, 1974. See Dziuba, Mosaic Press, pp. 46–7.

58. A. H. Muller, W. M. Reisinger and V. L. Heslin, 'Public Support for New Political Institutions in Russia, the Ukraine and Lithuania', *Journal of Soviet Nationalities*, vol. 1, no. 4 (Winter 1990–1), p. 97. Faith

in the centre progressively declined in 1990–1, and collapsed after the August coup. But the natural streak of Ukrainian conservatism could explain both the strong position of the CPU and longevity of Shcherbytskyi until 1989, as well as the overwhelming support for the 'centrist' presidential candidate, Leonid Kravchuk, in the elections on 1 December 1991. See the commentary by the editor of *Vechirnii Kyïv* (10 December 1991).

59. See the articles on 'The Lessons of the Elections', in *Filosofs'ka i sotsiolohichna dumka*, no. 8 (1990) pp. 3–41.
60. See L. Alexeyeva, *Soviet Dissent. Contemporary Movements for National, Religious, and Human Rights* (Middletown, Conn.: Wesleyan University Press, 1985) pp. 50 and 55.
61. Ivan L. Rudnytsky, 'The Political Thought of Soviet Ukrainian Dissent', *Journal of Ukrainian Studies*, vol. 6, no. 2 (Winter 1981) p. 5.
62. See B. Nahaylo, 'Dzyuba's Internationalism or Russification? Revisited: A Reappraisal of Dzyuba's Treatment of Leninist Nationality Policy', *Journal of Ukrainian Studies*, vol. 2, no. 2 (Winter 1977) pp. 31–53.
63. See B. Stenchuk, *What I. Dzyuba Stands for, and How He Does It (Once More about the Book 'Internationalism or Russification?')* (Kyiv: Society for Cultural Relations with Ukrainians Abroad, 1969 and 1970).
64. R. Solchanyk, 'Literaturna Ukraina Marks Ivan Dzyuba's Fiftieth Birthday', *Radio Liberty Research*, RL 304/81 (4 August 1981).
65. *Literaturna Ukraïna*, 9 November 1973; and *Visti z Ukraïny*, 22 May 1975.
66. Valentyn Moroz was forced to emigrate from the USSR in 1979 and settled in Toronto, Canada, where he began to publish the journal *Anabasis*. Originally allied to the Bandera faction of OUN, he later split from them. See Y. Bihun (ed.), *Boomerang. The Works of Valentyn Moroz* (Baltimore, Md.: Smoloskyp Publishers, 1974).
67. Rudnytsky, p. 6. In the view of Rudnytsky, the call by dissidents such as Pliushch and Badzo for 'democratic Marxism' was a 'symptom of intellectual confusion': Ukrainian dissent was less intellectually sophisticated and provincial, owing to a limited access to world literature and thought (in comparison to Russian dissidents in Moscow).
68. Danylo Shumuk, for example, passed through both national communism and integral nationalism as a member of the Communist Party of West Ukraine and then OUN, going on to join the Ukrainian Helsinki Group. See D. Shumuk, *Perezhyte i peredumane* (Detroit: Ukraïns'ki visti, 1983) and *Life Sentence: Memoirs of a Ukrainian Political Prisoner* (Edmonton: Canadian Institute of Ukrainian Studies, 1984). Leonid Pliushch also dropped his allegiance to Euro-Communism after being expelled to France in the 1970s and joined the external branch of the UHG. Iurii Badzo was also a Euro-Communist during the late 1970s, but was elected chairman of the Democratic Party of Ukraine in December 1990. See his 'Open Letter to the Soviet Leaders', *Journal of Ukrainian Studies*, vol. 9, no. 1 (1984) pp. 74–94; and vol. 9, no. 2 (Winter–Summer 1984) pp. 47–70.
69. Krawchenko, 1983, pp. 250–1. During the Gorbachev era, the large Russian minority in Ukraine produced surprisingly few *samizdat* publications or political parties. Political groups in Russia also seemed to have been relatively unsuccessful in establishing branches in Ukraine,

apart from in the Crimea. See Taras Kuzio, 'Independent (Samizdat) Press in Ukraine under Gorbachev', *Soviet Analyst*, 19 and 29 August, 13 September 1990.

70. See R. S. Clem (ed.), *The Soviet West: Interplay between Nationality and Social Organization* (New York: Praeger, 1975).

71. See articles by P. Herlihy, S. L. Guthier, R. Szporluk and P. Woroby in I. L. Rudnytsky (ed.), *Rethinking Ukranian History* (Edmonton: Canadian Institute of Ukrainian Studies, 1981) pp. 135–215.

72. Armstrong, p. 106.

73. R. Szporluk, 'West Ukraine and West Belorussia. Historical tradition, social communication and lingustic assimilation', *Soviet Studies*, vol. XXX, no. 1 (January 1979) pp. 76–98. See also Y. Bilinsky, 'The Incorporation of Western Ukraine and its Impact on Politics and Society in Soviet Ukraine', in R. Szporluk (ed.), *The Influence of East Europe and the Soviet West on the USSR* (London: Collins & Harvill Press, 1979) pp. 180–228.

74. L. Pliushch, *History's Carnival. A Dissident's Autobiography* (New York: 1977) pp. 177–8.

75. See V. Boysenko, 'Ukrainian Opposition to the Soviet Regime, 1956–59', *Problems of the Peoples of the USSR*, 1960, pp. 24–30.

76. *Ukrainian Review*, vol. VII, no. 1 (Spring 1960) p. 88; and vol. VII, no. 2 (Summer 1960) pp. 84–5. On members of the OUN-UPA in the Gulag see the memoirs of the Jewish dissident, M. Heifets, *Ukraïns'ki syliuety* (Munich: Suchasnist', 1984) pp. 175–204.

77. Nationalist opposition in Western Ukraine was 'rooted heavily in traditional, rural Ukrainian values', which had been, on the whole, destroyed during the artificial famine of 1933 in eastern Ukraine. In eastern Ukraine dissent was more 'defensive, protective activism', calling for greater autonomy and sometimes linked to workers' protests. See J. Birch, 'The Nature and Sources of Dissidence in Ukraine' in Potichnyj, 1975, pp. 308–10. See also his *The Ukrainian Nationalist Movement in the USSR since 1956* (London: Ukrainian Information Service, 1971) p. 13.

78. This rural and religious base was a handicap when the Ukrainian National Front attempted to expand beyond Galicia. Its contemporary counterpart is the political party known by its Ukrainian acronym DSU, Federation for State Independence of Ukrainian. Both the Ukrainian National Front and the DSU claimed to be following the tradition of the integral nationalists from the Bandera faction of the OUN.

79. Nina Strokata, 'Ukraïns'kyi natsionalnyi front, 1962–1975', *Suchasnist'*, June 1985, pp. 67–75.

80. See John-Paul Himka, 'The Opposition in Ukraine', *Labour Focus on Eastern Europe*, vol. 5, no. 3–4 (Summer 1982) p. 36. *Literaturna Ukraïna* (20 September 1978) linked Ukrainian dissidents to émigré nationalists, even accusing some of the dissidents of links to Western security services.

81. See *Pravda*, 6 March 1971; *Pravda*, 12 July 1972; *Molod' Ukraïny*, 26 September 1984; *Radians'ka Ukraïna*, 27 September 1984; *The Daily Telegraph*, 12 October 1984; *Sel'skaia zhizn'*, 17 January 1985; *Radians'ka Ukraïna*, 7 July 1985; *Sil's'ki visti*, 13 August 1985; and *Radio Kyiv*, 23 August 1985.

82. *Ukranian Weekly*, 30 October 1983. These continued into the early part of the Gorbachev era. See *Pravda Ukraïny*, 13 January 1987; *Svoboda*, 22 October 1987; *TASS*, 9 February 1988; and *Radio Moscow*, 5 August 1988.
83. 'The Triumph of the Émigrés in A. Motyl, *Sovietology, Rationality, Nationality: Coming to Grips with Nationalism in the USSR* (New York: Columbia University Press, 1990) pp. 132–45.
84. See articles in part II of Y. Boshyk, *Ukraine During World War II. History and Its Aftermath. A Symposium* (Edmonton: Canadian Institute of Ukrainian Studies, 1986) pp. 107–64. See also M. Warder, 'Collaborating with Communists to Prosecute Nazis', *Freedom at Issue*, May–June 1987, pp. 17–24; and E. Meyer, 'Efforts to Block Anti-Ukrainian Backlash ... Despite History of Mutual Mistrust', *The Jerusalem Post*, 20 March 1987.
85. Alexeyeva, pp. 29–30.
86. The trials are documented in Viacheslav Chornovil, *Lykho z rozumu (Portrety dvadtsiaty 'zlochyntsiv')* (Paris: PIUF, 1968 and L'viv: Memorial, 1991). English translation as *The Chornovil Papers* (New York: McGraw-Hill, 1968). Chornovil was arrested in August 1967, and sentenced to three years' imprisonment. He later played a prominent role in the new national-democratic movement during the Gorbachev era. He was elected chairman of the L'viv *oblast'* council in March 1990 and came second in the presidential elections on 1 December 1991. On the arrests in Ukraine see also M. Browne (ed.), *Ferment in the Ukraine* (London: Macmillan, 1971); and R. Kupchyns'ki *Pohrom v Ukraïni, 1972–1979* (n.p.: Suchasnist', 1980).
87. Glenny, pp. 85–7.
88. Alexeyeva, pp. 46 and 50. After 1974 secret instructions permitted locals only 25 per cent of places in universities in western Ukraine.
89. Nahaylo, in B. Krawchenko, 1983, p. 37. See also V. Swoboda, 'Cat and Mouse in the Ukraine', *Index on Censorship*, no. 1 (1973) pp. 81–9.
90. See Viktor Haynes, 'The Ukrainian Helsinki Group: A Postmortem', *Journal of Ukrainian Studies*, vol. 8, no. 2 (Winter 1983) pp. 102–13, which reviews all of the collections of UHG documents republished in the West.
91. Alexeyeva, pp. 51–2. The absence of support for worker's rights was criticised by Vasyl' Stus. See *Suchasnist'*, November 1983, pp. 89–90.
92. Nahaylo, in B. Krawchenko, 1983, p. 45.
93. Krawchenko, Winter 1983. See also Jaroslav Bilocerkowycz, *Soviet Ukrainian Dissent: a Case Study in Political Alienation* (Boulder, Col.: Westview Press, 1988).
94. Railway lines used to transport Soviet troops to Hungary were report-edly blown up and thousands of Ukrainian servicemen deserted, some joining the Hungarian partisans. See *Observer*, 16 December 1956 and *Daily Express*, 17 December 1956.
95. See G. Hodnett and P. J. Potichnyj, *The Ukraine and the Czechoslovak Crisis*, Occasional Paper no. 6 (Canberra: Department of Political Science, Research School of Social Sciences, Australian National University, 1970); and R. H. Anderson, 'Czech Ferment Spreads to the Ukraine', *New York Times*, 14 July 1968.
96. *Nasha kul'tura*, no. 3, 1963.

97. See three articles by R. Solchanyk, 'Poland's Impact Inside the USSR', *Soviet Analyst*, 9 September 1981; 'Nervous Neighbours: The Soviets and Solidarity', *Workers under Communism*, vol. 1, no. 1 (1982) pp. 16–16; and 'Poland and the Soviet West', in S. Enders Wimbush (ed.), *Soviet Nationalities in Strategic Perspective* (London: Croom Helm, 1985) pp. 158–80; and Taras Kuzio, 'Can Solidarity Spread to the USSR?', *Soviet Analyst*, 26 June 1985.

98. *Komunist*, no. 12, August 1984. See also *Soviet Nationality Survey*, vol. 1, nos 9–10 (September–October 1984) and the positive remarks about Solidarity by Vasyl' Stus written in the Gulag, *Suchasnist'* (November 1983) pp. 89–90. A *samizdat* text on Solidarity from the USSR was republished in the West as *Pol'skania revoliutsiia* (London: Overseas Publications Interchange, 1985).

99. See Stepan Hoverla [Ivan Hel], *The Facets of Culture* (London: Ukrainian Publishers, 1984 [Ukrainian-language edition] and London: Ukrainian Central Information Service, 1988 [English-language edition]). Ivan Hel became the chairman of the Committee in Defence of the Ukrainian Catholic Church in 1987–90, and was elected deputy chairman of the L'viv *oblast'* council in March 1990.

100. Alexeyeva, pp. 53 and 55. See also R. Solchanyk, 'Trials of Human Rights Activists in the Ukraine', *Radio Liberty Research*, RL 16/80 (8 January 1980).

101. 'More Helsinki Monitors Resentenced Prior to Their Scheduled Release', *News Release Communique, Human Rights Commission of the World Congress of Free Ukrainians*, 6 October 1982; and B. Nahaylo, 'Two More Ukrainian Human Rights Activists Face New Charges', *Radio Liberty Research*, RL 435/84 (13 November 1984).

102. R. Solchanyk, 'Dissidents in Ukraine: The Pressure to Conform', *Radio Liberty Research*, RL 61/78 (21 March 1978).

103. N. Svitlychna, 'The Death of Vasyl Stus', *Index on Censorship*, no. 2 (1986) pp. 34–6.

104. See 'Conditions in the USSR Perm Camp 36–1', *News Release Communique of the Human Rights Commission of the World Congress of Free Ukrainians*, 4 December 1986; and the full-page advertisement 'Will these men be on the summit agenda?', *New York Times*, 10 November 1985.

105. B. Nahaylo, 'The owls did it', *Index on Censorship*, no. 1 (1980) p. 64.

106. Nahaylo, in B. Krawchenko, 1983, p. 45.

107. Y. Suslensky, 'The Treatment of Activists of Russian and Non-Russian Nationality by the Soviet Regime: A Comparative Analysis'. *Nationalities Papers*, vol. XI, no. 2 (Summer 1983) p. 237. See also S. P. de Boer, E. J. Driessen and H. L. Verhaar, *Biographical Dictionary of Dissents in the Soviet Union, 1956–1975* (The Hague: Martinus Nijhoff Publishers, 1982), which lists 415 Ukrainian dissidents (excluding Jews, Tatars and Baptists from Ukraine, who are normally included in figures calculated in republican dissent). Another study compiled a list of 975 Ukrainian dissidents. See B. Krawchenko and J. Carter, 'A Statistical Profile of Dissidents in Ukraine before 1972', *Journal of Ukrainian Studies*, vol. 8, no. 2 (Winter 1983) pp. 85–8.

108. I. Korsun, 'The Political Opposition in Ukraine', *Meta*, vol. 2, no. 1 (1978) p. 6.

109. *Narodna hazeta*, no. 18 (December 1991).
110. Peter Reddaway, 'Dissent in the Soviet Union', *Problems of Communism*, vol. XXXII, no. 6 (November–December 1983) pp. 12 and 15.
111. See the texts by the Ukrainian National-Liberation Movember (1979) and Ukrainian Patriotic Movement (1980) reprinted in Taras Hunchak and R. Solchanyk (eds), *Ukraïns'ka suspil'no-politychna dumka v 20 stolitti* (New York: Suchasnist', 1983) pp. 370–8. See also *Documents of the Ukranian Patriotic Movement. Supplement to the Herald of Repression in the Ukraine* (External Representation of the Ukrainian Helsinki Group, 1980). A document signed by 'Ukraïns'ki Patrioty' was reprinted in *Shliakh peremohy* 3 February 1985.
112. See Radio Liberty, 'Soviet Area and Audience Opinion Research', SBN 4–84, September 1984.
113. Radio Liberty, *Arkhiv samizdata*, no. 4771. See also *Toronto Sun*, 8 June 1984; *The Ukrainian Weekly*, 9 January 1983; and *Ukraïns'ke slovo*, 4 November 1984.
114. *Sovetskaia kultura*, 8 September 1984.
115. Radio Liberty, *Arkhiv samizdata*, no. 5419.
116. *Shliakh peremohy*, 26 June 1988. Zenon Krasivskyi, a leading member of both the Ukrainian National Front and DSU was also reported after his death in September 1991 to have been the head of the underground OUN in Ukraine. See *Shliakh peremohy*, 6 October 1991.
117. Economist Intelligence Unit, *Foreign Report*, 23 May 1985.
118. The figure of 4000 functioning Russian Orthodox Churches in Ukraine is provided by *Radians'ka Ukraïna* (27 March 1988) out of a total of 6794 Russian Orthodox communities in the USSR in 1986 (*Nauka i relihiia*, no. 11, 1988). The single largest Russian Orthodox eparchy, with over 1000 Churches, was L'viv-Ternopil'. See *Sotsiologicheskie issledovaniia* (no. 4, 1987).
119. See Vasyl Markus, *Religion and Nationalism in Soviet Ukraine after 1945* (Cambridge: Ukrainian Studies Fund, 1985); *Soviet Persecution of Religion in Ukraine* (Toronto: World Congress of Free Ukrainians, 1976); and the two volumes on the Ukrainian Catholic and Orthodox Churches: *Martyrolohiia Ukraïnskykh tserkov, dokumenty, materialy, khrystyianskyi samvydav Ukraïny*, O. Zinkevych and O. Voronyn, (eds), vol. 1; and O. Zinkevych and Rev. T. R. Lonchyna (ed.), vol. 2 (Baltimore, Md.: Smoloskyp Publishers, 1987 and 1985). A first-hand account of Soviet actions against the Ukrainian Catholic Church is given in Rev. Dr. I. Hrynioch, 'The Destruction of the Ukrainian Catholic Church in the Soviet Union', *Prologue Quarterly*, vol. IV, nos 1–2 (1960) pp. 5–51. For an account of the ties between the Russian Orthodox Church and Stalin in destroying the Ukrainian Catholic Church see I. Hvat, 'The Moscow Patriarchate and the Liquidation of the Eastern-rite Catholic Church in Ukraine', *Religion in Communist Lands*, vol. 13, no. 2 (Summer 1985) pp. 182–8.
120. Bohdan Bociurkiw, 'Soviet Religious Policy in Ukraine in Historical Perspective' in Michael Pap (ed.), *Russian Empire: Some Aspects of Tsarist and Soviet Colonial Practices* (Cleveland: Institute for Soviet and East European Studies, John Carroll University and Ukrainian Historical Association, 1985) pp. 95–112.

121. H. L. Biddulph, 'Religious Participation of Youth in the USSR', *Soviet Studies*, vol. XXXI, no. 3 (July 1979) p. 423.

122. See B. R. Bociurkow, 'The Catacomb Church: Ukrainian Greek Catholics in the USSR', *Religion in Communist Lands*, vol. 5, no. 1 (Spring 1977) pp. 4–12.

123. Frank Sysyn, 'The Ukrainian Orthodox Question in the USSR', *Religion in Communist Lands*, vol. II, no. 3 (Winter 1983) pp. 251–63.

124. R. P. Moroziuk, 'Antireligious Propaganda in Ukraine' in M. S. Pap (ed.), pp. 113–30.

125. See L. J. Wollemborg, 'John Paul II and Ukrainian Catholics', *Freedom at Issue* (May/June 1988) pp. 28–30.

126. I. Hvat, 'The Ukrainian Catholic Church, the Vatican and the Soviet Union during the Pontificate of Pope John Paul II', *Religion in Communist Lands*, vol. II, no. 3 (Winter 1983) pp. 264–79.

127. J. Bilocerkowycz, 1988, pp. 93–8. See also Stephen Courtier, 'Ukrainian Catholics in the Catacombs', *Soviet Analyst*, 9 March 1983.

128. The close links already documented between the Ukrainian National Front (the ideological successor to the OUN in Ukraine) and the Ukrainian Catholic Church were openly admitted to in the euology on the 75th birthday of the deceased leader of the OUN–Bandera faction Iaroslav Stetsko, who was credited with having organised 'close joint activities' between the Ukrainian Catholic Church and 'the national-liberation underground'. See *Shliakh peremohy*, 25 January 1987.

129. Iosyf Terelia settled in Toronto, Canada, where he launched the journal *Khrest*.

130. See Bohdan Gidwitz, 'Labor Unrest in the Soviet Union', *Problems of Communism*, vol. XXXI, no. 6 (November–December 1982) pp. 25–42; and ch. 18, 'The Movement for Social and Economic Justice', in L. Alexeyeva, 1985, pp. 401–27.

131. M. Holubenko, 'The Soviet Working Class: Discontent and Opposition', *Critique*, no. 4 (1975) p. 8. See also T. Kuzio, 'Workers' Opposition in Ukraine', *Labour Focus on Eastern Europe*, vol. 5, nos 5–6 (1982–3) pp. 30–1.

132. *The Ukrainian Review*, vol. IX, no. 4 (Winter 1962) p. 85; and 'The Massacre of Workers at Novocherkas′k', *The Ukrainian Review*, vol. XXXII, no. 2 (Summer 1984) pp. 79–85.

133. Kelvin Klose, *Russia and the Russians. Inside the Closed Society* (New York: W. W. Norton, 1984) p. 9. The two original articles were printed in the *Financial Times*, 9 January 1981, and the *Guardian*, 22 February 1981.

134. Klose, p. 43.

135. M. Pohyba, 'Capitalist Russia versus the workers', *Observer*, 16 August 1981.

136. Solchanyk, 'Ukrainian Dissidents Call for Free Trade Unions', *Radio Liberty Research*, RL 338/80 (18 September 1980) and Radio Liberty, *Arkhiv samizdata*, no. 4071.

137. Klose, p. 45. One author found that, apart from the Soviet West (including Ukraine), Soviet workers were lukewarm and even hostile towards Solidarity. See E. Teague, *Solidarity and the Soviet Worker* (London: Croom Helm, 1988). The *Chronicle of the Ukrainian*

Catholic Church includes a letter to Lech Walesa from Iosyf Terelia expressing support for Solidarity. See Radio Liberty, *Arkhiv samizdata*, no. 5373.

138. R. Solchanyk, 'Labor Problems in the Ukraine', *Radio Liberty Research*, RL 389/81 (29 September 1981).

139. V. Haynes and Olga Semyonova (eds), *Workers Against the Gulag. The New Opposition in the Soviet Union* (London: Pluto Press, 1979).

140. The Donbas miners had an all-Union perspective on issues well into the Gorbachev era, often looking to Moscow and their fellow Russian miners as closer allies in the 1989–90 strikes and organisation of an independent miners' union, than Ukrainian opposition groups or Kyiv. See Chapters 6–7.

141. B. Nahaylo, 'The Death of Soviet Workers' Rights Activist Alexei Nikitin', *Radio Liberty Research*, RL 166/84 (25 April 1984).

142. Alexeyeva, p. 65. See also M. Corti, 'Repression of a Dissident Miner', *Workers under Communism*, vol. 1, no. 2 (1982) pp. 27–9.

143. On the immediate pre-Gorbachev era in Ukraine see two articles by B. Nahaylo, 'Ukraine: Moscow's Recalcitrant Republic', *Soviet Analyst*, 17 August 1983; and 'Moscow's Ukraine Predicament', *The Wall Street Journal*, 31 October 1984.

144. *Narodna hazeta*, no. 18 (December 1991).

4 Gorbachev, Dissent and the New Opposition (1987–8)

1. Zbigniew Rau, 'Four Stages of One Path Out of Socialism' (unpublished manuscript, University of Texas at Austin). See also Vladimir Brovkin, 'Revolution from Below: Informal Political Associations in Russia 1988–1989', *Soviet Studies*, vol. 42, no. 2 (April 1990) pp. 233–57.

2. On this period, see Anatol' Kamins'kyi, *Na perekhidnomu etapi: 'Hlasnist'', 'Perebudova' i 'Demokratyzatsiia Ukraïni* (Munich: Ukrainian Free University, 1990).

3. Bohdan Krawchenko (ed.), *Ukraine After Shelest* (Edmonton: Canadian Institute of Ukrainian Studies, 1983).

4. Roman Solchanyk, 'The Perils of Prognostication', *Soviet Analyst*, 5 March 1986; and 'Shcherbitsky Leaves the Political Arena: The End of an Era?' *Report on the USSR*, RL 457/89 (28 September 1989).

5. Kathleen Mihalisko, 'Ukrainian Party Takes Stock After Election Defeat in Republic', *Report on the USSR*, RL 278/89 (7 June 1990), and *Shliakh peremohy*, 23 April 1990.

6. Bohdan Nahaylo and Kathleen Mihalisko, 'Interview with Ukrainian Supreme Soviet Chairman Leonid Kravchuk', *Report on the USSR*, RL 483/90 (23 November 1990).

7. See The Ukrainian Helsinki Group, *Helsinki Guarantees for Ukraine Committee, Five Years of Struggle in Defense of Rights* (Ellicott City: Smoloskyp Publishers, 1981) and Human Rights Commission of the World Congress of Free Ukrainians, *Persecution of the Ukrainian Helsinki Group* (np: 1980 and 1985). The article by V. Haynes,

'Postmortem of the Ukrainian Helsinki Group', *Journal of Ukrainian Studies*, vol. 2, no. 2 (Winter 1983) pp. 102–13, provides a summary of the activities of the UHG and reviews the various books published about them in the West.

8. Borys Lewytzkyj, *Politics and Society in Soviet Ukraine, 1953–1980* (Edmonton: Canadian Institute of Ukrainian Studies, 1984) p. 113.

9. Taras Kuzio (ed.) *Dissent in Ukraine under Gorbachev. A Collection of Samizdat Documents* (London: Ukrainian Press Agency, 1989) p. 6.

10. While Chornovil was editor of the *Ukrainian Herald* between 1970 and 1972 six issues appeared. After the arrest of Chornovil in 1972 nos 7 and 8 (Spring 1974) appeared, edited by Maksym Sahaidak (the pseudonymn of Stepan Khmara), reflecting a more nationalistic position after the clampdown on Ukrainian dissent in 1972. Relaunching the *Ukrainian Herald* in 1987 as editor, Chornovil therefore chose to begin from where he had left off, from no. 7.

    Eight issues of the *Ukrainian Herald* appeared in Ukraine (7, 8, 9–10, 11–12 and 13–14). Only numbers 7–12 have been republished in the West by Ukrainian Publishers, London, 1987, and Suchasnist', Munich and New York 1988, the external representation of the Ukrainian Helsinki Union, New York, 1988 (nos 8 and 9–10), 1989 (nos 11–12). Four issues of the *Express Herald*, numbered 1, 8, 9 and 12, were also reprinted by the External Representation of the UHU between 1988 and 1989.

11. *L'vivs'ki novyny*, no. 22, 1990.

12. Levko Lukianenko, *What Next?* (London: Ukrainian Central Information Service, 1990; Ukrainian edition, 1989). Quotations are taken from pp. 4–5, 35, 41 and 43 of the English edition.

13. *Ukrainian Weekly*, 27 March 1988; and *Ukrainian Press Agency*, London, press release no. 63, 1988. The Declaration of Principles are translated in Kuzio (ed.), pp. 24–34. See also *Suchasnist'*, December 1988, pp. 92–9; and *Russkaia mysl'* 19 August 1989.

14. Levko Lukianenko, *Viruiu v Boha i v Ukraïnu* (Kyiv: Pam'iatky Ukraïny, 1991); and *Za Ukraïnu, za ïï voliu* (Kyiv:Fastivs'ka Drukarnia, 1991), pp. 55–8.

15. *Ukrainian Press Agency*, press release no. 23, 1987. See also Bohdan Nahaylo, 'Ukrainian Association of Independent Creative Intelligentsia Formed', *Radio Liberty Research*, RL 489/87 (25 November 1987).

16. *Shliakh peremohy* 12 March 1989.

17. The return of the remains of the four dissident writers was reported by the Ukrainian Press Agency, 21 November 1989; *Vechirnii Kyïv*, 21 November 1989; and *News from Ukraine*, no. 49, 1989. The UANTI declaration is reported in *Ukrainian Press Agency*, press release no. 35, 1989.

18. *Ukrainian Press Agency*, press release nos 32 and 33, 1987.

19. See Vasyl' Stus, *Poesiï* (Kyiv: Radians'kyi Pys'mennyk, 1990). Reprints of his works and articles calling for his rehabilitation include: *Molod' Ukraïny*, 13 April 1989; *Literaturna Ukraïna*, 25 January 1990; *Moloda Halychyna*, 31 July 1990 published Stus's 1982 article 'I accuse the KGB'.

20. *Kafedra* has been republished in the West by the External Representation of the Ukrainian Helsinki Union, New York, 1989, no. 2 and Association of Ukrainians, London, 1990, nos 2–3.

21. *USSR News Brief*, nos 17/18, 1987.

22. Bohdan Nahaylo, RL 57/88, 'Informal Ukrainian Culturological Club Helps to Break New Ground for Glasnost', *Radio Liberty Research*, RL 57/88 (8 February 1988). See also *USSR News Brief*, nos 19/20, 1987 and Andrew Brown, 'Dissident's Route to Faith on the Bleak Streets of Kyiv', *The Independent*, 11 June 1988.

23. See *Ukraïns'ke slovo*, 27 March 1988; *Russkaia mysl'*, 27 May 1988; *Ukraïnian Press Agency*, press release nos 29 and 74, 1987, and 25 and 26, 1988.

24. See also Bohdan Nahaylo, '"Informal" Ukrainian Culturological Club under Attack', *Radio Liberty Research*, RL 477/87 (23 November 1987); *Vechirnii Kyïv*, 19 October 1987 (14 November 1987), 2 December 1987 and 26 May 1988; *Russkaia mysl'*, 30 October 1987; *Radians'ka Ukraïna*, 12 and 13 May 1988.

25. The Chornobyl' anniversary meeting was reported by the *Ukrainian Press Agency*, press releases nos 73 and 80; *Associated Press*, 27 April 1988; *Ukraïns'ke slovo*, 19 June 1988; *News from Ukraine*, no. 21, 1988; and Roman Solchanyk, 'Soviet Press Reports on Antinuclear Demonstration in Kyiv', *Radio Liberty Research*, RL 249/88 (8 June 1988). The spread of similar Clubs was reported by the *Ukrainian Press Agency*, press release no. 67, 1988 and the *Ukranian Weekly*, 29 May 1988. The unofficial millennium celebrations were reported in *Ukrainian Weekly*, 19 June 1988; *Ukraïns'ke slovo*, 26 June 1988; *Ukrainian Press Agency*, press release no. 95, 1988; and 'Ukrainians stage protest', *Independent*, 6 June 1988.

26. See Kyivs'ki neformaly: Khto vony?', *Vechirnii Kyïv*, 2 September 1989.

27. David Marples, 'Mass demonstration in Kyiv focuses on ecological issues and political situation in Ukraine', *Radio Liberty Research*, RL 325/88 (5 December 1988).

28. See *USSR News Brief*, nos 21 and 23, 1988; and Kathleen Mihalisko, 'Report from Kyiv University on Future of Students Military Obligations', *Report on the USSR*, RL 36/89 (12 January 1989).

29. *News from Ukraine*, no. 4, 1988.

30. *Ukrainian Press Agency*, press release no. 173, 1988.

31. *Ukrainian Press Agency*, press release no. 17, 1989; *Kyivs'kyi universytet*, 15 April, 22 April, 27 May, 23 September, 2 December and 9 December 1988; and *Molod' Ukraïny*, 8 December 1988.

32. See Ivan Hvat, 'The Ukrainian Catholic Church, the Vatican and the Soviet Union during the Pontificate of Pope John Paul II', *Religion in Communist Lands*, vol. II, no. 3 (Winter 1983) pp. 264–79. On the contemporary period see Bohdan Bociurkiw, 'The Ukraine Catholic Church in the USSR under Gorbachev', *Problems of Communism*, vol. XXXIX, no. 6 (November–December 1990) pp. 1–19; and 'The Church in Ukraine–1988', *Religion in Communist Lands*, vol. 17, no. 2 (Summer 1989) pp. 152–6.

33. *Ukrainian Press Agency*, press release no. 18, 1987; and X. Smiley, 'Ukraine bishops open approach tests *glasnost*'', *Daily Telegraph*, 23 December 1987.

34. See Taras Kuzio (ed.), pp. 40–9; and L. J. Wollemberg, 'John Paul II and Ukrainian Catholics', *Freedom at Issue*, May–June 1988, pp. 28–30.
35. *Ukrainian Press Service* (Rome), 1988.
36. See V. Shevelyov, 'The Inertia of Simplification', *Moscow News*, no. 37, 1987; F. Barringer, 'Ukrainian Miracle Perplexes Communists', *International Herald Tribune*, 16 October 1987.
37. *Nove zhyttia*, 15 April 1988.
38. *Sotsialistychna kul'tura*, 1988, no. 6, p. 11.
39. *Molod' Ukraïny*, 6 March 1988; and *Ukrainian Press Agency*, press release no. 56, 1988.
40. *The Ukrainian Weekly*, 12 June 1988.
41. *Radians'ka Ukraïna*, 6 October 1988.
42. *Molod' Ukraïny*, 15 August 1988.
43. Marco Drohobycky, 'The Lion Society: Profile of a Ukrainian Patriotic "Informal" Group', *Radio Liberty Research*, RL 325/88 (18 July 1988). See also *Ukrainian Press Agency*, press release no. 22, 1988; and A. Serikov, 'Koho boïtsia Tovarystvo Leva?', *Ukraïna*, July 1988, pp. 20–2.
44. *Ukrainian Press Agency*, press release no. 199, 1988.
45. *Ukrainian Press Agency*, press release no. 65, 1988. See *Radians'ka Ukraïna*, 27 February 1988 and *Pravda Ukraïny*, 19 March 1988 for early actions by the Green World Association.
46. *Ukrainian Press Service*, April 1988.
47. *Ukrainian Central Information Service* (London), no. 18, 1988.
48. *Radians'ka Ukraïna*, 30 July 1989.
49. *News from Ukraine*, no. 18, 1988.
50. Chronology supplied by Green World Association office in Kyiv.
51. Op. cit., ref. 26; *News from Ukraine*, no. 48, 1988 and *Associated Press*, 13 November 1990.
52. See the description of new regulations in *Visti z Ukraïny*, no. 43, 1988, and the media campaign in *Vil'na Ukraïna*, 21 June, 14 and 20 July 1988; *L'vovskaia pravda*, 21 June 1988; *Pravda Ukraïny*, 14 July 1988; and *Komsomol'skaia pravda*, 10 July 1988. See also *Ukrainian Press Agency*, press release no. 122, 1988.
53. Oleksyi Haran', *Ukraïna bahatopartiina* (Kyiv: Pam'iatky Ukraïny, 1991) p. 7.
54. Taras Kuzio, 'Nationalist Ferment in Western Ukraine', *Soviet Analyst*, 3 August 1988; R. Solchanyk, 'Democratic Front to Promote Perestroika Formed in Ukraine', *Radio Liberty Research*, RL 324/88 (17 July 1988); and *Ukrainian Press Agency*, press release no. 112, 1988.
55. 'Ukrainian Party under attack', *Independent*, 26 July 1988.
56. *Lenins'ka molod'*, 28 July 1988, advertised the first meeting of the DFSP which was scheduled for 3 August.
57. Ukrainian Press Agency, press release no. 156, 1988 and UHU Press Service no. 8. See also R. Solchanyk, 'Lvov Authorities Begin Criminal Proceedings Against Ukrainian Activists'' *Radio Liberty Research*, RL 327/88 (26 July 1988).
58. Iurii Kyrychuk, 'Narys istoriï UHS-URP', *Respublikanets'* [theoretical journal of the L'viv UHU, later Ukrainian Republican Party], no. 2

(November–December 1991) p. 86; and Bohdan Horyn', 'Nash shliakh do URP', *Respublikanets'*, no. 1 (October 1990) p. 6.
59. *USSR News Brief*, 12 and 13, 1988.
60. *Radians'ka osvita*, 30 September 1988; and *Robitnycha hazeta*, 4 October 1988.
61. Haran', p. 6.
62. Bohdan Nahaylo, 'Representatives of non-Russian national movements establish coordinating committee', *Radio Liberty Research*, RL 283/88 (22 June 1988).
63. Bohdan Nahaylo, 'Non-Russian National-Democratic Movements Hold Another Meeting', *Radio Liberty Research*, RL 465/88 (10 October 1988) and *Ukrainian Press Agency*, no. 161, 1988.
64. Bohdan Nahaylo, 'Non-Russian National-Democrats Adopt Charter and Issue Appeal to the Russian Intelligentsia', *Report on the USSR*, RL 87/89 (5 February 1989) and *Ukrainian Press Agency*, press release no. 19, 1989.

5 Consolidation (1988–9)

1. *Soviet Nationality Survey*, vol. 5, no. 2 (February 1988).
2. Only Shcherbitskyi was a non-Russian voting member of the 13-member Politburo. All seven non-voting Politburo members were Russians and, of the 12 secretaries, only one was a non-Russian. See 'Union of Unequals: the Nationality Question in the USSR', *Soviet Nationality Survey*, vol. 5, no. 3 (March 1988); and Dawn Mann, 'Gorbachev's Personnel Policy: The Non-Russian Republic's', *Report on the USSR*, vol. 1, no. 48 (1 December 1989).
3. *Soviet Nationality Survey*, vol. 5, no. 7 (July 1988).
4. *Literaturna Ukraïna*, 7 November 1988.
5. *Vechirnii Kyïv*, 1 December 1988.
6. *Literaturna Ukraïna*, 15 December 1988.
7. David Marples, 'Current Events in the Ukraine (III)', *Soviet Analyst*, 28 June 1989.
8. See Taras Lekhyj, 'On the Current Situation in Ukraine', *Labour Focus on Eastern Europe*, vol. 12, no. 2, (1989) pp. 17–2; and Chrystia Freedland, 'Popular Movement Shakes Up the Ukraine', *Across Frontiers* (Summer 1989), pp. 9 and 50.
9. *Ukrainian Central Information Service*, no. 22, 1989.
10. An English translation of the draft *Rukh* programme can be found in *Soviet Ukrainian Affairs*, vol. 2, no. 4 (Winter 1988), pp. 20–3.
11. David Marples, 'Interview with Editor of Vechirniy Kyiv. The Voice of Perestroika in Ukraine', *Report on the USSR*, RL 353/89 (16 July 1989).
12. *Literaturna Ukraïna*, 9 March 1989. The same issue carried letters both for and against the draft *Rukh* programme.
13. The media campaign, orchestrated by the then Ideological Secretary of the CPU, Leonid Kravchuk, continued relentlessly throughout the period, but especially during February–May 1989. See B. Nahaylo,

'Confrontation over Creation of Ukrainian Popular Front.' *Report on the USSR* RL 101/89 (15 February 1989), and 'Draft Program of Ukraine Baltic-Style Popular Movement under Strong Attack', *Report on the USSR* RL 106/89 (1 March 1989). Some of the attacks are contained in *Radians'ka Ukraïna*, 11 February, 3 March, 17 March, 25 March, 20 April 1989; *Pravda Ukraïny*, 1 March, 1989; *Robitnycha hazeta*, 21 February, 23 February, 26 February, 3 March, 27 March 1989; *Molod Ukraïny*, 2 March and *Sil's'ki visti*, 22 March 1989.

14. *Radians'ka Ukraïna*, 8 March 1989.
15. *Radians'ka Ukraïna*, 7 Feburary 1989.
16. *Pravda Ukraïny*, 18 February 1989.
17. *Pravda Ukraïny*, 19 March 1989.
18. *Sovetskaia kul'tura*, 28 September 1989.
19. See Roman Solchanyk, 'Party and Writers at Loggerheads Over Popular Front', *Report on the USSR*, RL 237/89 (22 May 1989).
20. *Pravda*, 21 May 1989.
21. *Literaturna Ukraïna*, 27 April 1989.
22. *Radians'ka Ukraïna*, 5 July 1989.
23. *Literaturna Ukraïna*, 13 July 1989. See also Roman Solchanyk, 'Constituent Conference of Kievan Regional Popular Front', *Report on the USSR*, RL 365/89 (27 July 1989).
24. *Ukrainian Press Agency*, press release no. 101, 1988.
25. *Ukrainian Press Agency*, press release no. 18, 1989.
26. *Ukrainian Press Agency*, press release no. 9, 1989.
27. *Ukrainian Press Agency*, press release no. 187, 1988.
28. *Ukrainian Press Agency*, press release no. 10 & 11, 1989.
29. *Ukrainian Press Agency*, press release no. 56, 1989.
30. *Ukrainian Press Agency*, press release, 26 & 31 July, 1989.
31. *Ukrainian Press Agency*, press release no. 25, 1989 and see Taras Kuzio, 'The Ukrainian Christian Democratic Party', *Christian Democracy, Bulletin of the Christian Democratic International on Eastern Europe* no. 8 (July–August 1990) pp. 8–11.
32. *Ukrainian Press Agency*, Warsaw, no. 26, 6 February 1990 and *Ukraïns'ki novyny*, no. 5, 3 September 1990.
33. *Ukrainian Central Information Service*, no. 77, 1989.
34. Op. cit., ref. 9.
35. *Ukrainian Central Information Service*, no. 109, 1989, and *Moloda Halychyna* 8 July 1990.
36. Copy in the possession of the authors.
37. *Shliakh peremohy*, 3 December 1989.
38. *The Washington Post*, 22 January 1989.
39. *Keston News Service*, 2 march 1989; *Ukrainian Press Agency*, press release no. 27, 1989 and Bohdan Nahaylo, 'Initiative Group for Restoration of Ukrainian Autocephalous Orthodox Church Founded', *Report on the USSR*, RL 105/89, 26 February 1989.
40. See Frank Sysyn, 'The Ukrainian Orthodox Question in the USSR,' *Religion in Communist Lands*, (Winter 1993) no. 3, pp. 251–63 and Bohdor Bociurkiw, 'The Ukrainian Autocephalous Church, 1920–1930: a Case Study in Religious Modernisation', in D. J. Dunn (ed.), *Religion*

and *Modernisation in the Soviet Union* Boulder (Boulder, Co: Westview Press, 1977) pp. 310–47.

41. J. B. Dunlop, 'The Russian Orthodox Church and Nationalism After 1988', *Religion in Communist Lands*, vol. 18, no. 4 (Winter 1990) pp. 292–306.
42. *Radians'ka Ukraïna*, 9 May 1989.
43. *News from Ukraine*, no. 49, 1990.
44. *News from Ukraine*, no. 22, 1989.
45. *Ukrainian Central Information Service*, no. 94, 1989.
46. *Ukrainian Press Bureau*, 26 June 1989 and *Literaturna Ukraïna*, 29 June 1989.
47. *Ukrainian Press Bureau*, 22 June 1989 and *Keston News Service*, 6 July 1989.
48. *Ukrainian Weekly*, 8 January 1989.
49. *Ukrainian Central Information Service*, no. 15, 1989.
50. *Ukrainian Press Agency*, 19 February 1989.
51. Q. Peel, 'Too-good-to-be-true milkmaids flight for the Ukrainian vote', *The Financial Times*, 3 March 1989; S. Cornwell, 'Crusading journalist beats Communist bosses in Ukrainian elections', *The Independent*, 28 March 1989, and Kathleen Mihalisko, 'Alla Yaroshyns'ka: Crusading Journalist from Zhitomir Becomes Peoples Deputy', *Report on the USSR*, RL 247/89 (24 May 1989).
52. Bohdan Horyn', pp. 8–9.
53. Ibid.
54. *TASS*, 3 May 1989.
55. *Sotsialisticheskaia industriia*, 27 March 1989.
56. *Radians'ka Ukraïna*, 16 May 1989.
57. *Radians'ka Ukraïna*, 5 March 1989.
58. Rupert Cornwell, 'Anti-Stalinist congress in Kiev underlines anger at present leadership', *The Independent*, 6 March 1989. See also Iu. Lukanov, 'Dobro bez kulakiv', Pam'iatky Ukraïny 1989, no. 2, pp. 63–4. See also L. Y. Luciuk and A. Chyczij (comps.), *Memorial* (n.p.: Kashtan Press, 1989).
59. See Taras Kuzio, 'Bykovnia – Ukraine's Kuropaty', *Soviet Analyst*, 22 February 1989; B. Keller, 'Behind Stalin's Green Fence: Who Filled the Mass Graves?', *The New York Times*, 6 March 1989; X. Smiley, 'Hidden Horrors of Kiev's Katyn', *The Daily Telegraph*, 6 March 1989, and R. Cornwell, 'Long Crusade for Justice in Silent Forest of Death', *The Independent*, 10 March 1989.
60. See note 54.
61. *Ukraïns'ke slovo*, 26 March 1989. See the attack upon the UHU for its influence in Memorial in Lviv, *Pravda Ukraïny*, 11 June 1989.
62. *News from Ukraine* no. 11, 1989.
63. *Associated Press*, 5 March 1989.
64. See B. Nahaylo, 'Inaugural Congress of Ukrainian Language Society Turns Into Major Political Demonstration,' *Report on the USSR*, RL 103/89 (13 February 1989).
65. *Radio Kyiv* 11 February 1989. See *Lenins'ka molod'*, *31 December 1988 for an early conference of the Ridna Mova Society in L'viv.*

66. *Pravda Ukraïny*, 12 February 1989.
67. *Radians'ka Ukraïna*, 8 February 1989.
68. *Literaturan Ukraïna*, 2 March 1989 and *News from Ukraine*, 1989, no. 11.
69. *Literaturan Ukraïna*, 2 March 1989.
70. *News from Ukraïne*, 1989, no. 9.
71. David Marples, 'The Shevchenko Ukrainian language Society: An Interview with Dmytro Pavlychko', *Report on the USSR*, RL 340/89 (29 June 1989).
72. Myroslav Hroch, *Social Preconditions of National Revival in Europe* (Cambridge: Cambridge University Press, 1985).
73. Ibid., p. 23.
74. See B. Nahaylo, 'Confrontation over Creation of Ukrainian Popular Front', *Report on the USSR*, RL 101/89 (3 March 1989).

6   The Birth of Mass Politics (1989–90)

1. Motyl, 1987, p. 170.
2. See Marco Bojcun, 'Interview with Volodymyr Ivashko', *Ukraine Today*, vol. 1, no. 2 (August 1990) pp. 19–23.
3. *The Globe and Mail*, 5 June 1990.
4. *The Independent*, 12 July 1990.
5. *The Times*, 5 June 1990.
6. *The Times*, 13 July 1990.
7. Ibid.
8. *Soviet Television*, 11 July 1990.
9. *Sovetskaia kul'tura*, 12 October 1989.
10. *Nezavisimaia gazeta*, 29 January 1991.
11. *Literaturna Ukraïna*, 13 July 1989.
12. *Visti z Ukraïny*, no. 20, 1989; and *Pravda Ukraïny*, 6 May 1989.
13. On the CPWU see J. Radziejowski, *The Communist Party of Western Ukraine, 1919–1929* (Edmonton: Canadian Institute of Ukrainian Studies, 1983); R. Solchanyk, 'The Foundation of the Communist Movement in Eastern Galicia, 1919–1921', *Slavic Review*, vol. 30, no. 4 (Winter 1971) pp. 774–94; and 'The Comintern and the Communist Party of Western Ukraine', *Canadian Slavonic Papers*, vol. 23, no. 2 (Summer 1981) pp. 181–97.
14. Letter to *Daily Telegraph*, 9 August 1989. See also T. Sherlock, 'New Thinking on the Nazi-Soviet Pact', *Report on the USSR*, RL 333/89, 13 July 1989.
15. See *Zlochyny komunistychnoï Moskvy v Ukraïni v liti 1941* (New York: Prolog, 1960) (serialised in the L'viv *oblast* Memorial newspaper *Poklyk sumlinnia*); M. Rudnyts'ka, *Zakhidnia Ukraïna pid bol'shevykamy* (New York: Shevchenko Scientific Society in the USA, 1958); and J. T. Gross, *Revolution From Abroad. The Soviet Conquest of Poland's Western Ukraine and Western Belorussia* (Princeton: Princeton University Press, 1988).
16. *Ukrainian Press Agency*, 26 July 1989.

17. *Ukraïns'kyi visnyk*, Vypusk 9–10, October–November 1987 (n.p.: External Representation of the Ukrainian Helsinki Union, 1988) pp. 269–75.
18. *Ukrainian Press Agency*, 1 August 1989. See also the views of the Russian Democratic Union in *Russkaia mysl'* 18 August 1989.
19. *Ukrainian Press Agency*, 26 July 1989.
20. *Ukrainian Press Agency*, 5 September 1989.
21. *Daily Telegraph, The Times, Independent*, 22 January 1990; *Ukrainian Press Agency*, 25, January 1990; B. Nahaylo, 'Human-Chain Demonstration: A Triumph for *Rukh*', *Report on the USSR*, RL 57/90 (2 February 1990).
22. See Elisabeth Teague, 'Perestroika and the Soviet Worker', *Government and Opposition*, vol. 25, no. 1 (Spring 1990) pp. 191–211.
23. *Robitnycha hazeta*, 17 April 1988.
24. *Radio Kyiv*, 23 September 1989.
25. *Nasha meta*, no. 20 (76), June 1990.
26. *Respublikanets'*, no. 1, June 1990.
27. *Financial Times*, 15 March 1988. See also V. Haynes and O. Semyonova (eds), *Workers Against the Gulag. The New Opposition in the Soviet Union* (London, Pluto Press, 1979); and Taras Kuzio, 'Workers' Opposition in Ukraine', *Labour Focus on Eastern Europe*, vol. 5, nos 5–6 (Winter 1982–3) pp. 30–1; and J. Cunningham, *Klebanov and Nikitin. The Story of two Ukrainian miners' fight against the Soviet bureaucracy* (Oxford: no publisher or date).
28. *Ukrainian Press Agency*, Warsaw, no. 12, 1989.
29. *Holos*, no. 5, 1989.
30. 'Perestroika from Below: The Soviet Miners' Strike and its Aftermath', *New Left Review*, May–June 1990, pp. 5–32; and D. Marples, *Ukraine Under Perestroika. Ecology, Economics and the Workers' Revolt* (London: Macmillan, 1991) ch. 6, 'The Donbas Miners and the 1989 Coal Strike', pp. 175–217.
31. O. V. Volovodova, 'Shakhtars'kyi rukh: vid stykhiinoho vystupu do demokratychnoï systemy samoorhanizatsiï', *Filosofs'ka i sotsiolohichna dumka*, no. 7 (1991) pp. 45–52; fig. p. 51.
32. See also David Marples, 'Why the Donbas Miners Went on Strike', *Report on the USSR*, RL 416/89 (8 September 1989).
33. *Guardian*, 24 July 1989.
34. Volovodova, 1991, pp. 47 and 49.
35. *Dosvitni vohni*, no. 3, November 1989. See also *Obizhnyk UHS*, Donets'k, August 1989.
36. *Independent*, 24 July 1989.
37. Copy in authors' files.
38. *The Times*, 27 July 1989.
39. *Independent*, 20 July 1989.
40. *Ukraïns'ke slovo*, 2 July 1989; and *Russkaia mysl'*, 23 July 1989.
41. *Ukrainian Press Agency*, no. 2, 1989.
42. *Na spolokh*, No. 6, 1989.
43. *Ukrainian Press Agency*, 1 March 1990.
44. *Holos vidrodzhennia*, no. 3, 1990.

45. See *Volia*, no. 1, August 1990, where the statute of the Solidarity Free Trade Unions of Ukraine is published.
46. *Rankovyi Kyïv*, 2 July 1990.
47. See D. Kowalewski, 'The Lviv Strike Committee – The Role of Workers in the Ukrainian National Movement', *International Viewpoint*, 26 March 1990, pp. 21–2; and *Viche*, no. 14, 1990.
48. *Komsomol'skaia pravda*, 15 October 1989.
49. *L'vivs'kyi visnyk*, 7 October 1989.
50. Y. Trofimov, 'Ukraine's Mandela tipped as president', *Daily Telegraph*, 22 October 1990.
51. See *Vil'na Ukraïna*, 13 October 1990, for a critical account of the strike.
52. *USSR News Brief*, nos 23–4, 1989; and *Informator UHU*, no. 55, 21 December 1989.
53. *Ukrainian Press Agency*, 23 March 1990.
54. *Russkaia mysl'*, 9 March 1990; *Sotsialisticheskii Donbass*, 9 February 1990; *Sunday Telegraph*, 14 February 1990; *Soviet Labour Review*, April 1990; *Ukrainian Press Agency*, 26 February 1990; and *Sunday Correspondent*, 4 March 1990.
55. *The Times*, 13 July 1990. See also *Independent* and *The Times*, 12 July 1990, on the strikes.
56. David Marples, 'Turmoil in the Donbas: The Political Situation', *Report on the USSR*, RL 423/90 (12 October 1990).
57. *Wall Street Journal*, 18 July 1990.
58. *Moloda Halychyna*, 12 July 1990.
59. David Marples, 'The Background of the Coal Strike on July 11', *Report on the USSR*, RL 325/90 (27 July 1990).
60. See Taras Kuzio, 'The Ukraine Stirs', *Soviet Analyst*, 27 September 1989; T. Fishlock, 'Kremlin faces challenge from Ukraine Front', *Daily Telegraph*, 9 September 1989; Rupert Cornwell, 'Ukrainians create popular front to push for reform', *Independent*, 11 September 1989; M. Dobbs, 'Moscow Eyes Ukraine Warily', *International Herald Tribune*, 12 September 1989.
61. See Vladimir Paniotto, 'The Ukrainian Movement for Perestroika–Rukh: A Sociological Survey', *Soviet Studies*, vol. 43, no. 1 (January 1991) pp. 177–81.
62. C. Freedland, 'Solidarity gives tips on how to wake Ukraine' *Independent*, 14 September 1989; *Gazeta Wyborcza*, 11, 12 and 14 September 1989; and B. Bakula, 'Dokiad zmierza Ukrainski Ruch?' *Kontakt*, 1990, no. 3, pp. 76–84.
63. Lukianenko's speech is reproduced in the special issues of *Suchasnist'*, December 1989, pp. 96–9 and translated in *Soviet Ukrainian Affairs*, vol. 3, nos 3–4 (Autumn–Winter 1989) pp. 35–6 dealing with the congress.
64. *Pravda*, 15 September 1989.
65. *Literaturna Ukraïna*, 30 November 1989.
66. *Soviet Ukranian Affairs*, vol. 2, nos 3–4 (Autumn–Winter 1989) pp. 43–52.
67. *Literaturna Ukraïna*, 21 September and 12 October 1989; *Holos*, no. 5 (1989).

68. *Literaturna Ukraïna*, 5 October 1989; and *Soviet Ukrainian Affairs*, vol. 2, nos 3–4 (Autumn–Winter 1989) p. 55.
69. *Literaturna Ukraïna*, 5 October 1989.
70. *Radio Kyiv*, 10 September 1989.
71. J. Steele, 'Police keep wary eye on Ukraine fronts launch', *Guardian*, 11 September 1989.
72. *Literaturna Ukraïna*, 21 September 1989.
73. *Radians'ka Ukraïna*, 16 September 1989.
74. *Radians'ka Ukraïna*, 15 September 1989.
75. *Izvestiia*, 9 September 1989.
76. *Radio Vilnius*, 14 September 1989.
77. *Molod' Ukraïny*, 4 October 1989.
78. *Ukrainian Weekly*, 15 December 1991.
79. *Moloda Halychyna*, 31 January 1991.
80. See Taras Kuzio, 'Nationalist Ferment in Western Ukraine', *Soviet Analyst*, 3 August 1989.
81. *Robitnycha hazeta*, 5 August 1989.
82. Both Bohdan Horyn and Mykola Horbal in their interviews in *Gazeta Wyborcza* (10 July and 28 August 1989 respectively) called for Ukrainian independence. Chornovil also called for independence at the Kyiv *oblast* Rukh congress. See *Ukranian Press Agency*, 6 July 1989.
83. *Radians'ka Ukraïna*, 5 August 1989; and *Ukrainian Press Agency*, 1 August 1989.
84. *USSR News Brief*, nos 17/18 (1989).
85. *News from Ukraine*, no. 44 (1989).
86. *Radians'ka Ukraïna*, 14 September 1989.
87. *Materialy pro rozvytok mov v Ukraïns'kii RSR* (Kyiv: ULS 'Prosvita', 1991), pp. 3–12.
88. Ibid., pp. 14–16.
89. *Izvestiia*, 7 September 1989.
90. TASS news agency, 27 October 1989.
91. A. S. Pigolkin and M. S. Studenikina, 'Republican Language Laws in the USSR: A Comparative Analysis', *Journal of Soviet Nationalities*, vol. 11, no. 1 (Spring 1991) pp. 38–76.
92. *Keston News Service*, no. 334, 1989. See also *Lenins'ka molod'*, 19 September 1989; and *Vil'na Ukraïna*, 20 September 1989; 150 000 Ukrainian Catholics also demonstrated on 18 June 1989 after Cardinal Myroslav Liubachivskyi designated the date as an international day of prayer for the legalisation of the Ukrainian Catholic Church. See *Ukrainian Press Bureau*, 22 June 1989.
93. *Ogonëk*, no. 38 (September 1989).
94. *Keston News Service*, no. 334, 1989.
95. *Ukrainian Press Bureau*, 19 September 1989. See also *Sunday Telegraph*, 17 September; *International Herald Tribune, Guardian Globe and Mail*, 18 September; *Guardian*, 21 September; *Catholic Herald, Independent*, 22 September 1989.
96. *Radio Kyiv*, 15 November 1989.
97. *Ukrainian Press Agency*, 1 and 14 December 1989.

98. *Zakhidnyi kurier*, 3 November 1990.
99. *Ukrainian Press Agency*, 21 November 1989.
100. *Radio Moscow*, 20 December 1989; *Soviet Television*, 21 January 1990; Rupert Cornwell, 'A Different Holy War Rages in Soviet Union', *Independent*, 22 December 1989; J. Steele, 'Ukrainian Catholics Accused of Seizing Churches', *Guardian*, 28 December 1989; and M. Binyon, 'Church Battle Sours new Soviet Religious Freedom', *The Times*, 14 April 1990.
101. *Radians'ka Ukraïna*, 13 May 1990.
102. *Radio Moscow*, 29 December 1989.
103. *Keston News Service*, 11 January 1990.
104. Roman Solchanyk, 'Ukrainian Catholics in the USSR: Towards Legalisation', *Radio Liberty Research*, RL 559/89, 15 December 1989.
105. *Moscow News*, no. 31, 1989; *Keston News Service*, 17 January 1990; and *Radians'ka Ukraïna*, 4 February 1990.
106. *Ukrainian Press Bureau*, 18 September 1990.
107. *Lenins'ka molod'*, 22 March 1990.
108. *Pravda Ukraïny*, 9 February 1990; and *Radians'ka Ukraïna*, 15 February 1990.
109. *Ukrainian Press Agency*, 27 June 1990.
110. *Keston News Service*, 7 June 1990.
111. D. Marples and O. Skrypnyk, 'Patriarch Mstyslav and the Revival of the Ukrainian Autocephalous Orthodox Church', *Report on the USSR*, RL 25/91, 4 January 1991; S. Viets, '*Rukh* MPs challenge "Russian" Church, *Independent*, 29 October 1990; and A. Krushelnycky, 'Ukraine Nightmare for Gorbachev', *The European*, 2–4 November 1990.
112. *Nasha vira*, no. 7, October 1990.
113. *News from Ukraine*, no. 37 (199).

7 1990: Ukrainian Elections and the Rise of a Multi-Party System

1. *Radians'ka Ukraïna*, 6 August 1989.
2. Kathleen Mihalisko, 'Reaching for Political Democracy in Belorussia and Ukraine', *Report on the USSR*, RL 555/89, (15 November 1989).
3. The Deputies Club later formed the organising committee of the DPU of Ukraine.
4. This was republished in *Pravda Ukraïny* and *Radians'ka Ukraïna*, 8 September 1989.
5. *Lenin'ska Molod'*, 15 August 1989. See also Kathleen Mihalisko, 'Dispute in Ukraine over Draft Law on Elections to Republican Parliament', *Report on the USSR*, RL 430/89 (15 September 1989). The UHU also released an alternative election law drawn up by S. Khmara. See *Ukrainian Press Agency*, 22 September 1989.
6. *Pravda Ukraïny*, 8 September 1989.
7. *Moscow News*, no. 45, 1989.

8. Kathleen Mihalisko, 'Shcherbytsky Must Go: An Open Letter to Gorbachev', *Report on the USSR*, RL 441/89 (13 September 1989).
9. *Ukrainian Press Agency*, 22 November 1989; *Slovo*, no. 3, November–December 1989; and *Vilne slovo*, no. 8, 1990.
10. Viacheslav Chronovil: *Ukrainian Press Agency*, 22 September 1989; Oles Shevchenko: *Ukrainian Press Agency*, Warsaw, no. 19, 1989; Leuko Lukianenko: *Ukrainian Press Agency*, 8 December 1989. Copies of Stepan Khmara's and *Tovarystvo Leva's* programmes are in the authors' files.
11. Serhii Naboka, a leading UHU member, refused to be a candidate because the Supreme Soviet was not a genuine parliament and participation in the elections was therefore 'immoral'. See *Ukrains'ke slovo*, 8 April 1990.
12. *Vechirnii Kyïv*, 21 February 1990.
13. *Ukrainian Press Agency*, 22 February and 26 February 1990; *Vechirnii Kyïv*, 31 January 1990.
14. *Krasnaia zvezda*, 18 February 1990.
15. Kathleen Mihalisko, 'Can Rukh Win the March 4 Elections in Ukraine?', *Report on the USSR*, RL 91/90 (23 February 1990); and Taras Kuzio, 'Elections and National Discontent in Ukraine', *Soviet Analyst*, 21 March 1990.
16. *Literaturna Ukraïna*, 22 February 1990; *Ukrainian Press Agency*, 5 February 1990; and David Marples, 'The Ukrainian Election Campaign: The Opposition', *Report on the USSR*, RL 115/90 (9 March 1990).
17. *Washington Times*, 18 October 1990.
18. *Pravda Ukraïny*, 21 January 1989.
19. *Literaturna Ukraïna*, 12 April 1990.
20. *Ukrainian Press Agency*, 4 March 1990.
21. See Peter J. Potichnyj, 'Elections in Ukraine', *Berichte des Bundesinstituts für ostwissenshafliche und internationale studien*, 1990, no. 36; and Dominique Arel, 'The Parliamentary Blocs in the Ukrainian Supreme Soviet: Who and What Do they Represent?', *Journal of Soviet Nationalities*, vol. 1, no. 4 (Winter 1990–1) pp. 108–54.
22. Arel, table 1, p. 112.
23. *Postup*, no. 7 (24), March 1990; and *Dosvitni vohni*, no. 3, April 1990.
24. Arel, table 8, p. 128.
25. *Moscow News*, no. 17, 1990.
26. *Radians'ka Ukraïna*, 18 April 1990.
27. *Izvestiia*, 19 April 1990.
28. *Pravda*, 4 February 1991.
29. *Pravda*, 20 April 1990.
30. Valentyn Moroz, 'The L'viv Oblast Soviet Attempts to Introduce a Market Economy', *Report on the USSR*, RL 475/90, 16 November 1990.
31. *Ternystyi shliakh*, 6 June 1990, p. 2.
32. *Literaturna Ukraïna*, 14 and 28 June 1990; 'Ukraine Democrats Join Forces', *The Times*, 12 June 1990.
33. Kathleen Mihalisko, 'Volodymyr Ivashko and Ukraine', *Report on the USSR*, RL 315/90, 20 July 1990.

34. The CPU election platform is published in *Radians'ka Ukraïna*, 3 December 1989.
35. *Pravda Ukraïny*, 3 April 1990.
36. Susan Viets, 'Ukraine to Vote on Sweeping Changes', *Independent*, 16 July 1990.
37. See Kathleen Mihalisko, 'Ukraine's Declaration of Sovereignty', *Report on the USSR*, RL 329/90 (27 July 1990); Peter Shutak, 'Ukraine's Declaration of Sovereignty', *Soviet Analyst*, 1 August 1990; J. Rettle, 'Ukraine Soviet Republic Proclaims Sovereignty', *Guardian*, 17 July 1990; F. Clines, 'Ukrainians Declare Republican Sovereignty Inside Soviet System', *New York Times*, 17 July 1990; Marta Dejevsky, 'Ukrainian Parliament Declares Its Sovereignty', *The Times*, 17 July 1990; P. Symon, 'Ukraine Votes to Break Away', *Daily Telegraph*, 17 July 1990; and Adrian Karatnycky, 'Now It's the Ukraine's Turn', *Wall Street Journal*, 18 July 1990.
38. *TASS*, 16 July 1990.
39. *Ukrainian Press Agency*, Warsaw, 16 July 1990; and *News from Ukraine*, 1990, no. 31.
40. David Marples, 'The First Session of the Ukrainian Parliament', *Report on the USSR*, RL 403/90 (28 September 1990).
41. Article by Volodymyr Iavorskyi in authors' files.
42. *Ustanovchyi z'izd Ukraïns'koï respublikans'koï partiï* (Kyiv: RUKH-inform, 1990) p. 52.
43. Report of the mandate commission, 2nd URP congress; in authors' possession.
44. *Ukrainian Press Agency*, 14 May 1990; *Halychyna*, 2 June 1990; and *Za vil'nu Ukraïnu*, 17 July 1990. See also 'Rights Group Form First Free Ukrainian Party in 70 Years', *The Times*, 1 May 1990.
45. *L'vivs'ki novyny*, no. 22, 1990. See *Ustanovchiy z'izd ...*, 1990, pp. 92–93.
46. Iurii Kyrychuk, 'Narys istoriï UHS-URP', *Respulikanets'*, no. 2. (November–December 1991) p. 95.
47. Ibid., p. 82.
48. Copy in authors' files.
49. *Prapor antykomunizmu*, no. 5, 1990.
50. *Ukrainian Press Agency*, 12 March 1990; *Literaturna Ukraïna*, 8 March 1990; and *Moloda Halychyna*, 7 April 1990.
51. See Chapter 1.
52. Angelo Pannebianco, *Political Parties, Organisation and Power* (Cambridge: Cambridge University Press, 1988) p. 194.
53. *Ukrainian Press Agency*, 18 June 1990; and *Russkaia mysl'*, 22 June 1990.
54. *Agro*, 9 June 1990; *Zemlia i volia*, no. 1, August 1990; and *Moloda Halychyna*, 26 September 1990.
55. *Visnyk Rukhu*, no. 6, 1990; and *Za vil'nu Ukraïnu*, 12 December 1990. See also *Literaturna Ukraïna*, 8 November 1990 for Serhiy Plachynda's views.
56. 'Appeal of the UCDF to the Ukrainian People', *Ukrainian Review*, vol. XXXVIII, no. 1 (Spring 1990) pp. 82–3.
57. *Moloda Halychyna*, 24 April 1990.
58. *Chervona dolyna*, 5 May 1990.

59. Ievhen Boltarovych, 'L'vivshchyna: politychni syly i potitychnyi spektr', *Respublikanets'*, no. 2 (November–December 1991) p. 30.
60. See Alexander J. Motyl, *The Turn to the Right: The Ideological Origins and Development of Ukrainian Nationalism, 1919–1929* (Boulder, Col.: East European Monographs, 1980) ch. 6; and M. Sosnows'kyi, *Dmytro Dontsov: Politychynyj portret: Z istorii rozvytku ideolohiï ukraïns'koho natsionalizmu* (New York/Toronto: Trident International, 1974).
61. *Visnyk UNR*, no. 1, June 1990.
62. Haran', 1991, p. 30.
63. *Visnyk Rukhu*, no. 6, 1990; *News from Ukraine*, no. 43, 1990; *Ukrainian Weekly*, 21 October 1990; and *Ratusha*, 18 October 1990.
64. The L'viv branch of the Ukrainian Peasants' DPU also participated initially.
65. The Bandera faction of the OUN was called the 'external branches' of the OUN in the 1950s, and during the 1960s renamed itself the OUN revolutionaries (OUNr).
66. *Visnyk UNR*, no. 1, June 1990.
67. The programme is published in the special edition of the Federation's organ *Poklyk voli*. See also *Moloda Halychyna*, 10 April 1990; and interview with a veteran of the Ukrainian Insurgent Army and member of the Federation in *Halychyna*, 22 July 1990.
68. *Ukrainian Press Agency*, 13 December 1989; *Kyïvs'kyi politekhnik*, 22 December 1990.
69. *Kameniar*, 22 and 29 May 1989.
70. On the Student Brotherhood, see *Komsomol's'ki prapor*, 27 January 1990; *Moloda Halychyna*, 20 December 1990; *Prosvita*, vol. 3, no. 23, 1991; and *L'vivs'kyi politekhnik*, 1 March 1991.
71. SB programme in authors' files.
72. *Ukrainian Press Agency*, 21 and 22 February 1990; *Radians'ka Ukraïna*, 14 February 1990; *Molod' Ukraïny*, 17 February 1990; and *Vechirnii Kyïv*, 2 March 1990.
73. *Ukrainian Press Agency*, 16 February 1990.
74. *Ukrainian Press Agency*, 26 March 1990.
75. *Radio Kyiv*, 11 February 1991; *Molod' Ukraïny*, 10 April 1991; *Moloda hvardiia*, 12 April 1991; *Za vil'nu Ukraïnu*, 25 April 1991; *Slovo*, no. 10, May 1991; and *Osvita*, 11 June 1991.
76. *Radians'ka Ukraïna*, 27 April 1991.
77. On Donii, see *Holos Ukraïny*, 2 February 1991; while on the Ukraine Students Union see *News from Ukraine*, nos 42 and 46, 1991.
78. *Ukrainian Press Agency*, 1 June, 21 August and 26 October 1990; *Radians'ke slovo*, 27 February 1990; *Halychyna*, 1 June 1990; *Za vil'nu Ukraïnu*, 1 July 1990; *Moloda Halychyna*, 28 August 1990; and *Ratusha*, 13 October 1990.
79. *Ukrainian Press Agency*, 1 June 1990; *Halychyna*, 1 June 1990; and *USSR News Brief*, nos 5–6, 1989.
80. *Ukrainian Press Agency*, 26 October 1989.
81. See the article 'SNUM: Alternatyva Komsomolu?', *Osvita*, 15 February 1991.

82. *Postup*, no. 1, October 1990.
83. *Molodyi respublikanets'*, no. 1, 1991.
84. See *Ukrainian Press Agency*, 21 August 1990. See also the interview with the people's deputy and chairman of SNUM, Ihor Derkach, in *Perturbatsii*, no. 1 (Autumn 1989) pp. 29–37.
85. *Moloda hvardiia*, 6 July 1991.
86. *Nashe slovo*, 4 November 1990; *Bratstvo*, no. 4, 1990; *Moloda Halychyna*, 10 April, 1 May, 22 May, 14 August and 23 August 1990; *Halychyna*, 28 August 1990; and *Svoboda*, 9 June 1990.
87. *Molod' Ukraïny*, 18 April 1991.
88. *Ukrainian Weekly*, 15 December 1991.
89. *Moloda Halychyna*, 8 March 1990; and *Halychyna* 19 May, 10 June and 17 July 1990.
90. (All-Ukrainian Society of the Repressed); *Ukrains'ke slovo*, 16 September 1990; and *Zona*, no. 1, 1990; (Union of Former Political Prisoners): *Za vil'nu Ukraïnu*, 14 November and 7 December 1990; (Helsinki-90): *Informatsiinyi biuleten ukraïnskoho komitetu 'Helsinki-90'*, no. 1, August 1990.
91. The sociological breakdown of *Rukh* is given in *Ukrainian Reporter*, vol. 1, no. 1 (1991); and David Marples, 'A Sociological Survey of *Rukh*', *Report on the USSR*, RL 21/90 (12 January 1990). For a comparison with Solidarity see Janusz Pakulski, 'Leaders of the Solidarity Movement: A Sociological Portrait', *Sociology*, vol. 20, no. 1 (1986) pp. 64–81; and *Social Movements. The Politics of Moral Protest* (Melbourne: Longman, 1991).
92. All figures from *Suchasni politychni partiï ta rukhy na Ukraïni* (Kyiv: Institute for Political Research', 1991) p. 230.
93. Figures supplied by Oleksyi Haran'.
94. For example, in an autumn 1991 poll of 2056 Ukrainians for Radio Liberty, 35.8 per cent evaluated *Rukh* positively, and 36.4 per cent negatively. *Vechirnii Kyïv*, 3 December 1991.
95. *Literaturna Ukraïna*, 7 November 1990.
96. *Druhi vseukraïns'ki zbory narodnoho Rukhu Ukraïny: Dokumenty* (Kyiv: Rukh Secretariat, 1990) pp. 4 & 44.
97. M. Dobbs, 'Group Calls for Ukrainian Independence', *The Washington Post*, 29 October 1990.
98. *Radio Moscow*, 25 October 1990.
99. *Radio Kyiv*, 3 November 1990; and *Kul'tura i zhyttia*, 4 November 1990.
100. *Druhi vseukraïns'ki …*, p. 16.
101. The Association was established in July 1990. See *Moloda Halychyna*, 2 August 1990; *Zakhidnyi kurier*, 3 August 1990; and *Ratusha*, 20 November 1990.
102. See Volodymyr Lytvyn, 'Suchasni sotsial-demokratychni partii Ukraïny, *Polityka i chas*, 8 June 1991, pp. 44–9.
103. *Ukrainian Press Agency*, press release nos 14 and 15, 1989.
104. Copy in authors' files.
105. *Ukraïna bahatopartiina: Prohramni dokumenty novykh partii* (Kyiv: Pam'iatky Ukraïny, 1991) p. 74.

106. See *Visnyk Rukhu*, no. 2, 1990; *Postup*, no. 1 (18) 1990; *Moloda Halychyna*, 19 May 1990; *Halychyna*, 8 July 1990; *Moloda Halychyna*, 12 July 1990; and *Ratusha*, 4 October 1990.
107. Copy in authors' files.
108. See *Zelenyi svit*, no. 1, April 1990; and no. 2, May 1990.
109. *Ukrainian Press Agency*, 30 September 1990; *Visti z Ukraïny*, no. 42, 1990; and *Kul'tura i zhyttia*, no. 14, 1990.
110. *Zelenyi svit*, no. 12, October 1990.
111. *Zelenyi svit*, no. 11, September 1990.
112. For example, 10.28 per cent, second only to the then CPU in August 1991; *Zelenyi svit*, no. 16, October 1991.
113. *Ukrainian Press Agency*, 26 September 1990; *Moloda Halychyna*, 7 April 1990; and *Literaturna Ukraïna*, 19 April and 23 August, 1990.
114. *Demokratychnyi vybir*, no. 11, 1991.
115. *Ukrains'ke slovo*, 23 December 1990. The programme was published in *Suchasnist'*, January 1991, pp. 191–6.
116. *Partiia demokraticheskogo vozrozhdeniia Ukrainy: Materialy uchreditel'nogo s'ezda* (Kyiv: Ukrniinti, 1990) p. i. See also Volodymyr Lytvyn on the UPDR in *Polityka i chas*, no. 1, January 1991, pp. 84–6.
117. *Holos*, no. 21, 1990.
118. *Ratusha*, 4 December 1990.
119. *Partiia demokraticheskogo ...*, 1990, p. 39. See also *Vechirnii Kyïv*, 11 December 1990.
120. O. Iemets to the party's second congress in June 1990. Quoted by Volodymyr Lytvyn, 'Novi orientyry novykh partii', *Polityka i chas*, 12 (August 1991) p. 52.
121. *Zelenyi svit*, no. 14, December 1990.
122. *Literaturna Ukraïna*, 31 May 1990.
123. Volodymyr Lytvyn, 'Demokratychna partii Ukraïny', *Polityka i chas*, 2 (January 1991) p. 56.
124. Membership figures presented to the Ministry of Justice for registration, 24 June 1991. Authors' files.
125. *Ikva* (DPU organ) no. 1, 22 June 1991.
126. *Ideini zasady demokratychnoï partiï Ukraïny: z materialiv ustanovchoho z'ïzdu* (Kyiv: Prosvita, 1990) p. 15.
127. Ibid., p. 24. Emphasis in original.
128. *Trybuna*, no. 4, 1991, p. 35.
129. *Zakarpats'ka pravda*, 30 April 1991.
130. See the article by Taras Kuzio in *Za vil'nu Ukraïnu*, 4 June 1991; and *Slovo*, no. 11, 1991.
131. Rostyslav Khotyn, 'Bahatopartiinist': diiovi osoby ta vykonavtsi (Politychna kar ta Ukraïny), *Nezalezhnyi ohliadach*, August–September 1991, pp. 12–20.
132. See also A. M. Sliusarenko and V. Tomenko, *Novi politychni partii Ukraïny* (Kyiv: Znannia, Seriia Chas i suspil'stvo, no. 12, 1990).
133. Volodymyr Lytvyn, 'Novi orientyry novykh partii', *Polityka i chas*, 12 August 1991, pp. 47–55.
134. *Kyïvs'kyi sotsial-demokrat*, no. 2 (December 1991).

135. *Postanova natsional'noï radi DPU*, no. NR-2-2-1, 18 May 1991. Authors' files.

8 Stalemate and the Rise of National Communism (1990–1)

1. David Marples, 'The Communist Party of Ukraine: A Fading Force?', *Report on the USSR*, RL 253/90 (8 June 1990).
2. *Vechirnii Kyïv*, 24 July 1990.
3. *Soviet Television*, 4 July 1990.
4. See Taras Karpalo, 'The Ukrainian Student Movement: A Brief Account', London: *Ukrainian Central Information Service*, 120/91 (8 November 1991).
5. David Marples, 'Ukrainian Premier on the Way Out?', *Report on the USSR*, RL 446/90 (26 October 1990).
6. Roman Solchanyk, 'Ukrainian Communist Party on the Offensive, *Report on the USSR*, RL 111/91 (8 March 1991).
7. *Literaturna Ukraïna*, 4 October 1990. For the latter point, see the remarks by V. Filenko in *Komsomol's'koie znamia*, 15 June 1991.
8. See *Materialy XXVII z'izdu Komunistychnoï partiï Ukraïny* (Kyiv: Ukraïna, 1991).
9. *Moloda Halychyna*, 6 August 1991.
10. *Za vil'nu Ukraïnu*, 1 May 1991.
11. *Zakhidnyi kurier*, 13 October 1990.
12. *Za vil'nu Ukraïnu*, 10 July 1991.
13. *Ideolohiia i taktyka URP: Materiialy teoretychnoï konferentsiï* (Kyiv: URP, 1991) especially pp. 14–17, 48–9, 57–8. Or see Volodymyr Iavors'kyi in *Prapor antykomunizmu*, no. 5 (December 1990).
14. The Cherkasy branch of the URP, for example, joined the Ukrainian National Party *en masse* in late 1990. *Visti*, no. 1, 1990.
15. David Marples, 'Radicalisation of the Political Spectrum in Ukraine', *Report on the USSR*, RL 306/91 (30 August 1991).
16. *Shliakh peremohy*, 16 December 1991.
17. Roman Koval', *Holos*, no. 8, 1991.
18. The disputes are summarised in *Holos*, nos. 8 and 9, 1991.
19. *L'vivs'ki novyny* (newsletter of L'viv URP) no. 16, 1991.
20. On the URP's second congress, see *Holos Halychyny: Rozdumy pro doliu Ukraïny na 2-mu z'izdi URP* (Boryslav: URP, September 1991).
21. See the speech by Lukianenko, 'URP na suchasnomu etapi', *Samostiina Ukraïna*, no. 5 (January 1992).
22. *News from Ukraine*, 1991, no. 1.
23. Protocol for the meetings of the DPU's party council 12 April 1991, and Grand Council 14 May 1991. Authors' files.
24. *Visnyk: Informatsiinyi biuleten' DPU*, no. 1 (28 June–19 July 1991), p. 8.
25. *Ukrainian Reporter*, vol. 1, no. 4; Ievhen Boltarovych. 'L'vivshchyna: Politychni syly i politychnyi spektr', *Respublikanets'*, no. 2 (November–December 1991) p. 25.
26. *Ukrainian Reporter*, vol. 1, no. 5 (March 1991).

27. For the resolutions of the Congress, see *Literaturna Ukraïna*, 7 February 1991.
28. Meetings were held in Erevan (12–15 January 1988); Tbilisi (19–20 March 1988); L'viv (11–12 June 1988); Riga (24–5 September 1988); Vilnius (28–9 January 1989); and Loodi, Estonia (29 April–1 May 1989). See Bohdan Nahaylo, 'Representatives of Non-Russian National Movements Establish Coordinating Committee', *Radio Liberty Research*, RL 283/88 (22 June 1988); 'Non-Russian Democratic Movements Hold Another Meeting', RL 465/88 (10 October 1988); and 'Non-Russian National-Democratic Movements Adopt Charter and Issue Appeal to Russian Intelligentsia', RL 87/89 (24 February 1989).
29. Joint declarations are in authors' files.
30. *Ukrainian Reporter*, vol. 1, no. 3 (February 1991).
31. *Pravda*, 4 February 1991.
32. Roman Solchanyk, 'Ukraine Considers a New Republican Constitution', *Report on the USSR*, RL 215/91 (7 June 1991); and 'The Changing Political Landscape in Ukraine', *Report on the USSR*, RL 222/91 (14 June 1991).
33. *Molod' Ukraïny*, 17 April 1991.
34. *Komsomol's'kaia pravda*, 27 April 1991.
35. Roman Solhanyk, 'The Changing Political Landscape in Ukraine', *Report on the USSR*, RL 222/91 (14 June 1991).
36. *Molod' Ukraïny*, 27 March 1991.
37. *Vechirnii Kyïv*, 20 June 1991.
38. Roman Solchanyk, 'The Draft Union Treaty and the "Big Five"', *Report on the USSR*, RL 177/91 (3 May 1991).
39. *Nezavisimaia gazeta*, 25 May 1991.
40. Roman Solchanyk, 'Ukraine and the Union Treaty', *Report on the USSR*, RL 263/91 (26 July 1991).
41. *Holos*, no. 20, November 1990 gives a list of those deputies who supported the motion. See also Dominique Arel, 'The Parliamentary Blocs in the Ukrainian Supreme Soviet: Who and What Do They Represent?', *Journal of Soviet Nationalities*, vol. 1, no. 4 (Winter 1990–1) pp. 109–11.
42. *Trud*, 26 June 1991.
43. *Ternopil' vechirnii*, 15 June 1991.
44. *Vechirnii Kyïv*, 17 June 1991.
45. See the series of articles by Hurenko in *Radians'ka Ukraïna*, 14, 15 and 18 June 1991; and *Holos*, no. 4, 1991.
46. Mark Beissinger, 'Ethnicity, the Personnel Weapon, and Neo-Imperial Integration: Ukrainian and RSFSR Provincial Party Officials Compared', *Studies in Comparative Communism*, vol. XXI, no. 1 (Spring 1988) pp. 71–85.
47. Steven L. Burg, 'National Elites and Political Change in the Soviet Union', in Lubomyr Hajda and Mark Beissinger (eds), *The Nationalities Factor in Soviet Politics and Society* (Boulder, Col.: Westview Press, 1990) pp. 31–2.
48. Arel, 1990–1, pp. 133–8.

49. When the PDRU, other centrist parties, government ministers and deputies and business organisations combined to form the 'New Ukraine' movement as a lobby for a market economy and as an alternative 'shadow cabinet' to the Fokin government. *Nezavisimost'*, 17 January 1992.

50. John A. Armstrong, 'The Ethnic Scene in the Soviet Union: The View of the Dictatorship', in Erich Goldhagen (ed.), *Ethnic Minorities in the Soviet Union* (New York: Praeger, 1968), especially the section on 'younger brothers'.

51. Burg, 1990, op. cit.

52. 'Prohramni pryntsypy diial'nosti kompartii Ukraïny' in *Suchasni polity-chni partii ta rukhy na Ukraïni* (Kyiv: Institute of Political Research, 1991) p. 32.

53. *Holos Ukraïny*, 14 July 1991.

54. Roman Solchanyk, 'Ukraine Considers a New Constitution', *Report on the USSR*, RL 215/91 (7 June 1991).

55. *Zakon Ukraïns'koï RSR pro vybory prezydenta Ukraïns'koï RSR (Kyiv: Ukraïna, 1991)* pp. 3–4.

56. *Holos Ukraïny* (Interview with Kravchuk) 15 August 1991.

57. On the evolution of Ukraine's relations with Russia, see Roman Solchanyk, 'Ukraine and Russia: Before and After the Coup', *Report on the USSR*, RL 316/91 (27 September 1991).

58. Natalie Melnyczuk, 'Ukraine Develops an Independent Foreign Policy: The First Year', *Report on the USSR*, RL 379/91 (25 October 1991).

59. See the TV address by Fokin, reprinted in *Radians'ka Ukraïna*, 8 August 1991.

60. *Ikva (Chasopys Demokratychnoï partiï Ukraïny)*, no. 1, 22 June 1991.

61. 'Narodna rada: 4 fraktsiï', *Holos*, no. 10, 1991.

62. Such as those again commemorating Ukrainian independence and unification on 22 January, the campaign to release Khmara in March–April, alternative 1 May rallies and mass demonstrations against Ukraine signing any Union treaty on 23 June.

63. Bohdan Krawchenko, *Social Change and National Consciousness in Twentieth-Century Ukraine* (London: Macmillan/St Antony's, 1985) p. 211.

64. Roman Solchanyk, '"Intermovement" Formed in Donbass', *Report on the USSR*, RL 513/90 (21 December 1990).

65. *Literaturna Ukraïna*, 15 November 1991.

66. *Za vil'nu Ukraïnu*, 20 March 1991, p. 1.

67. 'Ohliad straikovoho rukhu na Ukraïni', *Nezalezhnist'*, no. 7, 1991, p. 1. (organ of the radical Ukrainian Peoples' Democratic Party).

68. *Ukrainian Reporter*, vol. 1, no. 10 (May 1991) p. 3.

69. *Ukrainian Reporter*, vol. 1, no. 17 (September 1991) pp. 4–5.

70. As each delegate represented 3000 workers, the minimum founding strength of VOST would be one million. The higher figure was claimed by People's Deputy Larysa Skoryk at the subsequent press conference. See *Moloda Halychyna*, 25 June 1991.

71. See the manifesto issued on 23 June. *Materialy z'ïzdu VOST* (Kyiv: Ukraïns'ka mizhpartiina asambliia, 1991).

72. Speech to the second URP congress.
73. *Za vil'nu Ukraïnu*, 27 June 1991.

9   From Soviet to Independent Ukraine: the Coup and Aftermath

1. Roman Laba, 'How Yeltsin's Exploitation of Ethnic Nationalism Brought down an Empire', *Transition*, vol. 2, no. 2 (12 January 1996), p. 10. See also Anita Inder Singh, 'Managing National Diversity through Political Structures and Ideologies: the Soviet Experience in Comparative Perspective', *Nations and Nationalism*, vol. 1, Part 2 (July 1995), pp. 197–220.
2. See Roman Solchanyk, 'The Gorbachev–Yeltsin Pact and the New Union Treaty', *Report on the USSR*, vol. 3, no. 19 (10 May 1991); and Ann Sheehy, 'The Union Treaty: A Further Setback', *Report on the USSR*, vol. 3, no. 49 (6 December 1991),
3. On the distinegration of the former USSR, see Bohdan Nahaylo and Victor Svoboda, *Soviet Disunion. A History of the Nationalities Problem in the USSR* (London: Hamish Hamilton, 1990); Ian Bremmer and Ray Taras, *Nations and Politics in the Soviet Successor States* (Cambridge: Cambridge University Press, 1993); and John Dunlop, *The Rise of Russia and the Fall of the Soviet Union* (Princeton: Princeton University Press, 1993).
4. Russian Television, 14 March 1996.
5. Nearly all references in this section are from the protocol of the Supreme Council's emergency session on 24 August: *Pozacherhova sesiia verkhovnoï rady Ukraïnskoï RSR: Dvanadtsiatoho sklykannia. Biuleten'* nos 1–2 (Kyiv: Verkhovna Rada URSR, 1991). This reference: Bulletin 1, p. 25.
6. Ibid., p. 26.
7. Ibid., p. 44.
8. Ibid., p. 90.
9. All quotes from leaflets distributed in Kyiv on the 19th and 20th. Copies are in the authors' files.
10. Two-page document in the authors' files.
11. Roman Solchanyk, 'Ukraine: Kravchuk's Role', *Report on the USSR*, RL 322/91 (6 September 1991).
12. *Pozacherhova ...*, pp. 91, 24 and 78–9.
13. Ibid., pp. 37 and 40.
14. Ibid., p. 93.
15. Ibid., p. 91.
16. Ibid., p. 92.
17. Solchanyk, p. 49.
18. *Pozacherhova ...*, Bulletin 2, p. 11.
19. *Vechirnii Kyïv*, 23 August 1991.
20. *Pozacherhova ...*, Bulletin 1, p. 18.
21. Ibid., p. 17.

22. Ibid., pp. 33–4 and 70.
23. Ibid., p. 73.
24. Ibid., p. 48.
25. Ibid., pp. 71–4.
26. Ibid., pp. 52 and 76.
27. Ibid., Bulletin 1, p. 84.
28. *Za vil'nu Ukraïnu*, 1 June 1991.
29. *Pozacherhova ...*, Bulletin 1, p. 74.
30. Ibid., p. 95.
31. Volodymyr Lytvyn, 'Sotsialistychna partiia Ukraïny', *Polityka i chas*, nos 17–18 (December 1991) pp. 80–5.
32. *Demokratychna Ukraïna*, 22 December 1991.
33. *Radians'ka Ukraïna*, 5 October 1991.
34. *Holos Ukraïny*, 30 October 1991.
35. For example, 100 according to the SPU's Mykola Zaludiak; *Slovo*, no. 21, December 1991.
36. *News from Ukraine*, no. 45, 1991. (Prof. Orlov's first name is not given).
37. Lytvyn, p. 83.
38. See the resolutions of the party's council on 11–12 January, attacking the economic reforms. *Pravda Ukraïny*, 14 January 1992.
39. 'Statut sotsialistichnoï partiï Ukraïny', *Polityka i chas*, nos 17–18 (December 1991) pp. 88–92. Quote on p. 89.
40. *Za vil'nu Ukraïnu*, 28 January 1992; *Holos Ukraïny*, 29 January and 14 February 1992.
41. *Literaturna Ukraïna*, 14 November 1991.
42. *Za vil'nu Ukraïnu*, 20 November 1991.
43. Ibid.
44. *Radians'ka Ukraïna*, 19 September 1991.
45. *Moloda hvardiia*, 18 November 1991.
46. *Samostiina Ukraïna*, no. 2 (January 1992).
47. *Nezavizimost'*, 17 January 1992.
48. *Holos Ukraïny*, 18 March 1992.
49. *Holos Ukraïny*, 18 December 1991.
50. *Holos Ukraïny*, 13 November 1991.
51. *Holos Ukraïny*, 29 October 1991.
52. TASS news agency, 6 November 1991.
53. *Molod Ukraïny*, 17 October 1991.
54. *Samostiina Ukraïna*, no. 12 (September 1991).
55. Both groups were listed in the URP's *Samostiina Ukraïna*, no. 7, February 1992, and no. 10, March 1992.
56. The flag was adopted on 28 January 1992, see *Holos Ukraïny*, 15 February 1992; the trident on 19 February, see *Holos Ukraïny*, 20 and 21 February; and the hymn on 15 January, see *Holos Ukraïny*, 18 January 1992. Even then, a compromise was reached whereby the trident would be part of, but not the whole of, the official state emblem. See *Vechirnii Kyïv*, 20 February 1992.
57. Both groups were listed in the URP's *Samostiina Ukraïna*, no. 7 (February 1992), and no. 10 (March 1992).

58. *Moloda Halychyna*, 22 February 1992; *Demokratychna Ukraïna*, 25 February 1992.
59. *Molod Ukraïny*, 20 December 1990.
60. On the first, see *Literaturna Ukraïna*, 25 July 1991; *Samostiina Ukraïna*, no. 10, August 1991; on the second, see *Literaturna Ukraïna*, 31 October and 7 November; and *Samostiina Ukraïna*, no. 17, November 1991.
61. See Kathleen Mihalisko, 'Laying the Foundations for the Armed Forces of Ukraine', *Report on the USSR*, RL 393/91 (8 November 1991); 'Defense and Security Planning in Ukraine', RL 417/91 (6 December 1991); and 'Ukraine Asserts Control Over Nonstrategic Forces', *RFE/RL Research Report*, vol. 1, no. 3 (24 January 1992).
62. *Za vil'nu Ukraïnu*, 7 September 1991. To all intents and purposes he was Ukraine's first Defence Minister, although the post had existed formally until 1945.
63. *Pravda*, 12 September 1991.
64. As Morozov explained at the Twelfth International Conference on Policy and Strategy in Munich on 17–19 November 1991.
65. *Izvestia*, 24 October 1991; *Holos Ukraïny*, 5 November 1991.
66. *Za vil'nu Ukraïnu*, 12 December 1991.
67. *Holos Ukraïny*, 18 December 1991.
68. *Za vil'nu Ukraïnu*, 14 December 1991; Radio Kyiv, 13 December 1991.
69. *Holos Ukraïny*, 26 October 1991.
70. *Neskorena natsiia*, no. 3, October 1991.
71. *Zelenyi svit*, September 1991.
72. On Ukrainian–Russian relations, see Roman Solchanyk, 'Ukraine and Russia: Before and After the Coup', *Report on the USSR*, RL 346/91 (27 September 1991); 'Ukraine, the Kremlin, and the Russian White House', RL 348/91 (1 November 1991) and 'Ukrainian–Russian Confrontation over the Crimea', *RFE/RL Research Report* (21 February 1992).
73. Such as at the all-Ukrainian *Viche* (Assembly) in St Sophia Square, Kyiv on 15 September: *URP-Inform* (press bulletin) no. 21, 17 September 1991.
74. *Pravda*, 21 October 1991; *Molod' Ukraïny*, 22 October 1991.
75. *Holos Ukraïny*, 15 November 1991.
76. *Holos Ukraïny*, 12 November 1991.
77. Kravchuk, ibid., p. 2.
78. Radio Kyiv, 25 October 1991.
79. In, of all places, *Paris Match*, no. 22–6, December 1991.
80. The text of the agreement was published in nearly all Ukrainian papers on 10 December 1991.
81. *Holos Ukraïny*, 11 and 21 December 1991.
82. *Holos Ukraïny*, 24 December 1991.
83. *Za vil'nu Ukraïnu*, 12 December 1991. See also Roman Solchanyk, 'Kravchuk Defines Ukrainian–CIS Relations', *RFE/RL Research Report* (13 March 1992).
84. The URP on 13 January (*URP-Inform*, no. 2, 15 January 1992); the DPU in the Declaration *Zvil'nytysia vid zahrozy novoho GKChP!* 18 January 1992, copy in the authors' files.

85. Douglas L. Clarke, 'The Saga of the Black Sea Fleet', *RFE/RL Research Report*, vol. 1, no. 3 (24 January 1992) and 'The Battle for the Black Sea Fleet', vol. 1, no. 4 (31 January 1992).
86. People's Council statement in *Za vil'nu Ukraïnu*, 18 January 1992.
87. Moroz in *Kyïvs'kyi visnyk*, 28 November 1991.
88. In September, 2 per cent considered themselves 'well-informed' about the IPA, 18.3 per cent about the DPU, 16.5 per cent about the URP, and 7.4 per cent about the PDRU. The Greens scored highest with 21.5 per cent. Even *Rukh* only managed 50.9 per cent. *Ukraïns'kyi tsentr sotsiolohichnykh doslidzhen'*, 20–24 September 1991. Information was supplied by Dmytro Vydrin, Director, International Institute for Global and Regional Security.
89. *URP–Inform*, no. 19, 3 September 1991.
90. *L'vivs'ki novyny* (URP newsletter) no. 39, 1991.
91. The Peasant Democratic and Christian Democratic parties were split between their support for Chornovil and Lukianenko respectively.
92. *Radio Kyiv*, 9 October 1991.
93. *Za vil'nu Ukraïna*, 8 February 1992.
94. *Literaturna Ukraïna*, 24 October 1991.
95. *Holos Ukraïny*, 21 November 1991.
96. On the regional definitions given in Chapter 2. See Table 9.1.
97. *Kyïvs'ka pravda*, 14 September 1991.
98. Institut Sotsiologii AN Ukraïny. *Obshchestvennoie mnenie naselieniia Ukrainy o predstoiashchikh vyborakh Prezidenta Ukrainy i respublikan-skom referendume o podtverzhdenii akta provozglasheniya nezavisimosti* (Kyiv: Institut Sotsiologii AN Ukrainy, September 1991) table 2.
99. Sekretariat verkhovnoï rady Ukraïny: Hrupa sotsiolohichnykh doslidzen', *Informatsiinyi biuleten'*, no. 14, 9–15 September 1991, table 5.
100. *Holos Ukraïny*, 1 November 1991.
101. Data obtained from a minority of *oblast'* electoral commissions, and copies in the authors' files. For example, Kravchuk obtained 65.3 per cent in the town of Dnipropetrovs'k, but up to 83.2 per cent in the surrounding countryside; 61.7 per cent in the town of Sumy, but up to 85.3 per cent outside.
102. *Sekretariat …; Biuleten'*, no. 13, 9–15 September 1991, p. 10.
103. Institut sotsiologii …
104. Sekretariat …
105. All the referendum evidence below is taken from Valerii Khmel'ko, *Khto pidtrymav i khto ne pidtrymav nezalezhnist' Ukraïny na referendumi*, by the kind permission of Eugene Paitha at RFE/RL in Munich.
106. *Holos Ukraïny*, 1 November 1991. Respondents could opt for up to four of the possibilities.
107. See also Khmel'ko.
108. See Roman Solchanyk, 'Centrifugal Movements in Ukraine and Independence', *Ukrainian Weekly*, 24 November 1991.
109. *Literaturna Ukraïna*, 7 November 1991.
110. *Ukrainian Weekly*, 24 November 1991.
111. For the URP see *Samostiina Ukraïna*, no. 15, October 1991. In *Zvernennia do prezydiï Verkhovnoï Rady, do uriadu ta heneral'noho*

prokurora Ukraïny, 2 October 1991, the DPU called for the new law to
be applied. Copy in the authors' files.
112. *Natsional'ni vidnosyny na Ukraïni* (Kyiv: Ukraïna, 1991) p. 32.
113. *Holos Ukraïny*, 4 October 1991.
114. *Radians'ka Ukraïna*, 18 September 1991.
115. *Avdet: Vozvrashcheniie*, nos 15–16, 11 July 1991.
116. Kathleen Mihalisko, 'The Other Side of Separation: Crimea Votes for
Autonomy', *Report on the USSR*, RL 60/91 (1 February 1991).
117. *Za vil'nu Ukraïny*, 11 October 1991.
118. *Holos*, nos 16 and 17, 1991.
119. *Holos Ukraïny*, 9 October 1991.
120. *Holos Ukraïny*, 4 October 1991.
121. Roman Solchanyk, 'Ukrainian–Russian Confrontation over the
Crimea', *RFE/RL Research Report*, vol. 1, no. 7 (21 February 1992).
122. Alfred A. Reisch, 'Transcarpathia's Hungarian Minority and the
Autonomy Issue', *RFE/RL Research Report* vol. 1, no. 5 (7 February
1992) and 'Transcarpathia and its Neighbors', ibid., vol. 1, no. 5
(14 February 1992).
123. *Za vil'nu Ukraïnu*, 31 August 1991.
124. *Robitnycha hazeta*, 27 November 1991.
125. Fedir Myshanych, 'Zakhystyty Zakarpattia', *Respublikanets'*, no. 2
(November–December 1991) pp. 41–6.
126. Reisch, 14 February 1992, p. 45.
127. *Za vil'nu Ukraïnu*, 23 October 1991.
128. *Demokratychna Ukraïna*, 5 December 1991.
129. *Novyny Zakarpattia*, no. 13, 1 February 1992.
130. *Pravda Ukraïny*, 3 December 1991.
131. See, for example, *Robitnychna hazeta*, 2 December 1990.
132. *Holos Ukraïny*, 22 and 26 November 1991.
133. *Robitnycha hazeta*, 19 September 1991.
134. *Samostiina Ukraïna*, no. 15, October 1991.
135. *Robitnycha hazeta*, 4 and 5 December 1991.
136. *Holos Ukraïny*, 4 January 1992.
137. Vladimir Socor, 'Creeping Putsch in Eastern Moldova', *RFE/RL
Research Report*, vol. 1, no. 2 (17 January 1992).
138. *Literaturna Ukraïna*, 29 August 1991.
139. *Za vil'nu Ukraïnu*, 29 October 1991.
140. *Za vil'nu Ukraïnu*, 17 October 1991.
141. *Holos Ukraïny*, 17 December 1991.

10 Conclusions

1. *Samostiina Ukraïna*, no. 20, May 1992.
2. See the voting analysis in *Narodna hazeta*, no. 12, April 1992, and in
Filenko's article summarised in *Ukraïns'kyi ohliadach* No. 2 (February
1992).
3. A Soviet perspective arguing that the primary factor generating nationalism was republican political institutions and the self-interests of the

elites they produced can be found in V. A. Tishkov, 'O novykh podkho-
dakh v teorii i praktike mezhnatsional'nykh otnoshenii', *Sovetskaia
etnografiia*, no. 5 (September–October 1989) pp. 3–14 and 'Etnichnost' i
vlast' v SSSR (etnopoliticheskii analiz respublikanskikh organov vlasti)'
Sovetskaia etnografiia, no. 3 (May–June 1991) pp. 3–12.

Select Bibliography

The following is a list of the more readily available English language works:

A. General Works on Ukraine and Soviet Nationality Problems

Arel, Dominique, 'The Parliamentary Blocks in the Ukrainian Supreme Soviet: Who and What do they Represent?', *Journal of Soviet Nationalities*, vol. I, no. 4 (Winter 1990–1), pp. 108–54. 'Language Politics in Independent Ukraine: Towards One or Two State Languages?' *Nationalities Papers*, vol. 23, no. 3 (September 1995), pp. 597–622.

Armstrong, John A., 'The Ethnic Scene in the Soviet Union: The View of the Dictatorship', reprinted with commentaries in *Journal of Soviet Nationalities*, vol. I, no. 1 (Spring 1990), pp. 66–75; and *Ukrainian Nationalism* (Lttlefon, Co: Ukrainian Academic Press, 1990).

Bahry, Remana. M. (ed.), *Echoes of Glasnost in Soviet Ukraine* (North York, Ontario: Captus Press, 1989).

Beissinger, Mark, 'Ethnicity, the Personnel Weapon and Neo-Imperial Integration: Ukrainian and RSFSR Provincial Party Officials Compared', *Studies in Comparative Communism*, vol. XXI, no. 1 (Spring 1988), pp. 71–85.

Bilinsky, Yaroslav, 'Shcherbytsky, Ukraine and Kremlin Politics', *Problems of Communism*, vol. XXXII, no. 4 (July–August 1983), pp. 1–20.

Bociurkiw, Bohdan R., 'The Ukrainian Catholic Church in the USSR Under Gorbachev', *Problems of Communism*, vol. XXXIX, no. 6 (November–December 1990), pp. 1–20.

Bremmer, Ian and Taras, Raymond (eds), *Nations and Politics in the Soviet Successor States* (Cambridge: Cambridge University Press, 1993).

Colton, Timothy J. and Legvold, Timothy (eds), *After the Soviet Union: From Empire to Nations* (New York: W. W. Norton, 1992).

Conquest, Robert, *The Harvest of Sorrow: Soviet Collectivisation and the Terror-Famine* (London: Hutchinson, 1986).

Dzyuba, Ivan, *Internationalism or Russification?* (London: Weidenfeld & Nicolson, 1968).

Farmer, Kenneth, *Ukrainian Nationalism in the Post-Stalin Era: Myths, Symbols and Ideology in Soviet Nationality Policy* (The Hague: Martinus Nijhoff, 1980).

Hodnett, Grey, 'The Views of Petro Shelest', *Annals of the Ukrainian Academy of Arts and Sciences in the United States*, vol. 14, no. 37–8 (1978–80), pp. 209–43.

Isajiw, Wsevolod, 'Urban Migration and Social Change in Contemporary Soviet Ukraine', *Canadian Slavonic Papers*, vol. XXII, no. 1 (March 1980), pp. 58–86.

Koropecckyj, I. S. (ed.), *The Ukraine within the USSR: An Economic Balance Sheet* (London: Praeger, 1977).

Krawchenko, Bohdan (ed.), *Ukraine After Shelest* (Edmonton: Canadian Institute of Ukrainian Studies, 1983); and *Social Change and National Consciousness in Twentieth-Century Ukraine* (London: Macmillan, 1985).

Kuzio, Taras, *Dissent in Ukraine Under Gorbachev* (London: Ukrainian Press Agency, 1989).

Kuzio, Taras, *Ukraine: The Unfinished Revolution. European Security Studies no. 16* (London: Institute for European Defence & Strategic Studies, 1992).

Kuzio, Taras, 'Nuclear Weapons and Military Policy in Independent Ukraine', *The Harriman Institute Forum*, vol. 6, no. 9 (May 1993).

Kuzio, Taras, *Ukrainian Security Policy* (Washington DC: Praeger and Csis, 1995).

Kuzio, Taras, *Ukraine under Kuchma. Political Reform, Economic Transformation and Security Policy in Independent Ukraine* (London: Macmillan, 1997).

Kuzio, Taras, *Ukraine. State and Nation Building* (London and New York: Routledge, 1998).

Kuzio, Taras, ed., *Contemporary Ukraine. Dynamics of Post-Soviet Transformation* (Armonk, NY: M. E. Sharpe, 1998).

Lewytzkyj, Borys, *Politics and Society in Soviet Ukraine, 1953–1980* (Edmonton: Canadian Institute of Ukrainian Studies, 1984).

Liber, George, *Soviet Nationality Policy, Urban Growth, and Identity Change in the Ukrainian SSR, 1923–1934* (Cambridge: Cambridge University Press, 1992).

Mace, James E., *Communism and the Dilemmas of National Liberation: National Communism in Soviet Ukraine, 1918–1933* (Cambridge, Mass.: Harvard University Press, 1983).

Magocsi, Paul R., *The Shaping of a National Identity: Subcarpathian Rus'* 1848–1948 (London: Harvard University Press, 1978); 'The Ukrainian National Revival: A New Analytical Framework', *Canadian Review of Studies in Nationalism*, vol. XVI, no. 1–2 (1989), pp. 45–62.

Markus, V., *Religion and Nationalism in Soviet Ukraine after 1945* (Cambridge: Ukrainian Studies Fund, 1985).

Marples, David, *Ukraine Under Perestroika: Ecology, Economics, and the Workers' Revolt* (London: Macmillan, 1991).

Motyl, Alexander J., *Will the Non-Russians Rebel? State, Ethnicity and Stability in the USSR* (Ithaca: Cornell University Press, 1987); *Sovietology, Rationality, Nationality: Coming to Grips with Nationalism in the USSR* (New York: Columbia University Press, 1991); and *Thinking Theoretically About Soviet Nationalities: Theory, History and Comparison in the Study of the USSR* (New York: Columbia University Press, 1992).

Motyl, A. J., *Dilemmas of Independence: Ukraine After Totalitarianism* (New York: Council on Foreign Relations Press, 1993).

Nahaylo, Bohdan, *The New Ukraine: Post-Soviet Business Forum* (London: The Royal Institute for International affairs, 1992).

Paniotto, Vlodimir, 'The Ukrainian Movement for Perestroika-Rukh: A Sociological Survey', *Soviet Studies*, vol. 43, no. 1 (January 1991), pp. 177–81.

Potichnyj, Peter J. (ed.), *Ukraine in the 1970s* (Ontario: Mosaic Press, 1975); and 'Elections in Ukraine', *Berichte des Bundesinstituts für ostwissenshafliche und internationale studien*, no. 36 (1990).

Rudnytsky, Ivan L. (ed.), *Rethinking Ukrainian History* and *Essays in Modern Ukrainian History* (both Edmonton: Canadian Institute of Ukrainian Studies, 1981 and 1987).

Solchanyk, Roman, ed., *Ukraine from Chernobyl' to Sovereignty: a Collection of Interviews* (London: Macmillan, 1992).

Saunders, David, 'Modern Ukrainian History (II)', *European History Quarterly*, vol. 21 no. 1 (1991), pp. 81–95.

Subtelny, Orest, *Ukraine: A History* (Toronto: University of Toronto Press, 1988).

Wilson Andrew, *Ukrainian Nationalism in the 1990s. A Minority Faith* (Cambridge: Cambridge University Press, 1997).

The following journals have been drawn on extensively; *Canadian Slavonic Papers, Harvard Ukrainian Studies, Journal of Soviet Nationalities, Journal of Ukrainian Studies, News from Ukraine, Problems of Communism, Religion in Communist Lands, Report on the USSR, RFE/RL Research Report, Soviet Analyst, Ukrainian Reporter, Ukrainian Review, Ukrainian Weekly.*

B.   General and Theoretical Works

Connor, Walker, *The National Question in Marxist-Leninist Theory and Strategy* (Princeton: Princeton University Press, 1984).

Eisenstadt, S. N., *The Political System of Empires* (New York: The Free Press, 1963).

Gleason, Gregory, *Federalism and Nationalism: The Struggle for Republican Rights in the USSR* (Boulder, Col.: Westview Press, 1990).

Hajda, Lubomyr and Mark Beissinger (eds), *The Nationalities Factor in Soviet Politics and Society* (Boulder, Col.: Westview Press, 1990).

Nahaylo, Bohdan and Swoboda, Viktor, *Soviet Disunion: A History of the Nationalities Problem in the USSR* (London: Hamish Hamilton, 1990).

Rakowska-Harmstone, Teresa, 'The Dialectics of Nationalism in the USSR', *Problems of Communism*, vol. XXIII, no. 3 (May–June 1974), pp. 1–22.

Smith, Anthony D., *Theories of Nationalism* (London: Holmes & Meier, 1983; and *National Identity* (London: Penguin, 1991).

Index